EFFECTIVE WRITING
A Guide for Social Science Students

Effective Writing

A Guide for Social Science Students

Pedro Pak-tao Ng

Department of Sociology
The Chinese University of Hong Kong

The Chinese University Press

Effective Writing: A Guide for Social Science Students
   By Pedro Pak-tao Ng

© **The Chinese University of Hong Kong**, 2003

ISBN 962-996-116-4

THE CHINESE UNIVERSITY PRESS
The Chinese University of Hong Kong
SHA TIN, N.T., HONG KONG

Fax: +852 2603 6692
       +852 2603 7355
E-mail: cup@cuhk.edu.hk
Web-site: www.chineseupress.com

Printed in Hong Kong

This book is dedicated to my parents

Contents

Appendices

Foreword

Ambrose Yeo-chi King
Vice-Chancellor and Professor of Sociology
The Chinese University of Hong Kong

Living in an "information age" when there is an endless flow and explosion of audio-visual images and simulation, we witness a concomitant (if not correlative) decline in the general capacity to write among students. We could safely set aside the problem only insofar as writing is no longer significant or relevant to our life. Yet the fact remains that effective writing is a skill desperately needed by the younger generation, no matter whether they come to work in business corporations, government or academic circles. Writing is not merely a medium of communication but also and more importantly the all-encompassing framework of conceptualization, analysis, elaboration, and, above all, thinking. We may thus rightly take the present deterioration in linguistic competence as one of the symptoms of the crisis of our age.

In this context I am pleased to learn that Professor Pedro Ng, my long time colleague at the Chinese University of Hong Kong, has compiled a monograph specifically addressing the issue of effective writing. The central message of this work, it seems to me, is that how to write is not something that should be taken for granted but is rather a skill that has to be acquired earnestly and systematically. I agree with Pedro's observation that "good writing skills are essential to every university student. They are instrumental for successful performance in any academic discipline and, indeed, in any profession after graduation." Deficiency in writing is thus tantamount to impotence in communication at the educated level.

But the value of effective writing proves to be more than instrumental. Writing is essentially *the* vehicle by which our ideas and feelings are articulated and expressed in the first place. Writing at once defines and constitutes our identity. If handwriting is one's costume, as an old Chinese saying puts it, then writing amounts to a disclosure of one's inner self. To a remarkable extent the quality of a person is manifested in his or her writing.

In this vein, Foucault's notion of "writing the self" reminds us of the significance of writing for self-care and self-cultivation, which had been the recurrent parlance and motif in Hellenic and Confucian thought. In contrast to its Western counterpart, in which self-care is accomplished by the pursuit of reason, moral perfection is considered paramount in the Confucian tradition. Be that as it may, it suggests that for modern individuals, writing may serve as a "technology" of fashioning a rational and moral self, which alone could resist the obsession with bodily appearance and with it subjection to the power of cosmetics and gymnastics. Viewed sociologically, therefore, the issue of writing is all the more important as it impinges upon the possibility of cultivating a truly autonomous and mature person, which is the ultimate ideal of liberal education.

More specifically, the contribution of Pedro's *Effective Writing* resides in its sensitivity to the peculiar need of students. He has been teaching the course "Writing for Sociology" in the Chinese University of Hong Kong since 1995. Over the years, he has accumulated considerable experience in handling students' problems in the learning of English in general and writing skills in particular.

Writing consists as much in the basic ability to command a language as the capacity to write. Writing guides and manuals are not altogether lacking in the book market; yet they have largely taken for granted the reader's linguistic competence and focused exclusively on the process of writing itself. In this regard Pedro's book is intended not only to teach the fundamental skills of academic writing, but also to help students to solve their language problems. To this end I think Professor Pedro Ng has done a good service to the community.

Foreword

David Heywood Parker
Professor of English
The Chinese University of Hong Kong

This excellent and useful book reminds us that accomplished academic writing is at the heart of a worthwhile liberal education. Writing is not simply the setting down, for the purposes of assessment, of what students already know and understand; it is often the means by which they come to know and to understand. Beginning with the notes and summaries students make in class or as they read, to the drafts they make of their assignments, to the final revised and proofread product, writing is a process that involves, among other things, grasping concepts, marshalling evidence and ideas, assessing alternative viewpoints, constructing logical and persuasive arguments, and refuting counter-arguments. In short, learning to write well is learning to think, learning to become an educated person.

Effective Writing will be especially useful in the Hong Kong context. As elsewhere, students have to deal with the fact that a large proportion of our store of knowledge in the social sciences, whether in print or electronic form, is in the English language. In order to participate fully in academic discourse and debate, to carry on conversation at the highest level in the world of learning, students need to be able to read and write effectively in English. As Dr. Pedro Ng clearly shows, this is a particular challenge for many Hong Kong students. Despite the long-term and widespread use of English in schools and in commerce, surprisingly few people in Hong Kong master the language. First-language syntax and habits of thought keep interfering with attempts at clear and accurate English expression. As Dr. Ng puts it, the basic problem is that writers are attempting to "translate" and are not yet "thinking in English".

Dr. Ng has put his finger on a very important point. For most Hong Kong tertiary students, there is a need to attend to a range of characteristic difficulties that Chinese-speaking learners have with English and which do not seem to be effectively addressed by thirteen years' study of the language at primary and secondary school. These include such obvious matters as agreements, tenses and the use of articles, but extend to much more subtle issues of English usage. Without explicit and conscious attention, common errors are endlessly repeated and reinforced. This is why it is so important that Dr. Ng has included appendices dealing with these difficulties clearly and head-on. I am especially impressed by the exercises he offers, which give practice in correct usage. The fact that Dr. Ng himself is inward with the first-language habits that need to be addressed makes his approach especially authoritative. And at the same time readers constantly have before them the example of his own ever lucid and graceful English.

This book will be useful both for undergraduates and for postgraduates. It will help students to prepare for and to write term papers; and at the same time it will help research students organize their data, set out their literature reviews and construct their bibliographies. Both ASA and APA methods of citation are given. Attention is also given to the citation of electronic sources and data.

Effective Writing is designed explicitly for students in the social sciences. My own view is that it could prove useful well beyond that target readership. Students in the humanities and the physical sciences will also find a great deal in this book to help them.

Acknowledgements

This book is a by-product of the "Integrated Programme for Enhancing Learning Skills in Sociology", a teaching development project (August 1999 to January 2003) supported jointly by the University Grants Committee, Hong Kong, and the Department of Sociology, The Chinese University of Hong Kong. The Programme aimed to promote sociology students' core learning skills, including reading, writing, understanding and using data, and critical thinking. The Programme's activities included offering skills courses, such as "Writing for Sociology" (now called "Research Writing") that I have been teaching two to three times a year since September 1995.

My experience in teaching the writing course for sociology students became the basis on which the book was conceived and planned. In the early phase of the Programme, Stephen Chiu, my colleague in the Department of Sociology who co-supervised the Programme with me, suggested that I produce a writing manual for students. The idea coincided with what I had wanted to do all along. During the course of the Programme, I was able to devote more time and energy to writing this book which, I hope, will give proper guidance to help students write better.

I wish to express my heartfelt appreciation to Professor Ambrose Yeo-chi King, Vice-Chancellor and Professor of Sociology of The Chinese University of Hong Kong, and to Professor David Heywood Parker, Professor of English of The Chinese University of Hong Kong, who have each so kindly graced this book with a foreword. Their inspiring words have strengthened my confidence that helping students to write better is indeed a worthy cause. As they have so eloquently indicated, learning to write well is "learning to think, learning to become an educated person" (Parker) and, at the same time, "cultivating a truly autonomous and mature person, which is the ultimate ideal of liberal education" (King). I cannot agree more.

I would like to thank all my students in the writing course, in the years since 1995, for giving me the opportunity to examine their writing closely and to understand their common problems, many of which I have tried to address in some way in this book. Many example sentences illustrating various kinds of flaws in Appendices 7, 8, and 9 are taken from their writing.

I have also included in this book exemplary writing from the work of several former students. When student readers see a good example, they are likely to find in it something useful to learn. Jade Lai (who after graduation in 2000 became a Rhodes Scholar at Oxford University), agreed to let me use a fine short essay she wrote for my course as illustration in Chapter 6 ("Writing a Well-organized Paper"). Two former postgraduate students, Amy Yuen Siu-man (M.Phil., 1997) and Frances Wong Kam-yuet (Ph.D., 1996) also agreed to let me use extracts from their theses for illustrating the presentation of qualitative findings in Chapter 9.

Through the generosity and cooperation of some colleagues in other social science disciplines—including psychology, social work, journalism and communication, and economics—I have been able to examine some samples of the writing of students in these fields. As a result, my discussion of the essentials of effective writing has, I hope, gained in relevance for the benefit of social science students more generally.

In summer periods, the Department of Sociology usually assigns postgraduate students to support various teaching and research activities. It is by this arrangement that several postgraduate students—Phoenix Yung, Chen Hon Fai, and Pansy Hoi—have, at various times, given me valuable assistance in collecting and sorting some of the material in Appendices 8 and 9. Pansy also helped me with some final-stage work in putting together the detailed chapter contents and the index. Funds from both the Integrated Programme and the Department also covered communication expenses and fees payable for obtaining permission to use copyright material for inclusion in this book.

I must thank Dr. Steven Luk, Director of The Chinese University Press, for his warm support of this book project and for his understanding in giving me ample time to complete the manuscript. My appreciation also goes to the staff of the Press, for their assistance in the publication of the book.

Last but certainly not least, I am grateful to my wife, Meliza, for her encouragement over the years as I worked on the manuscript. She has always been my motivation that enables me to climb mental mountains. Without her support, writing this book would have been a much more daunting undertaking.

Pedro Pak-tao Ng
Department of Sociology
The Chinese University of Hong Kong

June 2003

Credits

Introduction for Students

Writing is a skill that we all need whatever we do. Writing well is even more important for effective communication and getting things done. As a student, you cannot avoid various writing tasks that are a necessary and important part of your course work. To complete your education fruitfully in whatever field of study, you need to write well.

This book has been written to help you improve your writing for academic purposes. Although I have social science students in mind in preparing this book, students studying other disciplines will also find many parts of the book useful. To improve your writing, whatever your field of study may be, you need to see writing in a new light and care about your writing tasks in every way at every level, from using words and phrases properly to writing coherent paragraphs to preparing a paper according to given standards.

In this book, I place much emphasis on recognizing the significant role of writing in learning and examining the basic principles and strategies of writing paragraphs and papers that are coherent, effective, and up to professional standards. The book consists of ten chapters. Their concerns are briefly as follows:

Chapter 1: The Importance of Writing. Writing is to learn about a chosen topic as well as to demonstrate what you have learned. As you write, you train yourself to think, to organize ideas and to present them in the best way possible.

Chapter 2: Characteristics of Academic Writing. Academic writing is always concerned with a main question that you want to answer systematically using material carefully researched and selected as evidence. The approach is objective and cautious, with attention given to organizing thoughts logically and citing sources thoroughly.

Chapter 3: Writing as a Process. Writing may be thought of as consisting of four major phases: planning, prewriting, drafting, and revising. You should treat each of these phases seriously if you want to achieve better results.

Chapter 4: Reading and Summarizing. The connection between good reading habits and effective writing must not be overlooked. Learn to read actively and responsively so that you can summarize accurately and succinctly what you have read. Good summarization skills are highly valuable to academic writing.

Chapter 5: Writing Effective Paragraphs. As building blocks to organize and develop the main ideas of a paper, paragraphs deserve careful attention. They must be unified and coherent. The whole paper develops around a thesis statement, and each paragraph develops around a topic sentence.

Chapter 6: Writing a Well-organized Paper. A paper is well-organized to the extent that its paragraphs are constructed and arranged in a coordinated and integrated manner, thus making the whole paper unified and coherent. For this purpose, you will learn to follow a basic three-part structure.

Chapter 7: Citing Sources in the Text, and **Chapter 8: Preparing the List of References**. To cite sources and list references properly is necessary for both library research papers and empirical research papers. These two "technical" chapters will guide you in matters of quoting, paraphrasing, in-text citation, and listing references to document all sources cited in the text. You will find examples of many different types of situations in citing sources and listing references, following both APA (American Psychological Association) style and ASA (American Sociological Association) style.

Chapter 9: Reporting Research Findings. Read this chapter carefully for all the basic technical details you will need to attend to in preparing a research report. You will find detailed explanations concerning how you present findings in tabular form and describe a relationship between two variables in quantitative research. You will also find guidelines for presenting qualitative data.

Chapter 10: Revising, Editing, and Proofreading. Much work remains to be done even when you have finished drafting your paper, for you still need to revise, edit, and proofread it. So much goes into these tasks that you should allow sufficient time for them to enhance the quality of your written work. You will also learn how to prepare the paper in its final form ready for submission.

While it is instrumental to understand the nature of writing and the methods of putting together a good paper, it is essential too that you have a good command of grammar and usage of the English language. To write well, you need both sound writing strategies and good word and sentence skills. Like many students for whom English is a second language, you may still be deficient in your knowledge of subject-verb agreement, word forms, use of articles, verb tenses, and use of words and phrases. To help you strengthen your linguistic skills, I have prepared nine appendices. Some of them contain exercises for your practice. Study the explanatory notes and example sentences in the material to sharpen your awareness of what it takes to use English correctly and idiomatically. Given greater care and serious attention, it should not be too difficult to improve the linguistic quality of your writing. The following describes the gist of the nine appendices:

Appendix 1: Subject-Verb Agreement. While it may sound simple that a singular subject takes a singular verb, there are some situations that could be tricky and puzzling. You will find many useful guidelines and examples here.

Appendix 2: Using the Correct Word Form: Verbs, Nouns, Adjectives. Learn to use verbs, nouns, and adjectives correctly; they are the most often-used classes of words. To do so, try to understand their functions in the context of sentences and make a conscious effort to distinguish one word form from another.

Appendix 3: Uncount Nouns, Variable Nouns, and Plural Nouns. Are you careful enough about the use of nouns? Nouns may cause difficulty in use if you do not understand well the feature of nouns known as "number." Uncount nouns that denote abstract ideas, for example, do not have a plural form, whereas some nouns are often used in a plural form because they usually refer to multiple entities.

Appendix 4: Use of Articles. The proper use (or non-use) of articles is a big problem most baffling to many students. If you find yourself using *the* rather frequently in your writing, chances are that you have used this word (the definite article) unnecessarily or erroneously at many places. Read this appendix and study its many example sentences.

Appendix 5: Verb Tenses in Research Papers. Rather than explaining the uses of the various verb tenses in English in general, I have chosen to concentrate on several tenses that are often used in social science research papers.

Appendix 6: Punctuation. Punctuation marks serve to clarify and specify the flow of ideas. Unfortunately, many students have not given sufficient attention to punctuation marks in their writing, which often consists of overly long sentences that are incorrectly punctuated. You will find notes to help you understand how to use various punctuation marks properly so that your writing will be more readable.

Appendix 7: Writing Clear and Effective Sentences. The information in Appendices 1 to 5 should help you come closer to writing correct sentences, but you need more ammunition to make your sentences both clear and effective. For this purpose, I have included thirteen principles in this appendix for your use. You will encounter a variety of grammatical terms, but their meaning should be clear as you read the material.

Appendix 8: Examples of Revision of Sentences with Comments. When you see errors in a sentence and understand not only the nature of the errors but also how they may be corrected, you should learn to recognize them and avoid making such errors yourself. I believe that this is a useful way to learn and have therefore selected twenty cases of faulty sentences, all taken from my students' writing, with suggested revisions and comments.

Appendix 9: Use of Selected Words and Phrases. Use this appendix to examine carefully the correct usage of more than 300 words and phrases that you may often come across in your readings. You may need to use many of them when you write. Most of the entries collected here are based on errors found in students' writing over the years. Study the comments and the example sentences that illustrate how a word or phrase may be used. Many of these sentences have content that is relevant to the study of society and human behaviour.

Such is the distribution of material in this book. You do not have to start with the first chapter; you can select a chapter that seems to be more relevant to your present need (such as citing sources in your text or reporting research findings) if that is more urgent to you. However, if you start with the first three chapters, you will be on firmer ground to put academic writing into perspective, which will perhaps make the rest of the book more sensible and understandable to you. At the same time, do try to make good use of the appendices. They are included in this book to remind you that you must give due attention to your language competence to achieve better results in your writing, academic or otherwise. Without adequate use of language that is grammatical, idiomatic, and clear, writing cannot be truly effective. Enjoy reading and practise better writing!

CHAPTER 1

The Importance of Writing

When you think of writing, the first thing that comes to your mind is probably that it is something you do as part of your course work. True, as a student, you may often need to complete written assignments, long or short. The form and nature of these assignments depend on the discipline in question. In the social sciences, they are likely to include tutorial papers, reading reports, field reports, research reports, and term papers. They may seem very demanding, especially when they serve as the basis on which your course performance is partly or largely assessed.

Are you among those students for whom having to do written assignments causes much anxiety? Are they nothing but a chore to you? Do you think of them as just something you have to do to get grades rather than to learn something well? If you really think so, you are not likely to go very far in the learning of your subject, be it psychology, social work, or sociology. On the other hand, if you are serious about learning and are curious enough to want to get more out of your writing tasks, then you should pause to ask yourself what writing really means beyond the fulfilment of an imposed requirement. This is a question you must ask earnestly if you want to do a good job about writing for your course work. It is even more so if you are interested in the subject you are studying. Indeed, by taking a serious attitude towards writing, which is the first step in improving it, your interest in the subject you are studying is likely to increase.

Written assignments have two interrelated purposes. First, you write to demonstrate what you have learned. This sounds obvious enough. Second, you write to learn. This may not be immediately obvious to you. Let us consider these purposes in some detail.

1.1 Writing to Demonstrate What You Have Learned

Understanding your subject and its issues is not enough; in addition, you need to communicate what you know and understand to your teacher. Some of the writing done for this purpose takes relatively little time, as in examinations that use essay questions. Otherwise, the writing may take anywhere from a few days to several months (as may be needed for a substantial term paper or senior thesis) before completion. Whatever the subject and whatever the length of time taken, the examinations and term papers you write should reflect as accurately as possible what you know so that you will be assessed in the best light possible.

Other things being equal, you as a student will be judged by your writing because it is both a concrete and a convenient indicator. Papers that are well written are more likely to display your observation or analysis clearly and convincingly to the reader, and hence are more likely to be favourably received. By contrast, papers that are written in error-ridden language and are poorly organized will be burdensome to read if only because the teacher has to guess what you are trying to say. In general, the odds are against you when it comes to grading if your written work cannot effectively demonstrate what you have learned.

1.2 Writing to Learn

Writing to produce a paper is a process consisting of many activities. If you look carefully at the various things you are supposed to do when you try to produce the required written assignment, you will see that they are all essentially learning activities whose purpose is to gain understanding. First, you focus on the topic, search your mind to see what you know of it, and scribble rudimentary notes to indicate what might be interesting or relevant. Then, you read about the topic, gather what seems to be useful information from various sources, and take notes to help you remember this information. At some point when you feel you have accumulated a substantial amount of information and notes, you begin to construct some kind of outline to guide yourself as you proceed to write the draft.

As this process continues, you need to think hard about "points" or ideas that are worth describing, explaining, or discussing. This sort of thinking is reflective thinking, which you can do well if you "objectify" your thoughts—that is, if you put yourself in the position of a cool-headed observer looking over the ideas that come to your attention. You need to practise thinking this way to gain understanding. As this understanding emerges, you will find that you can start to think creatively to put certain ideas together in some meaningful order and express them accordingly in words, sentences, and paragraphs. An element of creativeness is always present in writing as you can shape the product in more ways than one, although some ways are likely to be better than others.

Reflective and creative thinking is what makes learning real and exciting since you use such thinking to process ideas selectively and often critically instead of merely receiving them passively. It is with such thinking that you commit your thoughts to paper. When your thoughts are expressed according to a carefully considered order, they become meaningful knowledge that you can communicate with your fellow students as well as your teacher. As you engage in these activities, you are certainly learning. Indeed, pause for a moment now and ask yourself whether your learning experience might have been different if you did not have to do any written assignment at all. Would you have learned less or less well? In all likelihood, you would, because without the training and discipline of writing you would have less opportunity to examine ideas rigorously and reflect on their meaning.

1.3 Writing to Deepen Understanding

The act of writing, in the sense just described, necessarily makes you think about the subject of your writing. The thoughts that you put down on paper become objective material that you can examine carefully. As you do so, you will think about this material not in a vacuum but in the context of your previous learning and of the knowledge that others have produced. Reading and examining your own writing allows you to evaluate the significance of a certain point, or to check whether your writing actually expresses what you want to say. Perhaps you discover that you have something better or more relevant to say. This is likely to occur if you examine your writing after some time during which you may have explored the topic further by reading or by discussing with others. As a result, you want to rewrite your draft so as to clarify or sharpen your ideas. Writing, to be as effective as it should be, is indeed rewriting, a point we will return to in Chapters 3 and 10. In this way, writing gives you the opportunity to deepen your understanding.

1.4 Relationship between Learning and Demonstrating What You Have Learned

Given the role of writing in your learning, you can see that it is closely related to writing to demonstrate learning. If you realize that your teachers use your written work to gauge how much you have learned and hence to assess your academic performance, that is all the more reason why you should treat your writing seriously and use it to show that you actually have learned something important. You should ask yourself this question: "What should I include in my paper and how should I approach the topic so that my presentation will show that I have something important and meaningful to say?" Thus, consideration of what is expected of you in demonstrating what you know and understand will be high on your agenda as you participate in the activities corresponding to writing to learn.

Suppose you are asked to write a paper on "The contemporary university as a means of consumption." Before you can write anything, you must examine carefully the nature of this topic to see what it means and what kinds of questions it involves. You may want to discuss with your teacher to help you understand better what you are expected to do in approaching this topic. After such preliminary effort, you will gradually clarify what your assignment calls for. In particular, you will perhaps have identified what the concept "means of consumption" means and the main ideas that this concept encompasses. You may decide that your analysis should include a variety of means of consumption—including, for example, fast-food restaurants, shopping malls, and theme parks—although your focus is on the "contemporary university." Further, you will decide whether your approach is one of explaining why the contemporary university can be seen as a means of consumption or one of critically evaluating such a view.

These, then, are some of the main considerations associated with writing to demonstrate learning. They are going to be on your mind as you take up your writing task in which you, in the manner explained above, learn about your topic. Indeed, such considerations may be seen as your guidelines when you treat writing as learning. As guidelines, they are often quite flexible, although some will be perhaps more prominent than others. Following them leads to not only a written product to fulfil a course requirement but also understanding that is new and rewarding to you.

1.5 Writing as Good Training

As writing to demonstrate learning in a very practical sense shapes your learning, it should be clear that writing to learn cannot be separate from writing to show learning. They take place simultaneously, and are two sides of the same coin. Undoubtedly, writing has a central role in your education. It trains you in developing effective thinking, organizing, and presentation skills, for to write well requires genuine effort given to planning, drafting, and revising. Good planning and preparatory work help you to generate useful ideas. Organizing ideas and arranging them clearly and logically help you to communicate effectively with your readers. Revising or rewriting, if done properly, enhances the effectiveness of your writing.

1.6 Improving Your Writing

As is true for any language, the ability to write well in English is the result of hard work and constant practice. To write well in English is even harder for students whose first language is not English. To improve your English writing skills, the following tasks are necessary: reading actively and extensively, strengthening your language awareness, and thinking in English.

1.6.1 Reading Actively and Extensively

As is discussed further in Chapter 4, you need to be an active and extensive reader if you want to be a good writer. Much of your learning in your major discipline and in language use comes from reading articles and books that others have written. The greater the variety of material you read, the better it is for you not only because it gives you more substantive information but also because it familiarizes you with ways of expressing and discussing ideas of all sorts. To be an active reader means not only that you read a lot but also that you read with much attentive involvement and response. Attentive involvement enables you to follow what you read carefully so that you will note how an idea is presented and developed. At the same time, attentive response occurs if you can associate what you read with certain relevant ideas that you have previously known from other sources. As you read along, perhaps you have questions concerning the validity of a point or the evidence the author uses for supporting the point. If you habitually notice these in other people's writing, you will find it important to check for such problems in your own writing.

From active reading you can distil not only information on a given subject but also knowledge of various uses of language that will become part of your language skills. Of course, for this to happen, you sometimes need to give a little extra attention to the language the author uses. If you are content with just knowing "roughly what it means," and hurry on with other matters because, as you might say, "I don't have time," then you simply are not making the best use of what reading can do for you. Naturally, sometimes you have to skim and scan for main points, without paying too much attention to how the material is actually written. But you should always allow yourself some time for slowing down so that you can learn more about methods of organization and patterns of presentation that will, in the long run, rub off on your writing. For this reason, no serious student intent on improving his or her writing can afford to overlook the value of active reading.

1.6.2 Strengthening Your Language Awareness

As you read extensively, you should become progressively more aware of the structure and idiomatic use of the English language. Such awareness is essential to the development of your language competence, particularly when it is not your first language. To nurture such awareness, you must pay special attention to the requirements of grammar and usage so that you will be better prepared to recognize what is correct and idiomatic. This awareness does not just happen by itself; it has to be created and developed through genuine and persistent effort. Do not, for instance, feel that you have learned enough English grammar in secondary school. You should feel an urge to improve your understanding and grasp of grammar and proper usage of words and phrases by consulting books on these subjects (for assistance, approach teachers or librarians).

But language awareness does not rest on knowledge of grammar and usage rules and conventions alone; it has to be strengthened and enhanced through seeing "real" English in action in newspapers, magazines, books, and on the Internet's many sites providing useful information. In these places, you see how the English language is actually used in this modern age, with all its richness and colour, in a great variety of domains, including business, politics, technology, travel, and entertainment. The more you see patterns of words, phrases, and sentences—I stress the word "see," which requires that you are actually aware of what is present before your eyes—the more they become lasting images that you can retrieve from your memory later on when the need arises. By exploring these places often, your personal vocabulary surely grows. Indeed, you should find it rewarding to see how ideas can be expressed clearly and effectively by identifying examples from what you read (and perhaps recording them in your notebook).

In essence, then, there is a two-way interaction between exposure to the language and language awareness. Now that English is truly a global language, you should foster such interaction as far as possible. The more you see various types of English writing, the more you become aware of the subtleties of the language. This, in turn, would motivate you to seek further improvement in writing in English.

1.6.3 Thinking in English

Many readers of this book are likely to be students for whom English is not their first language. Some comments on thinking in English are thus in order.

Language is a communication tool. The use of a language is the result of some integration of experiences of listening, speaking, reading, and writing. The mental faculty that makes this integration possible and that gives meaning to or derives meaning from the content of communication is, of course, thinking, which functions simultaneously with listening, speaking, reading, and writing. In the case of a first language, all these activities, including thinking, proceed in the same language. When people learn and use a second language, however, the more familiar first language often tends to interfere with the way in which ideas come out in the second language. In Hong Kong, for example, despite the common use of English in business and the learning of the language in schools, most students lack opportunities of using English, particularly in listening and in speaking. When students speak and write in English, the thinking that is responsible for putting ideas together in words often operates not in English but in Chinese. They then take an intermediate step of "translation" to turn Chinese words and phrases into English, often rendering the resulting English speech or text unidiomatic at best and fragmented at worst.

This is an issue beyond the scope of this book. But it seems fair to say that your command of the English language will be hampered if you rely too much on thinking in Chinese first and then trying to translate the idea into English. Such reliance is likely to make you write in patterns that follow the syntax of Chinese rather than that of English. You are likely to make mistakes in English grammar without realizing so. Just to illustrate this, examine the following sentence written by a student:

```
My friend choose to be vegetarian is because of her
belief.
```

Two points may be noted. First, because verbs do not inflect in Chinese as they do in English, Chinese students may not be too acutely aware of the *-s* ending of English verbs used in the present tense for the singular third person. Hence this student writes *My friend choose* instead of *My friend chooses*. Second, in Chinese the verb *shi* (是, roughly the equivalent of *be*) is often used, particularly in speech, to link not only a simple subject and a comment on the subject but also a finite clause and a comment on such a clause. Thinking in Chinese first would therefore cause the student to subconsciously use the verb *be* without realizing that in English syntax it cannot be used to link a finite clause such as *My friend chooses to be vegetarian* and a prepositional phrase such as *because of her belief*. Thinking in English, on the other hand, should more likely give the following correct sentence:

```
My friend chooses to be vegetarian because of her
belief.
```

For most learners of English lacking a firm grasp of the language, thinking in English is not easy. If you are one of them, you probably agree. But this does not mean that you should not try. If you have fairly large exposure to English through reading and listening (whatever you can get on television and in films), you may find thinking in English not impossible. Thinking is your inner voice that speaks silently. To keep this silent voice working, try using questions of *what?* (e.g., What does this concept mean?) *why?* (Why is it important?) and *how?* (How does it compare with ___?) As you ponder these questions, you can also try making statements with such introductory words as: *I think it means ___; there are at least two reasons why it is important; it is very much like the concept of ___.* Make a conscious effort to do something like this regularly, and gradually you should see significant differences— even improvements—in your writing.

Obviously, it takes great determination and much patience to change language habits. The weak writing skills of many students can be said to be the result of "unhealthy" language habits. There will not be any breakthrough unless a critical mass is obtained in the interaction, as pointed out above, between exposure to the language and language awareness. When that happens, thinking in English comes rather more naturally, making writing in English its direct outcome.

Of course, this is a simplified description of what happens in improving your writing, but I think the essence is there.

1.7 Writing is Serious Business

Good writing skills are essential to every university student. They are instrumental for successful performance in any academic discipline and, indeed, in any profess-sion after graduation.

Like other communication skills and skills in research and problem-solving, good writing skills are transferable from one situation to another. Clear and well-organized writing is essential to effective communication and leadership in the work world. To a considerable degree, the quality of your writing reflects your personal quality as a student now and as a professional or business executive in the future.

It should be clear that you must not think of writing in terms of simply completing a requirement imposed on you. The importance of writing must be seen in the broader context of learning. If learning is important to you, then writing is essential because it fosters your learning and it demonstrates what you have learned in a way that you, your teacher, and others can all see. If you value the opportunity of learning at the university and are keen on maximizing that opportunity so as to be solidly equipped for a career of your choice, then you should treat writing with all eagerness and seriousness because so much of what you want to achieve depends on it.

If the importance of writing is no longer in doubt, you should then familiarize yourself with the kind of writing that is expected for academic purposes. This is what the next chapter will explore.

1.8 Summing Up the Importance of Writing

- Writing is to demonstrate what you have learned. Writing that is error-free and well organized is always in your favour.
- Writing is also to learn because:
  (a) You need to think reflectively to understand better.
  (b) You need to think creatively to put ideas together.
  (c) Writing makes you think about your topic in relation to what you have previously learned.
- Writing to learn and writing to demonstrate what you have learned are two sides of the same coin: you have to really learn sufficiently about your topic before you can show what you know about it.
- Writing trains your thinking, organizing, and presentation skills.
- To improve your writing, do the following:
  (a) Read actively (i.e., responsively) and extensively.
  (b) Strengthen your awareness of the structure and idiomatic use of English.
  (c) (For those whose first language is not English) Think in English when you write.

CHAPTER 2

Characteristics of Academic Writing

Writing comes in many forms and styles. Just look around in your own home and in public libraries, and you will easily see that there is quite a variety: news reports, personal columns in newspapers, business communication (e.g., recruitment advertisements, records of annual meetings), fiction, biographies, and stories about celebrities in popular culture magazines. The list could go on. Then there is academic writing as found in books and articles on academic topics such as those available in a university library.

Academic writing is the kind of writing that you read in your studies and also the kind of writing you are expected to produce yourself as a university student. To improve your writing skills so that you can perform better as a student, you need to be familiar with the characteristics of academic writing, which is in many ways quite different from non-academic writing.

2.1 What is Academic Writing?

Loosely defined, academic writing is writing for academic purposes. That is, it is writing that explores or examines some aspect of knowledge. Generically, it is the kind of writing that scholars or academics produce (as philosophers, historians, social scientists, natural scientists, and so forth) as can be seen in academic books and articles in academic journals. There are, of course, differences in such aspects as organization, vocabulary, and academic conventions from one discipline to another.

Written assignments are required of students in practically all academic disciplines. In general, you are supposed to take the kind of writing normally found in the literature of your discipline as a model for your writing. In the social sciences, written assignments include tutorial discussion papers, brief summaries, reading reports, case reports, and term papers (which may be in the form of reports of library research or empirical research). They may vary in length from specific summaries of one or two pages to term papers running to 20 or 30 pages. You use them to assimilate and process what you know from reading, discussing, listening to lectures, and first-hand or secondary data. Your teacher expects your work to show your understanding of some given topic and to be written in conformity with the norms of writing applicable in your discipline.

As you can imagine, there are many forms of academic writing, depending on the discipline. Thus, you can expect to find considerable differences between a literary criticism essay and a sociological article on life quality in Hong Kong. Likewise, you will also find differences between quantitative research reports in sociology or psychology and qualitative ethnographic studies in anthropology or educational research. The form of writing also varies according to the special field within the same discipline. Within sociology, for example, a paper that evaluates the contribution of a contemporary theorist looks very different from one written about social problems of the old walled city in Kowloon of Hong Kong as a kind of oral history through interviewing qualified informants.

Regardless of such differences, you use academic writing to demonstrate how well you can research a certain topic, how observant you are of happenings in a given situation, how carefully you analyze an issue, how systematically you argue a point of view, how adequately you use and evaluate evidence that may support your argument, and how logically you organize your thinking. You may not do all of these things equally extensively in a given written assignment, but during the years of your university studies you are likely to have experienced them all to varying degrees.

In the following, we shall examine the characteristics of academic writing under seven aspects: purpose, objectivity, evidence, generalizations, structure, citation, and language. These are particularly relevant to the writing of essays or papers.

2.2 Purpose

All academic essays have a purpose: to write about a topic. In writing about a topic, you need to consider what you want to accomplish. Do you want to inform or to persuade your readers? If you want to inform, you may explain or describe a concept, an idea, a theory, an event, or an issue. What is the meaning of the concept or content of the idea? What is the theory all about? How does it help us to understand certain social events or issues? If you want to persuade, you need to gather enough evidence so that your readers may accept your viewpoint. You may want to convince them of the need for a new approach to an old problem. Depending on the topic, you may also want to both inform and persuade, such as when you review the penetration of the mass media and the Internet into the lives of adolescents and propose that parents are having less and less control over the development of their children. In any case, you have to find out what your purpose is before deciding on subsequent steps. Your purpose will determine the approach you will take and the tasks that are appropriate.

The purpose of your academic writing task, then, is more than just choosing a topic. It requires you to consider carefully what you intend to do about the topic that you have chosen (or one that has been assigned to you). While the topic may look straightforward as a phrase, say, "The role of the mass media in family life in Hong Kong," you must clarify for yourself the purpose for writing about this topic. That is, you need to construct a question or a set of questions about the topic for which you are to supply adequate answers. Of course, this depends very much on what you know about the topic and what seems important to you about this topic. For the topic just mentioned, you may want to examine how the mass media—television especially—are used by family members to provide not just content for information and relaxation but also a context for promoting interaction among themselves. You will then need to describe in some detail with examples how this indeed is the case. Such will then be your purpose.

2.3 Objectivity

If a writer focuses on the subject of discussion, whatever it is, without bringing in personal feelings or opinions, he or she is writing objectively. Personal diaries are often highly subjective, whereas news reports are objective to the extent that they are based on observable facts. In academic writing, room for objectivity may vary. Writing in the natural sciences is typically objective as the natural world is examined objectively while writing in the humanities, such as art and music, may suitably contain subjectivity to accommodate personal interpretation or appreciation. In the social sciences, writing can contain both objective and subjective elements. In sociology, for example, writing is predominantly objective in a research report based on survey data but may incorporate personal interpretations and opinions when discussing social policy options or when critically reviewing an article on gender differences in shopping. In economics, writing about how production of goods and services changes with the rapid development of a global economy also demands a high degree of objectivity in description and analysis, calling for the use of perhaps a large amount of statistics.

In essays that intend to inform, your approach is one that seeks to describe and explain what goes on in the world "out there" or what "facts" are associated with people, objects, and events. Where persuasion is the purpose, your task is largely analytical by showing, for instance, what factors are responsible for the emergence of a problem or why certain actions do not actually help to solve the problem. To approach a topic in such a manner is to be objective rather than subjective although it is still possible to develop your own approach as long as you do not forget to place it within an analytical frame in which you appeal to logic, not personal feelings.

2.4 Use of Evidence

Since objectivity is often necessary in social science writing, evidence rather than personal judgment is used to support observations or claims that you make. In your written assignments, you may have to evaluate an opinion concerning a certain policy, account for the emergence of a social trend, or consider the implications of some current state of affairs. To do so adequately, you need the help of evidence, such as the following:

- Facts (verifiable descriptions of conditions or states of affairs)
- Statistics (from Government or other credible sources)
- Research findings
- Specific cases as examples
- Expert opinion (from scholars, professionals, and other reputable opinion leaders)

Using such evidence means doing research. Your research would include not only finding and selecting the suitable (both in quality and in quantity) evidence but also documenting, or recording, the details of the sources of information so that they may be properly cited for the benefit of the reader.

2.5 Generalizations

Generalizations, as statements that are expected to be true in most cases, have an important role in academic writing. In the exploration of knowledge, they may be the result of careful analysis at times and the reason for rethinking and questioning at others. Where evidence is ample and strong, you can make generalizations with confidence. Where evidence is only partial and weak, you should qualify your generalizations to allow for exceptions, discrepancies, or other types of error.

If presented as part of a conclusion, a generalization is often treated as tentative, subject to further testing and verification. At the same time, the conditions under which the generalization is to be treated as plausible should always be indicated. This characteristic is important because of the nature of society and human behaviour—the subject matter of the social sciences. Patterns of social phenomena and human behaviour are more likely to be probabilistic than deterministic. Thus, a qualified general statement such as the following is often seen in social research reports:

```
Both men and women--and women in particular--who are
less than 50 years old and who have a post-secondary
education are highly likely to reject the idea of
male dominance in the household.
```

This is a statement made with the support of research findings, implying that it is subject to further verification in other research. As a qualified generalization, it is more precise than a sweeping statement such as: *People now no longer accept the idea of male dominance in the household.* Indeed, sweeping generalizations are dangerous because they are oversimplified and easily challenged. Since the evidence you have is often specific to certain categories of people under certain conditions, you must be careful not to make too large a leap in describing the "general pattern." That is, you must not over-generalize; academic writing is responsible and cautious writing.

2.6 Structure

In personal writing, such as a diary or a letter to a friend, there is no definite order or pattern governing how you present your ideas: you simply write whatever comes to your mind. It may not even have a clear or relevant ending. But such writing is still valid because it is all about the thoughts and feelings of the writer. In journalistic writing, as in news reports, there is usually the brief announcement or report of what happened followed by a detailed account of the event that may include the background or historical account of what led to the event. Academic essays, in sharp contrast, are usually written in a three-part structure: introduction, body, and conclusion.

The introduction presents the topic that you want to write about. It states your thesis, or the position you intend to take. At the same time, it also places your thesis in some larger picture by summarizing what other scholars have said or found about the topic. This is technically known as "literature review." How extensive this review ought to be depends on the nature of your topic and on the length of the essay.

The body is the main part of your essay in which you develop the main idea presented in the introduction. It may consist of any number of paragraphs, depending on largely the complexity of the topic. Each paragraph should have its own focus, dealing with one point related to the overall main idea. The paragraphs must be constructed to show a logical connection between them. Your readers will expect to see not only clear statements of what the focal idea of each paragraph is but also sentences that indicate how the paragraphs are linked so that the essay is an integrated whole.

The conclusion is, of course, where you sum up the points discussed in the body and bring those points to bear on your thesis. It should be clear that you have given your topic a systematic and thoughtful treatment so that your readers will find your claim or position acceptable. The conclusion is also the place where you may want to raise questions that need further exploration.

If you follow this structure in writing your essay, it stands a good chance of becoming better organized and more readable. Chapter 6 discusses this further.

2.7 Citation

Since the goal of academic writing is to explore some aspect of knowledge, the stock of knowledge that others have contributed to is a source of ideas and insights that can help you approach your topic. When you take ideas or words from other authors to illustrate a point or to support a claim or argument, you must acknowledge such authors by accurately indicating the sources, published or otherwise, at appropriate places in your text. This is called citation, a distinctive mark of responsible academic writing.

In your written assignments, you are obliged to cite sources whether you quote the exact words or rephrase them in your own words. In either case, you need to include the full citation of the sources in a list of references at the end of your essay. This is the norm—and a very important one—in academic writing demonstrating the principle of academic honesty. If you use ideas and words originating in other sources without acknowledging them by citing, you commit plagiarism, a serious offence. By upholding this norm, with all sources consulted and used in the process of writing properly recorded, you are giving them proper credit. Your readers, including those in the larger academic community, can then go to these sources if they need more details to enhance their understanding of your topic.

Citing other relevant sources is commonly practised in academic writing to provide a context for approaching and developing a topic. To do so properly requires familiarity with many conventions, which are covered in detail in Chapters 7 and 8.

2.8 Language

Since academic writing places much emphasis on objectivity of approach and logical organization of ideas, this goal is more conveniently attained if the writer uses language seriously and carefully. In casual conversation and personal writing, you use informal and colloquial language, because you communicate with friends or people whom you know well. Contractions (*I'm fine, we don't know*) are frequent and sentences are sometimes incomplete, but this does not matter too much as communication in speech is often aided by gestures and facial expressions, and people whom you know well are likely to be capable of understanding what you mean even if you use a subjective style with incomplete sentences. In writing about academic topics, however, the written language itself must bear the whole burden of making your messages clear to those who read them. You must use words that are precise in meaning, make statements that are complete in structure and content, and avoid contractions.

Two characteristics of the language used in academic writing may be mentioned here. First, it contains subject-specific terminology or vocabulary. Second, it is formal rather than informal.

2.8.1 Subject-specific Vocabulary

In writing about phenomena and issues in the social sciences, words used may have specific meanings known to scholars following a particular field or problem area. Used properly, they facilitate communication among parties interested in the field or area. If not, your writing may fail to achieve its academic purpose effectively. Problems, however, may arise where the social science terms are also part of everyday language, which may attach certain connotations to such terms or simplify their meaning. Thus, for example, in common everyday usage, the word *bureaucracy* connotes inflexibility and official arrogance of "red tape." While inflexibility and arrogance may well be a consequence of *bureaucracy*, they are not part of the essential meaning of the concept of *bureaucracy,* which is the hierarchical structure of authority based on recognized positions. When you use such a term in writing about organizations of any kind, you must use it correctly. Another example is the commonly used word *role*. In everyday language, a person's *role* in a given situation is likely to be understood as simply what that person does. Strictly speaking, of course, what a person does is not entirely the same as what that person *is expected* to do. In the social sciences, particularly in sociology, such distinction is necessary, as can be demonstrated by the distinction between *role expectations* and *role performance.* Performance may fall short of or exceed expectations: their difference is often a subject for study. Thus, you need to think twice about what you really mean to say when you plan to write about "the role of working mothers in family interaction."

2.8.2 Formal Language: Authoritative and Emotionally Neutral

The other characteristic of academic writing is that its language is formal. That subject-specific vocabulary is used in academic writing is a factor that contributes to the formality of the language of such writing. Formality is a matter of the "level of usage," which ranges from the very formal level, as seen in legal documents that have a highly impersonal tone and use long and cumbersome sentence structures, to the very informal level as in conversation between close friends. On this continuum, social science writing may be placed as moderately formal.

The main features of formal language include the following:

- It is authoritative and serious in tone. By using subject-specific vocabulary that has specialized reference to the phenomena under study or discussion, the writing that results maintains an authoritative and serious tone.
- It is not emotionally charged, but is neutral and avoids jumping to personal judgements. Thus, for example, you would never write something like *All politicians are liars* or *The government is so stupid as to follow a course of action that is absolutely senseless.*

To illustrate these two features, let us take a paragraph from Johnson's (1991) *The Forest for the Trees* and examine its language closely.

```
Sociological thinking requires a sensitivity to the
existence of social systems and their cultural,
structural, population, and ecological characteris-
tics. These basic characteristics--and concepts such
as value, role, and group that are related to and
derived from them--make up a conceptual framework we
can use to observe the world in a sociological way.
This kind of framework is the foundation of any
discipline, because it defines basic subject matter,
whether it be the origins of the universe, the
properties of living organisms, or the varieties of
family life.
```

The first sentence of Johnson's paragraph declares, with a tone of authoritativeness and seriousness, that "sociological thinking requires a sensitivity to the existence of social systems and their cultural, structural, population, and ecological characteristics." Such words as *sensitivity* and *social systems* quickly draw our attention to what happens when we think sociologically. The rest of the paragraph carries on with the same tone of seriousness to point to the kind of *conceptual framework* that enables us to "observe the world in a sociological way." Note that the writing contains nothing about the writer's own personal feelings of what sociological thinking is. Rather, the paragraph takes an objective position to explain to its readers the elements that make up the conceptual framework used for thinking sociologically. Indeed, Johnson tells us, this kind of conceptual framework "defines basic subject matter" in any discipline.

2.8.3 *Formal Language: Expressing Meanings Precisely*

A third main feature of formal language in academic writing is that it is particularly concerned with expressing meanings precisely. Readers must not be left to guess what exactly it is that you want to say. Meanings must be made as clear as possible. You will find it useful to recognize several ways of achieving this goal: (a) using examples, (b) choosing the right words, (c) being clear about what you are discussing, and (d) expressing the same idea in another way.

2.8.3a *Using examples*

Examples serve to clarify or elaborate a point or an idea. Thus, in the illustrative paragraph shown above, Johnson mentions "value, role, and group" as examples of concepts related to social systems, and "the origins of the universe, the properties of living organisms, or the varieties of family life" as examples of various kinds of basic subject matter. The use of examples in academic writing ensures that you convey meanings precisely and that your readers understand your ideas clearly.

2.8.3b *Choosing the right words*

Choosing the right words for what you really want to say is a basic skill in academic writing. Take the word *result* for example. It is a neutral word because it does not indicate the nature or kind of result that you may have in mind. If the result is desirable, you should consider using the word *benefit* instead of *result.* If the result is undesirable, you probably should use *harm* or *repercussion.* Further, if you are thinking about unexpected results, which could be either good or bad, then what you need is perhaps *ramifications* or *implications.*

If you are trying to gather evidence to support an argument (P), what you can say in conclusion depends heavily on the strength of the evidence (X) you have. Partial evidence does not allow you to claim that you have *proven* P; you can only say that X *suggests* (or *implies*) that P *probably stands*. On the other hand, if you believe that you have got very strong evidence, then you can choose from such words as *confirm, demonstrate,* or *substantiate*, and say that X *confirms* P.

2.8.3c *Being clear about what you are discussing*

What you are discussing must be clear to your readers, or they will find it difficult to follow your discussion. The following are some possible situations for each of which an example sentence is given:

- Classifying a term into types:

      Groups may be classified into in-groups and out-
      groups.

- Indicating the characteristic(s) of an entity (e.g., people, event, collectivity, society):

      Hong Kong society is characterized by its emphasis
      on work efficiency.

- Defining a term:

      By "identity crisis," we mean a condition in which
      people are uncertain and confused about who they
      are.

- Specifying what is not included in your discussion:

      While leisure is as much a state of mind as it is
      a pattern of time use for pleasure, we shall focus
      our discussion on the latter.

2.8.3d *Expressing the same idea in another way*

To ensure that your readers see exactly what you mean, especially when you are discussing an important idea, you can try to put it in some other way, as done in the following:

    Language is our guide to social reality. That is to
    say, language gives us the tool for establishing the

```
meanings of the experience we obtain in our world:
what we see, think, and do.
```

Of course, you can always find other ways to say the same thing. Thus, the second sentence in the above example can be alternatively introduced by *In other words, Put differently,* or *This means that.* Such phrases to explain or elaborate an idea are indeed often used in academic writing.

2.9 Informal and Formal Styles Compared

Since formal language is so important in academic writing, we will put its main features here once again against those of the informal style so that you can get a better idea of the kind of language you should use in your papers.

Informal style	**Formal style**
(1) Relaxed and personal in tone:	(1) Serious and impersonal in tone:
`Many of my classmates enjoy the book.`	`The book is well received by many readers.`
`When we think, we try to get something done.`	`Thinking is purposive.`
(2) Often expressing meanings imprecisely:	(2) Expressing meanings precisely:
`The article is about the problems of working couples.`	`The article reports how younger and older dual-income couples cope with the problems of having to live apart in pursuing a career.`
`We will talk about . . .`	`We will examine (or analyze, evaluate) . . .`
(3) Frequent use of contractions:	(3) Use of contractions avoided:
`We don't know what's missing.`	`We do not know what is missing.`
(4) Sentences tend to be short and simple: See first example sentence in (2).	(4) Sentences vary in length and structure: See first example sentence in (2).

2.10 Your Written Assignments for Different Purposes

The characteristics of academic writing described above may be present to varying degrees depending on the type of written assignment. In term papers using library research, empirical research reports, and theses based on empirical research, the characteristics of being objective, using evidence, and citing other sources are particularly prominent. Your teachers will expect you to demonstrate these qualities clearly. In other types of assignment, such as reading reports and tutorial discussion papers—or assignments that are more limited in scope and purpose—the statement of the problem or specification of the topic is less elaborate and there is likely to be less need for citing sources. Moreover, some degree of personal response to and evaluation of an event or a process may be justifiably included along with reasons in some assignments, such as case reports and qualitative research reports.

In preparing to write your assignment, always think carefully about its purpose and try to visualize what this means for the kind of academic writing you are expected to produce. While there are differences such as those just mentioned, you should bear in mind that the academic style is the model that applies to your writing task as a university student. In particular, pay special attention to how you organize ideas and how you express them in a language that is used carefully and thoughtfully to convey precise meanings.

2.11 Checklist for Academic Writing in the Social Sciences

The main characteristics of academic writing are essentially the following:

- Identify as your writing purpose the main question to which you want to provide the answers.
- Prefer objective facts to personal feelings or opinions.
- Use evidence (e.g., verifiable facts, documented statistics, case material, expert opinion) to support claims.
- Make generalizations cautiously: qualify your generalizations whenever evidence is only partial.
- Use a basic three-part structure (introduction, body, and conclusion) to organize your thoughts.
- Always cite sources that you have used for ideas, whether you quote directly or rephrase in your own words.
- Write in a formal style using words carefully to convey meanings precisely.

CHAPTER 3

Writing as a Process

Like building a house or putting on a stage performance, writing is a process because it takes time and effort. The process results in a product. Like a house or a performance, a written essay or term paper is a product that, if crafted well, we can admire and remember. A good house needs a competent architect and careful execution of his or her plans; a good performance requires seasoned artists and meticulous rehearsals. Likewise, a good paper is written by someone who not only has something to say but who also understands that good writing is always the result of care and patience.

What does the writing process involve? As you can imagine, it must begin in small and humble ways before taking shape, and anything that takes shape must be carefully developed and polished before there is any acceptable written product. This sounds natural enough; it is true whether the desired product is a short essay or a full-length term paper or even a thesis. For simplicity, let us think of the writing process as consisting of four main stages: (a) planning, (b) prewriting, (c) drafting, and (d) revising. In planning, you want to have an overall picture of how you are going to tackle your written assignment. Then you need to search for ideas and try to shape them into some meaningful basic form through prewriting activities. Once you have a main theme and some usable ideas roughly structured, you can start drafting to give "body and flesh" to your paper. But do not forget that you must leave time for revision, which is to see if changes are necessary to improve the quality of your paper both in content and in presentation. Let us now consider these stages in some detail so that you may recognize their importance.

3.1 Planning

In planning, you consider several basic questions that will set the stage for your writing task. You need to consider (a) the nature of your writing task, (b) your audience, (c) the sources of information required, and (d) your constraints.

3.1.1 *What Is the Nature of Your Writing Task?*

Your assignment may be a two-page reading report or a fifteen-page term paper on a topic of your choice. Given this basic ground, you need to identify what the reading report or the term paper will require. Thus, the reading report is likely to require both a brief summary of a designated article and a critical evaluation of it. The term paper may require you to compare two theories of deviant behaviour and assess their usefulness for explaining why young people join gangs. In the case of the reading report, you need to know that "critical evaluation" means looking for both strengths and weaknesses according to some clearly stated criteria. In the case of the term paper, you should realize that comparison involves an examination of similarities and differences. Depending on the topic chosen, your writing task may call for an analysis of what a problem may consist of or what may be the problem's causes and consequences. Alternatively, your writing task may require you to put forward an argument and to seek suitable evidence to support it. Knowing what your writing task involves at the planning stage is important because it draws your attention to the kinds of activities you should engage in so that your writing will proceed in the right direction.

3.1.2 *Whom Are You Writing For?*

All writing is written to be read. In your case, your written assignment will most likely be read by your professor or someone assisting him or her in the role of a teaching assistant. What does your professor expect you to do? Does he or she expect you to do very little in the summary part but much more in the evaluation part of your reading report? In that hypothetical term paper on deviant behaviour, does your professor expect you to be rather thorough in comparing the two selected theories of deviant behaviour to the extent that all basic concepts and assumptions relevant to those theories should be explained? Remember to ask yourself such questions and perhaps clarify them with your professor so that you have clear guidelines. Not all professors think alike and expect the same kinds of ingredients in their students' writing. In one sense, this may look like giving your professor what he or she wants. In another sense—and this is more important for your learning—you can think of your professor as the person who interprets for you the standards that may be used to assess your academic work. In this sense, your writing is done for a larger academic audience as represented by your professor.

3.1.3 *What Sources of Information Do You Need?*

You should first check what you already know about your topic. Personal knowledge is often a starting point. This probably being not much, you may need to do some direct observation and perhaps interviewing with people as additional sources. Sometimes, personal knowledge and observation can be the main types of information necessary for writing, as in the case of social work students' keeping progress records of their clients at the agency to which they are assigned for their fieldwork training. Students in other social sciences may also use direct observation and interviewing for writing about social problems, events, snapshots of modern living, and certain kinds of news stories.

For many writing tasks, though, you need other sources of information as well. You may need information that other people have collected or written. If you are writing a reading report on an assigned article, you may need not just that article but perhaps also some other articles that are relevant to the ideas contained in the main article. You may need them to stimulate your thinking so that you will have a handle on some way to evaluate it critically. If you are writing a term paper based largely on library research, you will need to spend some time selecting, locating, and obtaining the library resources that are potentially useful. You may also need to scan many electronic resources available on the Internet. If you are writing a research proposal, you need to review some studies others have done on a similar topic, read up on the methodology appropriate to your proposed research, and perhaps also collect certain relevant kinds of statistics from some organizations or government departments.

In thinking about sources of information, you should consider how much you will depend on different kinds of information so that you will prepare to allocate your time and effort accordingly. It may turn out that some of the information is not available or is not really suitable for your purposes, in which case you may decide to enlarge your search for information or, at some point, change your topic instead.

3.1.4 *What Are Your Constraints?*

Train yourself to be keenly conscious of your time constraint. Whether your paper is due in a week, a month, or three months, you should always plan your use of time sensibly and practically. That means you should allocate time for getting your information through various activities including research if that is necessary, shaping ideas into a draft, and revising it. The last stage, revision, as will be discussed later, is so important for enhancing the quality of your work that you must allow sufficient time for it before submitting your product.

Another constraint is length. The length of your writing often determines the amount of time and effort required. The length also has implications for both the breadth and depth of what you can say. Thus, for example, a topic that is appropriate for a term paper of 15 to 20 pages can hardly be treated with justice in just three or four pages. If length is imposed on you as a strict requirement—which it often is—you have to think clearly about how to approach the topic in the most practicable manner. On the other hand, if you are free to select your topic without a fixed length requirement, just remember that the complexity of your topic will largely dictate your paper's length.

3.2 Prewriting

Prewriting consists of various preparatory activities before you start drafting your paper. Here the word "paper" is used in a somewhat loose sense to mean any academic written work, long or short, for which some amount of reading is normally necessary. In the social sciences, it could be a reading report based on an article or a book, a tutorial discussion paper based on assigned readings, a short essay on a given topic, a proposal describing a small project, a report of an empirical study, a case progress record, or a term paper based on library research. Whichever kind of paper you may be writing, you need to consider carefully what you are going to write about.

Depending on the type of paper in question, prewriting can take more or less time. Generally, it takes longer if you have to set your own topic, if your topic requires a substantial review of relevant literature, if it is a term paper rather than a relatively short discussion paper, or if it is an empirical research paper.

What do you do for prewriting? There are several activities that you can engage in, the extent of which depends on the kind of paper you intend to write.

3.2.1 *Listing Ideas*

You can jot down ideas that you may have about the topic based on your current knowledge of the topic, limited as it may be. They may be random thoughts, questions, and facts that you are aware of. Make a list of such items. One or more of these items may be selected as sub-topics about which you can make other lists of ideas. As you make these lists, you can also freely write whatever comes to your mind that you believe may have something to do with the items on your lists. Suppose you are asked to write on "Why do we study sociology?" A brief list of items with some freely written material may look like this:

Why do we study sociology?

- The nature of sociology—a social science that has much in common with the humanities.
- We live in society, but do not understand it well.
- Sociology studies society.
- Society is people in all kinds of interaction—something we all seem to know and yet can be very complex and therefore hard to understand clearly.
- Are we free to do what we like or are we influenced and even controlled by others?
- We need concepts and theories for studying individuals and society—sociology gives us such concepts and theories. (But are they unique or similar to those used in some other social science disciplines?)
- Sociological imagination—sociology trains us to think about individuals in broader contexts.

3.2.2 Taking Notes

You can take notes based on reading material relevant to the topic. Keep your notes (brief summaries of important ideas and questions, if any, arising from them) on 3-inch-by-5-inch index cards for easy reference and sorting, at a later time, to help you develop ideas for your paper. But initially, your notes should help you construct the lists of ideas as described above.

3.2.3 Brainstorming

Third, you should try to discuss with fellow students who are working on the same assignment so that you can brainstorm and think aloud. Indeed, although students in Hong Kong seldom do this outside of the classroom, you have much to gain by brainstorming with your classmates who have some interest in your topic or with those with whom you may be engaged in some group project. As a result of brainstorming, you are likely to obtain some useful ideas and to clarify certain questions that may have arisen earlier. You can thus use brainstorming to modify the lists of ideas that you are working on.

3.2.4 Diagramming and Outlining

On the basis of the above activities, you can make some graphic representation of the ideas that you believe are most relevant to your topic. By using lines, circles, and symbols that are meaningful to you, you can make your diagram serve as a kind of map or overall view of the structure of your paper. In addition, try to use such a diagram to construct an outline that contains the main elements of your paper listed in roughly the order in which you may want to develop or elaborate them.

As an illustration, the following is a simple "idea map" that I used in planning to write a paper on "Leisure and social life in Hong Kong" some years ago. I thought of leisure as occurring in a network of roles (family, work, and leisure) that can be called "life space" which takes shape within some social context meaningful to each individual. Then I tried to examine four areas of social change—demographic factors, education, technology and mass communication, leisure services and facilities—which should have certain consequences for a person's social context and hence affecting that person's leisure behaviour.

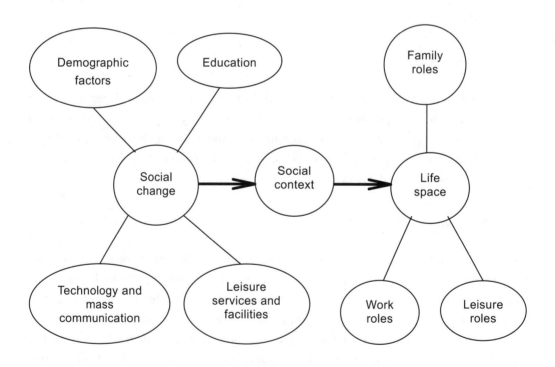

An idea map

Corresponding to the idea map but with some additional details is the following outline (showing only the main parts here) that guided my thinking somewhat further.

I. Main conceptual idea that guides the examination of leisure

    A. "Life space": Total ways of spending time in a network of roles

        1. Family

        2. Work

        3. Leisure

    B. Life space reflects a person's social context

II. Areas of change that shape a person's social context

    A. Demographic factors

        1. Singlehood

        2. Parenthood

        3. Post-parenthood

    B. Education

        1. Resources of leisure

        2. Attitudes

        3. Occupational roles

        4. Life styles

    C. Technology and mass communication

        1. Home as leisure centre

        2. Perception of time and distance

        3. Leisure expectations

    D. Leisure services and facilities

        1. Promotion of activities

        2. Creation of leisure interests

        3. Establishment of new expectations

Mapping ideas in a diagram can help you see the overall connection between ideas that you may want to examine. Listing these ideas with certain details in an outline can help you gain a better notion of not only the relationship between ideas but also their relative importance. Thus, in the outline shown above, the four areas of social change (A, B, C, and D under II) are of equal weight, whereas the points listed under each of them are examples that illustrate change in that particular area.

You may have greater or less need for a diagram and an outline, depending on the complexity of your topic. Although not many students actually use such aids in their writing process, you need to realize that, in general, diagrams and outlines enable you to have a sense of how ideas relevant to your topic are related and a sense of both the scope and depth of what you could include in your paper. Of course, you may treat your diagram and outline as tentative and there is no reason why you cannot modify your ideas as you write the draft, perhaps even departing considerably from your preliminary outline. But thinking the ideas through and putting them down on paper in rough diagrams and more or less organized steps constitute an important beginning.

3.3 Drafting

Having planned for your written assignment and taken some initial steps to lay down your thoughts in an outline, you should be ready to start writing the draft of your paper. Using your outline as a rough guide, it is only natural that you should focus on a part or a section at a time, from the introduction to the conclusion of the paper. As you proceed, however, you may find that some of your earlier ideas need changing and that you need to read more sources for supporting points and evidence. Consequently, your outline may have to be modified, sometimes perhaps substantially.

Not only do you use your outline to guide your drafting, but if your planning has been active you will also have various kinds of notes and material that you have already written in rough form that you can now use for your first draft.

As you write your draft, bear in mind that you need to develop your ideas systematically and effectively. That essentially means that your paragraphs should be so constructed that they each present a main idea clearly and coherently, and that together they form an integrated whole. This is the paper's structure or organization. A well-written paper is tightly organized. We shall discuss this in Chapter 6.

Should you draft as much as possible at one sitting or just a small portion at a time? If it is only a short paper two or three pages long and if you have a pretty good idea of what to include, you may want to draft the whole paper all at once. On the other hand, if it is a more substantial paper running to ten or twenty pages and if your ideas for it are still rather fluid, it may be better to divide the content into a number of segments so that you can write just one or two segments at a time. In general, if you have a deadline to meet, you must allow enough time for not only drafting but also revising after that. To maximize results, you should try drafting as much as you can at one sitting when you are concentrating on ideas and when they seem to be flowing smoothly.

Most students now do their writing on a computer, which is indeed highly convenient and efficient. You can change, add, delete, move, insert, and transpose text so easily that drafting a paper can be almost effortless. At least, it is far less cumbersome than it was in the pre-computer days. Some of you may feel the need to write your draft in longhand first and will not use the computer until you have a fairly well laid-out draft. This is fine if it works well for you, but I would strongly recommend that you start the drafting on the computer right from the beginning if you already know how to use it. The ease of making whatever changes you desire and the satisfaction from seeing your draft in clear, double-spaced type on the computer screen are advantages that drafting in longhand does not have.

With the convenience provided by the computer, you should try to proceed boldly in your first draft without worrying too much about language correctness and coherence of structure. You do so with the understanding that you will come back to the draft to check language matters, improve organization, or make any other necessary changes. Of course, you will be watching these matters to some extent even when you are writing the first draft, but you will get more done and move on faster if you concentrate on writing as much as you can in one sitting until you have come to some appropriate break (such as the end of a section or a main idea). Indeed, a clear advantage of this approach is that at the end of each drafting session you will have a sizeable amount of work done. You will feel a sense of achievement from seeing pages of draft accumulating.

At the same time, though, you must not let the words on your draft pages lead you to believe that they are good enough to need no change. They are only your first draft; much remains to be done.

3.4 Revising

In a real sense, revision is the most important part of the writing process. When the draft of the entire paper is complete, you need to go over it carefully to make all the necessary revisions. But do not hurry: it is much better if you put your draft away for a while, like a couple of days, before you return to it. This way, you have a chance to "cool off" from the intense involvement of your thoughts during the drafting phase, and are therefore more likely to see your own work in a more objective and critical light.

The importance of revision must be clearly recognized. Regardless of how much time and effort you have spent on your draft, you must not think of it as the final product. When your first draft is largely complete, you should be able to think about the paper as a whole. This being the case, you should not be surprised to find problems large and small if you take the time to read carefully what you have written. To revise is basically to re-examine and to improve. If you examine carefully, you will certainly identify places in your draft where improvement is possible and necessary. The following are some questions you can ask to identify what revisions will be necessary:

- Is my thesis (theme) clearly stated?
- Have I followed my thesis faithfully? Are there places where I have wandered away from the thesis without good reason?
- Are my main ideas presented in an appropriate sequence?
- Are there any main ideas not explained or discussed clearly enough?
- Have I included all the ideas or points that are necessary?
- Do I need more examples for some particular points?
- Are there any points that are actually irrelevant?
- Are the sentences in each paragraph connected logically?
- Are the paragraphs connected logically?
- Have I summarized my main points clearly and included any necessary comments in the conclusion?

Seeing the paper as a whole is necessary so that you will be more aware of the paper's structure. Its content must be crafted to show a well laid-out structure that helps you to achieve the purpose of the paper.

At the same time, you must also pay attention to sentence-level matters. To make your paper as effective and as readable as it should be, you should aim at correctness of language use and compliance with the appropriate convention and style of academic writing. Your revision includes checking such matters as spelling, grammar, punctuation, sentence construction, choice of words, and acknowledgement of sources. (These tasks are more appropriately called "editing," although you may think of them as part of the revision process. See more detailed discussion in Chapter 10.) The quality of your paper will suffer greatly

- if there are numerous misspellings,
- if your verbs often do not agree with their subject,
- if you use punctuation marks indiscriminately,
- if your sentences are usually wordy and entangled, and
- if your citation of sources is unconventional.

To demonstrate the importance of revision, I will use a paragraph written by a student in my writing course in a short essay on the topic "Why do we study sociology?" By using just one paragraph, we cannot illustrate changes to improve the structure of the paper. But it does show how ideas can become more clearly stated and how the connection between sentences becomes smoother and more logical. While the revision you see here shows how a teacher has proposed to change the text

instead of how the student writer has actually revised it, you can use it as a model for
your reference.

I asked my class to focus on the benefits offered by the study of sociology. One
of the readings they had done before writing the essay was the opening chapter "The
Promise" in C. Wright Mills' classic, *The Sociological Imagination.* Mills uses the
concept of "sociological imagination" to stress the importance of trying to examine
the relationship between individual experiences ("biography") and larger societal
processes ("history"). The following is the student's paragraph:

> The sociological imagination enables us to correctly
> conscious of our position in society. It helps us to
> develop reasons in order to have a clear view of what
> is happening in the world. To understand the rela-
> tions between history and our own experience is the
> biggest achievement. Individual can only be aware of
> their personal fate and own chance of life before. We
> do not realize the difficulties they faced are also
> becoming aware of all individuals in the circum-
> stances. With help of relating history and biography,
> we are able to recognize our human behaviour is
> shaping and formulating by the societal forces. The
> interactions between the two means we can have better
> means to cope with circumstances happening in the
> world.

The revised paragraph reads as follows:

> The sociological imagination enables us to be
> conscious of our position in society. That means it
> helps us to relate our own experience to what is
> happening in the world. This is rewarding because we
> see our experience not so much as our personal fate
> but as something that is like what others have in
> similar circumstances. We see this even better if we
> put ourselves in a larger historical context. This is
> what Mills wants us to do. We need to recognize that

> our behaviour is shaped by societal forces. If we
> understand the interaction between these forces and
> individuals, we are in a better position to cope with
> personal difficulties. For example, the sudden loss
> of a job exerts great psychological pressure on us.
> However, we may realize that this is common in our
> society when the unemployment rate increases dramat-
> ically.

Notice that not only are several grammatical errors corrected, but sentences are reconstructed so that they connect with each other better. Ungrammatical or vague parts are reworded or deleted. (The sentence "We do not realize the difficulties they faced . . ." is deleted, but a new sentence "This is rewarding . . ." is introduced to bring out the student's intended meaning.) Imprecise expressions are made clear and specific. ("To cope with circumstances happening in the world" is imprecise; "to cope with personal difficulties" is more specific and idiomatic.) The reconstruction of sentences, together with added elements, sharpens the idea that it is important to understand the interaction between society and the individual. The student's paragraph has no examples to illustrate the point "If we understand the interaction between these forces and individuals, we are in a better position to cope with personal difficulties." She later supplied one concerning unemployment which, after my revision, is shown here.

3.5 The Writing Process in Perspective

The above description of the four basic stages of the writing process is intended to outline the major activities that are likely to occur in most written assignments. Two qualifications, however, must be pointed out.

First, depending on the actual written assignment, the extent to which these activities are engaged in varies. For instance, a tutorial discussion paper—if it intends to raise one or two major questions based on an assigned article or book chapter—will not demand as much planning and prewriting as will a term paper. On the other hand, a project proposal, in some ways like a term paper, may require careful planning and a good amount of prewriting because it is supposed to review some relevant literature so as to build a convincing argument why the proposed study is worth pursuing and supporting.

Second, although we visualize the writing process as consisting of four main stages, some activities may have to straddle or be repeated in different stages. For example, the consideration of whom you are writing for is a thought or a reminder that you should have not only when you first plan for your writing but also practically throughout the entire duration of work on your assignment. Then, as you write the draft of your paper, especially in the case of a term paper based on library research, you probably will keep reading and checking with relevant sources, although perhaps not as extensively as in the planning and prewriting stages. Further, revising or rewriting does not necessarily begin after you have completed your first draft. For a substantial term paper that has several distinct parts, you may find it worthwhile to revise each part once the draft of the part is done.

With these qualifications in mind, you should see that the writing process does involve a variety of activities and that you can expect to have a better product if you give your writing job the attention and care it requires. Of course, the level of competence in using the English language makes an important difference in the quality of writing; but language use *per se* is not the only determinant of writing well. Students whose writing is less than satisfactory certainly need to work hard on such matters as vocabulary, usage, and sentence construction. But they would not go very far if they do not (a) treat planning, time management, and prewriting seriously, (b) learn to organize ideas effectively, and (c) put enough time and effort into rewriting and revising for better result. We shall consider the task of revision in further detail in Chapter 10.

CHAPTER 4

Reading and Summarizing

Like most social science students, you are expected to read a large variety of assigned or recommended material (e.g., selections from books, articles) in your course work. You may associate reading with preparing for tests and examinations. While that is true, you must not forget that you often need to read to get ideas and various kinds of information for your written assignments. In the first chapter, I explained that writing is important because it helps you to learn as well as to demonstrate what you have learned. Either way, reading gives you the substance of learning and thereby stimulates your mind so that you will be ready to select and organize ideas for inclusion in your writing. What many students overlook, however, is the importance of taking notes and summarizing as they read so as to improve the quality of their learning.

In the following, I begin by discussing two main ideas. First, you should establish the habit of reading actively if you want to write well. Second, to be an active reader you must learn to write good summaries of what you have read. After that, let us consider the qualities of a good summary and see how a summary may be presented. Finally, I use a few examples to demonstrate some ways of writing a summary.

4.1 Active Reading

When you are reading a book or an article, are you aware of the reason for reading it? You read it because it gives you some information that is relevant to some topic in a course; because you are preparing for a test or examination; or because you are asked to review it and write a reading report. Naturally, you may read for any of these reasons. But whatever the reason, you are not likely to obtain the understanding that you need for your particular purpose if you do not read actively.

What does active reading mean? There is not much sense in reading if you do not gain any understanding from doing it. To gain understanding, you need to involve yourself actively in the reading process. This means that you need to search for information and respond with observation, feelings, and questions.

First, when you search for information, the word to note is "search." Look carefully for various cues in the text (the article, the book or part thereof) such as the abstract (if given), headings and subheadings, key sentences, and tables (if provided) to help you grasp the author's main and supporting ideas. After skimming the material and reading through it once or twice, you are likely to have found what the reading is basically about and may even have identified those parts of it that are particularly meaningful or relevant to you.

Second, as you read with involvement, you will feel in particular ways about the author's points and how he or she develops those points. You may agree with or respond positively to some of them but feel uncertain or even uncomfortable about some others. To remind yourself of these feelings, you should write them down on the margin of the article or book (only if it is your own copy) as notes that you can read when you review the material later.

Third, active reading requires you to read with a critical eye so that you do not accept everything given without a thought. You should raise various kinds of questions that will help you understand the material better. What does this really mean? Why does the author say this? Is it really so? Does it apply to Hong Kong society? What may the author have overlooked? Is this a good example of the kind of issue that the author is analyzing? Has the author given us enough evidence to support his or her argument?

If you find yourself doing most of these activities as you read, you are reading actively. But what has this got to do with writing? A great deal. Most obvious is that you will be in a better position to obtain material that you need for writing. For example, you may be reading to review the relevant literature for a research paper on the social effects of television. For this purpose, you need to read a number of articles and book chapters in order to survey the variety of approaches to the topic that have appeared, say, in the last two decades. You need some sources that deal with theoretical conceptualizations of "social effects" as well as empirical studies that demonstrate some such effects. Reading the relevant literature actively, you will surely gather responsive (particularly evaluative) as well as substantive notes which you will use for your paper. Indeed, you should try to formulate and accumulate as many evaluative thoughts as possible so that you become ready to write a more analytical and critical paper on the topic.

I said in Chapter 1 that there are two interrelated purposes of writing: to learn and to demonstrate what you have learned. Reading plays an instrumental role for both these purposes. In the example just mentioned of reading the literature on the social effects of television, you learn about the discussion of this topic by reading. Since you expect to produce a paper on the topic, you write to demonstrate your knowledge of the ideas and arguments involved. At the same time, you will actually learn more about the topic as a result of the reading you do and the writing that you produce to make sense of what you have read.

Not only do you gather ideas for writing through reading, but you also learn something about writing although you may not realize that this happens. By reading actively, you will have a clear picture of how the author approaches a given topic. This means both (a) how the author organizes ideas and supporting examples, and (b) how the author expresses these ideas clearly and effectively by writing in a readable style. Sometimes, the author may choose to build a suitable context before disclosing his or her real position on a certain issue. You can recognize and learn such a rhetorical device if you read actively. Thus, by reading with active involvement, you not only understand the text better, but you also see what effective writing is like if what you read is truly well written. The more you read in this manner, the more likely it is for you to know what to aim at when you write.

4.2 Why Is Summary Writing Important?

A summary is a brief statement in your own words of the essential information of some original text. Depending on your purpose and the text in question, the length of a summary can vary anywhere from one sentence to a few pages. Of course, the longer the summary, the more details it contains. On the other hand, the shorter the summary, the more selective you have to be about what to include.

To practise active reading, you should be involved and responsive. This means you should be taking notes to summarize, even if in only a few words, important points or ideas. Not only will you have notes for specific parts of an article or book chapter that you read, but you will also find it helpful to write a short overall summary for the whole piece so that you will remember the reading better. This is probably the most practical way to nurture your ability to write summaries. Practice makes perfect, as you surely know.

Indeed, the more often you write summaries of what you read, the better you hone your skills of being an active reader. Reading and summarizing interact to improve your understanding of what you read as you become more aware of how ideas are developed, expressed, and related to one another. With more practice, you can learn to do something similar in your own writing.

4.2.1 Summary Writing and Learning

Summary writing may seem simple and, because it is about other people's ideas rather than your own, peripheral to the main task of writing. Little wonder, then, that students may not be paying as much attention to summary writing as they should. The truth is, summary writing is not as simple as it seems because it depends so much on identifying the most important information contained in the original work. If we say that learning depends on grasping the most important information of something, then there is a close connection between summary writing and learning. Undoubtedly, the ability to write clear and accurate summaries is one of the most important skills you need in order to do well academically.

When you write a summary in your own words, you need to examine the text's meaning carefully before you can find the words to express the gist of that meaning. Consequently, you are more likely to remember what you have read. By organizing the main ideas in such a way as to indicate the author's intention and point of view, you will end up with a clearer understanding of the material.

4.2.2 Summary Writing and Preparing for Examinations

If you are proficient in summary writing, you remember and understand the material better. If you have the habit of writing summaries of what you read for your courses, then you are in an advantageous position when you study for examinations. Since summaries represent the result of what you have distilled from a large amount of material, going over them in preparing for examinations is the logical thing to do. You can use your summaries to refresh your memory of the most important points of the material. Using them as a study aid, you can always go back to the original material concerned for details if you need to. You can thus see how useful your summaries can be when you must use your time efficiently and judiciously when preparing for examinations.

4.2.3 Summary Writing and Preparing for Writing

If your writing task requires a great deal of reading, as when you prepare to write the literature review section of a research report to put your research problem in a larger picture, the notes you take and the summaries you write will be important raw material that you use to shape your paper. Certainly, you do not simply include all the summaries you have written: you will probably say more of some and less of others. You will need to synthesize them in a way that serves the purpose of your discussion. In any case, the point is that your reading notes and summaries become a kind of bridge between the authors of these readings and the paper that you work on.

4.2.4 Summarizing Your Own Writing

Whether or not you use other sources in your writing, you need to summarize what you have said when your paper is about to conclude so as to help readers see and remember your main points. On the basis of such a summary, you may raise some questions concerning the implications of your conclusions or findings, as the case may be. You may also discuss a point or two that call for further study.

4.3 Basic Steps in Writing a Summary

As a rule, always write a summary in your own words because such a summary makes more sense to you and you will learn more about the original text. Never just piece together selected parts from the original text to form a summary. Not only does it look truncated and unnatural, you will also be uncertain whether you really understand the material. At the same time, using the author's own words and phrases as if they were yours is an act of plagiarism, a serious offence in academic work. Try to use the following steps in writing a summary:

(1) Read through the text to identify its main sections and to find out the main idea of each section.
(2) Give each section a suitable label that makes sense to you, and place such labels on a tree diagram to show the structure of the text.
(3) Write a one-sentence summary of each main section.
(4) When you have finished doing this for all sections, write one or two sentences to indicate the overall central idea (the thesis or theme).
(5) Review this central idea and the one-sentence summaries of the sections until you see clearly how they are related.
(6) In your own words write a paragraph, whose length depends on your requirement, as the summary of the whole text. (Sometimes, your summary may need more than one paragraph when you are summarizing a lengthy text.)

4.4 What Should a Good Summary Be Like?

4.4.1 It Should Contain the Main Idea and, If Space Allows, Important Supporting Points

With some practice, it should not be difficult to identify an author's central or main idea (also called "controlling" idea). Of course, what constitutes a main idea depends on the amount of text which you are trying to summarize. If you are summarizing an entire book chapter, for instance, the main idea would be more general than is the case if you are summarizing only a portion of the same chapter. In either case, you should identify the important points that support the main idea. In an earlier section (4.2) on why summary writing is important, for example, the main idea was that summary writing helps you or any reader to remember the material read. Supporting points included that the ability to write good summaries helps learning, that summarizing also helps preparing for examinations and other writing tasks, and that including a summary in your writing makes it easier for your reader to understand what you have to say. If one wishes to summarize that section, these points should be included.

4.4.2 It Should Be Accurate

Your summary should reflect accurately not only the main idea in the original text, but also the relationship between supporting points. You should not change the tone of the original by, for example, overstressing one point and understating another. Neither should you include any evaluation or criticism of your own.

4.4.3 It Should Be Brief

To be brief is to be short, using as few words as appropriate for a summary of a given length. Brevity is not absolute but relative, depending on how much detail you want your summary to include. If you intend to use the summary for highlighting a point or describing an idea related to your paper topic, or for inclusion in the literature review section of your research paper, a summary of one or two sentences will probably be adequate. If you find that some sources are particularly useful for illustrating a complicated point, you may write longer summaries of them later.

4.4.4 It Should Be Written in Your Own Words

To strengthen your understanding of the source read and to avoid committing plagiarism, you should write the summary in your own words, as pointed out earlier. It would be best if you put the source out of sight when you write the summary so that you will write from your understanding in your own words. Do not even think of looking at it as you compose your summary, or you will be tempted to copy words and phrases from the original text. This means you should not attempt to write the summary before you have a firm grasp of what the author has written.

4.5 An Example: Towards an Appropriate Summary

The following is a passage taken from a chapter on "Thinking Sociologically" in Allan Johnson's (1991) book on sociological thinking. It is quite straightforward and not difficult to understand. Read it now and try to write a one-sentence summary of the passage. Then you can compare with the several sample summaries given.

Sociological thinking requires a sensitivity to the existence of social systems and their cultural, structural, population, and ecological characteristics. These basic characteristics--and concepts such as value, role, and group that are related to and derived from them--make up a conceptual framework we can use to observe the world in a sociological way. This kind of framework is the foundation of any discipline, because it defines basic subject matter, whether it be the origins of the universe, the properties of living organisms, or the varieties of family life.

 Although they sensitize us to perceive the world in particular ways, these concepts are only the beginning of what is meant by sociological thinking, because a conceptual framework is only a point of departure to answer questions of what can be known about social life and alternative ways of coming to know it. We could, for example, use sociological concepts to describe the differences between Industrial and nonindustrial societies, just as we could describe differences between various types of family systems, including the division of labor between men and women within families, how stable and enduring they are, and the incidence of various kinds of violence. But if we went no further than this, we would have said nothing about *why* such differences occur or what connections link them together. What, for example, are the social forces that bring indus-

trialization about, and how do they and industriali-
zation affect the family as an institution?

For these kinds of questions, mere description
will not do. We can use concepts such as system and
culture to become more aware about social systems and
their various characteristics, but we also need
frameworks that are theoretical--in other words, that
organize how we think about social systems in order
to explain what goes on in them. If conceptual frameworks direct our attention and tell us *what* to
observe, theoretical frameworks tell us how to
interpret and *understand* what we observe. The study
of social systems requires a framework that includes
basic assumptions about how they work and defines the
kinds of questions we need to ask not only about how
they work but also about the consequences they
produce and how they change.

In the sociological literature you will not find
a single unified theoretical perspective, for over
the years sociologists have gone about this work in a
variety of ways, resulting in several approaches, the
most prominent being the functional, conflict, ecological, and interactionist perspectives. As is often
the case in a discipline still establishing itself,
the history of sociology includes a fair amount of
disagreement among adherents to these several perspectives. Some of the issues have been primarily
intellectual: Is social structure, for example, an
external network of statuses and roles that shape
human behavior, or is structure the actual patterns
of behavior that result from what people do? Other
issues have been as much political as intellectual:
Is the conflict perspective superior because it
reveals conditions of inequality and injustice, or
does it lend itself to such excesses of advocacy of
radical social change that it loses its intellectual
usefulness? Does the functional framework support the
status quo and, therefore, social inequality and

> injustice? Do we have to choose one or the other? (pp. 109–111)

You will notice that in the first paragraph Johnson introduces the term "conceptual framework" which he stresses is the "foundation of any discipline." In the second paragraph, he explains that while concepts help us describe what we observe, they are only the "beginning" of sociological thinking. To understand why social systems operate the way they do and how they change, we need theoretical frameworks. This is Johnson's main idea in the third paragraph. In the fourth paragraph, he tells us that, like other relatively new disciplines, sociology has not just one but a variety of theoretical frameworks each of which being concerned with particular questions.

Did you grasp these points? If so, you should be ready to write a summary. The following is a sample summary:

Sample Summary 1

> In describing the nature of sociological thinking, Johnson says that, as in any discipline, concepts describing the various characteristics of social systems constitute a framework that we can use to describe what we want to observe. We need concepts, for example, to describe family systems. Built on this foundation, sociological thinking uses a number of theoretical frameworks or perspectives to guide us in our effort to interpret and understand how social systems operate and change. Thus, we use theoretical perspectives, such as functionalism or ecological perspective, to try to account for changes in family systems. While we do this, we should realize that proponents of the various perspectives do not have the same views on certain issues. (117 words)

This summary is about one-fifth of the length of the original passage (540 words). For general purposes, including collecting ideas that you may later use or refer to in a term paper, this is adequate. Note that it mentions "family system" as an example of what conceptual and theoretical frameworks may be used for. It is one of the examples that Johnson mentions explicitly in his second paragraph but only implicitly in the third.

In principle, a summary should always contain the most important idea;

supporting points or examples may be included also when space allows and if you feel it is necessary to do so. If reference to the example of "family systems" is deleted from Sample Summary 1, the last sentence is also deleted but its idea is retained by the phrase "despite their differences in certain issues" inserted immediately after "a number of theoretical frameworks or perspectives." Overall, the main controlling idea regarding the use of concepts and theoretical perspectives still remains in Sample Summary 2.

Sample Summary 2

> In describing the nature of sociological thinking, Johnson says that, as in any discipline, concepts describing the various characteristics of social systems constitute a framework that we can use to describe what we want to observe. Built on this foundation, sociological thinking uses a number of theoretical frameworks or perspectives--despite their differences in certain issues--to guide us in our effort to interpret and understand how social systems operate and change. (72 words)

Sometimes it is necessary to keep your summary really short. For example, you may want to use just one sentence to record the most significant message, and keep this separately from perhaps a somewhat longer and more detailed summary of the same passage. You may use the one-sentence summary for a quick review in studying for examinations or in compiling items for your literature review section of a library research paper. If you need more details, you can check the longer summary if you have written one. The following are three versions of trimming the summary of Johnson's passage down to just one sentence. In each version, the main idea of the use of conceptual and theoretical frameworks is retained.

Sample Summary 3

> In sociology, we have conceptual frameworks that guide us in observing the social world and theoretical frameworks that help us understand what goes on in it. (26 words)

Sample Summary 4

> Whereas there are concepts that describe various

phenomena in social life, we need theoretical frameworks to make sense of how these phenomena occur and
what results they bring about. **(29 words)**

Sample Summary 5

Sociological thinking begins with using conceptual
frameworks to see our social world and develops as we
apply theoretical frameworks, representing different
perspectives, to ask questions about how different
parts of society interrelate and change. **(34 words)**

Before commenting on these three sample summaries, we should note that it is
customary to introduce a summary with a reference to the author (as is done in
Summary 1), especially when you are using the summary to write a literature review.
If you record your summary on a note card, it does not matter too much if you do not
include the author's name in the summary sentence itself, but you must always
record the source with full citation, including the author's name, on the same card so
that you will have all the citation information when you actually use the item in your
writing. To illustrate how you may indicate the author when using the summary in
your writing, Summary 3 is now modified in two forms, as shown below. You will
read about the details of citing sources in Chapter 7.

Sample Summary 3 modified, with author mentioned in summary's text

Johnson (1991, pp. 109-111) points out that in
sociology, we have conceptual frameworks that guide us
in observing the social world and theoretical frameworks that help us understand what goes on in it.

Sample Summary 3 modified, with author mentioned not in summary's text

In sociology, we have conceptual frameworks that
guide us in observing the social world and theoretical frameworks that help us understand what goes on
in it (Johnson 1991, pp. 109-111).

While Summaries 3 to 5 all indicate the main idea of Johnson's passage, each
carries a slightly different "message" because of the way the sentence is constructed.
Summary 3 mentions conceptual frameworks and theoretical frameworks in a
"balanced" manner, but Summary 4 places emphasis on theoretical frameworks by

using a sentence structure that subordinates one idea to another. If you read Johnson's passage carefully, you will find that Johnson does mention that just having sociological concepts as descriptive tools is not enough for us to understand what goes on in social systems. For this reason, Summary 4 would be better than Summary 3 if you had to choose between the two.

What about Summary 5? The last paragraph of Johnson's passage indicates that sociological theorizing has been evolving even as considerable disagreement exists among sociologists. Indeed, Johnson refers to sociology as "a discipline still establishing itself." With this in mind, it seems fair to say that Summary 5 captures the idea that sociological thinking is something that has been developing over the years. It is just somewhat longer than the other two versions, but it is probably the best of the three as a one-sentence summary of the given passage.

4.6 Checklist for Reading and Summarizing

- Be aware of your purpose when you read.
- Read actively with involvement so that you may learn something about others' writing.
- Read to recognize important points and to understand how ideas are developed and organized.
- Read to feel in particular ways about those points. (e.g., Does it make sense to you? Is it clear and convincing? Is there anything special about the writing itself that impresses you?)
- Take notes to record both important points and your reaction.
- Write summaries of what you have read to strengthen your understanding.
- Before writing your summary, read the original text carefully to identify its central idea.
- Identify the points that support the text's central idea and see how they are related to each other.
- Put away the original text when you write the summary in your own words. Write from your understanding of the material.
- Do not add your own comments or any additional information. Your summary must be accurate.

CHAPTER 5

Writing Effective Paragraphs

You know from your reading experience that essays and many other written documents consist of paragraphs. Imagine how much harder it would have been for you to read them if these documents were not divided into paragraphs. You would have found it more troublesome to identify main ideas and to recognize how the essay is organized. So paragraphs are a device to make a piece of writing more readable and understandable.

Undoubtedly, you, like many of your fellow students, are familiar with reading something presented in paragraphs. But have you ever given serious thought to what makes a well-written paragraph? Do you know how you can increase the effectiveness of a paragraph? These are important questions for you if you want your paragraphs to organize and clarify ideas the way they should.

5.1 Writing Is Paragraph Construction

A paragraph is the basic unit of most kinds of writing. The task of writing is also the task of constructing paragraphs, each of which is a group of related sentences about an idea. A paragraph is effective if it presents this idea clearly and if its sentences are all related to this idea in such a way that the idea is adequately described, explained, and developed with the necessary details.

When you have finished putting together one paragraph, you go on to another paragraph to present another idea that is related in some way to the idea contained in the preceding paragraph. It may be an extension of the earlier idea; it may also be an additional idea that, together with other ideas to be included in the essay, supports the same overall central idea.

By organizing your essay into paragraphs, you signal to your reader that one unit of thought has been completed and a new one is about to begin. Again, you want to construct the sentences of the succeeding paragraph in such a manner that the new idea is clearly stated and developed. And the process goes on. Writing is therefore a process of constructing strong and effective paragraphs. As building blocks of an essay, paragraphs deserve careful attention no matter how ordinary or inconsequential they may seem to you.

5.2 What Does a Paragraph Do?

You can use a paragraph to do any of the following:

- To introduce your essay.
- To present one of the main ideas of your essay with the support of examples, facts, or quoted material from other sources.
- To discuss in greater detail a particular point that has been introduced by using other examples or citing other evidence.
- To shift from one approach to another, such as from a theoretical perspective to another, from for to against, and from past to current thinking.
- To review the works of other scholars that bear upon a particular point.
- To introduce a substantial amount of quoted material.
- To conclude your essay.

You can thus see how versatile a paragraph can be in presenting and organizing ideas.

5.3 Using the Topic Sentence to Announce Your Purpose

Each paragraph, wherever it appears in the main body of an essay, ought to be concerned with one main idea. When you start to write a paragraph, be sure that you know what that idea is. You want to write your paragraph in such a way that it will show and develop that idea. That is the purpose of the paragraph, and that is what your readers expect to know. The usual practice is to announce the purpose of a paragraph in the form of a topic sentence, so called because it is about the "topic" of the paragraph.

The topic sentence helps you organize your paragraph more effectively around a clear focus so that the paragraph can be unified. It helps your reader to grasp what you have to say in that paragraph. Other sentences in the paragraph usually provide details that expand or illustrate the main idea contained in the topic sentence.

5.3.1 *Topic Sentence at Beginning of Paragraph*

Very often, the topic sentence is placed at or near the beginning of the paragraph although, as we shall see later, this is not always the case. Let us take, as an example, the following two paragraphs from Thurow's (1996) *The Future of Capitalism*; the topic sentences are boldfaced.

For the first time in human history, anything can be made anywhere and sold everywhere. In capitalistic economies that means making each component and performing each activity at the place on the globe where it can be most cheaply done and selling the resulting products or services wherever prices and profits are highest. Minimizing costs and maximizing revenues is what profit maximization, the heart of capitalism, is all about. Sentimental attachment to some geographic part of the world is not part of the system.

Technologically, transportation and communication costs have fallen dramatically and the speed with which both can be done has risen exponentially. This has made possible completely new systems of communications, command, and control within the business sector. Research and design groups can be coordinated in different parts of the world; components can be made wherever in the world it is cheapest to do so and shipped to assembly points that minimize total costs. Assembled products can be quickly shipped to wherever they are needed with just-in-time air freight delivery systems. Sales can be global. From 1964 to 1992, first world production was up 9 percent, but exports were up 12 percent, and cross-border lending was up 23 percent. (p. 115)

These two paragraphs tell us that today's economy is a global one and that technology has made this possible. In the first paragraph, the main idea is explicitly indicated in the first sentence asserting that "anything can be made anywhere and sold everywhere." The second sentence immediately explains what that means: production takes place where production costs are cheapest and products are sold where profits are highest. Then Thurow goes on in the third sentence to point out that this is typical of capitalism. The fourth and last sentence of this paragraph emphasizes the main idea of the paragraph, but Thurow does so by saying that "sentimental attachment to some geographical part of the world" has no place in a global economy.

The second paragraph develops the main idea of the first paragraph. If you examine the paragraph carefully, you will find that it consists of two parts. The opening topic sentence and the second sentence that amplifies it form the first part, which tells us that technology, by reducing costs, has brought about "new systems of communications, command, and control" in business. In the rest of this paragraph, Thurow illustrates this by referring to the ease of coordinating research and development, shipping of components to assembly points, and shipping of products to where they are needed. To end the paragraph, Thurow cites figures, including exports of the first world, to indicate the presence of a global economy.

From this example, we can see how the topic sentence provides a direction for the presentation and amplification of an idea, thus integrating the sentences in a paragraph to make the paragraph both unified and coherent. Readers will therefore find the paragraph clear and easy to follow.

5.3.2 Topic Sentence in Middle of Paragraph

Although it is common for the topic sentence to appear at or near the beginning of the paragraph, the position of the topic sentence can actually vary. It could be in the middle of a paragraph, after some transitional statements made in reference to preceding paragraphs. We can find an example of this in the third paragraph of Johnson's passage (1991) on sociological thinking quoted in Chapter 4. The following is that paragraph quoted here once again:

> For these kinds of questions, mere descriptions will
> not do. We can use concepts such as system and
> culture to become more aware about social systems and
> their various characteristics, but we also need
> frameworks that are theoretical--in other words, that
> organize how we think about social systems in order
> to explain what goes on in them. **If conceptual
> frameworks direct our attention and tell us what to
> observe, theoretical frameworks tell us how to
> interpret and understand what we observe.** The study
> of social systems requires a framework that includes

```
basic assumptions about how they work and defines the
kinds of questions we need to ask not only about how
they  work  but  also  about  the  consequences  they
produce and how they change. (p. 110)
```

If you read this paragraph after reading the paragraph that comes before it (see 4.5 in Chapter 4), you will notice how Johnson uses the first two sentences—and particularly the second—in this paragraph to reiterate the point made in the preceding paragraph, namely, that using concepts to describe the characteristics of social systems is not enough. In the second sentence, he begins to point to the need for theoretical frameworks that go beyond mere description to organize our thinking so that we can explain how social systems work. Indeed, referring back to a point already mentioned in the preceding paragraph as a backdrop for turning to something new is useful for establishing connection as you move from one point to the next in an essay.

Having made this transition, Johnson uses the third sentence to indicate the difference between conceptual frameworks and theoretical frameworks. This, then, is the topic sentence. The remaining sentence of the paragraph amplifies this difference to specify the use of theoretical frameworks.

5.3.3 Topic Sentence at End of Paragraph

Sometimes, the topic sentence may appear at the end of a paragraph. In an introductory paragraph of an essay, for example, the author may choose to set the stage for discussion by first making a few prefatory statements that are relevant to the essay's theme but they keep the reader in a kind of suspense until the end of the paragraph where the author announces the main idea clearly. This is the case in the following introductory paragraph on labelling theory by Rubington and Weinberg (1995):

```
Perspectives differ in the questions they ask and the
answers they yield. The sociology of deviant behavior,
for example, initially asks why people commit crimes
or other deviant acts. Sociologists in this tradition
attempt  to  determine  the  necessary  and  sufficient
conditions that produce deviant acts. The labeling
perspective, on the contrary, examines the social
definition of deviance. Sociologists in this tradi-
tion want to know how people define situations,
persons, processes, or events as problematic. (p. 179)
```

In the above example, the main idea is, strictly speaking, contained in the last two sentences. The authors point out that the labelling perspective is quite different from the traditional sociological perspective in the study of deviance, and then they specify the concern of the labelling perspective in approaching deviance. Thus, sometimes it may take more than one sentence to deliver the main message of a paragraph. If it takes two sentences to announce the topic of the paragraph clearly, you should not hesitate to do so although in many instances a single sentence may be sufficient.

When you conclude an essay, consider placing the topic sentence at the end of the paragraph to sum up the discussion or to restate the main idea of your essay. In exploring the relation between rationalization and enchantment of such modern means of consumption as shopping malls and cruise ships, Ritzer (1999) concludes his chapter on this topic as follows:

> This chapter has made three related points: First, the cathedrals of consumption can be described as being highly rationalized; second, rationalization leads to disenchantment; third, rational means of consumption can themselves have enchanting qualities inherent in their rationalized natures. **In spite of the latter, the central problems confronting the cathedrals of consumption remain rationalization and the disenchantment engendered by it.** (p. 103)

5.3.4 Topic Sentence at Beginning and End of Paragraph

A variation of putting the topic sentence at the end of the paragraph is to have, in addition, a different form of the topic sentence at the beginning of the paragraph. In the next example, Barber (1992) opens his paragraph by mentioning the existence of "two possible political futures." He goes on to give examples of each scenario, one in which people are torn apart by conflict and another in which different cultures are brought together by such factors as technology and commerce. At the end of the paragraph, he claims that both "futures" are actually occurring at the same time.

> **Just beyond the horizon of current events lie two possible political futures--both bleak, neither demo- cratic.** The first is a retribalization of large swaths of humankind by war and bloodshed: a threaten- ed Lebanonization of national states in which culture

is pitted against culture, people against people,
tribe against tribe—-a Jihad in the name of a hundred
narrowly conceived faiths against every kind of
interdependence, every kind of artificial social
cooperation and civic mutuality. The second is being
borne in on us by the onrush of economic and ecological forces that demand integration and uniformity
and that mesmerize the world with fast music, fast
computers, and fast food—-with MTC, Macintosh, and
McDonald's, pressing nations into one commercially
homogenous global network: one McWorld tied together
by technology, ecology, communications, and commerce.
**The planet is falling precipitantly apart and coming
reluctantly together at the very same moment.** (p. 53)

After reading Barber's paragraph, you should see that using a topic sentence at the beginning and another at the end of a paragraph does have the effect of strengthening the main idea, thus enhancing the unity of the paragraph. Of course, if this arrangement is used, the two topic sentences would not be the same. The first topic sentence may be quite general whereas the second should be more specific. Alternatively, the first could be a question and the second, being at the end of the paragraph, could be an answer to the question.

5.4 Absence of a Topic Sentence

There are times when a paragraph does not really have a topic sentence because the main idea or theme is apparent or because the topic sentence is implied. This is particularly so in a narrative or descriptive paragraph, such as in paragraphs describing procedures of sampling and data collection in research reports. The following example is taken from Ng and Man's (1988) study of the leisure and life satisfaction of young people in Hong Kong's Eastern District.

With the assistance of the Census and Statistics
Department, a sampling frame of all permanent structure living quarters in Eastern District was made
available. It contained about 139,000 living quarters.
A systematic sample, using a selection interval of 1
out of 73, was taken to give 1898 addresses of living

> quarters. If temporary structures were also included, the same procedure would produce an additional 104 addresses. Considering the many possible problems in fieldwork dealing with temporary structures (e.g., difficult access), it was decided that all temporary structures would be excluded from the survey. (p. 3)

Obviously, in such a paragraph, a topic sentence is unnecessary. The same is true of the following paragraph in which Chao (1983) describes a Chinese custom of the Ching Ming festival.

> Another custom on the day of Ch'ing Ming is the wearing of willow branches and evergreen. Women and youngsters wear a thin twig hanging from the hair knot or tie it to their dresses. Willow branches are also inserted between the tiles of the roof and hung above the doors and windows of the house. In North China willow trees are the first to blossom and herald the spring. (p. 176)

In paragraphs that review the literature relevant to a certain problem, a topic sentence may not be needed when the author makes some comments about certain studies and then prepares to move on to review some other works, as is done in the following example from Ng (1984) in a research report on the leisure behaviour of adolescents in Hong Kong. Note the in-text citations of sources (not given in this book because they do not bear directly on our purposes).

> The study of leisure is a relatively neglected topic in sociology. It is only in the last two decades or so that the sociological approach to the many aspects of leisure has attracted the attention of a small number of scholars. Understandably, a primary concern has long been the conceptualization of leisure in contradistinction to work (e.g., Anderson, 1961; Parker, 1965; Dunkerley, 1975; Johannis and Bull, 1971; Dumazedier, 1967, 1974). Other scholars have paid more attention to leisure as an integral part of social life: work is not the only framework in which the meaning of leisure may be understood (e.g., Cheek and Burch, 1976; Katz and Gurevitch, 1976; Roberts,

1978; Kelly, 1982). More recently, the leisure of young people has received particular attention among some writers who have attempted to relate leisure behaviour of youth to the expectations and concerns of young people in their period of growth and development during which school life looms large (e.g., Emmett, 1971; Rapoport and Rapoport, 1975; Poole, 1983; Hendry, 1978, 1983). (pp. 1-2)

From these examples, you can see that although there may not be any single sentence to serve as a topic sentence in narrative and descriptive paragraphs, paragraph unity is still maintained by keeping all sentences related to the same theme. The theme in Ng and Man's (1988) paragraph is obviously the method of sampling adopted; that in Chao's (1983) paragraph is the custom of wearing willow branches on Ch'ing Ming; and that in Ng's (1984) paragraph is a brief review of research concerns in the sociological study of leisure.

5.5 The Thesis Statement

The "thesis" of an essay is its main or controlling idea. What the topic sentence does for a paragraph, the thesis statement does for the whole essay. That is, the thesis statement announces the main idea of the essay and indicates how that idea will be approached or taken up. At the end of the first or sometimes the second paragraph, you will usually write a thesis statement to set the stage and announce the main idea of the whole essay. If you are writing a long paper in which the introduction may take a few pages, then your thesis statement may appear not after the first or second paragraph but at some later location after you have presented some background information. We shall soon see some examples of where the thesis statement is placed, but let us first examine the nature and qualities of the thesis statement itself.

5.5.1 *Thesis Statement Distinguished from Topic*

A thesis is not the same as a topic: a thesis is always some observation or analysis of a topic. While a topic is an area or a subject, a thesis is your position on or treatment of that subject. For instance, if your topic is women's employment, your thesis might be that women still face much discrimination although their participation in the labour force has been increasing. Indeed, this is one possible thesis statement for the topic of women's employment. Thus, a thesis statement is not just an announcement of the subject matter, but it includes an indication of the author's position or view concerning the subject.

The following are several examples to show the difference between a topic and a thesis:

Topic   Social sciences and general education

Thesis   As disciplines studying various domains of social
           life, the social sciences should make an important
           contribution to one's general education, thus
           justifying the inclusion of certain social science
           subjects in a university programme of general
           education.

Topic   Education reform in Hong Kong

Thesis   To reform education in Hong Kong, the Government must
           first identify and address the basic issues of
           teaching and learning before working on any action
           plan.

Topic   Leisure in modern society

Thesis   Contrary to popular belief, people in modern society
           are working more but having less leisure, with the
           consequence that the distinction between work and
           leisure becomes increasingly blurred.

As you can see from the above examples, topics are like labels that indicate domains of knowledge or areas selected for study. To write about such domains or areas, you have to narrow them down to something very specific that brings out some particular belief or view. If you succeed in doing so, you have moved from a topic to a thesis.

You should also note that whereas topics are indicated by noun phrases, thesis statements are always written in sentences that contain verbs. You can name a topic using a noun phrase, but you must use verbs to state a position, an opinion, a claim, or a view.

5.5.2 *Qualities of a Good Thesis Statement*

From the explanation and examples given above, you can see that a well-written thesis statement must meet three important criteria:

- It must be *unified* to include only one main idea although it may contain several related parts.
- It must be *specific* enough for the reader to see your position on the topic and hence the direction in which you will develop your paper.
- It must show, although in a limited way, the overall *structure* of the paper by mentioning what aspects you plan to include and even the order in which you will discuss them.

Let us examine once again the example concerning the topic "Leisure in modern society." The thesis will be unsatisfactory if it is written as follows:

```
We shall explore the nature of leisure in modern
society.
```

Although it seems to contain one main idea, it is not really an idea that can be argued about or defended. Simply saying that you plan to "explore" or study something is not saying much. It is not specific enough to indicate the author's view on leisure in modern society. It does not tell us anything about how the author will address the topic in the paper.

In contrast, the thesis written as follows is much improved:

```
Contrary to popular belief, people in modern society
are working more but having less leisure, with the
consequence that the distinction between work and
leisure becomes increasingly blurred.
```

This thesis is far better because not only does it contain a main idea (*that people in modern society are working more but having less leisure*), it specifically indicates the author's position (*which differs from what popular belief would expect*). The statement also clearly reveals the structure of the paper. The reader can expect that the author will first report that conventional wisdom portrays growing abundance of leisure in modern society, only to be refuted by evidence showing that reality is otherwise. The author will then show us how work and leisure become more and more indistinguishable.

5.5.3 *Thesis Statement Helps You to Plan Your Paper*

Since the thesis statement indicates your position or view concerning the subject, you should compose it with care and tact to ensure that it contains what you believe to be worth saying about the subject. If you express it clearly, it can help you greatly in planning the rest of your paper because it gives you a blueprint for developing your thoughts about the subject. At the same time, it is like a map with which your readers will more easily follow the content of your paper.

5.6 Position of the Thesis Statement

Like the topic sentence in any paragraph, the thesis statement may be placed in various positions. More commonly, however, it follows some introductory material about the topic of the essay. Thus, it may appear at the end of the first paragraph, as in Gill's (1998) opening paragraph in his discussion of Japanese children's programmes on television:

> In any culture, there are elements of change and elements of continuity. The literature on Japan tends to overemphasize either change (such as in technology) or continuity (for example, cherry blossom viewing, haiku, sumo, etc.). **In this chapter, I hope to show how cultural continuities may be found even in an area of popular culture which is subject to countless fast-changing influences: commercial television dramas for children.** (p. 33)

The following paragraph from Pearson's (1996) examination of the social position of Hong Kong women also places the thesis statement at the end of the opening paragraph:

> The end of the saying "The past is another country" is "and they do things differently there." The irony for Hong Kong is that the past is also the future: China. And indeed, they do things differently there. It is not uncommon to hear Hong Kong people wistfully talking of a return to "traditional Chinese values," which they contrast negatively with the more modern and certainly more Westernized ways of Hong Kong. Like most things, however, traditional values were a mixed blessing, particularly for women. Both Hong Kong and China have moved away from such values, one under the influence of colonialism and capitalism, and the other under the influence of communism. **This**

article attempts to demonstrate that while changes in law and official policy do wield influence over cultural mores, such mores show a good deal of tenacity in their effects on individual behavior. (p. 92)

In book-length treatises, the placement of the thesis statement can be highly variable. The first chapter is usually devoted to an overall view of the book's theme. You might say that the whole introductory chapter amounts to a presentation of that theme, or thesis. The author may have several versions of the thesis statement placed at different positions throughout the introductory chapter, separated by explanation and elaboration of the main ideas embraced by the thesis. This is what you find in, for example, Ritzer's (1993) introductory chapter of his book *The McDonaldization of Society.*

Ritzer has his thesis in at least three places. In his second paragraph, Ritzer says:

McDonald's is treated here as the major example, the "paradigm case," of a wide-ranging process I call *McDonaldization*, that is *the process by which the principles of the fast-food restaurant are coming to dominate more and more sectors of American society as well as of the rest of the world.* (p. 1)

About midway in the same chapter, he announces:

Even if some domains are able to resist McDonaldization, this book intends to demonstrate that many other aspects of society are being, or will be, McDonaldized. (p. 9)

Then, in about the middle of the conclusion of the chapter, we are reminded clearly once again of the book's thesis:

Overall, the central thesis is that McDonald's represents a monumentally important development and the process that it has helped spawn, McDonaldization, is engulfing more and more sectors of society and areas of the world. It has yielded a number of benefits to society, but it also entails a considerable number of costs and risks. (p. 16)

5.7 Qualities of a Well-written Paragraph

5.7.1 Unity

So far we have seen the use of a thesis statement to indicate the main idea of an entire paper or book in much the same way that a topic sentence indicates the main idea of a paragraph. The paragraph's purpose is to clarify what that main idea is. Even when no single sentence stands out as the topic sentence, a paragraph should still be about a single main idea. That is, a paragraph should be unified. It must have a clear focus. Never ramble in different directions or try to deal with several main ideas in the same paragraph. You should remember this as the essential requirement of a well-written paragraph.

5.7.2 Development

At the same time, a well-written paragraph must contain appropriate details as you go about clarifying its main idea. This is called *development* of the paragraph. Developing a paragraph could involve any task similar to those in the following, or some combination of them, depending on the main idea you have:

- describing a concept (e.g., professionalization of nursing),
- explaining why factor A is related to factor B (e.g., education and political liberalism),
- offering examples to illustrate what is meant by a certain idea (e.g., Parkinson's law saying that work expands to fill the time available for its completion), or
- arguing why a certain policy will or will not work (e.g., Can increasing taxes help solve Hong Kong's fiscal deficit problem?)

We cannot define precisely how much development is "enough" or "appropriate," but the development of the substance of a paragraph should be reasonably "complete" for the paragraph to stand as a unified segment of your paper with the main idea of that segment clearly explained.

5.7.3 Coherence

You may have no problem understanding the importance of keeping a paragraph unified (all that you say is about one main idea) and developing it sufficiently (so that it covers enough ground to make that main idea clear to your reader). But you still need to pay considerable attention to the paragraph's *coherence*.

A paragraph is coherent to the extent that its sentences are related to each other logically so that the paragraph holds together. Reading a coherent paragraph, your readers will feel that relationships between one point and another are clear and that the sentences flow along smoothly. To achieve coherence, the construction of sentences and their sequence are vital. If unity and development concern essentially what you say, then coherence is a function of how you say it. They are all fundamental qualities of a well-written paragraph.

We shall next see in somewhat greater detail how you develop a paragraph and how you make it coherent.

5.8 Developing Paragraphs

In social science writing, you can develop a paragraph in one or more of the following ways:

(1) Giving examples
(2) Giving a definition
(3) Giving specific details or facts
(4) Making comparison and contrast
(5) Using analogy
(6) Exploring causes and effects
(7) Using a general-to-particular or particular-to-general sequence

Not always mutually exclusive, these methods may be used in combination. For example, you may need to have a diversity of details when you compare or contrast. Likewise, a number of examples can be cited to illustrate the effects resulting from a given cause. Let us now see how each method works.

5.8.1 Giving Examples

This is probably the most common way of substantiating or clarifying an idea. You almost always need examples when you want your readers to understand and to accept a generalization, a statement of opinion, or a concept that is not immediately clear. Below, in his essay "The Clash of Civilizations?" Huntington (1993) uses examples to explain what he means by "civilization":

```
What do we mean when we talk of a civilization? A
civilization is a cultural entity. Villages, regions,
```

```
ethnic groups, nationalities, religious groups, all
have  distinct   cultures   at   different   levels   of
cultural heterogeneity. The culture of a village in
southern   Italy   may   be   different   from   that   of   a
village in northern Italy, but both will share in a
common Italian culture that distinguishes them from
German villages. European communities, in turn, will
share cultural features that distinguish them from
Arab   or   Chinese   communities.   Arabs,   Chinese   and
Westerners,   however,   are   not   part   of   any   broader
cultural   entity.   They   constitute   civilizations.   A
civilization is thus the highest cultural grouping of
people  and  the  broadest  level  of  cultural  identity
people have short of that which distinguishes humans
from other species. (p. 23)
```

5.8.2 Giving a Definition

Sometimes you need to define a term clearly to show its meaning by using not only a
general statement but also examples and, if appropriate, quoted material from other
sources. Actually, part of the paragraph in the preceding illustration involves the
giving of a simple and short definition ("a civilization is a cultural entity") followed
by examples. There are times, however, when you may have to focus on the task of
not only giving a clear definition but also discussing certain conceptual or theoretical
aspects based on the definition. Such a task appears in the following paragraph from
Ng's (1974) paper on "population-related norms," in which the concept of "norm"
and its implications for behaviour are discussed.

```
A  norm  is  essentially  a  standard  or  principle  of
behaviour  that  is  socially  acceptable.  It  defines  or
prescribes  the  right  thing  to  do--although  often  a
range  of  behaviour  is  allowed--under  a  particular
situation.  Such  definition  or  prescription  is  typi-
cally  shared  to  some  extent  by  others  to  give  the
norm  a  social  significance  in  terms  of  providing
certain  sanctions  to  enforce  conformity.  However,
conformity   varies,   depending   on   the   situation,
because  although  norms  do  exercise  some  influence  on
behaviour,  they  do  not  necessarily  determine  behav-
```

iour completely. To understand an individual's
behaviour, we must examine the norms, some more
influential than others, that are relevant to the
individual and that have been learned and accepted by
him or her as guidelines for action. (p. 2)

5.8.3 *Giving Specific Details or Facts*

To develop a main point, you sometimes need to give concrete descriptive details,
such as numerical facts or statistical data. Of course, you should make sure that these
details or facts are correct and be ready to indicate their sources if possible. You can
easily spot the specific details that Croteau and Hoynes (2000) use to develop the
following paragraph on one dimension of the influence of television:

At the dawn of the twenty-first century, television
so permeates our lives that it's easy to forget how
recent its growth has been. Think of it this way:
People who were over 55 years old in the year 2000--
roughly 30 percent of the U.S. population--were born
before the commercial introduction of television. It
wasn't that long ago--as anyone over 55 will be happy
to confirm! On the other hand, most Americans who
were under the age of 45 in the year 2000 have a
difficult time imagining life without the near-
constant presence of television. That's how quickly
the influence of television has spread. (p. 12)

5.8.4 *Making Comparison and Contrast*

The qualities of something, whether it be a concept, a phenomenon, or a view, are
often made clear by comparing it with another entity. When you compare, you are
more concerned with the similarities; when you contrast, you are more interested in
the differences. Depending on the nature of the entities and your purpose, you may
want to concentrate on either comparison or contrast or both. Thus, for example, you
may choose to describe the similarities of Chinese and Japanese family values or
examine the differences between two types of organizations, one professional and the
other commercial. In the following paragraph describing the practice of *karaoke* in
Japan, Kelly (1998) observes a main difference between participation in *karaoke* in
Japan and such participation in the United States or England. In so doing, Kelly is

also giving some specific details about the expectation of skill improvement associated with participating in the singing:

> An activity in which all can participate, karaoke is perhaps more vitally one in which all participants can improve their performance. An important aspect of the solo performance is the implicit expectation that some degree of preparation and effort will be invested by the performer into polishing his or her act. Whereas participation in karaoke or other forms of amateur singing in the United States or England might depend on talent--a good voice for example, particularly if an audience is involved--in Japan, anybody, regardless of ability, is provided the opportunity to do their best and is generally accorded patience and even encouragement along the way. Furthermore, there seems to exist a standard of singing, a sort of ideal model, set by professional pop or *enka* (ballad) singers, which participants can strive to emulate and against which their relative ability can be gauged. There has thus developed a "way of karaoke" (*karaoke-do*) which, with discipline and practice, enables one to perfect a chosen piece, performing it with a minimum of effort when the occasion arises. (p. 80)

5.8.5 Using Analogy

Sometimes you can use an analogy to explain an idea by comparing it with something, usually familiar to many people, on the basis of certain shared characteristics. This way, your readers will understand the idea more easily. In the following paragraph, I use the analogy of a Chinese painting being more than the sum of all its landscape segments to stress the point that the whole of society is more than the sum of its parts.

> While society is certainly made up of individuals, we cannot understand society adequately simply by putting together what we know about individuals. When individuals come together in various relations that

form part of the larger society, it takes much more than their own characteristics as individuals. As the saying goes, the whole is more than the sum of its parts. Take, for example, a Chinese traditional landscape painting that depicts the following: in the foreground a hermit sitting in a pavilion by the side of a stream in the hills, in the mid-ground layers of mist hovering over a valley, and in the background plenty of empty space accompanying the soft outlines of some distant hills. You can, of course, examine any part of the painting and be amazed by how the artist's brush strokes bring out all kinds of details and images. Even if you remember these details and images well, you cannot really claim to understand the whole painting. *It is not just a collection of details and images that make the painting; it is how they are arranged within the space of the rectangular scroll so that they bear some particular relationship with one another that results in a work of art that evokes our admiration.* Indeed, as is typical of Chinese paintings, even seemingly empty space adds a certain philosophical meaning or aesthetic quality to the painting. The hermit, the pavilion, the stream, the trees, the mist hanging over the valley, and the distant hills at which the hermit seems to be gazing all come together to tell a story. But such a story is possible only if we take all the ingredients of the painting not individually but together as a whole so that we see their arrangement and hence their relationship. Thus, the whole painting has a character that is not present in the parts that make up the painting. Similarly, *society as a whole has a character that is not present in individual persons although they are part of society.* It is not just a collection of individuals that makes society, but how they interact directly and indirectly in patterned ways that gives meaning to "society." (Written for this book)

5.8.6 *Exploring Causes and Effects*

In thinking about the development of events or the emergence of "new" phenomena, you are likely to consider causes and effects. Sometimes the concern is more with causes, such as when you try to write about the causes of family violence. At other times, you may want to explore the possible consequences of a certain phenomenon, such as the effects on social life brought about by the increasingly widespread use of information technology. You should try to pick out this kind of thinking contained in the following paragraph in which Schor (1991) questions the validity of the economist's view on spending behaviour.

> Most economists regard the spending spree that Americans indulged in throughout the postwar decades as an unambiguous blessing, on the assumption that more is always better. And there is a certain sense in this approach. It's hard to imagine how having more of a desired good could make one worse off, especially since it is always possible to ignore the additional quantity. Relying on this little bit of common sense, economists have championed the closely related ideas that more goods yield more satisfaction, that desires are infinite, and that people act to satisfy those desires as fully as they can. (p. 9)

5.8.7 *Using a General-to-particular or Particular-to-general Sequence*

In developing a paragraph that starts with a topic sentence, which is often a general statement, you can continue with details and examples that support the statement. This pattern, from the general to the particular, is quite common. Conversely, you may start with details, examples, and reasons and end with a general statement. This would be going from the particular to the general, placing the topic sentence at or near the end of the paragraph. The following paragraph is my own summary of C. Wright Mills' (1959) idea of the sociological imagination as described in the opening chapter of his classic *The Sociological Imagination*. You will notice that it uses the general-to-particular pattern of development:

> The sociological imagination is developed through sharpening our awareness of how individual experi-ences both contribute to and are shaped by macro societal processes. We should not restrict our vision

```
to our immediate surroundings; neither should we be
distracted or overwhelmed by sweeping social changes
without recognizing their impact on us as individuals.
Insofar as we can exercise our sociological imagina-
tion, we shall be able to distinguish between
"personal troubles" occurring in our immediate
confines and "public issues" present in society at
large.
```

Note that the paragraph is introduced by a general statement that indicates how the sociological imagination is developed. This is followed by two sentences that explain what this statement means by spelling out clearly, though briefly, the relation between "individual experiences" and "societal processes." Compare it with the next example which takes the reverse route, from the particular to the general. In this other summary of Mills, I open immediately with references to personal experiences and societal processes, but without mentioning the term "sociological imagination" at all. After some elaboration, the paragraph concludes with a general statement that reveals Mills' well-known phrase at the very end. Of course, not every specific detail needs to be expressed in this version of the summary.

```
To understand the meaning of our life experiences, we
must relate them to broad societal processes.
Conversely, to comprehend the significance of these
processes, we need to examine their implications for
individuals. The characteristics of a society and its
dynamics of change constitute a context for the
unfolding of individual lives. At the same time,
personal endeavours certainly contribute to the
character of society. To recognize this and to
incorporate it in our consciousness is to exercise
the sociological imagination.
```

5.9 Paragraph Coherence

It is not enough that a paragraph is unified (all its content related to one main idea) and well developed (elaborating the idea in adequate detail). To be effective, your paragraph has also to be coherent. That is, your sentences must be related logically as you develop the topic or main idea. Their sequence and organization must be such that the paragraph holds together as a meaningful whole. Your reader will then be able to follow your train of thought without difficulty.

Of course, if you do poorly in unifying and developing your paragraph, your paragraph will not cohere well because poor unity means lack of focus and poor development means unclear relationship between sentences as well as insufficient details. On the other hand, if your paragraph is clearly focused and contains well-developed details, you will come closer to having a coherent, hence readable, paragraph. You can do the following to add coherence to your paragraph:

(1)   Using pronouns as cues
(2)   Using verb tenses properly
(3)   Repeating important words and phrases
(4)   Using parallel structures
(5)   Supplying transitional markers

5.9.1 Using Pronouns as Cues

As words that stand for or refer to a noun, pronouns are often used in sentences when you need to make such references. They are cues for your readers to follow who is doing what or what is the object of attention. In using pronouns as cues, you should keep their references both consistent and clear. Note the use of pronouns in the following two sentences from my second (particular-to-general) summary of Mills' notion of the sociological imagination shown to you in 5.8.7.

> To understand the meaning of **our** experiences, **we** must relate **them** to broad societal processes. Conversely, to comprehend the significance of these processes, **we** need to examine **their** implications for individuals.

5.9.2 Using Verb Tenses Properly

Verbs are important words in writing because they express actions and indicate various states of being (e.g., *The elderly feel isolated from society*). Without verbs, sentences become lifeless. But the aspect of tense is always associated with verbs. Chinese students tend to have considerable difficulty with verb tenses largely because verbs in the Chinese language do not inflect as verbs in English do. You must take great care to use verb tenses correctly and consistently. Tense errors and shifting from one tense to another without due reason weaken the relationship among the elements making up your sentences and hence reduce the coherence of the paragraph.

Note that, in the two sentences shown in 5.9.1 and also in the paragraph you just read, the predominant verb tense is the simple present to indicate that all statements are supposed to have general validity at all times.

5.9.3 *Repeating important words and phrases*

At various points in your paragraph, you need to repeat certain key words and phrases, sometimes using synonyms and alternative phrases with similar meanings, to sharpen your paragraph's focus and to help your reader see how your points are linked in the paragraph.

If you examine again the illustrative paragraphs given above, you will find that repeating important words and phrases is a common strategy indeed in writing coherently. Let us take Schor's (1991) paragraph in 5.8.6 on spending behaviour for example. Repeated or similar words and phrases are boldfaced:

```
Most  economists  regard  the  spending  spree  that
Americans  indulged  in  throughout  the  postwar  decades
as  an  unambiguous  blessing,  on  the  assumption  that
more  is  always  better.  And  there  is  a  certain  sense
in  this  approach.  It's  hard  to  imagine  how  having
more of a desired good  could  make  one  worse  off,
especially  since  it  is  always  possible  to  ignore  the
additional quantity.  Relying  on  this  little  bit  of
common  sense,  economists  have  championed  the  closely
related  ideas  that  more goods  yield  more satisfaction,
that  desires  are  infinite,  and  that  people  act  to
satisfy  those  desires  as  fully  as  they  can.
```

5.9.4 *Using Parallel Structures/Constructions*

Parallel structures are constructions of words or phrases that are grammatically identical. You may use them to express similar or related ideas, such as when you give a series of items, make comparison and contrast, describe characteristics of something, raise questions, or give reasons for some phenomenon. (Note that the preceding sentence itself contains parallel structures in a series.)

Parallel structures can occur within the same sentence, as in the following sentence that gives two specific points:

```
Our  purpose  in  conducting  this  survey  is  to find out
```

```
what young people think about leisure and to examine
how they use their leisure.
```

Parallel structures can also occur across sentences, as in the following two sentences that provide a comparison:

```
Some people like television because it gives them
free entertainment. Others hate it because it has too
much unrealistic content.
```

In the following paragraph from Best's (2001) book *Damned Lies and Statistics,* you can see examples of both within-sentence and across-sentence parallel structures. You can also see how coherence is achieved by the other strategies described above. Note, for example, that Best repeats the word "statistics" several times to emphasize his message. Note also that he uses the simple present tense throughout to indicate that the statements are regarded as generally valid.

```
This is a book about bad statistics, where they come
from, and why they won't go away. Some statistics are
born bad--they aren't much good from the start,
because they are based on nothing more than guesses
or dubious data. Other statistics mutate; they become
bad after being mangled. . . . Either way, bad
statistics are potentially important: they can be
used to stir up public outrage or fear; they can
distort our understanding of our world; and they can
lead us to make poor policy choices. (p. 5)
```

5.9.5 Supplying Transitional Markers

As you develop your paragraph, you will need to indicate, at various places, how a particular point is related to one that is mentioned earlier, or what is to come next. This you can do with the help of words or phrases known as "transitional markers" (also called "transitional expressions," "connectives," or simply "transitions"). They are usually placed at or near the beginning of a sentence, sometimes in mid-sentence, to show how it is related to the preceding sentence or to an idea developed in the preceding sentences. Used suitably, transitional markers clarify the logical connection between ideas and thus add to the coherence of the paragraph. However, you must be careful not to overuse them. The following is a list of commonly used transitional markers:

To add

also, and, additionally, again, as well, besides, equally important, further, furthermore, in addition, moreover, then

To emphasize a point

certainly, definitely, even, indeed, inevitably, in fact, of course, that is, really, surely, truly, undoubtedly, undeniably

To give examples

for example, for instance, in particular, namely, specifically, to illustrate

To repeat

as has been said, in a word, in brief, in other words, in short, in simpler terms, that is, to put it differently

To show cause and effect

accordingly, as a result, as a result of, because, because of, consequently, for this purpose, given, hence, otherwise, since, so, subsequently, then, therefore, thus, to this end

To show concession

after all, although, at the same time, but, despite, even though, in spite of, of course, regardless of the fact that, while

To show contrast

although, but, despite, however, in contrast, in spite of, nevertheless, nonetheless, notwithstanding, on the contrary, on the one hand . . . on the other hand, regardless, still, yet

To show place

above, adjacent to, below, beyond, elsewhere, everywhere, here, in back, in front, near, nearby, on the other side, opposite to, to the left, to the right, there

To show sequence

first, second, third, next, then, finally

To show similarity

also, in the same way, just as . . . so too, likewise, similarly

To show time

after, afterwards, after a while, as long as, as soon as, at last, before, currently, during, earlier, immediately, in the meantime, in the past, meanwhile, later, now, recently, shortly, simultaneously, soon, subsequently, then, thereafter, until, when

To summarize or conclude

all considered, in a nutshell, in brief, in conclusion, in short, on the whole, therefore, thus, to conclude, to sum up, to summarize

Here is an example paragraph taken from Campbell's (1997) report on the results of a study of women's and men's attitudes towards shopping. Transitional markers used have been removed. Read the paragraph to see how it sounds to you.

```
. . . the results suggest that women were much more
likely to express positive attitudes toward shopping
than were men, and . . . that men were far more
likely to express negative attitudes toward shopping
than women. . . . , women were far more likely to
express a strong positive attitude-- . . . , to say
that they 'loved' shopping rather than that they
merely 'liked' it. . . . , men were far more likely
to express a strong negative attitude-- . . . , to
say that they 'hated' it rather than merely
'disliked' it. . . . , women were more prone to
express positive attitudes toward a range of
different kinds of shopping, . . . when males
expressed a positive attitude it was more likely to
be toward a very product-specific form of shopping
( . . . , shopping for records, computers or electric
goods). . . . , women were also much more likely than
men to express a preference for shopping above other
forms of leisure-time activity, . . . watching a film
or eating in a restaurant. (p. 167)
```

Well, how did it sound? Rather choppy and not very clear at some places? Now read the same paragraph again, this time with the author's transitional markers put back in. You should feel a big difference, in that the paragraph becomes so much clearer and smoother.

```
Essentially the results suggest that women were much
more likely to express positive attitudes toward
shopping than were men, and correspondingly that men
were far more likely to express negative attitudes
toward shopping than women. What is more, women were
far more likely to express a strong positive
```

attitude--**that is,** to say that they 'loved' shopping
rather than that they merely 'liked' it. **Corre-**
spondingly, men were far more likely to express a
strong negative attitude--**that is,** to say that they
'hated' it rather than merely 'disliked' it. **In**
addition, women were more prone to express positive
attitudes toward a range of different kinds of
shopping, **whilst** when males expressed a positive
attitude it was more likely to be toward a very
product-specific form of shopping (**for example,**
shopping for records, computers or electric goods).
Finally, women were also much more likely than men to
express a preference for shopping above other forms
of leisure-time activity, **such as** watching a film or
eating in a restaurant.

Thus, you see how transitional markers are like signposts that help the reader
follow the author's line of thought. Without them, sentences may appear disjointed,
and the reader will easily get lost in a maze of ideas.

5.10 Using the Devices of Maintaining Paragraph Coherence

Let us now see how all these devices of maintaining coherence are used in the second
of the two brief summaries of C. Wright Mills' idea of the sociological imagination
you read earlier (5.8.7). You may remember that it is a paragraph developed
inductively (from the particular to the general). After a series of specific explanations,
the concluding sentence declares that the result is the sociological imagination. (For
your convenience, I have numbered the sentences, italicized pronouns, and boldfaced
transitional markers.)

(1) To understand the meaning of *our* life experiences,
we must relate *them* to broad societal processes. (2)
Conversely, to comprehend the significance of these
processes, *we* need to examine *their* implications for
individuals. (3) The characteristics of a society and
its dynamics of change constitute a context for the
unfolding of individual lives. (4) **At the same time,**
personal endeavours **certainly** contribute to the

```
character of society. (5) To recognize this and to
incorporate it in our consciousness is to exercise
the sociological imagination.
```

5.10.1 Pronouns

The first person plural pronoun is used in sentences 1, 2, and 5 to include not just the author but all readers as well. This indicates that the meaning of the sentences (not only 1, 2, and 5 explicitly but also 3 and 4 implicitly) applies to everybody. Further, clearly, *them* in sentence 1 refers to "our life experiences," and the possessive pronoun *their* (used as an adjective or determiner) in sentence 2 refers to "societal processes" mentioned in the first sentence. In sentence 3, the possessive *its* before *dynamics of change* obviously refers to "society." Finally, in sentence 5, the demonstrative pronoun *this* and the nominative *it* both refer to the entire statement in the preceding sentence. You can see how various forms of pronouns are used to tell the reader what references are intended and in so doing give meaning to the connection between the sentences in the paragraph.

5.10.2 Verb Tense

As all the statements are supposed to be still true and continue to be so, the present tense is used throughout the paragraph. The consistency of the use of this verb tense stresses the generality of the idea conveyed in the paragraph.

5.10.3 Repetition of Important Words and Phrases

The paragraph contains two sets of important words and phrases. The first set includes phrases referring to society in general: *broad societal processes* (sentence 1), *these processes* (sentence 2), *characteristics of a society* (sentence 3), *character of society* (sentence 4). The second set includes words and phrases concerning individuals and their experiences: *our life experiences* (sentence 1), *individuals* (sentence 2), *individual lives* (sentence 3), *personal endeavours* (sentence 4). By repeating such more or less synonymous terms, the sentences make it clear that the sociological imagination functions to explore the connection between society and the individual. Moreover, several words and phrases indicating closely allied cognitive activities are used in the paragraph when referring to what is done with the connection between society and the individual: *understand* (sentence 1), *relate to* (sentence 1), *comprehend* (sentence 2), *examine* (sentence 2), *recognize* (sentence 5), and *incorporate in* (sentence 5). The use of these words and phrases contribute to underscoring the main idea of what the sociological imagination is all about.

5.10.4 *Parallel Structures*

The use of parallel structures adds a rhythm to what we write by expressing similar ideas in similar grammatical forms, thus making our text more readable. You can identify parallel structures in sentences 1 and 2 (*to comprehend* parallels *to understand; we need to examine their . . .* parallels *we must relate them to . . .*). In sentence 5, you can see three elements in parallel (using infinitive phrases): *to recognize this, to incorporate it,* and *to exercise the sociological imagination.*

5.10.5 *Transitional Markers*

The mental activity prescribed in sentence 1 is to relate the individual to society; that in sentence 2 is just the reverse, relating society to the individual. This difference is made clearer by the use of the transitional marker *conversely* at the beginning of sentence 2. Reading on, you will see that sentences 3 and 4 carry on this mental activity a bit further. Sentence 3 draws the reader's attention to the "characteristics of a society," while sentence 4 returns to the significance of "personal endeavours." To show that these two views are equally important, sentence 4 begins with the transitional marker *at the same time*, and in mid-sentence adds emphasis with the adverb *certainly*.

5.11 Guidelines for Writing Effective Paragraphs

- In principle, a paragraph should have a topic sentence that announces your purpose or the main idea that you will develop in the paragraph.
- The topic sentence usually appears early in the paragraph, but may be placed anywhere else.
- Occasionally, the topic sentence representing the main idea is not present but is implied.
- Extending the principle to the entire paper, you announce the purpose of the paper in the introductory paragraph. Such an announcement is called a thesis statement, which must clearly indicate your position or view on the topic. It should also show how you will approach the topic.
- Plan your paper around your thesis statement.

- A good paragraph must be unified in that it is about one main idea, giving the reader a clear focus of attention.

- A good paragraph must be well developed. To achieve this goal, you can choose from the following methods, which can be used in combination: giving examples, giving a definition, giving details, making comparison and contrast, using analogy, and exploring causes and effects. You can develop your paragraph in a general-to-particular or particular-to-general sequence.

- A good paragraph must also be coherent, with all its sentences related to one another logically. That is, the sentences "hang together" as a whole to make the main idea of the paragraph clear to the reader.

- To construct a coherent paragraph, you can use pronouns, proper verb tenses, repeated important words and phrases, parallel structures, and transitional markers.

CHAPTER 6

Writing a Well-organized Paper

6.1 From Paragraphs to a Paper

If you can write a well-constructed paragraph using the methods described in Chapter 5, writing a multi-paragraph paper should not be too difficult because whatever the writing task, the basic principles of writing clear and effective paragraphs remain the same. You will make sure that each paragraph is unified, well developed, and coherent. What you need to consider, though, is how you put multiple paragraphs together so that they are just as effective and powerful as a whole.

Just as a paragraph should be unified, well developed, and coherent, so, too, a paper should be unified around a thesis, developed with sufficient supporting points and examples, and coherent with each paragraph making its contribution to the thesis of the paper in a coordinated and integrated manner. When paragraphs combine to produce a paper that fits the bill in this way, the paper is effective.

6.2 The Basic Three-part Structure of a Paper

Generally, a paper consists of three main parts: introduction, body, and conclusion. Each part may include one or more paragraphs. The introduction announces your purpose of writing the paper. The body elaborates your thesis and brings in various kinds of related or relevant supporting points to help your readers to understand the overall central or controlling idea of the paper. The conclusion sums up the main ideas to reinforce the weight of your thesis.

Not every piece of academic writing displays the "introduction, body, conclusion" structure, but many do, although the proportion of each part may vary a great deal. The "three-part" structure is logical and applicable to practically any topic. It helps you to keep focused and organized as you write. You will find writing not a haphazard activity but a disciplined process if you follow the three-part structure as a basic model. Let us now briefly examine what you should do in each part.

6.3 The Introduction

The introduction has three important functions:

- It attracts your readers' attention to and interest in what you have to say.
- It provides background information so that your readers understand the nature of your topic and are able to follow your thinking.
- It clarifies your central idea as described in your thesis statement.

All of the above three elements are necessary to make your introduction effective. The opening sentence or sentences must attract your readers' attention and keep them sufficiently curious about what you have to offer so that they will keep on reading. As you are doing this, you should also include some relevant background information (e.g., past events, main points of a controversy, recent research, meaning of an important concept) to guide readers to your paper. How much of this is appropriate depends on the length of the paper as well as the nature of the topic itself. Naturally, you must not overdo this or risk boring your readers. Then, as I explained in Chapter 5, you should include a carefully constructed thesis statement to indicate your position on the topic and how you will develop the paper to clarify and support your position. Done properly, this statement will give your paper a sense of purpose and direction. If you have all these elements included in the introduction, which may be one or more paragraphs long, you are off to a good start. But remember: once you have settled with the introduction, you must write the paper in the direction shown there. That is, the introduction is where you make a kind of commitment. You must later deliver what you promise.

The following introduction (written by a student) to a short essay on "Leisure and social life" is weak because the opening sentence is not quite forceful enough to capture attention and interest. What the author continues to say is more about the nature of leisure rather than the relationship between leisure and social life, which is what the title suggests. Worst of all is the absence of any statement to indicate the thesis of the paper, making it impossible for the reader to see how the paper will be developed.

```
Leisure makes social life easy and comfortable. In
social life, interaction with work colleagues is
important. But interaction in work is rather imperson-
al and is quite routine. On the contrary, when
participating in leisure activities, we feel it easier
and more comfortable to interact with other people.
```

```
For instance, in a friend's birthday party, we chat
delightedly with our friends about a trip to the Great
Wall and discuss the destination of the next one. But
we never do so at a business meeting.
```

Another student wrote the following introduction. It is more effective because the opening sentence immediately focuses on leisure as contrasted with work. The next two sentences point to both how leisure may benefit social life and how social life may shape leisure. The last sentence generalizes this idea to make a thesis statement, which then guides the reader's expectation of the kind of discussion that will follow.

```
Leisure activities serve as an escape from both
boredom and stress of the work environment. They are
generally regarded as beneficial to our social life
because they provide opportunities for us to cultivate
and maintain friendship in a more relaxing way. At the
same time, our social life shapes the forms of leisure
activities--individual and collective--that are avail-
able to us. Leisure and social life are thus inter-
active and interrelated: each affects the other both
explicitly and subtly.
```

6.4 The Body

The body of your paper is where you expand and develop the main idea announced in your thesis statement. The length of the body depends on the complexity of your thesis and the extent to which you intend to elaborate ideas contained in it. Thus, you could have a relatively short body of just two paragraphs or one of perhaps twenty or more.

Whatever the length of the body, its content should relate to the thesis clearly. If your thesis statement indicates, as it should, the basic structure of your paper, the construction of the body ought to reflect this structure. Assuming that you have done sufficient preparatory work in reading, taking notes, and that, more importantly, you have an outline to guide your writing, you should be able to sort your material according to the organization indicated in the thesis statement. Of course, while it may be more detailed, the organizational plan should basically match what you have promised to deliver in the introduction. You may find yourself deviating from the original outline as you proceed with the writing. This does often happen because you may see the organization of your paper in a somewhat different light if you come across new information or some bright idea suddenly dawns on you. That notwithstanding, you are obliged to show how ideas arising from your preparatory work are put together in a well-organized way to illustrate and support your thesis.

6.4.1 Some Ways of Organizing a Paper

As indicated in Chapter 5, a single paragraph can be developed in various ways, such as giving examples, comparing or contrasting, and analyzing causes. In writing the body of a paper, you may use one of these ways, or combinations of them, to develop the paragraphs. The following three simplified illustrations represent what you can do if you choose to use one main pattern to develop the paragraphs of the body.

If your paper is mainly about proposing an idea or arguing that an idea is a valid one, you may organize your paper as follows:

> Introduction: thesis (that a certain idea is valid)
> Argument 1 with examples
> Argument 2 with examples
> Argument 3 with examples
> Conclusion

If you want to compare or contrast two subjects, A and B (such as two approaches to a specific problem), you may organize your paper around several points or aspects, as follows:

> Introduction: thesis (that B is the better approach to a problem than A)
> Subject A
>> Point 1
>> Point 2
>> Point 3
> Subject B
>> Point 1
>> Point 2
>> Point 3
> Conclusion

Notice that in the above development involving comparison, the discussion of the more "important" of the two subjects comes last. Thus, if your thesis is that A, rather than B, is the better approach to the problem in question, you should discuss Subject A last. The pattern of development shown above is called "block organization." Alternatively, you can use "point-by-point organization," which requires you to refer to both A and B for each of the points you choose to include for discussion.

> Introduction: thesis (that B is the better approach to a problem than A)
> Point 1
>   Subject A and Subject B
> Point 2
>   Subject A and Subject B
> Point 3
>   Subject A and Subject B
> Conclusion

If you want to examine the causes of a phenomenon, you may arrange your paper as follows:

> Introduction: thesis (that the causes of a certain effort are 1, 2, and 3)
> Cause 1 (most important)
> Cause 2 (less important)
> Cause 3 (least important)
> Conclusion

Surely, one paper may use one method of development rather than others, but you should always consider the possibility of using various methods in combination. Indeed, it is often the case that one method becomes embedded in another. For instance, you are likely to need examples when you compare and you probably need both examples and comparison to study causes and effects. If necessary, use quoted material or summarize other authors' views, but do this judiciously.

As you construct the paragraphs of the body, keep in mind that each paragraph addresses one main point which is actually related to the thesis. If each paragraph is one argument, make sure that it is part of the central idea of the thesis. Similarly, if you analyze the causes of something, they should also be anticipated by the thesis statement, and each cause should be discussed by one or more paragraphs. Whatever method of development you choose for the paragraphs, the thesis statement that you have in the introduction should determine the topic sentence of each paragraph. It is in this way that you establish an interlocking frame that ensures the unity and coherence of the whole paper.

Whatever you do in writing the body paragraphs, be particularly careful that you do not drift away from the main theme or thesis of the paper. Whatever you say must have a purpose that is related to that theme. *Just as you keep each paragraph well focused, so you should also keep the whole paper integrated around the overall thesis.*

6.4.2 Linking Paragraphs

In writing the paragraphs of the body of the paper, you should pay attention to how the paragraphs are linked together in a natural and sensible way. While each paragraph has its own focus, the paragraphs of the paper should work together towards addressing the overall thesis or establishing what it claims to demonstrate. As is evident in the preceding section's brief sketch of organizing papers, the paragraphs are supposed to relate to one another in a way that is determined by the thesis. As you move from one paragraph to another, their mutual relationship as far as the paper's thesis is concerned should be clear.

In a paper that examines the pros and cons of a certain social policy, for example, you will want to describe what that policy is, mention the criteria by which you are going to evaluate it and justify why these criteria are relevant. The body of such a paper will explain first the pros and then the cons of that policy, followed by an overall evaluation. For linkage, the paragraphs should follow the right sequence, and all turning points (e.g., going from the pros to the cons, returning to the pros later on when these are seen to be dominant) should be clearly indicated. The following are some sentence constructions that announce transitions:

- While the advantages of X are easily seen, as shown above, we must not overlook the problems that it is likely to cause.
- Despite the advantages accompanying X, it is also true that a number of disadvantages will follow. It is to these disadvantages that we will now turn.
- Some people may find the strengths of X rather obvious without, however, taking time to consider its weaknesses. The following inadequacies are among the most serious.

6.5 The Conclusion

After having gone to some length developing and substantiating your points, you need to bring all that to a close. Before you write the conclusion, however, take time to go through what you have written to check if you have covered your points sufficiently and in the right proportions. You should then gather your thoughts to plan for a strong conclusion.

A strong conclusion is hard to write, because it should tie the whole paper together without sounding simply repetitive. Just as your introduction has to interest your readers in what you have to say, so your conclusion must satisfy your readers in seeing that you have brought your ideas to a logical end. *A well-written conclusion should leave a good lasting impression.*

What should you say in the conclusion? The following are some tasks that are usually taken up in the concluding paragraphs (the conclusion may consist of more than one paragraph):

(1) *Summarize your main points.* You summarize your main points, generally in the order in which they appear in your paper. You should not, however, merely provide a dull summary, but should try to present them in such a way that their overall relevance to the topic of the paper is clear. As a result, your readers will remember them well.

(2) *Restate your thesis.* The main points all relate to the thesis. It is usually a good idea to restate your thesis so that your readers can focus once again on it as the central theme of your paper. But you should phrase the thesis in different words. Since you are stating it after all the development and expansion in the body of the paper, you should state it in more specific and assertive terms than when you first mention it in your introduction. Following the restatement of the thesis, you could make a generalization that puts the thesis into perspective. (See example student essay below.)

(3) *Point out any significant implication that places your thesis in a larger context.* If you see a significant implication of your thesis that places the thesis in a larger context, it is worth pointing out in your conclusion. In doing so, you may raise a question or two to sharpen your readers' awareness of the implication. For instance, if you are writing about how sociology or psychology helps to improve our understanding of ourselves as individuals living in society, you could conclude with the idea that sociology or psychology probably ought to be made a required component of a general education programme at the university. Try to pick a key word or phrase (e.g., *knowing the self through others*) mentioned in your introduction, and use it to point to the implication that sociology or psychology has an important place in general education. You might then want to raise the question whether a course in introductory sociology or introductory psychology designed for major students should be made

available for general education or another parallel course should be designed, perhaps with modification, especially for general education. Although you may have no ready answer to the question, you leave the reader something to think about. That sometimes can be quite effective.

6.6 Pitfalls to Avoid in Writing Conclusions

- *Do not simply "cut and paste" your thesis statement.* Always try to recast your thesis statement in a stronger form to underscore your purpose in writing the paper. Your tone should be more affirmative than that in the introduction. After all, you have given the topic due elaboration.
- *Do not bring up an entirely new idea.* You should not introduce anything that has not been mentioned directly or indirectly in the paper, although you may raise questions that invite further thought on your topic. That is, do not write anything in your conclusion that sounds like beginning an essay on a new topic.
- *Do not contradict your thesis.* Do not include any reference to minor points or anything that contradicts your main thesis. Remember that you are supposed to have given your main thesis a full development as far as the length of the paper allows. Let your conclusion confirm that.
- *Do not quote or paraphrase extensively from other sources.* Such material, if needed, belongs more to the main body than to the conclusion. Your voice should dominate in the conclusion. Remember that you must now give your readers the strongest impression possible.
- *Do not make any unsupported assertion.* What you have presented as likely must not be restated as definite; what you have treated as doubtful must remain the same. This way, you will be honest and fair; your conclusion will be trustworthy and strong.

6.7 A Sample Student Essay

To illustrate some of the main principles in organizing a multi-paragraph paper, let us now examine a sample short essay entitled "Why do we need to study sociology?" It was written by a final-year sociology student named Jade Lai in my course "Writing for Sociology" under the specification that it was to contain only four paragraphs. As you would expect, the first paragraph is introduction, the second and the third paragraphs are the main body that elaborates the thesis, and the fourth paragraph the conclusion. For convenience of our discussion, the sentences in each paragraph are numbered sequentially. Jade's essay has been edited slightly for use here.

Why Do We Need to Study Sociology?

By

Jade Lai

(1) Oftentimes, people with pragmatic but myopic concerns regard sociology as abstract and irrelevant to their lives. (2) Yet, it is precisely our lives that sociology examines very thoroughly and of which it offers some of the most accurate depictions and revealing explanations. (3) Since we each, as a social being, owe our identity to the larger collectivity that defines and circumscribes us, society is what we must investigate for a better understanding of ourselves: sociology is the scientific study of society. (4) **Through sociology, we can look into society to understand the socialization processes that determine who we are and the social structures that pattern how we live.**

(1) Socialization, "the process by which a child learns to be a participant member of society" (Berger 1963, p. 116), is a major subject matter that sociology deals with. (2) While our dispositions certainly play a role in expressing who we are, socialization has a much larger influence on the way we think, feel, and act. (3) Through the work of the all-embracing socializing agents, such as family, school, and the mass media, society defines and shapes us to become who we are. (4) That is what Berger means when he writes: "Identity is socially bestowed, socially sustained and socially transformed" (p. 116). (5) Moreover, even something as "personal" as our self-concept is mostly a product of socialization. (6) As George Herbert Mead theorizes, it is through

---

imitating and interacting with his or her significant and generalized others, or members of society in general, that a child learns to take up his or her various roles and participate in society (p. 117). (7) **By analyzing the process that makes us who we are, sociology gives us a better understanding of ourselves vis-à-vis the larger collectivity surrounding us.**

(1) **Besides socialization, sociology also examines the social structures that pattern our lives.** (2) Each of us is born into a structured society, and it is within the frame of the structures in it that we live out our lives and make our choices. (3) It is no exaggeration to say that people living in the same society always exhibit basically the same general pattern of life. (4) For instance, in well-integrated and highly conforming Japanese society, the ages at which women get married, have children, and retire from work are strikingly similar. (5) Experientially, each Japanese woman seems to be the person who decides on her own life path; analytically, the uniformity of these women's "time-table" proves the powerfulness of institutional governance. (6) Should we scrutinize the lives of upper-middle class Anglo-Saxon Americans, we would, most likely, discover that they read similar books, prefer similar designer labels, watch similar movies, hang around similar places and even pick similar resorts to spend their holidays. (7) Again, these similarities are more than random overlaps of taste; they are results mediated by social factors such as class, race, and educational background. (8) Evidently, **through sociology, we get to explore the social structures that frame our everyday life.**

(1) **Since society largely determines who we are and how we live, sociology, by studying the interplay between individuals and society, gives us not only insights into our social environment, but also knowledge of our inner selves.** (2) Although having sociological knowledge, as a form of consciousness,

> does not guarantee optimal moves in life, especially
> considering the limited power of individuals in
> society, not having it does lead to a lot of
> confusions and mysteries that are otherwise avoidable.

Jade's first paragraph. Jade opens her introduction with a brief statement that some people (those "with pragmatic but myopic concerns") view sociology as "abstract and irrelevant," but rebuts immediately in sentences 2 and 3 that sociology gives us "revealing explanations" of our lives and helps us understand society so that we may better understand ourselves. With this as backdrop, she presents her thesis statement in sentence 4, the ending sentence of the introduction. Note that not only does Jade indicate in the thesis statement the role of sociology as generally described in sentences 2 and 3, she also mentions two specific aspects—"socialization processes that determine who we are" and "social structures that pattern how we live"—that will be discussed in the main body of her essay.

Jade's second paragraph. This paragraph develops the first of the two elements mentioned in the thesis statement: socialization. Jade announces this clearly in the first sentence in which she uses a brief quote from Berger to define socialization. She then expands the idea of socialization to focus on two related supporting points. One is that various socializing agents shape our identity (sentences 2, 3, and 4). Another is that our self-concept is also very much a result of socialization (sentences 5 and 6). Note that she uses two more quotes as she develops these points: one from Berger for the first point, and one from Mead for the second. In closing this paragraph, Jade reiterates its theme that sociology promotes better self-understanding by studying socialization. If we compare this last sentence with the first, we may say that the last sentence is more appropriately the topic sentence of the paragraph.

Jade's third paragraph. Jade devotes her third paragraph to the other element mentioned in her thesis statement, namely, social structures. Her first sentence begins with the words "Besides socialization" to mark a clear transition away from the topic of the preceding paragraph. It clearly announces that the topic now is social structures. The second sentence stresses that these structures frame our lives, an idea that is further underscored in sentence 3 ("people living in the same society always exhibit basically the same general pattern of life"). She then proceeds to give examples to illustrate this, referring to Japanese women in sentences 4 and 5, and to upper-middle class Anglo-Saxon Americans in sentence 6. In each of these two situations, noticeable similarity, if not uniformity, exists in how people live their lives. In sentence 7, as she does in sentence 5, she attributes this similarity to social factors. Summing all this up, sentence 8 repeats the idea that sociology is concerned with "the social structures that frame our everyday life."

Jade's concluding paragraph. This is a brief conclusion to a short essay. The two ideas mentioned so far—shaping forces of socialization and those of social structures—are picked up once again in closing to remind the reader that this has been the main substance discussed. Indeed, the first sentence of the last paragraph is both a reiteration and an expansion of the thesis statement that appears at the end of the first paragraph, with a clear message now that sociology gives us "insights into our social environment" and "knowledge of our inner selves." To bring the essay to a smooth close, Jade writes in the second and last sentence that while sociological knowledge "does not guarantee optimal moves in life," the lack of it can bring about "confusions and mysteries." An example or two of what these confusions and mysteries might be would be more helpful to the reader. Anyhow, concluding the essay in this way does make the reader think, with wonderment perhaps, about the use of sociology.

Having analyzed Jade's essay this way, you can see that it is tightly organized, giving careful attention to all the ingredients, including unity and coherence, that make a piece of writing effective.

6.8 Guidelines for Writing a Well-organized Paper

To write a well-organized paper, follow these guidelines:

The introduction

- Capture the attention and interest of your readers.
- Give enough background to enable your readers to understand what you want to say.
- Always pay special attention to the crafting of a good thesis statement, which will help you organize your paper. Remember that the thesis statement must indicate your position on the topic and the basic structure of the paper.

The body

- All paragraphs in the body should relate to the thesis.
- The topic sentence of each paragraph is derived from expanding ideas contained in the thesis statement.
- Use one or more methods, such as giving examples, comparing, and examining causes and effects, to develop the paragraphs.

- Check that the paragraphs are linked smoothly and all turning points are clearly indicated.

The conclusion
- Aim at giving your readers a strong and lasting impression.
- Summarize your main points to show that collectively they demonstrate your central (controlling) idea.
- State your thesis once again, concretely and assertively.
- Indicate the implication of your discussion, if you see any; raise questions if appropriate. But do not bring up any entirely new idea.

CHAPTER 7

Citing Sources in the Text

7.1 What Does Citing Sources Mean?

In writing a research paper, it is often necessary for you to consult certain sources for ideas. Such sources may include books (either in whole or in part), journal articles, newspaper articles, or other forms of published material, including material available on the Internet. If you have used these sources and included ideas taken from them in your paper, you must indicate the sources clearly to give them proper credit.

Giving proper credit to authors from whom you obtain ideas is not the only reason why you cite them. You cite them also to make it possible for readers to consult these sources if they want more information, as we do when we review the relevant literature in research papers. Academic work depends heavily on the accumulation of knowledge, which is possible if the sources of ideas are clearly documented. When all academic authors observe the requirement of citation, it will be possible to identify and build up a body of literature for any topic or subject.

7.2 Upholding Academic Honesty and Avoiding Plagiarism

To use an idea from a source, you may quote the original words or express the idea in your own words. Either way, you should cite the source. If you do not indicate sources used but have presented ideas and words taken from them, you are committing plagiarism, which is a serious academic offence. If your teacher discovers such an act and can prove that it indeed is plagiarism, you can be punished according to university rules. The offence is likely to remain even if you claim to have unintentionally forgotten to cite the sources.

Words and ideas are intellectual property, which must be respected and protected. Since others have made the effort to communicate to the academic community their thoughts and understanding as a result of their research and analysis, you should make no pretence of "borrowing" words and ideas from them as if these were your own. If you use them for good reason to support some point you are making, just observe the principle of academic honesty by acknowledging the source and citing it properly.

7.3 Examples of Plagiarism

Plagiarism occurs when you copy whole sentences or sentence parts without indicating the source, or when you express an idea taken from a source largely in your own words but without indicating the source.

Let us first see an original passage on television and its audience, taken from Abercrombie (1996):

> Television does not involve its audience to the extent that other media can. It is usually watched in distracting circumstances in the home, while a lot of other activities are going on. The result is that people do not always concentrate intently on the television and, indeed, the medium frequently does not demand such attention. (p. 153) (Nicholas Abercrombie. 1996. *Television and Society.* Cambridge, England: Polity Press. Courtesy of Polity Press.)

The following representation of the content of the original passage is an example of plagiarism (the boldfaced parts are taken directly from the original). With the exception of the first sentence, wording is practically the same as the original.

> Television is a very different medium compared with other media. **It is usually watched in distracting circumstances in the home, while a lot of other activities are going on.** Therefore, **people do not always concentrate on the television. Indeed,** television **frequently does not demand such attention.**

The next rendition is also an example of plagiarism. Much of the original sentence structure remains, with quite a few words replaced by their synonyms (boldfaced). The writer may think that with some change in wording the reworked version can pass as the writer's own. This is simply a dishonest and fraudulent act, particularly when no citation is given.

```
Television is very different from other media, because
it is normally watched in the home where many other
activities are going on. The consequence is that we do
not always focus on the television when it is turned
on. In fact, this medium does not always require our
attention.
```

The following represents one way in which you might express Abercrombie's idea in your own words (that is, a paraphrase), but it would still be considered plagiarism if you did not give the source.

```
Television does not really involve its viewers as much
as other media do. In the home where many activities
occur at the same time, it is difficult for people to
pay full attention to television when they are
watching it.
```

From the above examples, you can see that to avoid plagiarism you must remember three important principles:

- Always indicate the source of the point or idea you are writing about, if that point or idea is not a matter of "common knowledge" but a subject of discussion in the source.
- Never try to simply rearrange or replace certain words in an original passage to give them the guise of your own writing.
- If you feel that certain words, phrases, or even sentences are so well chosen or so well said that you want to include them as part of your text, enclose them in quotation marks and indicate the source (details of which you will see later in this chapter).

7.4 Summarizing, Paraphrasing, Quoting, and In-text Citation

To introduce someone's idea because it illustrates a point, answers a question, or supports an argument, you can summarize it, paraphrase it, or quote the original words. Whichever way you choose, you must indicate the source explicitly by noting the author(s), the year of publication of the work, and the page location where appropriate. This you do to acknowledge or give proper credit to the source.

What is involved in summarizing, paraphrasing, and quoting?

7.4.1 *Summarizing*

As discussed in Chapter 4, to summarize is to capture the main idea of some text in your own words. It is always a brief statement of what is considerably longer in the original. You summarize when you try to refer to the main idea of an author in a journal article, a book or some portion (e.g., chapter) of it. Sometimes, you can even summarize ideas involving several sources.

7.4.2 *Paraphrasing*

To paraphrase, on the other hand, is to "translate" an original piece, usually a sentence or a short passage, into your own words. The paraphrase is about the same length as, or somewhat shorter than, the original. When the original passage is transformed and rewritten in a more condensed form, you hope that your readers will understand it more readily.

7.4.3 *Quoting*

To quote is to use certain words, phrases, or sentences as they appear in the original. If the source's words are, in your opinion, authoritative, powerful, or even unique, you may quote them in part or in full to illustrate or to support a point you are making in your writing. Typically, quoted material is enclosed in quotation marks, except when it is introduced as a separate block set apart from your text.

7.4.4 *In-text Citation*

Whichever option you choose, you should always cite the source by giving the author's name and year of publication of the work you have used. If the idea or words are specific to some page or pages in the source, then the page location is given as well. This information is given in your text as you mention the idea or words, rather than in footnotes or elsewhere. The citation, with or without page location information, is therefore called *in-text citation.* As you will see in greater detail later in this chapter, some or all of the citation information is given in parentheses so that all sources mentioned can be briefly identified. It is essentially an *author-date system of citation.* Full documentation of the sources used is given in a list of references at the end of the paper.

    To illustrate what in-text citation may look like, let us use Abercrombie's passage mentioned earlier. If you decide that all three sentences in the passage are

important enough for your purpose, you might introduce them as a quote in this
manner:

```
Abercrombie (1996) reminds us that people do not watch
television with the kind of concentration that is
typical of reading books or seeing a movie. As he puts
it: "Television does not involve its audience to the
extent that other media can. It is usually watched in
distracting circumstances in the home, while a lot of
other activities are going on. The result is that
people do not always concentrate intently on the
television and, indeed, the medium frequently does not
demand such attention." (p. 153)
```

You may choose to paraphrase instead of quoting directly. One paraphrased
version was shown earlier. There, without citing the source, it would be considered a
case of plagiarism. Let us therefore make it proper by putting in the citation, as
follows:

```
In discussing the nature of television, Abercrombie
(1996, p. 153) points out that television does not
really involve its viewers as much as other media do.
In the home where many activities occur at the same
time, it is difficult for people to pay full attention
to television when they are watching it.
```

If you want to refer to a source only generally, without spelling out any further
detail, page reference is inappropriate and thus not needed. This also applies when
you want to summarize the essence of an entire article or even book. Using the same
example, you may want to mention Abercrombie as one of any number of sources
that see television as a medium not particularly involving the audience, as follows:

```
Television is different from some other media in that
it does not always capture the full attention of the
audience (see, for example, Abercrombie 1996).
```

When the reader sees the source (surname of an author) mentioned, he or she
can check from the list of references at the end of the paper (more about this in
Chapter 8) the full description of the source so that it may be retrieved, if necessary,
from the library or elsewhere to permit a closer examination of the relevant text.

7.5 Keeping Notes for Use in Citation

To prepare well for citing material, you need to have an effective system of note-taking as you read relevant sources. For best results, use 3" × 5" *index cards* (lined or unlined) on which you record notes and, separately, full documentation of sources. Cards are most suitable because they can be selected, shuffled, sorted, and rearranged according to how you want to organize ideas that you feel should be included in your writing.

7.5.1 Recording Notes

- Use each note card for only one piece of information. This may refer to a single article or book, or any specific part of it.
- Write a short summary (a few sentences will normally be sufficient) if you refer to an entire work or a substantial part of it. Alternatively, if you refer to a specific sentence or short passage (say, a few lines), you may quote the exact words from the source or write a paraphrase using your own words. If you include any original words or phrases in your paraphrase because you feel that they are special, remember to enclose them in quotation marks.
- Record specific page number(s) for each summary, quotation, or paraphrase.
- At the bottom of the card, record the source in an author-date form, e.g., Abercrombie 1996.
- Write a suitable subject heading on the top of the card, e.g., *Non-involving TV audience.* The subject heading should be clear and precise for your purpose: you need subject headings to classify your cards into meaningful groups to represent main topics and supporting ideas to be included in your paper.

7.5.2 Recording Documentation of Sources

So that you have all the bibliographic information of sources necessary for locating them if needed, you should record such information accurately on separate cards. This information usually includes the following:

- Author(s) (last name, i.e., surname first, followed by given name)
- Year of publication
- Title of work (book, monograph, journal article) (If the work is a chapter in an edited book, record name(s) of editor(s) and book title.)
- Place of publication (city, and state for works published in the USA)
- Publishing agency (including institutions, societies, and government bodies).

When you become familiar with the format in which a source is given in a list of references (see Chapter 8), you can actually record a source according to such format. For convenient organization, each card should contain only one source. Those sources that are eventually selected for citing in your text will need to be indicated in the list of references at the end of your paper.

7.6 Basic Format of In-text Citations

In this section, you will see a variety of situations in which you may cite sources. Two styles are commonly in use: the style used by the American Sociological Association (ASA) and that by the American Psychological Association (APA). While the ASA style is mainly used by sociologists, the APA style is generally used in the social sciences. Both styles are given, as indicated by their corresponding abbreviation, ASA and APA. If these initials are not shown, it means that the two styles are the same.

After you are familiar with the basic format of in-text citation, you can apply it along with quotations, which we will examine later.

7.6.1 One Work by One Author, with Author's Name in Your Text

```
In a recent study of consumption, Ritzer (1999) shows
us how various new "means of consumption" manage to
lure us into big spending.
```

7.6.2 One Work by One Author, with Author's Name not in Your Text

ASA   In a recent study of consumption (Ritzer 1999), we find in-depth description of how various new "means of consumption" manage to lure us into big spending.

APA   In a recent study of consumption (Ritzer, 1999), we find in-depth description of how various new "means of consumption" manage to lure us into big spending.

If you do not refer to some specific study explicitly within your sentence, you should place the source and the year at the end of the sentence. Note also the following two points:

- The period (full-stop) that ends the sentence is placed not after the last word of the sentence itself but after the citation if it is placed at the end of the sentence.
- APA style requires a comma between author name and year in the parenthetical citation.

Check these two points in the following example:

ASA New "means of consumption" have managed to lure us into big spending (Ritzer 1999).

APA New "means of consumption" have managed to lure us into big spending (Ritzer, 1999).

7.6.3 *One Work by Two Authors, with Authors' Names in Your Text*

In their study of mass media and society, Croteau and Hoynes (2000) claim that . . .

7.6.4 *One Work by Two Authors, with Authors' Names Not in Your Text*

ASA In a study of mass media and society (Croteau and Hoynes 2000), it is claimed that . . .

APA In a study of mass media and society (Croteau & Hoynes, 2000), it is claimed that . . .

Note that, in APA style, the names are joined by an ampersand (&) when they appear in parentheses.

7.6.5 *One Work by Three or More Authors*

If you are citing a work by two authors, you must cite both names every time you mention the work. For works by three to five authors, use the last names of all authors the first time you mention the work; in subsequent citations, use the last name of the first author followed by "et al." (Latin, et alibi, meaning "and others," not italicized and with a period after "al"). For works by six or more authors, use the last name of the first author followed by "et al." even the first time you mention the work.

In the examples that follow, no separate listings will be given to show how you put authors' names in or not in your text because this will be similar to the examples shown above. Only one of the two alternatives (that is, either the authors' names are in your text or they are not) will be shown. However, remember that when both author name(s) and the year appear in parentheses, a comma separates them in APA style but no comma is used in ASA style. That is:

ASA   `(Gamson 1990)`

APA   `(Gamson, 1990)`

For works by three to five authors, the last names of all authors are given the first time you refer to such a work:

```
Gamson, Croteau, Hoynes, and Sasson (1992) found
that . . .
```

Subsequently, if you refer to the same work in the same paragraph, you may omit the year:

```
Gamson et al. also found that . . .
```

But you need to indicate the year again if you refer to the same work for the first time in any subsequent paragraph:

```
Gamson et al. (1992) stressed that . . .
```

For works by six or more authors, mention the last name of the first author followed by `et al.` for the first and all subsequent citations:

```
Simon et al. (1990) proposed that . . .
```

Although you do not indicate all authors when you cite works by multiple authors in your text, in general you need to include all authors when you include them in the reference list at the end of your paper.

7.6.6   *Works by the Same Author (or Same Two or More Authors in the Same Order) with the Same Year of Publication*

If you cite several works by the same author published in the same year, attach suffixes a, b, c, and so on after the year. (In the reference list, these items are ordered alphabetically according to the title of the work.)

ASA   `This has been discussed elsewhere (e.g., Clark 1991a, 1991b).`

APA   `This has been discussed elsewhere (e.g., Clark, 1991a, 1991b).`

7.6.7 *Multiple Works All Relevant to a Specific Idea*

Sometimes you may want to cite several works that illustrate or discuss a specific idea. In reviewing the literature, you may find that a number of researchers have obtained similar results. To indicate this, both ASA and APA require that you put them in alphabetical order by the author's last name. Separate the sources with semicolons.

ASA   (Ellison 1994; Levin 1994; Taylor and Chatters 1988)

APA   (Ellison, 1994; Levin, 1994; Taylor & Chatters, 1988)

If you want to indicate a major citation followed by others, the major citation is mentioned first, followed by some appropriate phrase, such as *see also*, and then the other citations. Suppose that, in the above example, Levin (1994) is the major citation, you would then have:

ASA   (Levin 1994; see also Ellison 1994; Taylor and Chatters 1988)

APA   (Levin, 1994; see also Ellison, 1994; Taylor & Chatters, 1988)

7.6.8 *Institutional Authors*

You may sometimes need to cite publications that bear no named authors but are published or sponsored by an association, a government department, a public body, or some other group. In such a situation, the name of that body or group may serve as the author both in text citations and in the reference list at the end of your paper.

Names of institutional authors are usually spelled out in full whenever they are cited. Alternatively, if the name is long enough to cause some inconvenience in citing, you may use a shortened version in the second and all subsequent citations. If the name has a commonly known acronym, e.g., UNESCO for United Nations Educational, Scientific, and Cultural Organization, you may use the acronym as its shortened name. Place the shortened name in square brackets after the full name so that the reader will know what the short form refers to upon seeing it in your subsequent reference to the same work:

FIRST CITATION:

(United Nations Educational, Scientific, and Cultural Organization [UNESCO], 1995)

SUBSEQUENT CITATIONS:

> (UNESCO, 1995)

If the name does not have a commonly known short form, you may devise your own. It should, however, contain sufficient information to enable your readers to locate the entry in the reference list. For example, if you have a paper published by a group that calls itself Advisory Committee on Tertiary Education Planning in Hong Kong, you may consider shortening it to just `Advisory Committee`.

If you are citing works published by universities in Hong Kong, you can use their commonly known abbreviations (e.g., CUHK, HKU, PolyU). However, if the work is published not by the university itself but by a specific unit or department of the university, you should use a shortened form of that unit or department instead. The full description of such a publisher must always be given in the reference list, followed by the shortened form you have given it. Take, for example, the Hong Kong Institute of Asia-Pacific Studies of The Chinese University of Hong Kong. First and subsequent citations of works published by it as an institutional author would be as follows:

FIRST CITATION:

> (Hong Kong Institute of Asia-Pacific Studies, The Chinese University of Hong Kong [IAPS], 2000)

SUBSEQUENT CITATIONS:

> (IAPS, 2000)

Again, remember that APA style puts a comma between the author and the year when these appear in parentheses; ASA style omits the comma.

Note that, whatever shortened names you have chosen or devised in your citations must also be indicated after the fully spelled out names in the reference list to help your reader in identifying the work involved.

7.6.9 *Authors with the Same Last Name*

If you cite two works whose authors have the same last name, you should include their initials in all text citations to avoid confusion even if they were published in different years:

> Both R. J. Gordon (1990) and D. M. Gordon (1996) believed . . .

7.6.10 Page Location for a Specific Part

You do not need to indicate page location in a citation if you want to describe the main theme of a work or if the statement you are making is relevant to the work as a whole. But you should always give the page location for a point or an idea that comes from a specific place in the source work:

```
Stokowski (1994, p. 37) points out that interpretive
approaches to leisure are primarily concerned with
micro-level interactions.
```

The above statement can be modified slightly to leave the source author's name out of the text and have it in parentheses if emphasis on the content of the statement is desired:

```
Interpretive approaches to leisure are primarily con-
cerned with micro-level interactions (Stokowski 1994,
p. 37).
```

7.7 Quotations

7.7.1 When Do You Use Quotations?

Do not use quotations just to make your paper look more "scholarly." Neither should you use them so frequently that the point of including them is unclear and that they interrupt the flow of the idea you want to present and discuss. You use direct quotations only when you believe that the source's words provide support because of their authority or that they strengthen the impact on readers because the words are especially insightful or powerful. Otherwise, you may do better by paraphrasing, that is, rewriting the original idea in your own words.

7.7.2 Quoting with Citation

When you quote, always indicate the author or authors, year, and page location. In general, a quotation with citation may take one of the following two arrangements:

- ```
  Ritzer (1993) maintains that McDonaldization "has
  yielded a number of benefits to society, but it also
  entails a considerable number of costs and risks" (p.
  16).
  ```
  ```

- One can surely see that McDonaldization "has yielded a
  number of benefits to society, but it also entails a
  considerable number of costs and risks" (Ritzer, 1993,
  p. 16).

As noted before, APA style (but not ASA style) requires that a comma separates author name and year when they both appear in parentheses.

Whether you place the author in your text is optional. If you mean to emphasize the idea more than the author, you can put the author's name in parentheses, together with the year and the page location. In any case, remember that the period (full stop) completing the sentence that contains the quotation is placed at the very end, after the parentheses containing the page location.

7.7.3 *Quotation Marks*

Use double quotation marks to enclose a quotation. If there are words enclosed in double quotation marks in the source, change such marks to single quotation marks in your quotation:

Ritzer (1993) remarks that "in shopping, the malls are
turning people into mall 'zombies'" (p. 120).

7.7.4 *Signal Phrases and Lead-in Verbs*

You should not let a quotation stand alone without introducing it with a signal phrase (also called attributive phrase). A signal phrase typically contains a lead-in verb that serves to tell us about a source author's opinion or conclusion from research. Helping to integrate the quotation with your own text, such a phrase can be placed before, interrupting, or following the quotation.

SIGNAL PHRASE BEFORE THE QUOTATION:

Ritzer (1993) remarks that "McDonaldization is
engulfing more and more sectors of society and areas
of the world" (p. 16).

SIGNAL PHRASE INTERRUPTING THE QUOTATION:

"McDonaldization," Ritzer (1993) remarks, "is engulfing more and more sectors of society and areas of the
world" (p. 16).

SIGNAL PHRASE FOLLOWING THE QUOTATION:

```
"McDonaldization is engulfing more and more sectors
of society and areas of the world," remarks Ritzer
(1993, p. 16).
```

You should compare and study these alternatives carefully to note the differences in word order and punctuation. Used skilfully, these patterns will add variety and colour to your writing. You should also choose an appropriate lead-in verb that reflects the context of the quotation and the attitude of the source author (e.g., does he say something with strong conviction or is he quite neutral about it?). The following are some lead-in verbs for your consideration. They are all present tense singular verbs (for single authors), and are suitable for introducing opinions and conclusions from research. The verbs that are boldfaced may be considered if you believe that the source author feels strongly about the idea in question.

> admits, agrees, **argues**, asks, **asserts**, **claims**,
> concludes, **contends**, **declares**, **emphasizes**, explains,
> feels, finds, indicates, **insists**, **maintains**, mentions,
> notes, observes, points out, proposes, recognizes,
> recommends, remarks, reports, says, sees, shows,
> states, **stresses**, suggests, thinks, writes

7.7.5 Run-in Quotations and Block Quotations

In principle, quotations that do not exceed three lines, such as the examples given above, are kept in the text as *run-in quotations*. They are enclosed by quotation marks as shown. Quotations that are longer than three lines (40 or more words, according to APA style) are set apart from the text as *block* (or *boxed*) quotations. They must not be enclosed by quotation marks. To introduce a block quotation, the last word of the text is often followed by a colon. Further arrangements depend on whether you use ASA style or APA style.

ASA   Type the block quotation single-spaced (with double spaces separating it from your text), and indent the whole block at least five spaces from the left margin. Since five-space paragraph indents are standard, this means the block quotation either aligns with the paragraph indent, or is set somewhat further to the right, indicating that the quotation is relevant to the current text paragraph.

APA   Type the block quotation double-spaced as for the text. Indent the block five spaces from the left margin. This places the block quotation in the same position as a new text paragraph.

The following is an example that contains both a run-in quotation and a block quotation. It is displayed in APA style. Like the paragraph, the block quotation is indented five spaces from the left margin. If ASA style is adopted, the block quotation should be typed single-spaced. (This and other examples in the rest of this chapter are taken from the classic, *Invitation to Sociology: A Humanistic Perspective* by Peter L. Berger, copyright © 1963 by Peter L. Berger. Used by permission of Doubleday, a division of Random House, Inc.)

> What is the sociologist interested in? Berger (1963) asks "not only what it is that the sociologist is doing but also what it is that drives him to it" (p. 17). To answer this question, Berger gives us this characterization of the sociologist:
>
> > The sociologist . . . is a person intensively, endlessly, shamelessly interested in the doings of men. . . . He will naturally be interested in the events that engage men's ultimate beliefs, their moments of tragedy and grandeur and ecstasy. But he will also be fascinated by the commonplace, the everyday. (p. 18)

Note that the final period ending the block quotation is placed immediately after the last quoted word. This is then followed by the page citation. By contrast, in a run-in quotation, the final period is placed after the page citation.

7.7.6 *Omitting Material by Using Ellipsis Dots*

To incorporate a quotation into your text suitably to illustrate or emphasize a point, you may sometimes need to delete words or phrases from the source. Use three spaced ellipsis dots (. . .) to indicate this. (Many students forget that these points must be spaced, making them look rather cramped: …)

7.7.7 *Omitting Material within a Sentence*

If there is no other punctuation mark before or after the ellipsis, simply place the ellipsis dots in place of the material omitted. *Remember that each of the three ellipsis dots is preceded and followed by one space.*

Source:

```
The sociological problem is always the understanding
of what goes on here in terms of social interaction.
(p. 37)
```

Your text with quotation:

```
Berger (1963) asserts that "the sociological problem
is always the understanding of . . . social inter-
action" (p. 37).
```

If you omit a phrase set off by commas within a sentence, those commas may be dropped if they are not essential to the grammar of the sentence and if dropping them improves readability. Sometimes, you may need to retain a comma, a semicolon, or a colon that comes before the words you want to omit.

Source:

```
Indeed, this very ability to look at a situation from
the vantage points of competing systems of inter-
pretation is, as we shall see more clearly later on,
one of the hallmarks of sociological consciousness.
(p. 38)
```

Your text with quotation:

```
For Berger (1963), the "ability to look at a situation
from the vantage points of competing systems of
interpretation is, . . . , one of the hallmarks of
sociological consciousness" (p. 38).
```

7.7.8 Omitting Material Following a Sentence

This is indicated by four dots. The first dot is the period (full stop) at the end of the sentence before the ellipsis.

Source:

```
The structures of society become the structures of our
own consciousness. Society does not stop at the
```

> surface of our skins. Society penetrates us as much as
> it envelops us. Our bondage to society is not so much
> established by conquest as by collusion. (p. 121)

Your text with quotation:

> In describing our tendency to accept what society
> expects of us, Berger (1963) has this to say: "The
> structures of society become the structures of our own
> consciousness. . . . Our bondage to society is not so
> much established by conquest as by collusion" (p. 121).

Note that, if you omit material following a sentence, but include in your quotation a subsequent sentence, as in the above example, the quotation can no longer be combined with your own text to form a single complete sentence. Hence, you must introduce such a quotation with a sentence ending with a colon.

That is, you *cannot* write:

> In describing our tendency to accept what society
> expects of us, Berger (1963) says that "the structures
> of society become the structures of our own conscious-
> ness. . . . Our bondage to society is not so much
> established by conquest as by collusion" (p. 121).

But you can split the quotation into two parts, avoiding the use of ellipsis dots:

> In describing our tendency to accept what society
> expects of us, Berger (1963) says that "the structures
> of society become the structures of our own conscious-
> ness," and that "our bondage to society is not so much
> established by conquest as by collusion" (p. 121).

If you choose to quote this way, you may change the period after the word "consciousness" to a comma because you are joining two quoted parts into a single complete sentence. You should also note that since you now have a single sentence, "the structures of society" and "our bondage to society" remain within the same sentence, thus justifying the change of uppercase letters at sentence beginnings in the source to lowercase in the sentence that is now your text.

If the sentence before the ellipsis ends with a question mark or exclamation mark, that mark is retained and followed by the three ellipsis dots. Without having to print all the material omitted after a sentence, the following illustrates this (using APA style). Since the quoted material exceeds three lines, it should be displayed as a block quotation. Remember that if you adopt ASA style, the block quotation should be typed single-spaced.

> While it is true that society's control systems have considerable effect on individuals, Berger (1963) observes that individuals are not really too troubled by this. Indeed, as he points out:
>
> > For most of us the yoke of society seems easy to bear. Why? . . . Why then do we not suffer more from this power? . . . The sociological answer to this question has already been alluded to-- because most of the time we ourselves desire just that which society expects of us. We *want* to obey the rules. We *want* the parts that society has assigned to us. (p. 93)

Now that you have seen some examples in which an introductory signal phrase ending with a colon is used before a block quotation or before a run-in quotation that contains more than one sentence, you should try to be familiar with the many ways in which such introductions are written. Here are just some more examples of introductory phrases:

- Berger (1963) notes:
- As Berger (1963) puts it:
- This is how Berger (1963) characterizes the social- ogist:
- Berger (1963) describes the sociologist's concern in this way:
- In essence, society shapes our identity. Berger (1963) explains it thus:
- For Berger (1963), a sociological problem can be understood as follows:
- Berger (1963) offers the following explanation of what "seeing through" things can do for us:
- This is the essence of Berger's (1963) argument:

7.7.9 Omitting Material from the End of a Sentence

If you want to conclude your sentence with a quotation that omits an ending part of a sentence in the source, you should delete whatever punctuation mark (comma, dash, semicolon), if any, that comes after the last quoted word in the source. Skip one space after the last quoted word, put in the three ellipsis dots and the closing quotation marks. This is followed by the page citation and the period that concludes your sentence.

Source:

> The sociologist, at his best, is a man with a taste for other lands, inwardly open to the measureless richness of human possibilities, eager for new horizons and new worlds of human meaning. (p. 53)

Your text with quotation:

> In declaring that sociological consciousness is characterized by cosmopolitanism, Berger (1963) contends that "the sociologist, at his best, is a man with a taste for other lands, inwardly open to the measureless richness of human possibilities . . . " (p. 53).

If you want your sentence with the quotation to continue, you should retain any punctuation mark that follows the last quoted word. In the above example, this is a comma. Then you add the ellipsis, the closing quotation marks, the page citation, a comma, and the rest of your sentence. In such a situation, make sure that what you say after the quoted material does follow in meaning and is grammatically integrated with the rest of your sentence.

> In declaring that sociological consciousness is characterized by cosmopolitanism, Berger (1963) contends that "the sociologist, at his best, is a man with a taste for other lands, inwardly open to the measureless richness of human possibilities, . . . " (p. 53), a point that is particularly relevant to us living in a globalized world.

7.7.10 *Incomplete Quoted Parts*

No ellipsis dots are used before or after quotations that consist of a few words or a fragment of a sentence. But if an omission occurs within the fragment, it should be indicated by ellipsis:

```
Berger  (1963)  describes  sociology  as  "an  attempt  to
understand"  which  "can  be  recommended  to  .  .  .  anyone
whose  goals  involve  the  manipulation  of  men"  (pp.  4-5).
```

7.7.11 Capitalization of First Word of Quotation

From the examples given above, you can see that capitalization of the first word of a quotation is governed by two principles:

- If the quotation is joined to your introductory words (signal phrase) to form a grammatical part of the sentence in which it occurs, the first word of the quotation begins with a lowercase letter, even if it is capitalized in the source.
- If your text introducing the quotation ends either with a period or with a colon (as when you introduce a block quotation or when the quoted material in a run-in quotation contains more than one sentence), the first word of the quotation is always capitalized, even if it is not capitalized in the source.

7.7.12 Inserting Material or Adding Emphasis

7.7.12a Explaining or clarifying

You may use square brackets [ ] to insert words to explain, clarify, or emphasize some point. Do not use parentheses ( ) for such purposes, because your readers may assume that any parenthetical element was placed in the original by the source author. By convention, anything contained in square brackets is supplied not by the source author but by the person quoting the source.

Study the following example to see how inserting appropriate words in brackets helps to clarify the meaning in the quotation and, indeed, improve the smoothness of the sentence when some part of the original material has been omitted.

Source:

```
The  game  of  the  sociologist,  then,  uses  scientific
rules.  As  a  result,  the  sociologist  must  be  clear  in
his  own  mind  as  to  the  meaning  of  these  rules.  That
is,  he  must  concern  himself  with  methodological
questions.  Methodology  does  not  constitute  his  goal.
The  latter,  let  us  recall  once  more,  is  the  attempt  to
understand  society.  Methodology  helps  in  reaching  this
goal.  (p.  17)
```

Your text with quotation:

> In describing the concerns of the sociologist, Berger
> (1963) has this to say: "The sociologist must be clear
> in his own mind as to the meaning of [scientific]
> rules. That is, he must concern himself with method-
> ological questions. . . . Methodology helps in
> reaching [the] goal [of understanding society]" (p.
> 17).

As you can see, since two sentences in the original have been omitted (after "questions") in which the "goal" of the sociologist is mentioned, the meaning of the sentence retained and placed at the end of the quotation would not be clear unless "reaching this goal" is modified to read "reaching the goal of understanding society." The words that are not the same as those in the original are thus enclosed in square brackets. In principle, the words you supply to clarify a point should, as far as possible, be incorporated into the original sentence.

7.7.12b Adding emphasis

If you feel that a certain word, phrase, or even an entire sentence is so special or important that you want to draw your reader's attention to it, you may type this part of the quotation in italics and put the words "italics mine," "italics added," or "emphasis added" within square brackets.

Source:

> Sociology is more like a passion. The sociological
> perspective is more like a demon that possesses one,
> that drives one compellingly, again and again, to the
> questions that are its own. (p. 24)

Your text with quotation:

> While Berger (1963) admits that sociology may not
> interest everybody alike, he compares sociology to
> "passion" for those who are interested. According to
> his description:
>
> > Sociology is more like a passion. The socio-
> > logical perspective is more like *a demon that*
> > *possesses one, that drives one compellingly,*

again and again, to the questions that are its
own [italics added]. (p. 24)

7.7.13 Integrating Quoted Material into Your Own Text

While you may quote a source to support or clarify a point, you must not lose sight
of the importance of integrating the quoted material into your own text. Some of the
examples above have illustrated this.

7.7.13a Forming a grammatically correct sentence

The quoted material must blend with your own text (particularly the part that
introduces the quotation). As example, let us take the following original text (which
you saw in 7.7.5), from Berger again:

We would like to ask not only what it is that the
sociologist is doing, but also what it is that drives
him to it. (p. 17)

Only a few of many possible ways of introducing the quotation are given here.
To focus your attention better on the sentence structure, the year is not shown in this
illustration. (The incorrect versions are all taken from student work.)

(1) Incorrect: Berger suggests that "not only what it is that
the sociologist is doing, but also what it is
that drives him to it" (p. 17).

Correct: Berger suggests that we should ask "not only
what it is that the sociologist is doing, but
also what it is that drives him to it" (p. 17).

(2) Incorrect: Berger states that "not only what it is that
the sociologist is doing, but also what it is
that drives him to it" (p. 17).

Correct: Berger states that we need to ask "not only
what it is that the sociologist is doing, but
also what it is that drives him to it" (p. 17).

(3) Incorrect: Berger concerns that "not only what it is that
the sociologist is doing, but also what it is
that drives him to it" (p. 17).

Correct: Berger is concerned with "not only what it is
            that the sociologist is doing, but also what it
            is that drives him to it" (p. 17).

(4) Incorrect: Berger   further   states   the   concern   on
            sociologist is "not only what it is that the
            sociologist is doing, but also what it is that
            drives him to it" (p. 17).

Correct: Berger further states that our question about
            the nature of the sociologist is "not only what
            it is that the sociologist is doing, but also
            what it is that drives him to it" (p. 17).

Other possible ways of introducing the quotation:

- Berger wants (or urges) us to consider (or grasp) "not
  only what it is that the sociologist is doing, but also
  what it is that drives him to it" (p. 17).
- We are interested in knowing, as Berger points out,
  "not only what it is that the sociologist is doing, but
  also what it is that drives him to it" (p. 17).

7.7.13b Achieving a smooth flow of thought

With care, you can weave quoted material into your sentences to achieve a smooth
flow of thought. Study the next example with this in mind.

Writing   on   sociology   as   a   form   of   consciousness,
Berger (1963) stresses the need for the sociologist to
engage in "a process of 'seeing through' the facades
of   social   structures"   (p.   31).   Essentially,   this
requires the sociologist to search for social mechanisms existing and operating underneath the surface.
Personally, the sociologist may take things at face
value like what most people do; but as a sociologist,
he or she is obliged not to take things for granted.
As Berger reminds us, "the roots of the debunking
motif in sociology are not psychological but method-
ological"(p. 38). This is what careful observation
calls for.

Note that, when quoted material from the same source appears closely in your text, as in this example, it is not necessary to repeat the year citation. Of course, if the same source is quoted again later but separated by quotations from other sources, the author and the year will need to be cited again at that point. More generally, if only one source is referred to throughout an essay, such as is likely to be the case in a book review, the year citation is given only once, that is, when the author's name is first mentioned.

7.8 Quoting and Paraphrasing Compared

When you use other authors' material in your paper, you have to decide between quoting directly and paraphrasing. Of course, as you should know by now, quoting will be your choice if you need the support of the strength or authority of the source. Otherwise, state the idea in your own words as accurately as you can.

Read the following text from Berger about the nature of a sociological problem before comparing the paraphrased and quoted versions.

> The sociological problem is always the understanding of what goes on here in terms of social interaction. Thus the sociological problem is not so much why some things "go wrong" from the viewpoint of the authorities and the management of the social scene, but how the whole system works in the first place, what are its presuppositions and by what means it is held together. (p. 37)

Paraphrasing

- As Berger (1963, p. 37) so emphatically claims, the sociological problem is not what some group defines as problematic but how some system operates through social interaction and integration.
- We need to realize that the sociological problem is not what some group defines as problematic but how some system operates through social interaction and integration (Berger, 1963, p. 37).

Quoting

- For Berger (1963), "the sociological problem is not so much why some things 'go wrong' from the viewpoint of the authorities . . . , but how the whole system works in the first place, what are its presuppositions and by what means it is held together" (p. 37).

- Distinguishing a "sociological problem" from a "social problem," Berger (1963) stresses that "the sociological problem is not so much why some things 'go wrong' from the viewpoint of the authorities . . . , but how the whole system works in the first place, what are its presuppositions and by what means it is held together" (p. 37).

7.9 Concluding Note on Citing Sources

Using source material is often necessary in many forms of academic writing, such as in expository essays, book reports, literature review in research proposals and reports, and theses. Learning how to summarize other authors' ideas, paraphrase them, quote from the original text when necessary, and cite the relevant sources in your writing is just as important as, if not more so than, reading them with understanding in preparation for your writing task. If you have cited properly, it helps your readers to relate what you say in your paper to other writings and to check the sources you cite for further details, if necessary. It also helps to demonstrate your willingness to maintain academic integrity. It is both proper academic style and sound strategy for the propagation of knowledge.

When you have cited sources in your text, you must prepare a list at the end of your paper to show a full documentation of all such sources. This is the list of references the details of which are explained in the next chapter.

CHAPTER 8

Preparing the List of References

8.1 What Is the Difference between a Bibliography and a List of References?

Many students are not too sure about how a bibliography differs from a list of references. A bibliography is a list of all the works that you have read or consulted in writing your paper. You may use some of these in a rather limited way as background reading and others much more extensively as they relate more directly to what you want to say in your paper. Some of the sources in your bibliography are not explicitly referred to or not quoted from in your text, but they are included in the list because you believe that they are important enough as part of the relevant literature concerning the topic of your paper. In this sense, the bibliography that you prepare is supposed to constitute a guide to the topic in the manner that you approach it. It could well include works for further reading on the topic or even on the more general area to which the topic belongs.

In contrast, a list of references is much more specific to a particular paper. As the name indicates, it includes only those sources that you have actually cited in summary, paraphrase, or quotation form. *Every work that you have referred to in your paper must, as a rule, appear in the list of references. Conversely, a list of references must not contain any item that is not mentioned in your paper.* The list usually goes under the name "References," but "Works Cited" may also be used to mean the same thing.

8.2 Accuracy and Completeness

All entries included in the list of references must be both accurate and complete. Each entry is usually (but not always) a published work for which four main elements are shown: (1) author, (2) year of publication, (3) title, and (4) publisher information. Details of these and other relevant elements will be explained later in this chapter. The description of these elements must not contain any inaccuracy, such as misspelling of names or incorrect year of publication, or any omission, such as the omission of a subtitle when there is one or that of the names of editors of an edited book when listing a component part of such a book.

As an author, you must learn to be very careful with all details of the information required for every entry in your reference list. Always check such details as you find them in the original work, since you are responsible for providing accurate and complete information so that readers can find and use any source appearing on your list if they want to.

8.3 Importance of Format Matters

By "format," we mean the way in which all relevant details—here referring to those of sources cited—are to be displayed. To facilitate reading and use by readers, it is necessary for the display of such details to follow a consistent pattern or style. Scholars in the same field are expected to be familiar with (they usually are) stylistic matters so that they will find it reasonably easy to share and transmit the product of their research and to engage in intellectual exchange.

In this chapter, you will see how reference lists are displayed in both ASA (American Sociological Association) and APA (American Psychological Association) styles. There are both similarities and differences between the two systems. Examples of only the more common types of sources are given. If you need to list a source that does not fit into any of the ones shown in this chapter, you should consult manuals published by the American Sociological Association and the American Psychological Association. The examples in this book follow principles given in these manuals:

American Psychological Association. 2001. *Publication Manual of the American Psychological Association,* 5th ed. Washington, DC: American Psychological Association.

Krenzin, Joan and James Kanan. 1997. *Handbook of the Mechanics of Paper, Thesis, and Dissertation Preparation,* 2nd ed. Washington, DC: ASA Teaching Resources Center, American Sociological Association.

Alternatively, you could consult any of the writing handbooks or manuals that are available at any large academic library. Most of them should include information about the APA style.

Since all reference list entries begin with author(s) and year, you should start by learning how the two styles handle these elements.

8.4 Some Basic Differences and Similarities between ASA and APA Styles

8.4.1 *Author Names and Year of Publication*

- In both APA and ASA styles, the names of authors of single-authored works are inverted. A name is inverted when the surname comes first, followed by the given name.
- For multi-authored works, the names of all authors are inverted in APA style.
- In ASA style, only the name of the first author of multi-authored works is inverted; other authors' names maintain their natural order (given name first, surname last, as is practised in Western countries).
- In ASA style, first names and initials follow exactly the way they are given in the original publication. This means using spelled-out first names if this is how you see them appearing in the original work.
- In APA style, only initials are used. Thus, a spelled-out first name in the original would be reduced to an initial in your reference list. You should also note that, in APA style, the ampersand (&) is used in place of "and," and the year of publication is enclosed in parentheses. Further, whereas there is no comma separating two authors' names in ASA style, there is such a comma in APA style.

The following examples illustrate the points just mentioned:

```
ASA     Johnson, Allan G. 1998.
        McLuhan, Marshall and Bruce R. Powers. 1989.

APA     Johnson, A. G. (1998).
        McLuhan, M., & Powers, B. R. (1989).
```

8.4.2 *Spacing between Lines*

- The entire reference list is typed double-spaced in both styles. Both styles accept single spacing within individual entries, but double spacing is required between entries.

- In both styles, all entries have a hanging indent. That is, if you need more than one line to display an entry, the runover lines should be indented. The exact extent of indentation is flexible, but five to seven characters are preferred. Whatever the amount of indentation you have chosen, you should adopt it for all entries. By letting the surname of the author stand out clearly, the indentation will help your readers locate any entry on your list conveniently.

8.4.3 Capitalization of Titles

- In ASA style, you capitalize all the main words, including the first word, of the title and the subtitle, if any. Conjunctions (e.g., *and, but, or*), articles (*a, an, the*), and prepositions of four or fewer letters (e.g., *in, on, by, to, at, for, with, from*) must not be capitalized unless they happen to be the first word of the title or the subtitle. This applies to titles of a main work (e.g., book, journal) and titles of component parts (e.g., chapter, article) of the main work.
- In APA style, you do not capitalize the words of titles and subtitles except the first word and proper nouns.
- What about the second word in a hyphenated compound? In ASA style, you capitalize it; in APA style, you do not.

8.4.4 Using Quotation Marks for Articles and Book Chapters

The titles of journal articles and book chapters or parts are enclosed in double quotation marks in ASA style but not in APA style.

ASA   "Title of Chapter."

APA   Title of chapter.

8.4.5 Using Italics for Titles of Books and Journals

In both ASA and APA styles, italics are used for titles of books and journals. If you do not have access to an italics function, you may underline these titles.

8.4.6 Basic Differences between ASA and APA Styles at a Glance

The following example demonstrates the differences in spacing, capitalization, and use of quotation marks and italics:

ASA   Crenshaw, Edward M., Ansari Z. Ameen, and Matthew
        Christenson. 1997. "Population Dynamics and
        Economic Development: Age-specific Population
        Growth Rates and Economic Growth in Developing
        Countries, 1965 to 1990." *American Sociolog-*
        ical Review 62: 974-984.

APA   Crenshaw, E. M., Ameen, A. Z., & Christenson, M.
        (1997). Population dynamics and economic
        development: Age-specific population growth
        rates and economic growth in developing
        countries, 1965 to 1990. *American Sociological*
        Review, 62, 974-984.

You will note that in ASA style, the volume number of the journal and page numbers are not italicized. In APA style, the volume number is italicized; the page numbers are not.

We shall next see how ASA and APA styles treat order of references and publisher information. After that, we shall examine a series of examples that demonstrate how reference items are listed for various situations.

8.5 Order of References

8.5.1 *General Alphabetical Order*

Entries appear in alphabetical order of the surname (last name) of the author or editor. If the authors of several entries have the same surname, alphabetize according to their given (first) names.

ASA   Burr, Vivien. 1995.
        Gordon, David M. 1996.
        Gordon, Robert J. 1990.

APA   Burr, V. (1995).
        Gordon, D. M. (1996).
        Gordon, R. J. (1990).

8.5.2   Works by the Same First Author and Different Second or Third Authors

Arrange them alphabetically by the surname of the second author. If the second author is the same, arrange according to the name of the third author.

ASA   Peterson, Richard A. and Roger M. Kern. 1996.
        Peterson, Richard A. and Albert Simkus. 1992.

APA   Peterson, R. A., & Kern, R. M. (1996).
        Peterson, R. A., & Simkus, A. (1992).

8.5.3 Multiple Works by the Same Author in Different Years

Arrange them by year of publication, beginning with the earliest publication. In ASA style, the name in the second and subsequent entries is replaced by an underline of seven spaces followed by a period (full stop). In APA style, the name is shown in every entry.

ASA   Campbell, Colin. 1987.
        _____. 1996.

APA   Campbell, C. (1987).
        Campbell, C. (1996).

8.5.4 Multiple Works by the Same Author (or Same Two or More Authors in the Same Order) in the Same Year

Place lowercase letters—*a, b, c,* and so on—immediately after the year of publication. The entries are listed alphabetically by the title (ignoring *A* or *The*) that follows the year.

ASA   Dittmat, Helga. 1994a. "Material Possessions . . . "
        _____. 1994b. "To Have is . . . "

APA   Dittmat, H. (1994a). Material possessions . . .
        Dittmat, H. (1994b). To have is . . .

8.5.5 Author's Single-authored and Jointly-authored Works

- Always place the single-authored works before jointly-authored ones.

- When you have multiple-authored works with the same first author, alphabetize according to the surname of the second author or that of the third if the second author is the same.

ASA   Faber, Ronald J. 1992.
          Faber, Ronald J., Gary A. Christenson, and James Mitchell. 1995.
          Faber, Ronald J. and Thomas C. O'Guinn. 1992.

APA   Faber, R. J. (1992).
          Faber, R. J., Christenson, G. A., & Mitchell, J. (1995).
          Faber, R. J., & O'Guinn, T. C. (1992).

8.5.6 Works by Different Authors with the Same Surname

Arrange these according to the first name or first initial.

ASA   Allen, Douglas E. 1994.
          Allen, Margaret. 1981.

APA   Allen, D. E. (1994)
          Allen, M. (1981).

8.5.7 Works by Group Authors

Group authors include government bodies, associations, and institutions (e.g., schools, churches). Works by these authors are alphabetized according to the first significant word (disregarding any article that may be present) of the group's name. Always indicate group names in full (e.g., The Chinese University of Hong Kong, not CUHK).

8.5.8 Works with No Authors

If no authors (or editors) at all—individuals or groups of any kind—are listed, use the first significant word of the title for alphabetizing. Place the title in the initial position normally used for authors, as shown below:

ASA   Television Awareness Training. 1980.

APA   Television awareness training. (1980).

8.6 Place of Publication and Name of Publisher

8.6.1 Check Title Page and Copyright Page

The place (city) of publication and the name of the publisher are usually indicated on the title page of a book. If more than one city is mentioned under or near the name of the publisher, the first-named city is what you need for the list of references. If you do not see any cities mentioned on the title page, check the copyright page, which is normally the backside of the title page. You may find one or more addresses of the publisher there. As a general rule, use the city named in the first address if there is more than one. (The other addresses may well be addresses of branches of the publisher or those of its affiliated publishing houses.)

8.6.2 List City and (If Needed) State or Country

Indicate the city where the work is published. This is normally followed by the state (for works published in the USA) or province (for works published in Canada), or the country (for works published elsewhere). For major cities well known for publishing, such as New York, Boston, Chicago, Los Angeles, San Francisco, London, Beijing, and Hong Kong, there is no need to give the name of the state or the country. Place a colon after the city, if only the city is named, or the fuller indication of place of publication. This is then followed by the name of the publisher:

City, State: Publisher (for works published in the USA)
City, Province: Publisher (for works published in Canada)
City, Country: Publisher (for works published in the UK or other countries)
City: Publisher (for works published in cities well known for publication, e.g., New York, London, Tokyo, Hong Kong, Beijing)

8.6.3 List Name of Publisher Briefly

Give the name of the publisher as briefly as is understandable to the reader. This means you should leave out such terms as *Ltd., Publishing Company, Publishers,* or *Associates Inc.* The initial article *The* should also be omitted. All such words are not essential for identifying the publisher. However, you should keep the words *Books* and *Press.* You should also give the names of organizations, government departments, and university presses in full, keeping any initial *The* if there is one.

8.6.4 *Examples of Listing Publisher Information*

Study the following examples, bearing in mind that both ASA and APA styles treat publisher information in the same way:

Thousand Oaks, CA: Pine Forge Press.   (CA = California)

Englewood Cliffs, NJ: Prentice Hall.   (NJ = New Jersey)

Scarborough, ON: Nelson Canada.   (ON = Ontario)

Cambridge, MA: Harvard University Press.   (MA = Massachusetts)

Cambridge, England: Cambridge University Press.

Aldershot, England: Gower.

London: Heinemann.

New York: McGraw-Hill.

Hong Kong: The Chinese University Press.

Beijing: Foreign Language Teaching and Research Press.

If you need to check the abbreviations of American states and Canadian provinces, you can consult any one of the following handbooks: American Psychological Association (2001), Gibaldi (2003), and Turabian (1996).

8.7 Examples of References (in ASA and APA Styles)

Now we shall give a series of examples of the kinds of references that social science students are likely to encounter. The following is first an outline of the examples before listing the examples themselves so that you can locate the ones you want easily. Use the following section numbers to look up the specific type of reference example that you need.

A.   Books

8.7.1	One author
8.7.2	Two authors
8.7.3	More than two authors
8.7.4	Written in a non-English language but translated into English
8.7.5	One editor
8.7.6	More than one editor
8.7.7	Chapter (or article) in an edited book

8.7.8   Corporate author
8.7.9   Editions other than the first edition
8.7.10   Republished book

B.   Professional journals
8.7.11   One author
8.7.12   Two authors
8.7.13   More than two authors

C.   Magazines and newspapers
8.7.14   Article in popular magazine with author listed
8.7.15   Article in popular magazine with no author listed
8.7.16   Newspaper article with author listed
8.7.17   Newspaper article with no author listed

D.   Theses and dissertations
8.7.18   Unpublished thesis or dissertation
8.7.19   Thesis or dissertation abstract

E.   Other print sources
8.7.20   Government document
8.7.21   Conference proceedings
8.7.22   Working paper
8.7.23   Unpublished paper

F.   Chinese sources
8.7.24   Book
8.7.25   Chapter in an edited book
8.7.26   Journal article
8.7.27   Newspaper article
8.7.28   Article in popular magazine

G.   Electronic sources
8.7.29   Electronic journal
8.7.30   Article in an online newspaper
8.7.31   Article in an online magazine
8.7.32   Information from government sources
8.7.33   Non-periodical documents

A. References to Books

8.7.1 One Author

ASA   Ritzer, George. 1993. *The McDonaldization of Society.* Thousand Oaks, CA: Pine Forge Press.

APA   Ritzer, George. (1993). *The McDonaldization of society.* Thousand Oaks, CA: Pine Forge Press.

8.7.2 Two Authors

ASA   Phelan, Peter and Peter Reynolds. 1996. Argument and Evidence: Critical Analysis for the Social Sciences. London: Routledge.

APA   Phelan, P., & Reynolds, P. (1996). Argument and evidence: Critical analysis for the social sciences. London: Routledge.

8.7.3 More than Two Authors

ASA   Tyson, Laura D'Andrea, William T. Dickens, and John Zysman. 1988. *The Dynamics of Trade and Employment.* Cambridge, MA: Ballinger.

APA   Tyson. L. D., Dickens, W. T., & Zysman, J. (1988). *The dynamics of trade and employment.* Cambridge, MA: Ballinger.

For books with more than six authors, abbreviate the seventh and subsequent authors as "et al." Do not italicize these words and make sure you put a period (full stop) after "al." Such multi-author books are rare in the sociological literature.

8.7.4 Written in a Non-English Language but Translated into English

ASA   Durkheim, Emile. [1893] 1964. *The Division of Labor in Society*, translated by George Simpson. New York: Free Press.

Use the following parenthetical citation in your text:

```
(Durkheim [1893] 1964)
```

APA   Durkheim, E. (1964). *The division of labor in society* (G. Simpson, Trans.). New York: Free Press. (Original work published 1893)

In your text your parenthetical citation should be:

```
(Durkheim, 1893/1964)
```

8.7.5 One Editor

ASA   Bond, Michael Harris, ed. 1986. *The Psychology of the Chinese People.* Hong Kong: Oxford University Press.

APA   Bond, M. H. (Ed.). (1986). *The psychology of the Chinese people.* Hong Kong: Oxford University Press.

8.7.6 More than One Editor

ASA   O'Meara, Patrick, Howard D. Mehlinger, and Matthew Krain, eds. 2000. *Globalization and the Challenges of a New Century: A Reader.* Bloomington, IN: Indiana University Press.

APA   O'Meara, P., Mehlinger, H. D., & Krain, M. (Eds.). (2000). Globalization and the challenge of a new century: A reader. Bloomington, IN: Indiana University Press.

8.7.7 Chapter (or Article) in an Edited Book

ASA   Scott, Janet Lee. 1997. "Traditional Values and Modern Meanings in the Paper Offering Industry of Hong Kong." Pp. 223-241 in *Hong Kong: The Anthropology of a Chinese Metropolis*, edited by Grant Evans and Maria Tam. Surrey, England: Curzon Press.

APA   Scott, J. L. (1997). Traditional values and modern meanings in the paper offering industry of Hong Kong. In G. Evans & M. Tam (Eds.), *Hong Kong: The anthropology of a Chinese metropolis* (pp. 223-241). Surrey, England: Curzon Press.

8.7.8 Corporate Author

ASA   Census and Statistics Department (Census). 1997. *Hong Kong Monthly Digest of Statistics: November 1997.* Hong Kong: Census.

      The Family Planning Association of Hong Kong (FPAHK). 1983. *A Study of Hong Kong School Youth: Report on the Family Life Education Survey.* Hong Kong: FPAHK.

Note: You may abbreviate long names of corporate or group authors when you use ASA style, but only after you have given the name in full. In APA style, however, you should use only the full name in the list of references although you may use an abbreviated form in text citations after the first citation in which the full name is given. In the reference list, use the word Author as the name of the publisher when the publisher is the same as the author, as given below:

APA   Census and Statistics Department. (1997). *Hong Kong monthly digest of statistics: November 1997.* Hong Kong: Author.

      The Family Planning Association of Hong Kong. (1983). *A study of Hong Kong youth: Report on the family life education survey.* Hong Kong: Author.

8.7.9 Editions Other than the First Edition

ASA   Goodale, Thomas L. and Peter A. Witt, eds. 1985. *Recreation and Leisure: Issues in an Era of Change,* rev. ed. State College, PA: Venture.

```
        Rubington, Earl and Martin S. Weinberg, eds. 1995.
             The Study of Social Problems: Seven Perspec-
             tives, 5th ed. New York: Oxford University
             Press.

APA     Goodale, T. L., & Witt, P. A. (Eds.). (1985).
             Recreation and leisure: Issues in an era of
             change (Rev. ed.). State College, PA: Venture.
        Rubington, E., & Weinberg, M. S. (Eds.). (1995).
             The study of social problems: Seven perspec-
             tives (5th ed.). New York: Oxford University
             Press.
```

8.7.10 Republished Book

Some classics may be republished, without changing the main content, many years after they were first published. These are not considered as revised or subsequent editions, although sometimes a new introduction or afterword may be added.

```
ASA     Berger, Peter L. [1963] 1991. Invitation to
             Sociology: A Humanistic Perspective. Reprint.
             London: Penguin Books.
```

Cite this in your text as:
```
        (Berger [1963] 1991)
```

```
APA     Berger, P. L. (1991). Invitation to sociology: A
             humanistic perspective. London: Penguin Books.
             (Original work published 1963)
```

Cite this in your text as:
```
        (Berger, 1963/1991)
```

B. References to Professional Journals

As pointed out earlier (8.4.4), the title of a journal article is enclosed in double quotation marks in ASA style but not in APA style. For journal articles, the place of publication and the name of the publisher are not indicated. To mark clearly the location of a journal article, however, the volume number and sometimes the issue number of the journal, as well as the exact pages, must be indicated. When each issue of a volume (there may be three or four issues in each volume) is paginated separately, the issue number is shown in parentheses after the volume number. When pagination is consecutive in a given volume, only the volume number is needed. Note that in APA style, the volume number is italicized along with the journal name.

8.7.11 One Author

ASA   Gamson, William A. 1995. "Hiroshima, the Holocaust, and the Politics of Exclusion." *American Sociological Review* 60: 1-20.

APA   Gamson, W. A. (1995). Hiroshima, the holocaust, and the politics of exclusion. *American Sociological Review, 60,* 1-20.

8.7.12 Two Authors

ASA   Morris, Merrill and Christine Ogan. 1966. "The Internet as Mass Medium." *Journal of Communication* 46: 39-50.

APA   Morris, M., & Ogan, C. (1996). The Internet as mass medium. *Journal of Communication, 46,* 39-50.

8.7.13 More than Two Authors

ASA   Yiu, Chun, Wing-tang Au, and Catherine So-kum Tang. 2001. "Burnout and Duration of Service Among Chinese Voluntary Workers." *Asian Journal of Social Psychology* 4: 103-111.

APA   Yiu, C., Au, W.-T., & Tang, S.-K. (2001). Burnout and duration of service among Chinese voluntary workers. *Asian Journal of Social Psychology, 4,* 103-111.

Note that in APA style, the hyphen in a hyphenated given name (as in many Chinese names) is retained.

C. References to Magazines and Newspapers

8.7.14 Article in Popular Magazine with Author Listed

ASA   Stein, Joel. 2002. "Braving a Life Without Tele-
        vision." *Time* 29 April, p. 72.

APA   Stein, J. (2002, April 29). Braving a life without
        television. *Time*, p. 72.

8.7.15 Article in Popular Magazine with No Author Listed

ASA   "China's Leverage." 2001. *Far Eastern Economic
        Review* 23 August, p. 6. (Note the absence of punctua-
        tion between magazine name and date.)

   Parenthetical in-text citation:

        ("China's Leverage" 2001)

APA   China's leverage. (2001, August 23). *Far Eastern
        Economic Review*, p. 6.

   Parenthetical in-text citation:

        ("China's Leverage," 2001)

Note that the comma comes before the closing quotation mark.

8.7.16 Newspaper Article with Author Listed

ASA   Chugani, Michael. 2002. "Asians Unite to Fight a
        Bad Name." *South China Morning Post* 22 April,
        p. 16.

APA   Chugani, M. (2002, April 22). Asians unite to fight
        a bad name. *South China Morning Post*, p. 16.

8.7.17 Newspaper Article with No Author Listed.

ASA   "SAR Still Leads Way." 2002. *South China Morning
        Post* 25 April, p. 15.

APA   SAR still leads way. (2002, April 25). *South China Morning Post*, p. 15.

D. References to Theses and Dissertations

8.7.18 Unpublished Thesis or Dissertation

ASA   Ngai, Sek Yum Steven. 1999. *The Politics of Identity Constitution Among Outreach Workers in Hong Kong.* Unpublished Ph.D. thesis. Hong Kong: Division of Sociology, Graduate School, The Chinese University of Hong Kong.

Yuen, Siu Man Amy. 1997. *Gendered Job and Clerical Workers in Hong Kong.* Unpublished master's thesis. Hong Kong: Division of Sociology, Graduate School, The Chinese University of Hong Kong.

APA   Ngai, S. Y. S. (1999). *The politics of identity constitution among outreach workers in Hong Kong.* Unpublished Ph.D. thesis, Division of Sociology, Graduate School, The Chinese University of Hong Kong, Hong Kong.

Yuen, S. M. A. (1997). *Gendered job and clerical workers in Hong Kong.* Unpublished master's thesis, Division of Sociology, Graduate School, The Chinese University of Hong Kong, Hong Kong.

If the thesis or dissertation is referred to in its unpublished form (as in the form of a bound copy kept in the library), it is listed as given above. Note that the title is italicized like a book title. If the thesis or dissertation is abstracted in *Dissertations Abstracts International (DAI)* and is obtained (by purchase) from University Microfilms International (UMI), then you should indicate the volume and page numbers of *DAI* and the UMI number. These numbers are given as you access the source online. The example below (8.7.19) illustrates how you list such a thesis or dissertation.

8.7.19 *Thesis or Dissertation Abstract*

ASA   Arnold, Margaret Lane. 1997. *The Relationship of
        Gender, Race, and Social Class to Leisure
        Constraints.* Doctoral dissertation, University
        of Illinois at Urbana-Champaign. *Dissertation
        Abstracts International,* 58 (06), 2389A. (UMI
        No. AAT 9737037)

APA   Arnold, M. L. (1997). The relationship of gender,
        race, and social class to leisure constraints
        (Doctoral dissertation, University of Illinois
        at Urbana-Champaign). *Dissertation Abstracts
        International, 58* (06), 2389A. (UMI No. AAT
        9737037)

Note: *DAI's* page numbering runs in two series: series A is for the humanities and social sciences, and series B is for the physical sciences and engineering. For a thesis abstracted in *DAI* or in *Masters Abstracts International*, APA style treats the thesis title like an article title (not italicized) whereas ASA style treats it like a book title (italicized).

E. References to Other Print Sources

8.7.20 *Government Documents*

ASA   Hong Kong SAR Government Information Services
        Department. 2000. *Hong Kong 1999.* Hong Kong:
        Hong Kong SAR Government Information Services
        Department.
        Census and Statistics Department. 1998. *A Collec-
        tion of Feature Articles.* Hong Kong: Census
        and Statistics Department.

APA   Hong Kong SAR Government Information Services
        Department. (2000). *Hong Kong 1999.* Hong Kong:
        Author.
        Census and Statistics Department. (1998). *A collec-
        tion of feature articles.* Hong Kong: Author.

Note: Some Hong Kong Government publications, especially those before 1997, were explicitly marked as printed and published by the Government Printer. For these publications, it is appropriate to mention Government Printer as publisher. Now the general pattern is that a given Government department publishes its own reports and other documents, as is the case in the two examples cited above.

8.7.21 Conference Proceedings

Papers presented at a conference are often (sometimes after selection) collated in a publication called "proceedings." In this form, the papers may be considered published although they may also be subsequently modified by authors and published in academic journals.

Sometimes, the proceedings may appear in the form of abstracts of papers presented, as in the following example in which the reference resembles that for journals:

ASA   Peters, Hans Peter. 1994. "How Mass Media Present Experts to the Public." *Sociological Abstracts Supplement 173* (XIIIth World Congress of Sociology): 240.

APA   Peters, H. P. (1994). How mass media present experts to the public. *Sociological Abstracts, Supplement 173* (XIIIth World Congress of Sociology), 240.

At other times, a paper printed in published proceedings is treated like a chapter in an edited book, as in the next example:

ASA   Rodriguez, G. and J. Cleland. 1981. "Socio-Economic Determinants of Marital Fertility in Twenty Countries: A Multivariate Analysis." Pp. 325-414 in *World Fertility Survey Conference 1980: Record of Proceedings,* Vol. 2. Voorburg: Internationial Statistics Institute.

APA   Rodriguez, G., & Cleland, J. (1981). Socio-economic determinants of marital fertility in twenty countries: A multivariate analysis. In *World fertility survey conference 1980: Record of*

proceedings, Vol. 2 (pp. 325-414). Voorburg:
International Statistics Institute.

8.7.22 *Working Paper*

ASA   Wong, Ka-fu and Linda Yung. 2002. "Does Our Time of
        Birth Determine Our Fate? An Analysis from an
        Economic Perspective." Working Paper Series No.
        140. Hong Kong: Department of Economics, The
        Chinese University of Hong Kong.

APA   Wong, K.-F., & Yung, L. (2002). *Does our time of
        birth determine our fate? An analysis from an
        economic perspective* (Working Paper Series No.
        140). Hong Kong: The Chinese University of
        Hong Kong, Department of Economics.

Note that the title of a working paper is treated like an article title in ASA style but like a book title in APA style. Note also that, in APA style, the document number that identifies the working paper is enclosed in parentheses following the paper title. The period (full stop) that normally appears at the end of the paper title now appears after the parentheses.

Another difference between the two styles concerns the order in which you indicate the name of the university and that of the specific department or unit that produces the paper. In ASA style, the department precedes the university; in APA style, the university comes first. Generally, the same principle holds for other university-produced reports.

ASA   Chan, Tak Wing. 1995. "Intergenerational Social
        Mobility in Hong Kong: A Review of Recent
        Studies." Occasional Paper No. 45. Hong Kong:
        Hong Kong Institute of Asia-Pacific Studies,
        The Chinese University of Hong Kong.

APA   Chan, T. W. (1995). *Intergenerational social mobil-
        ity in Hong Kong: A review of recent studies*
        (Occasional Paper No. 45). Hong Kong: The
        Chinese University of Hong Kong, Hong Kong
        Institute of Asia-Pacific Studies.

8.7.23 *Unpublished Paper*

ASA   Power, Sally and Geoff Whitty. 1996. "Teaching New
         Subjects? The Hidden Curriculum of Marketised
         Education Systems." London: London Institute
         of Education. Unpublished paper.

APA   Power, S., & Whitty, G. (1996). *Teaching new sub-*
         jects? The hidden curriculum of marketised
         education systems. Unpublished paper, London
         Institute of Education. (The name of the city is not
         mentioned separately when it is included in the name of the
         university.)

F. References to Chinese Sources

If you use and cite Chinese sources in a paper written in English, it is legitimate to assume that your reader may or may not be able to read Chinese. The least you can do as a writer is to give sufficient information of these sources in English so that any reader will be able to identify and understand what sources they are. Romanization of author names and titles of works is necessary to enable a reader, if he or she so wishes, to search for such sources. Academic libraries in Hong Kong use *pinyin* romanization for Chinese materials. Hence, you should adopt this system (but without indicating tone marks) in principle for any Chinese sources that you use. At the same time, Chinese characters for author and title of work should be given because these are often necessary to ensure that the specific work is found. Specifically, note the following points:

- Author name: Use *pinyin* or the author's own romanization if known, followed by Chinese characters. (Normally, Cantonese romanization is adopted for Hong Kong authors.)
- Book and article title: Use *pinyin* romanization, followed by Chinese characters and an English translation (sometimes available in the publication).
- The first word of a romanized title—books and articles included—and proper nouns are capitalized.
- Publication place and publisher: Use *pinyin* or English if the English name is better known (thus Hong Kong rather than *Xianggang).*

Although neither ASA nor APA style deals with Chinese sources explicitly, you can list them in such a way that they appear compatible with the system of your choice. Follow the chosen style's way of showing each of the four main elements of a reference entry: author, year of publication, title of work, and publisher information. You should realize that if you prepare references to Chinese sources as illustrated in the following examples, they can be combined and placed alphabetically along with your English language sources.

With this in mind, you should regard the designations ASA and APA in this section as essentially guidelines modified to apply to Chinese sources rather than as either style's own stipulations. I have also given the standard all-Chinese version of these examples for your reference. They would be appropriate for papers written in Chinese. Slight modifications may be required by individual publishers.

8.7.24 Books

ASA   Liu, Xinping. 劉心平 2002. *Xiuxian Zhongguo* 休閒中國 [Leisure in China]. Beijing: Zhongguo Gongren Chu-banshe.

Sun, Lung Kee. 孫隆基 1990. *Zhongguo wenhua de shenceng jiegou* 中國文化的深層結構 [The Deep-Seated Structure of Chinese Culture], rev. ed. Taibei: Tangshan Chubanshe.

Wong, Sing Wing. 黃成榮 1999. *Qingshaonian jiazhi-guan ji weiguixingwei tansuo* 青少年價值觀及違規行為探索 [An Exploratory Examination of Young People's Values and Deviant Behaviour]. Hong Kong: Joint Publishing.

Note: The romanization of the names of these three authors follows their own version. If in doubt, you can check with the catalogues of your university library. If you can locate the work in question by a particular version of romanization of the author's name, that is probably how the author's name should be shown in your list of references.

APA   Liu, X. P. 劉心平 (2002). *Xiuxian Zhongguo* 休閒中國 [Leisure China]. Beijing: Zhongguo Gongren Chubanshe.

Sun, L. K. 孫隆基 (1990). *Zhongguo wenhua de shen-ceng jiegou* 中國文化的深層結構 [The deep-seated

structure of Chinese culture] (Rev. ed.).
Taibei: Tangshan Chubanshe.

Wong, S. W. 黃成榮 (1999). *Qingshaonian jiazhiguan
ji weiguixingwei tansuo* 青少年價值觀及違規行為探索
[An exploratory examination of young people's
values and deviant behaviour]. Hong Kong:
Joint Publishing.

CHINESE

劉心平。2002。《休閒中國》。北京：中國工人出版社.

孫隆基。1990。《中國文化的深層結構》，修訂版。台北：唐山出版社。

黃成榮。1999。《青少年價值觀及違規行為探索》。香港：三聯書店。

8.7.25 Chapter in an Edited Book

ASA   Ng, Pak Tao. 吳白弢 1998. "Xianggangren dui xianxia
       de qiwang ji manzu" 香港人對閒暇的期望及滿足
       [Leisure Expectations and Leisure Satisfaction
       of Hong Kong People]. Pp. 399—420 in *Huaren
       shehui de bianmao: shehui zhibiao de fenxi* 華人
       社會的變貌：社會指標的分析 [*Changing Chinese
       Societies: Social Indicators Analysis*], edited
       by Siu-kai Lau, Ming-kwan Lee, Po-san Wan, and
       Siu-lun Wong. 劉兆佳、李明堃、尹寶珊、黃紹倫 編 Hong
       Kong: Hong Kong Institute of Asia-Pacific
       Studies, The Chinese University of Hong Kong.

APA   Ng, P. T. 吳白弢 (1998). Xianggangren dui xianxia de
       qiwang ji manzu 香港人對閒暇的期望及滿足 [Leisure
       expectations and leisure satisfaction of Hong
       Kong people]. In S. K. Lau, M. K. Lee, P. S.
       Wan, & S. L. Wong (Eds.) 劉兆佳、李明堃、尹寶珊、黃
       紹倫 編 *Huaren shehui de bianmao: shehui
       zhibiao de fenxi* 華人社會的變貌：社會指標的分析
       [Changing Chinese societies: Social indicators
       analysis](pp. 399—420). Hong Kong: Hong Kong
       Institute of Asia-Pacific Studies, The Chinese
       University of Hong Kong.

CHINESE

> 吳白弢。1998。〈香港人對閒暇的期望及滿足〉。劉兆佳、李明堃、尹
> 寶珊、黃紹倫編,《華人社會的變貌:社會指標的分析》,頁
> 399–420。香港:香港中文大學香港亞太研究所。

Note that when references are listed in all-Chinese style for papers written in Chinese, the entries are listed in the order according to the number of strokes of the surname of the author, starting with names having the smallest number of strokes. All personal names, wherever they appear in the entry, are given in the natural order of Chinese names, with the surname coming first. The 〈 〉 mark is used for titles of articles and book chapters; the 《 》 mark is used for titles of books and journals.

8.7.26 Journal Article

ASA   Hwang, Yih-Jyh. 黃毅志 2000. "Wenhua ziben shehui
       wangluo yu jieceng rentong jieji jiexian" 文化
       資本、社會網絡與階層認同、階級界限 [Cultural Capital,
       Social Network, Strata Identification, and
       Class Boundaries]. *National Chengchi Univer-
       sity Sociology Journal* 30: 1–42.

APA   Hwang, Y.-J. 黃毅志 (2000). Wenhua ziben shehui
       wangluo yu jieceng rentong jieji jiexian 文化資
       本、社會網絡與階層認同、階級界限 [Cultural capital,
       social network, strata identification, and
       class boundaries]. *National Chengchi Univer-
       sity Sociology Journal* 30: 1–42.

CHINESE

> 黃毅志。 2000。〈文化資本、社會網絡與階層認同、階級界限〉。《政
> 大社會學報》,第三十期: 1–42。

8.7.27 Newspaper Article

As in the case of articles in English language newspapers, you should check whether the article you use from a Chinese language newspaper is "signed." A signed article is one that prints the author's name. The author's name must be shown in your reference if it is given in the newspaper. If no author is given, the romanized title of

the article moves to the author position in the reference. In the following, you will
see first an example of a signed article, and then one of an unsigned article.

ASA   Song, Ligong. 宋立功 2002. "Jiangou xinjizhi chuli
        tigai wenti" 建構新機制處理體改問題 [Constructing
        New Mechanisms to Handle System Reform
        Problems]. *Hong Kong Economic Journal* 6 May,
        p. 6.

        "Gongwuyuan jianxin fudu zhengfu xian liangnan" 公務
        員減薪幅度政府陷兩難 [Government's Dilemma in
        Scope of Civil Servants' Pay Cut]. 2002. *Ming
        Pao* 7 May, p. A2.

APA   Song, L. G. 宋立功 (2002, May 6). Jiangou xinjizhi
        chuli tigai wenti 建構新機制處理體改問題
        [Constructing new mechanisms to handle system
        reform problems]. *Hong Kong Economic Journal*,
        p. 6.

        Gongwuyuan jianxin fudu zhengfu xian liangnan 公務員
        減薪幅度政府陷兩難 [Government's dilemma in scope
        of civil servants' pay cut]. (2002, May 7).
        Ming Pao, p. A2.

CHINESE

        宋立功。2002。〈建構新機制處理體改問題〉。《信報》5月6日，頁6。
        〈公務員減薪幅度 政府陷兩難〉。2002。《明報》5月7日，頁A2。

8.7.28 Article in Popular Magazine

ASA   Sun, Xupei. 孫旭培 2001. "Rushi dui Zhongguo xinwen-
        meiti de chongji" 「入世」對中國新聞媒體的衝擊 [The
        Impact of Joining WTO on China's News Media].
        Ming Pao Monthly 36 (3) : 34-39.

        Li, Oufan. 李歐梵 2001. "Shijie wenming de chongtu？"
        世界文明的衝突？ [The Conflict of World Civili-
        zations?] *Yazhou Zhoukan* 8 October, p. 9.

APA   Sun, X. P. 孫旭培 (2001). Rushi dui Zhongguo xinwen-
        meiti de chongji 「入世」對中國新聞媒體的衝擊 [The

impact of joining WTO on China's news media].
Ming Pao Monthly, 36(3), 34-39.
Li, O. F. 李歐梵 (2001, October 8). Shijie wenming
de chongtu？ 世界文明的衝突？ [The conflict of
world civilizations?] *Yazhou Zhoukan*, p. 9.

CHINESE

孫旭培。2001。〈「入世」對中國新聞媒體的衝擊〉《明報月刊》
36（3）：頁 34-39。
李歐梵。2001。〈世界文明的衝突？〉《亞洲週刊》8 月 5 日，頁 9。

G. References to Electronic Sources

Sometimes you may find it necessary to use and cite sources available on the Internet's World Wide Web. You need to be careful, however, about the appropriateness of the use of such information for the purpose of your academic writing. Depending on the nature of the source, the trustworthiness and accuracy of the information may sometimes be open to question. In addition, the document you are using may have been modified or no longer available. If in doubt, you should consult your teacher.

In referencing an electronic source, note the following:

- The URL (Uniform Resource Locator), which is the most important element as the address for finding the document, must be shown in full.
- Pay extra attention to typing the URL correctly. The host name part of a URL (e.g., www.cuhk.edu.hk) is not "case sensitive," which means it does not matter whether you type it all or partly in lowercase or uppercase letters. Usually though, for consistency and ease of reading, you should type it all in lowercase letters.
- Other than the host name, the rest of the URL is case sensitive, so you must make sure that it is all correct in lowercase and uppercase (if any) letters and punctuation. You can copy a URL directly from the address window on your monitor screen and paste it into where you need it.
- If you have to break a URL across lines, break it after a slash (stroke) or before a period (full stop), but do *not* place a hyphen at the break.
- Finally, do not put a period (full stop) at the end of a URL even when it appears at the end of the reference in order not to mislead the reader to think that the period is part of the URL when in fact it is not.

8.7.29 *Electronic Journal*

ASA style requires that paragraph numbers (if given in the online journal article) should be included in the citation. Not so in APA style, but APA style includes the complete publication date if this is known.

ASA   Collins, Peter. 1998. "Negotiating Selves: Reflections on 'Unstructured' Interviewing." *Sociological Research Online* 3(3):1.1-4.5. Available at <http://www.socresonline.org.uk/3/3/2.html> accessed 24 May, 2002.

Note: ASA style also accepts the indication of accessing the URL as follows:

Retrieved May 24, 2002 (http://www.socresonline.org.uk/3/3/2.html).

Since the URL is enclosed within parentheses in this way, you can place a period after the parentheses.

APA   Collins, P. (1998, September 30). Negotiating selves: Reflections on "unstructured" interviewing. *Sociological Research Online, 3*(3). Retrieved May 24, 2002, from http://www.socresonline.org.uk/3/3/2.html

Note: If you follow APA style, do not put a period (full stop) after the URL although that is the end of a reference entry.

8.7.30 *Article in an Online Newspaper*

ASA   Levy, Clifford J. 2002. "Here, Life Is Squalor and Chaos." *New York Times* 29 April. Available at <http://www.nytimes.com/2002/04/29/nyregion/29HOME.html> accessed 27 May, 2002.

APA   Levy, C. J. (2002, April 29). Here, life is squalor and chaos. *New York Times*. Retrieved May 27, 2002, from http://www.nytimes.com/2002/04/29/nyregion/29HOME.html

8.7.31 Article in an Online Magazine

ASA   Drucker, Peter. 2001. "The Next Society." *The Economist* 1 November. Available at <http://www.economist.com/library/articlesBySubject/PrinterFriendly.cfm?Story_ID=7708198subjectID=423172> accessed 28 May, 2002.

APA   Drucker, P. (2001, November 1). The next society. *The Economist.* Retrieved May 28, 2002, from http://www.economist.com/library/articlesBySubject/PrinterFriendly.cfm?Story_ID=7708198subjectID=423172

8.7.32 Information from Government Sources

ASA   Census and Statistics Department. 2002. *Environmental Report 2001.* Available at <http://www.info.gov.hk/censtatd/eng/aboutus/environment/environment.htm> accessed 28 May, 2002.
      Home Affairs Bureau. 2002. *Report of the Sports Policy Review Team.* Available at <http://www.info.gov.hk/Policy.htm#ConsultationPapers> accessed 29 May, 2002.

APA   Census and Statistics Department. (2002). *Environmental report 2001.* Retrieved May 28, 2002, from http://www.info.gov.hk/censtatd/eng/aboutus/environment/environment.htm
      Home Affairs Bureau. (2002). *Report of the sports policy review team.* Retrieved May 29, 2002, from http://www.info.gov.hk/policy.htm#ConsultationPapers

In the second of the above two items from Hong Kong government sources, the URL given will lead the reader to the index page showing a number of "consultation papers" one of which is the specified report (Report of the Sports Policy Review Team) in the reference. The reader will then have to click on this report from the list shown on the index page which is thus an entry page for the document. This means that the URL shown in the reference is not a full address in that it does not lead directly to the document, but it is adequate enough since once reaching the index page, the remaining retrieving action should be fairly obvious and easy to execute. Indeed, when the document has multiple sections, as is the case of the sports policy report, each section may have a different URL. It is then best to provide a URL that leads to the entry page for the document. This URL is more stable and reliable than the full URL that leads to the document because the full URL may no longer work if the document is repositioned later.

8.7.33 Non-periodical Documents

Conceivably, there could be a large variety of non-periodical documents available on the Internet. They actually include documents from government sources which are separately treated above. Articles on special topics or reports by working parties may be carried on the Web sites of organizations and universities. APA style recommends that if the author of the document is different from the host organization or the provider of the site, you should identify the host organization in the retrieval statement. Although ASA style makes no such recommendation, you may insert such information as shown in the following two examples:

ASA   Abbott, Roberta. 1998. "Population Control in the People's Republic of China and Its Place in the Global Population Debate." Available at the International Development Studies Network Web site <http://www.idsnet.org/Papers/Essays-1998/Abbott/abbott.html> accessed 30 May, 2002.

        University Grants Committee. 1996. *Teaching and Learning Quality Process Review Report.* Available at the Chinese University of Hong Kong Web site <http://www.cuhk.edu.hk/aas/tlqpr/tlqpr.htm> accessed 30 May, 2002.

APA   Abbott, R. (1998). Population control in the People's Republic of China and its place in the global population debate. Retrieved May 30, 2002, from the International Development Studies Network Web site: http://www.idsnet.org/Papers/Essays-1998/Abbott/abbott.html

```
University Grants Committee. (1996). Teaching and
    learning quality process review report.
    Retrieved May 30, 2002, from the Chinese Uni-
    versity of Hong Kong Web site: http://www.cuhk
    .edu.hk/aas/tlqpr/tlqpr.htm
```

Note that a "report" may be treated as a book, as shown in the way its title is typed. In the retrieval statement in APA style, there is a colon just before the URL if you indicate the host organization.

8.8 General Points to Remember in Preparing the List of References

Having seen the many seemingly tedious details of listing reference sources displayed in this chapter, you probably feel somewhat daunted by the complexity of it all. You do not need to, if you realize that all such details are intended to present your references clearly and consistently in a way that ensures accuracy and completeness. Readers will then be able to use the information given in your list of references to check and explore the cited material further if needed. As other researchers do the same in carefully listing their reference sources, it will enhance the cross-fertilization of research. Thus, it is not an exaggeration to say that a meticulously prepared list of references, not at all less than the substantive content of the paper itself, plays an important part in the transmission and accumulation of knowledge.

To do a good job in preparing the reference list, remember the following general points and review the checklist that follows in 8.9:

- Any item on a list of references must contain four basic elements: author, year of publication, title of the work, and publisher information (place of publication and name of publisher). There may be additional elements (such as page location and edition); there may be exceptions (as when no publication information is necessary for journals and magazines). In any case, check the format details required by the system you adopt (ASA or APA), and follow the requirements faithfully.
- Pay great attention to such matters as spelling of names, punctuation, capitalization, indentation where appropriate and necessary, and spacing between words and after punctuation marks.
- Your presentation of details describing each and every reference entry must be accurate, complete, and done consistently throughout the entire list.

- Sources that you may have consulted but not referred to should not be included in the list. Remember that the list is called "References" rather than "Bibliography." As such, the list is more restrictive than a bibliography.

8.9 Checklist for Preparing the List of References

This checklist contains reminders of most of the basic format requirements of a list of references. For details, read 8.4 to 8.6 and use the list of different types of examples in 8.7 to check how to display your references properly.

- **Inclusion of entries.** Every source you have referred to in your text must appear in the reference list; every source appearing in the reference list must have been mentioned in your paper.
- **Title.** Place the title (References) at the centre and top of a fresh page following the end of your text. ASA style prefers capitalizing the entire word (REFERENCES).
- **Alphabetical order of entries.** Arrange the entries in the reference list alphabetically by the last name (surname) of the author. For entries without an author, use the first word, not counting articles (*A, An, The*), if any, of the title of work for alphabetizing.
- **Author names.** Indicate author names in accordance with the following:
  ASA style: All first names are indicated as you find them in the source. For multiple-author items, second and subsequent authors are given in their natural, rather than inverted, order. If the item is part of an edited work, names of editors are given in their natural order.
  APA style: Indicate initials only for first names of all authors and editors. Give the names of second and subsequent authors of multiple-author items in their inverted order. If the item is part of an edited work, names of editors are given in their natural order.
- **Capitalization.** Capitalization of title and subtitle of book or article differs between the two styles:
  ASA style: Capitalize first word and all other words except articles, conjunctions, and short prepositions (four letters or fewer).
  APA style: Capitalize first word and proper nouns only.
- **Runover lines.** The first line of each entry starts from the left margin, but the second and other runover lines are indented five spaces.
- **Spacing between lines.** Double-space all entries.

- **Punctuation.** Be careful with the use of punctuation marks in each entry. The period (full stop) is used at the end of each main element (author, year of publication, title of work, publisher information). Do not forget the period at the end of each entry which usually is publisher information. However, entries that end with an Internet address must not carry an ending period. In APA style, the year of publication is enclosed in parentheses. For other punctuation marks within entries, follow details shown in this chapter's examples (8.7.1 to 8.7.33).

- **Several works by the same author.** List multiple works by the same author by year of publication, beginning with the earliest. If there are several works published in the same year, list them alphabetically by the title (ignoring *A, An,* or *The*).

  ASA style: Author's name in the second and subsequent entries is replaced by an underline of seven spaces followed by a period.

  APA style: Author's name is shown in every entry.

Reporting Research Findings

Empirical research in the social sciences usually uses such methods as questionnaire or interview survey, experiment, field research, and secondary analysis of existing data (e.g., census statistics). If you are writing a research paper based on survey, experiment, or some form of numerical data, you will have to put your data to quantitative analysis. On the other hand, if you engage in field research in which you focus on observation and description of behaviour and experiences of people, your data will be more qualitative. Even so, the report of some form of quantitative data is still possible (e.g., frequencies of certain types of interaction in a particular field setting) in addition to qualitative analysis.

As a student studying human behaviour in various areas of social life, your ability to write about research findings properly is an important part of your learning. You can learn a great deal from reading research articles written by social scientists. Of course, these articles differ from one another in such aspects as subject matter, research method used, and analyses undertaken. But their authors are well aware that they must communicate their findings effectively to their readers. This often means that they need to select, organize, and describe their findings so that numbers or whatever phenomena that are observed become meaningful information in the context of the research problem.

Even if you think you can write a clear and well-organized essay, you may still feel uneasy about writing up the findings of a research paper. This is true of many students. You have more to learn about the use of writing to describe what is important in some quantitative or qualitative data. If you do not learn this well, your report of research findings is likely to be cumbersome if you say more than is necessary, confusing if you set up tables improperly, and misleading if your use of language fails to reflect the tendencies and patterns of behaviour that you attempt to describe.

In this chapter, I shall draw your attention to nine topics:

1. Basic structure of the research report
2. The research report as a context for presenting research findings

3.   Important guidelines for presenting quantitative findings
4.   Describing univariate distributions, or values of one variable at a time
5.   Describing bivariate relationships, or relationships between two variables
6.   Variations on the same theme: Writing different statements that describe the same relationship
7.   Presenting qualitative data
8.   Verb tenses in reporting research
9.   Expressing numbers.

9.1 Basic Structure of the Research Report

Although individual research reports may be organized differently according to the social science discipline (or a given field in it) and the nature of the research topic or problem, they generally contain these basic elements:

1.   Introduction
2.   Literature review
3.   Methodology
4.   Results
5.   Discussion

9.1.1 Introduction

What is your research question or problem? Why is it worth studying? Do you have any hypotheses to test? If not, what do you intend to obtain in your research? Essentially, the introduction directs the reader to your research. In it you delineate your research problem and place it in some theoretical or historical context so that the nature and justification of your study are clear. To establish this context, you need to include a review of selected works from the relevant literature. Sometimes, if you plan to do this more extensively, as in a thesis, the literature review may constitute a separate section following the introduction.

9.1.2 Literature Review

What have other researchers found or said about the general problem to which your research problem is related? In what ways do they shed light on your study? Are there any knowledge gaps that you may want to fill? Your purpose in the literature review is not only to summarize past research but also to comment on how your study relates to other similar studies or other writings that are relevant to your research problem. Of course, you need to exercise judgement on what studies to review so that you include both works done in the more distant past (but are perhaps classics) and works that are good representatives of more recent studies. To write an adequate literature review, you will need to apply the skills of reading and summary writing (Chapter 4) and those of quoting and citing sources (Chapter 7).

9.1.3 Methodology

While the introduction and the literature review orient the reader to your study, the methodology section explains to the reader exactly how your study was conducted. The main ingredients that make up this section should include: What method(s) or research design did you use to collect your data? How did you select the subjects and how many were included? How were the data actually collected and what problems were encountered in the process of data collection? How did you measure the variables under study? Generally, and especially when you are conducting a qualitative study, you should also provide necessary details of the setting in which the data were collected through, for example, interviewing. All such information about how you accomplished the study tends to lend credibility to your report of findings.

9.1.4 Results

The results section is the heart of your research paper. If yours is a quantitative research report, the results section contains typically tables and, where appropriate and necessary, figures (charts and graphs). These you must use only sparingly. They are accompanied by your description of patterns and/or trends indicated by the percentages and other numerical information contained in the tables and diagrams. In addition, you will need to make sense of the findings (what the data show) to see if they support any hypotheses you may have or if, in the absence of hypotheses, they allow you to make certain generalizations. The guiding principle is that *you should analyze the data in terms of what they indicate about your research problem.*

In a qualitative research report, you can arrange the findings according to certain conceptual topics under each of which you present the relevant observations and interpretations, including quotations from respondents or dialogues between respondents and researcher where appropriate. Other arrangements are possible depending on the nature of the study, such as separating the findings (observations, descriptions, quotations) themselves from the analysis (interpretations of the meaning of the findings).

9.1.5 *Discussion*

How do your findings relate to theory and previous research (which you have reviewed)? Can you construct any meaning for your research problem given the findings you have? In the concluding discussion section, you have the opportunity to elaborate on your findings so that you can put key points into sharper focus and report any insights you may have from the research. At the same time, you should attempt to examine any shortcomings in your completed project (e.g., conditions that limit the generalizability of the findings) and indicate those areas of your research problem that still require further study.

9.2 The Research Report as a Context for Presenting Your (and Others') Findings

While reporting research findings belongs squarely in the results section of your research report, you should bear in mind the content of your introduction section as you process and analyze your data. This means that your effort in data analysis and reporting should be guided by the theoretical concerns of your research. More specifically, you should select and organize your data analysis in such a way that what you present in the results section is all related to those theoretical concerns.

Writing about findings may occur in other sections also. In the introduction, or in the literature review section if you have it as separate from the introduction, you may need to refer to results from past research. If so, make sure that you do not misinterpret or misrepresent the research results you refer to. Then, if your research uses indexes constructed from certain questionnaire items, you need to report how well the index values correlate with those individual items to show the reliability of the index, and with another conceptually relevant item to check the validity of the index. This you can do in the methods section or at the beginning of the results section.

Further, in the discussion section, where you are supposed to give special attention to the meaning of the findings as they bear upon the central concerns of your research paper, you will quite likely refer to those parts of the findings that supply the material for your consideration. Of course, you would be doing much more than merely summarizing those findings, for you would perhaps be asking questions that remain unresolved after your study or pointing to certain deficiencies in the data that you hope will be rectified in future research. Whatever you choose to say in the discussion section, the reference to at least some of your findings is inevitable.

9.3 Important Guidelines for Presenting Quantitative Findings

There are quite a few conventions that govern how you construct tables and display percentages. But you should first be familiar with some important guidelines for presenting quantitative findings.

9.3.1 Do Not Include Too Much Information

Although you could have very extensive analyses generated by computer programs, do not expect to put them all in your results section. Plan your analyses from which you will further organize the results that you need.

9.3.2 Organize Findings

First give a profile of your sample (respondents or cases) and perhaps a description of each of several important variables, particularly dependent variables. These will be all summaries of univariate (single-variable) distributions. You will then proceed to a number of bivariate (two-variable) analyses that are your main research concerns, including testing certain hypotheses, if you have any.

9.3.3 Use Tables and Figures Sparingly

While you can present your results in tabular or graphic (figures) form, the major force of your presentation is your text. Use tables and figures sparingly and judiciously as an aid to your textual description. (For example: "As shown in Table 2, educational attainment makes substantial differences in the rate of participation in cultural activities, . . .") If the information can be stated briefly and clearly— distribution of respondents by sex, for example—you need not repeat such information by making a table for it.

9.3.4 Statements Describing Findings Must be "Factual"

What you write about the findings should reflect nothing more than what is supported and justified by the numerical information you have. For instance, if your data show that 70 per cent of the husbands in your sample reported that they regularly helped with household chores, you should not say anything like "This is quite against what we would expect" or "We were quite surprised to observe this." Comments like these do not belong in the results section; they tend to colour your reader's reading of your results.

9.4 Describing Univariate Distributions (Values of One Variable at a Time)

9.4.1 Describing Background Variables

In describing univariate distributions, a single average (mean, median, or mode, depending on the nature of the variable and your research purpose) will serve to summarize the values as found in your sample:

```
Respondents ranged in age from 18 to 64 with a mean
age of 32.5 years.
```

For nominal variables (e.g., sex, occupation, and religion), you will use the percentages of the values concerned instead:

```
Of the 228 subjects who were interviewed, 61 per cent
were female and 39 per cent were male.
```

For variables with a few values, such as sex or marital status, you do not need a table to show the distribution of the values; just describe the distribution in words, such as the above two examples. You might make other similar statements, as in the following: (Note that any number mentioned at the beginning of a sentence must be spelled out.)

```
Sixty-five per cent of the respondents were female, 35
per cent were male.
```

```
The married were most numerous (72 per cent) in the
sample, followed by those who were single (26 per cent)
and those who were divorced (2 per cent).
```

However, if your study includes several groups and the sex distribution in each group is to be noted, it would be better to present such information in a table because it will make comparison easier.

If you have variables that have many value categories, such as occupation or age (depending on how you set up the value categories), it would be helpful if you prepare tables to show the distribution of values in detail. You should, in your text, point to certain characteristics in the distribution, as in the following:

```
As shown in Table 1, while our sample includes a
sizeable proportion (28 per cent) of production
workers, it also has a comparable proportion (25 per
cent) of sales and service workers.
```

Table 1 Occupation of Respondents

Occupation	% (N=228)
Professional, technical and related workers	18.9
Administrative and managerial workers	13.5
Clerical workers	11.3
Sales workers	10.2
Service workers	14.8
Production workers	28.1
Others	3.2

Source: Hypothetical

Notice that when you have a table whose content you refer to in your text, the table should be mentioned by its number in your text (e.g., "As shown in Table 1" or "As we can see from Table 1"). You can include a phrase referring to the table as part of your sentence, or you can simply put the table number within parentheses at the end of your sentence. If you choose the latter, the above example statement becomes:

> While our sample includes a sizeable proportion (28 per cent) of production workers, it also has a comparable proportion (25 per cent) of sales and service workers (Table 1).

It is sometimes convenient to present the information concerning the demographics of the sample in one table, as the next example illustrates. Of course, the number of variables to be included in the table must not be too large, or the table will become too cumbersome to read.

> The demographics of the sample are shown in Table 2. Fifty-one per cent of the respondents were female. As many as 66 per cent of the sample were married, while 28 per cent were never married. Subjects ranged in age from 18 to 78 with a mean age of 34.5 years. More than half (53.5 per cent) of them belonged to the 25 to 44 age group. Of all the respondents, 11 per cent had a post-secondary education, 48 per cent had not gone beyond secondary school, and 28 per cent had only a primary education.

Table 2   Demographics of the Sample

Variable	% (N=408)
Sex	
Male	48.8
Female	51.2
Marital Status	
Never married	27.7
Married	66.2
Separated/Divorced	4.4
Widowed	1.7
Age	
18–24	17.0
25–44	53.5
45–64	20.8
65–78	8.8
Education	
No schooling/Kindergarten	13.7
Primary	27.7
Lower secondary	16.9
Upper secondary	30.7
Post secondary	11.0

Source: Hypothetical

9.4.2 Presenting Percentage Results

You should note the following points when presenting percentage results:

- Tables are always numbered and given appropriate titles.
- Only horizontal lines are used in constructing a table.
- In a distribution, only percentages and their "base N" (base number) are normally shown. Actual frequencies are unnecessary not only because they tend to clutter the table but also because they can always be recovered from the base number and the relevant percentage if needed.
- Percentages in a table usually show no more than one figure after the decimal point.
- Your text quoting percentages is more readable if you round them to the nearest integer since the more precise figures are easily identified in the relevant table.
- You may refer to a given percentage with a phrase that describes the

approximate quantity (such as "more than half," "nearly one-third," and "about a quarter"), which is more readily grasped by the reader. For accuracy, however, these descriptions should be followed by the specific percentage given in parentheses). If you use such words as "sizeable" or "substantial" because you want to mean that they are not to be overlooked, make sure you insert the corresponding percentage numbers after them so that the reader understands their meaning clearly.

• Use the percentage symbol (%) only in tables. In text, use "per cent" (two words) instead. "Percent" is also considered acceptable. Whichever form you choose, be consistent.

9.4.3 *Describing Variables under Study*

Describing the demographics of the sample is merely the first step in reporting research findings. Following it is usually a description of the distributions of some key variables under study. Suppose one such variable in your study is "life satisfaction." Suppose also that, like a host of other questions asking about satisfaction with given domains (e.g., family life, friends, leisure), the item has five response categories: "very dissatisfied," "dissatisfied," "average," "satisfied," and "very satisfied."

Your table showing the results may look like this:

Table 3 Satisfaction with Life and Its Various Domains

Domain of satisfaction	Degree of satisfaction (%)					(N)
	Very dissatisfied	Dissatisfied	Average	Satisfied	Very satisfied	
General life satisfaction	1.1	10.8	39.1	45.3	3.7	(2,267)
Family life	0.4	4.8	23.4	62.9	8.5	(2,251)
Friends	0.4	2.6	30.8	60.6	5.7	(2,212)
Leisure	0.9	9.0	49.2	38.3	2.6	(2,132)

Source: Adapted from Table 2.2 in Wan (1997)

Please note that this form of table is suitable for presenting multiple items that have the same response categories, with percentages adding up to 100 horizontally.

Since the number of respondents who actually answer may vary from question to question, it is customary to indicate the base N of each question.

Your statements that describe findings presented in a table are supposed to help your readers understand the information contained in the table. To do so, you certainly need not refer to every numerical entry in it, but should instead point to what is notable or unusual.

With this in mind, your statement could be:

> Among the individuals interviewed, the percentages that were "satisfied" or "very satisfied" with family life, friends, and leisure were 71 per cent, 66 per cent, and 41 per cent, respectively. Asked how satisfied they were with life generally, 49 per cent indicated they were "satisfied" or "very satisfied."

9.4.4 Making the Frame of Reference Clear

The broader substantive meaning of a percentage depends on its relevant base that serves as a frame of reference. Interpretation of a reported percentage easily becomes problematic if its base is not clearly indicated. The proper base may be the entire sample or a part of it, depending on the item (variable) in question. In writing statements to describe your findings, you should then be very careful to differentiate between findings that apply to the entire sample and those that apply to certain groups within the sample.

Study the following example in which one percentage figure is mentioned that represents the extent to which a sample of Hong Kong people believe that the feeling of "peace of mind" associated with leisure is important. Then, the reader's attention is drawn to those members of the sample who hold such a belief and to the percentage of these people who say that their own leisure always gives them peace of mind.

> An overwhelming 86 per cent of our 397 respondents said that "peace of mind" as a characteristic of leisure was important. Of these, however, only 32 per cent indicated that their leisure "always" gave them such feeling, and 26 per cent admitted that their leisure in fact "rarely" or "never" gave them the peace of mind that they regarded as important. (See: Table 10.12 in Ng (1997))

As you can see, the words "of these" at the beginning of the second sentence guide the reader to that part of the sample to which the percentage figures in that sentence apply. That is, "32 per cent" and "26 per cent" do not refer to all the 397 respondents as base but to only those who regarded "peace of mind" as an important characteristic of leisure.

Here is one final note about reporting findings before we move on to bivariate relationships. When you use the same words to represent certain response categories as the ones that actually appear in the questionnaire, you should enclose them in quotation marks the first time they appear in your statement describing the finding, such as "peace of mind," "always," "rarely," and "never" that you just saw in the above example.

9.5 Describing Bivariate Relationships

In social research, the researcher often wants to see if a relationship (association) exists between two variables. One of these variables may be regarded as the independent variable and the other the dependent variable. The dependent variable is the variable whose values are supposed to depend on or be caused by values of the independent variable. If, for example, you want to study how life satisfaction varies with or depends on educational background, you can treat life satisfaction as the dependent variable and educational background as the independent variable.

With the aid of computers, you can without too much difficulty process and analyze your data in a diversity of ways that will enable you to obtain the necessary results for constructing tables to display bivariate distributions.

In describing findings concerning bivariate relationships, you will rely more heavily on tables. You should learn to set them up properly and understand how to use them for making the right statements in your paper's results section. We shall now proceed to consider the following:

1.   the parts of a bivariate table,
2.   some basic conventions governing how you construct and use a bivariate table,
3.   the idea of association between two variables, and
4.   how bivariate findings may be reported (with examples).

9.5.1 *The Parts of a Bivariate Table*

A bivariate table (also called a cross-tabulation) is a table that shows the joint distribution of two variables. Although such a table can vary in design and complexity, depending on the variables in question, its basic structure is largely like that shown below. Like univariate tables, a bivariate table has a table number, a title that succinctly and accurately describes the table content, and headings that indicate the organization of the table's content. Unlike univariate tables, however, a bivariate table shows the occurrence of *pairs of values* (since there are two variables) rather than single values.

Table Number   Title (Dependent Variable by Independent Variable)

Dependent variable (Y) name	Independent variable (X) name		
	Category X_1	Category X_2	Category X_3
	%	%	%
Category Y_1			
Category Y_2			
Category Y_3			
Total	100	100	100
(n)	(n_1)	(n_2)	(n_3)

9.5.2 *Some Conventions for Constructing and Using Bivariate Tables*

Use the following points to guide you in setting up and using bivariate tables:

9.5.2a *Table title*

The dependent variable is mentioned first in the table title, and the word "by" is used to introduce the independent variable. This means that the table displays distribution of the dependent variable according to subgroups of the independent variable.

9.5.2b *Columns and rows*

The independent variable is usually the column variable and the dependent variable the row variable. Thus, the columns represent the categories of the independent variable and the rows represent the categories of the dependent variable. Sometimes, however, these are reversed so that the column variable becomes the dependent variable and the row variable the independent variable. This may be done if you want to construct a composite table in which the same dependent variable is cross-tabulated against three or four independent variables.

9.5.2c Percentaging

Initially, the cells of the table register the frequencies of cases with a particular pair of values (one from each variable). But they are converted to percentages when the table is presented. *As a general rule, the percentaging is done within the categories of the independent variable.* Thus, most of the time, with the independent variable as the column variable, the percentaging is done within each column, using the column total as base number. For instance, the percentage of y_1 within the category x_1 of the independent variable is the frequency in that cell divided by n_1 (column total of x_1) and multiplied by 100.

9.5.2d Overall distribution

Sometimes there may be an additional rightmost column (or topmost row if you choose to use rows for the independent variable) to show the overall distribution of the dependent variable. Make sure you understand this point.

9.5.3 *The Idea of Association between Two Variables*

The distribution of the dependent variable (more accurately: percentage distribution of the values of the dependent variable) within each category of the independent variable is called a *conditional distribution*. When you have entered all information, i.e., all percentages within each column, into a cross-tabulation (assuming that you follow the convention of making the column variable the independent variable), you should compare the conditional distributions displayed down the columns.

If the two variables are totally unrelated, each conditional distribution of the dependent variable should be just like any other. Indeed, they should each be no different from the distribution of the dependent variable itself. This means knowing a person's value on the independent variable does not at all help us predict that person's value on the dependent variable. If the conditional distributions are different, then the two variables are related, with the extent of the relationship (association) depending on how different the conditional distributions are. This means that *knowledge of the independent variable helps us guess better or more accurately about the dependent variable.*

Examine Table 4, which has been percentaged down the columns to show three conditional distributions, one for each of the three levels of educational attainment. You can see that they are noticeably different from one another and, with perhaps the exception of the conditional distribution corresponding to secondary education, quite different from the overall univariate distribution of the dependent variable "importance of using time freely." This being the case, you can claim that there is an association between educational attainment and the belief in the importance of being able to use time freely. To indicate the strength of the association, you will need to compute an appropriate measure of association. Check your social statistics or research methods books for details.

Table 4 Importance of Using Time Freely by Educational Attainment

Importance of using time freely	Educational attainment			All
	Primary	Secondary	Tertiary	
	%	%	%	%
"Important" or "Very important"	57.0	69.4	81.2	66.8
"Average"	30.6	23.6	14.6	24.7
"Unimportant" or "very unimportant"	12.4	7.0	4.2	8.5
Total	100.0	100.0	100.0	100.0
(N)	(121)	(199)	(48)	(368)

$\chi^2 = 15.99$, $p < .05$

Source: Table 2 in Ng (1998)

9.5.4 Examples of Describing Bivariate Findings

It is difficult, if not impossible, to cover exhaustively the many details and nuances pertaining to describing bivariate findings, especially as these vary according to the nature of the variables involved and the specific kind of question the researcher wants to answer. However, to help you grasp the essence of what goes into describing findings concerning two variables at a time, I shall focus on a few typical situations.

9.5.4a Both the independent variable and the dependent variable are ordinal

First, let us consider the situation where both the independent variable and the dependent variable are ordinal (values on some kind of rank order). Table 4 referred to in the preceding section (9.5.3) represents such a situation, since both educational attainment and degree of importance attached to using time freely contain values or categories that are ranked from low to high.

If you compare the three conditional distributions of importance of using time freely, you will notice that they are quite different from one another. While on the whole about two-thirds of the respondents believe that using time freely is "important" or "very important," the percentage of those who so believe varies with the level of educational attainment, being lowest among the primary-educated and highest among the tertiary-educated. The two variables do appear to be associated. You might describe this table as follows:

> From Table 4, we can see that the tendency to believe that using time freely is important or very important increases with educational attainment. The percentage holding such belief rises from 57 per cent among the primary-educated to 81 per cent among those who have had a tertiary education. This is certainly higher than the 67 per cent among the whole sample.

Since both "importance of using time freely" and "educational attainment" have ordered values, it makes sense to say whether the values of the former increase or decrease with those of the latter. That is, we can examine the covariation between the values of the two ordinal variables when considering the association between these variables. As indicated by the results in Table 4, the association between the two variables is positive. In describing such an association, you can choose to focus on the "high-high" connection (the higher the independent variable, the higher the dependent variable) or the "low-low" connection. The statement you just read is an example of mentioning the "high-high" connection. Now consider the following alternative which underscores the "low-low" connection (the lower the independent variable, the lower the dependent variable):

> Table 4 indicates that while about two-thirds (66.8 per cent) of the respondents believe that using time freely is important or very important, there are still some (8.5 per cent) who think otherwise. The size of this minority clearly varies according to educational attainment, from only 4.2 per cent among the tertiary-educated to a not-so-small 12.4 per cent among those who have only a primary education.

Both statements, and others similar to them, may be made about the same table of results. The choice depends on whether you are more concerned with what makes people see the free use of time as important. In any case, you should be aware that in describing bivariate relationships, your statement should be concise enough to indicate the nature of the relationship clearly. Just point to those parts of the table that you think are notable for understanding that relationship: you never need to refer to more details than are necessary for supporting what you say.

9.5.4b   Both the independent variable and the dependent variable are nominal (categorical)

A nominal or categorical variable is one whose values differ in kind only. Variables such as sex, religion, occupation, voting preference, and area of residence are all of this type. The idea of association between two nominal variables is not whether one increases or decreases as the other increases or decreases, but rather whether certain categories of one tend to occur together with certain categories of the other. In other words, *association between nominal variables is understood not in terms of co-variation but in terms of "joint occurrence."* If, for instance, you are studying the association between gender and drink preference for either tea or coffee and find that proportionally more men choose coffee while proportionally more women choose tea, then an association is said to exist. Such an association may be simply stated as follows:

```
Men are more likely than women to choose coffee while
women are more likely than men to choose tea.
```

Of course, depending on the strength of the association, you can place a suitable modifier before "more likely":

```
Men are somewhat more likely than women to choose
coffee while women are somewhat more likely than men
to choose tea.
```

In describing the association between two variables, it is common practice to use a noun phrase to label a particular variable. (In the example in 9.5.4a, we had "the tendency to believe . . ." and "educational attainment.") You could write the statement describing men's choosing coffee by using nouns or noun phrases:

```
Maleness is associated with preference for coffee;
femaleness is associated with preference for tea.
```

While such a sentence is not incorrect, it may sound somewhat abstract and impersonal. The previous statement (Men are more likely than women to choose coffee . . .) that brings the "actors" into the picture is more easily understood, and thus is a better choice.

Table 5 is typical of cross-tabulations of two nominal variables. Here the independent variable is "leisure associates" or whether the respondents in a Hong Kong survey of leisure behaviour usually spend their leisure alone or with others such as friends or family. The dependent variable is "most desired leisure." As in Table 4, the column variable is the independent variable and the row variable the dependent. Percentages representing the distribution of the dependent variable's values are shown down the columns within each category of the independent variable. These are the conditional distributions, i.e., distributions of the values of the dependent variable for each value of the independent variable. Then the rightmost column under the label "all" is the overall distribution of the values of the dependent variable.

Table 5 Most Desired Use of Leisure by Leisure Associates

Use of leisure	Leisure associates			
	Alone	Family	Friends	All
	%	%	%	%
Television	4.0	7.1	----	4.2
Other entertainment	2.9	2.0	5.0	3.0
Personal activities	38.4	2.0	5.0	21.5
Social activities	5.2	43.9	45.0	23.9
Domestic activities	15.7	6.1	----	10.0
Physical activities	5.2	37.8	45.0	22.1
Resting	28.5	1.0	----	15.2
Total	100.0	100.0	100.0	100.0
(n)*	(172)	(98)	(60)	(330)

*Number of respondents
Source: Table 3 in Ng (1997)

Faced with such a cross-tabulation, you should normally first inspect the dependent variable's overall distribution to note if there is one value that stands out above the rest or if there is more than one such value. Then you should inspect the conditional distributions to see if the independent variable makes any difference in the distribution of the values of the dependent variable. Using Table 5 as an example, we can consider two main questions: What are the most desired uses of leisure? What is the picture like when we know their leisure associates? The following passage is one way of reporting the findings with these two questions in mind.

As indicated in Table 5, the three most desired uses
of leisure among the 330 respondents are social activities (23.9 per cent), physical activities (22.1 per
cent), and personal activities (21.5 per cent).

Among those who spend their leisure with their
friends, the likelihood of naming social activities as
most desired almost doubles to 45 per cent. The same
is true for physical activities.

For those who spend their leisure with their
family, the preference for social and physical activities is almost as strong, being 43.9 per cent and 37.8
per cent respectively. In addition, these respondents
are somewhat more likely (but only 7.1 per cent) than
others to mention television watching as most desired
leisure use.

Finally, those who usually spend leisure alone
(and they account for slightly more than half of the
respondents) show a rather different pattern of
desired leisure use. For instance, there is a considerably greater tendency to prefer personal activities
(38.4 per cent) to social activities (5.2 per cent).
At the same time, quite interestingly, the second most
frequently mentioned (28.5 per cent) desired use of
leisure among these respondents is simply taking a
rest.

For this cross-tabulation (Table 5), the length of the description is about right. If
you read the sample description carefully, you will notice the following:

- Not all percentages are described; only the more "dominant" or the more
  "peculiar" ones are selected for description.
- The present tense is used to describe the findings, implying that you assume the
  pattern will be the same at the time the report is read.
- Percentage figures are placed in parentheses closest to words that refer to these
  figures to explain what a strong tendency or a different likelihood means in
  numerical terms. They are placed in parentheses so as not to interrupt the flow
  of the text. Sometimes, however, it may be necessary or more convenient to put
  the percentage figures as part of the text.

Naturally, you can describe your findings in more ways than one. Using the same cross-tabulation, let us now see another sample description. This time, there is a greater effort to stress the association between desired use of leisure and leisure companionship.

> Figures in Table 5 indicate an association between most desired use of leisure and leisure companionship. If leisure is usually spent with family, then the most preferred leisure uses are social activities (43.9 per cent) and physical activities (37.8 per cent). Trailing far behind are television watching and domestic activities which together account for about 13 per cent.
>
>   A similar pattern applies to those who usually spend their leisure with friends, for the most preferred leisure uses are also social activities and physical activities (each carrying 45 per cent). However, none of them care for television or domestic activities.
>
>   By comparison, those who are usually alone during their leisure are typically in favour of personal activities (38.4 per cent), simply resting (28.5 per cent), or domestic activities (15.7 per cent).

You can see that this alternative description starts with a statement that the results indicate the presence of an association between the two variables. That has the effect of shaping the rest of the description to point to such an association. Throughout, the concern is to describe the most typical desired uses of leisure in each subgroup of respondents. The resulting description is, as you have just read, somewhat shorter than the first version.

One of the things that you need to learn about describing findings is to see clearly how you refer to the variables and their values or categories. To refer to them, you can always vary your choice of words and phrases. Thus, "leisure associates" can be written as "leisure companions." The three subgroups of respondents according to difference in this variable are "those who usually spend their leisure with friends," "those who usually spend their leisure with family," and "those who are usually alone during their leisure." Of course, you can alternatively say "those who have friends as leisure associates," "those who have family leisure associates," and "those who have no leisure associates."

Coming to the dependent variable—most desired use of leisure—you must first remember not to confuse it with how the respondents actually use their leisure. "Most desired" is synonymous with "most preferred." To refer to the values of this variable, you can say "the most desired uses of leisure are . . ." or "the most preferred uses of leisure are . . . " Instead of the noun phrase "the most preferred uses of leisure," you can use "desire" as a verb by saying "they most desire . . . in their leisure." You can also say "they are in favour of . . ." This is used in the last paragraph of the second sample description above. If you vary your wording carefully, your writing will sound more interesting rather than monotonous.

While you vary your wording, your main concern in describing findings about two nominal variables is still to highlight joint occurrences. Association between two nominal variables is shown by examining which values of one variable tend to occur jointly with which values of the other variable.

9.5.4c *The independent variable is nominal (categorical) and the dependent variable is interval*

There are occasions when scales are constructed to measure how people rate themselves in certain aspects. This is one way of studying people's subjective feelings, such as life satisfaction. If a scale (5-point, 7-point, 9-point, etc.) is used to measure life satisfaction, the variable is treated as an interval variable since the distance between one point and the next on the scale is assumed to be the same throughout the scale. Mean scores and standard deviations can be computed for different groups of respondents. Some groups may be differentiated according to ordinal variables (e.g., educational attainment, social class), which may be reduced to and considered as nominal if needed; others may be classified by straightforwardly nominal variables (e.g., sex, marital status). The mean scores of different groups may be compared to see if the differences are statistically significant.

The following illustrative description includes a brief reference to the measurement of "life satisfaction" and "general happiness."

> Respondents were asked two questions: "How satisfied are you with your life as a whole right now?" and "How happy are you about your life as a whole?" Both questions offered a scale of seven points for response, with "1" representing the lowest degree and "7" the highest. A response of "4" represented "mixed feelings."

Table 6 Comparison of Overall Life Satisfaction and Happiness
among Different Socio-demographic Groups

Socio-demographic group	Life satisfaction Mean (SD)	General happiness Mean (SD)
Overall	4.56 (1.24)	4.83 (1.33)
Gender		
Male	4.49 (1.32)	4.73 (1.34)
Female	4.62 (1.16)	4.91 (1.31)
F-ratio	2.153	4.057*
Education		
Primary	4.46 (1.27)	4.76 (1.41)
Secondary	4.53 (1.23)	4.83 (1.31)
Tertiary	4.81 (1.19)	4.91 (1.23)
F-ratio	3.578*	0.544
Marital status		
Married	4.59 (1.26)	4.90 (1.32)
Single	4.49 (1.15)	4.69 (1.26)
Others	4.36 (1.31)	4.51 (1.64)
F-ratio	1.039	3.153*
Occupation		
Manual	4.40 (1.27)	4.71 (1.40)
Clerical/Sales/Service/Disciplinary forces	4.52 (1.16)	4.84 (1.24)
Managerial/Professional	4.65 (1.17)	4.90 (1.23)
F-ratio	1.685	0.876

*$p < 0.05$
Source: Adapted from Table 7.2 in Wan (2001)

Table 6 compares the mean scores and standard deviations among different socio-demographic groups, that is, groups classifying respondents by sex, education, marital status, and occupation.

We may make two observations about the findings in Table 6. First, the average level of general happiness is higher than that of life satisfaction among all respondents (4.83 versus 4.56) and within each socio-demographic subgroup. Second, variation (measured by standard deviations) in general happiness tends to be greater than that in life satisfaction. Again, this is true in the whole sample and within each socio-demographic subgroup.

```
     Inter-group    variations    in    satisfaction    and
happiness   scores   show   that   those   who   are   female,
better-educated,  married,  or  engaged  in  managerial  and
professional   work   generally   hold   a   higher   level   of
satisfaction   and   happiness.   However,   ANOVA   (analysis
of   variance)   test   results   indicate   that   for   life
satisfaction,   only   inter-group   variations   related   to
education   are   statistically   significant.   For   general
happiness,   only   inter-group   variations   related   to
gender   and   marital   status   are   statistically   signif-
icant.
```

You will notice that in this description of findings, numerical results are almost not mentioned at all. This is largely because verbal interpretation of the results rather than citing numbers is more meaningful for this particular table. If there is some conspicuous pattern (e.g., happiness scores being higher and more dispersed than satisfaction scores) that applies to subgroups as well as the overall sample, we need to point it out.

You may recall that when both variables are ordinal (i.e., have ordered values), you can refer to an association between them in terms of one variable increasing or decreasing with the other variable (covariation). But when the independent variable is nominal, you describe its association with an interval dependent variable by specifying the particular subgroup of respondents in which the mean score of the dependent variable is highest. Let us inspect once again the sentence in the above sample description that draws the reader's attention to the association:

```
[T]hose  who  are  female,  better-educated,  married,  or
engaged  in  managerial  and  professional  work  generally
hold  a  higher  level  of  satisfaction  and  happiness.
```

In describing the relationship between two variables, you should thus bear in mind the nature of the variables involved so that you will say the pertinent things in your statement.

9.6 Writing Different Statements that Describe the Same Relationship

As you can see from the above examples, there are indeed many ways in which you can describe a relationship between two variables, depending on how much detail you want and what kind of emphasis you wish to bring to your reader. It is therefore worth your while to study the following additional examples so that you will have a better idea of how to write sentences to describe relationships that you may find.

For our present purposes, let us focus on the situation in which both the independent variable (X) and the dependent variable (Y) are ordinal, which often occurs in social research (e.g., educational attainment, income level, social class, extent of agreement with a given view on an issue, intensity of some kind of orientation or motivation, length of time lived in a community). When both X and Y are measured at the ordinal (or interval) level, rankings from low to high are meaningful. We have noted earlier that given such a situation, it makes sense to say whether the values of the dependent variable (Y) increase or decrease with those of the independent variable (X). To describe the relationship between two such variables, there are at least three main ways:

- Write a general statement that describes how Y varies as X varies.
- Describe how subjects who have a certain value on X tend to behave or tend to be on Y.
- Describe more specifically, with the aid of percentage figures, the different extents to which a certain value on Y is found among subjects of different categories (i.e., ordinal values) of X.

The data that generated Table 7 were collected from the Social Indicators Survey carried out in 1995 by researchers, including myself, from The Chinese University of Hong Kong, the University of Hong Kong, and the Hong Kong

Table 7 Leisure Satisfaction by Educational Attainment

Leisure satisfaction	Educational attainment		
	Primary	Secondary	Post-secondary
	%	%	%
Not satisfied	5.9	10.2	16.0
Average	24.3	37.9	34.0
Satisfied	69.8	51.9	50.0
Total	100.0	100.0	100.0
(n)*	(136)	(206)	(50)

* Base number for percentage

Source: Table 10.15 in Ng (1997)

Polytechnic University. About 400 respondents were asked to indicate their degree of satisfaction with the things they were able to do during their leisure. Responses were trichotomized (divided into three categories) into "not satisfied," "average," and "satisfied." Educational attainment was classified as "primary," "secondary," or "post-secondary." (Note that statements describing the data on which certain analyses are performed can read like the ones you just read. Of course, in a real research report, more details may be necessary.)

Now, let us see how you can describe the relationship between the respondents' leisure satisfaction and their level of educational attainment according to the three ways mentioned above.

9.6.1 Describing How the Dependent Variable (Y) Varies with the Independent Variable (X)

Without quoting numbers, you can write a general statement to focus on how the dependent variable varies with the independent variable, such as the following:

- As the level of educational attainment increases, the level of leisure satisfaction decreases. (Note the use of "level" in referring to both educational attainment and leisure satisfaction.)
- Leisure satisfaction varies inversely with educational attainment.
- The higher the respondents' educational attainment (is), the lower their leisure satisfaction (is).
- As education increases, leisure satisfaction decreases. (Simple and straightforward)

9.6.2 Describing How Subjects Who Have a Certain Value on X Tend to Behave or Tend to Be on Y

Sometimes it may be necessary to single out a certain subgroup (as defined by the independent variable X) and describe its standing on the dependent variable Y. You do not usually need numbers to describe such a pattern. The following are some possible descriptions:

- Those who are less well educated tend to be more satisfied with leisure.
- Those who are better educated tend to be less satisfied with leisure.

- The best-educated (i.e., those with a post-secondary education) tend to be the least satisfied with leisure.
- Those with a post-secondary education are most likely to be the least satisfied with leisure.
- Those who are only primary-educated tend to be the most satisfied with leisure.

(Note that in the above, "tend to be" is equivalent to "are likely to be.")

9.6.3 Describing the Different Extents to Which a Certain Value on Y is Found among Subjects of Different Categories of X

This is somewhat similar to the preceding (9.6.2) strategy, but here you want to emphasize a certain value on the dependent variable (Y), because it may be the focus of attention in your paper, and show how the extent of its occurrence varies among different subgroups as defined by the independent variable (X). Study the following descriptions, noting particularly how you can refer to relevant percentage figures from the data:

- The level of satisfaction with leisure is highest (69.8 per cent) among the primary-educated and lowest (50.0 per cent) among the post-secondary-educated.
- As many as 69.8 per cent of those with primary education are satisfied with their leisure as compared with 50.0 per cent of those with post-secondary education.
- We see that as many as 69.8 per cent of those with primary education, but only 50.0 per cent of those with post-secondary education, are satisfied with their leisure.
- Satisfaction with leisure is most likely to be found among those with primary education (69.8 per cent) whereas dissatisfaction is most often found among those with post-secondary education (16.0 per cent).
- The level of leisure satisfaction falls from 69.8 per cent among the primary-educated to only 50.0 per cent among the post-secondary-educated.
- The level of leisure dissatisfaction rises substantially from 5.9 per cent among the primary-educated to 16.0 per cent among the post-secondary-educated.
- Respondents who are tertiary-educated are more likely (16.0

per cent) than those who are primary-educated (5.9 per cent)
to be satisfied with leisure.

9.7 Presenting Qualitative Data

9.7.1 Differences between Qualitative Studies and Quantitative Studies

A qualitative study differs from a quantitative one in that it is more concerned with understanding social processes through information about actors, settings, interactions, and events. Such information is often not in numerical form. In quantitative studies, survey questionnaires and structured interviews are often used to generate large quantities of numerical data for statistical analysis and, where appropriate and necessary, tabular or graphic presentation. In qualitative studies, such methods as participant or non-participant observation, in-depth interviews, official records, or historical documents are used to produce descriptions of how something happens or why something is the case.

In quantitative research, the presentation of findings usually takes standard forms. We construct tables—and figures if necessary—to show the numerical results concerning the main research questions, and we write text to describe them. In qualitative research, by contrast, there is no standard way of presenting findings. Much room for variation is possible from one study to another, depending on the nature and purpose of the study. However, some guiding principles are useful to help you organize and prepare your report.

9.7.2 Some Guiding Principles

As in quantitative research reports, organize your findings according to your study purpose and major questions.

- Determine the approach that is most effective for presenting your findings. For example, consider whether it is appropriate for you to report unfolding events as you discovered or experienced them. Alternatively, perhaps you can identify certain main themes (e.g., ways of coping with the SARS epidemic, modifying life style at a time of economic downturn) that can be used to organize your material.
- Look for patterns, although you will probably need to use certain individual subjects as illustration of such patterns.
- In presenting the findings, you should try to show the attitudes or perspectives

of your subjects. Avoid infusing your personal attitudes or feelings into your presentation. This is a very important principle.

- Protect the privacy of your subjects by using disguised names. Depending on the nature of the study, their exact locations in the field may need to be concealed.

- If you are directly involved in the study's setting (field research), you may use the first personal pronoun *I*. This is natural since you interacted with your subjects and you are reporting your observations.

- In recording dialogues and in quoting what your subjects said, you may use contractions (e.g., *don't, it's, that's, we've*)

9.7.3 *Field Research and Narrative*

One type of qualitative research that social scientists often do is field research. It can take various forms, including participant observation, non-participant observation, and case study. In field research, if your findings are based on patterns emerging from the notes you have kept about your observations of the goings-on in the field and the conversations you had with your subjects, your task is to write about these patterns. You should do so in such a way that your reader can visualize and feel the "story" that you have to tell.

Typically, you would be writing about your findings in the form of a *narrative*. Not all narratives are prepared in the same way though. The form that is often adopted is one consisting of descriptions of the context in which some process or interaction was observed and summaries of your observation. At suitable places, you need to quote either in full or in part what your subjects said to illustrate or clarify a point.

How much you want to identify the subject depends in part on how representative the subject is and what kinds of background information the reader should know about the subject, apart from the collective descriptive data of all your subjects you should have presented earlier in your report, in order to better understand what that subject has to say.

If, for instance, you are studying a group of sales workers, you might introduce a quote in one of the following ways:

- These sales workers were seemingly very enthusiastic about their work. All of them spoke positively about the importance of service. The following is a typical description of how they felt about service:

- Most of the younger (mid- to late-twenties) sales workers

were newcomers to their field with a noticeably strong
concern with working hard to win customers. Asked what was
most important to him, one of them said:

- Suet-ling had been with the company for a little over eight
  years, which was long for her company. She was well liked
  by her colleagues. Asked what was most important in her
  work, she had this to say:

In the first of the above three examples, no specific information is given about
the identity of the subject from whom a quote is given because what that subject has
to say is taken as representative of all other subjects. In the second example, the
writer indicates that the subject is one of the younger sales workers; what is said is
supposed to be typical of these younger workers. In the third example, one particular
individual is singled out, given a made-up name, probably because there will be more
references to her as one of several key persons in the study. If one individual is
singled out, usually more information about the person's identity is given so that all
statements quoted from him or her can be understood accordingly.

In general, then, if the quote comes from someone who is among those given
individual attention in your story or if you wish to present a dialogue between two
subjects or between a subject and you as researcher (or some interviewer assisting
you), then the subject or subjects need to be identified, albeit under made-up names.

In presenting your field research findings, then, you will be weaving a story
with your observations and descriptions, which can be as detailed as your research
concerns and questions require. To illustrate or expand a point, you need to include
quotes from the subjects whom you study. At appropriate places, you may also want
to insert generalizations that are based on and supported by the evidence you present
(the descriptions and quotes).

9.7.4 Two Examples of Reporting Qualitative Results

To give you a clearer picture of how qualitative results may be reported, here are two
excerpts from the theses of two former graduate students.

The first excerpt comes from Yuen's (1997) M.Phil. thesis, a study of the
gender segregation of clerical work in Hong Kong. She focuses on how clerical
workers react to the constraints of their employment and what strategies they adopt
to enlarge their employment opportunities. Yuen interviewed 26 clerical workers (17
women and 9 men) between July 1996 and March 1997. She found that, for young
male workers, the typical working strategy was leaving clerical work. Clerical work

to them was only temporary; they wanted to move into a different occupation to become upwardly mobile. The following is how Yuen describes two cases, King-on and Sidney (both fictitious names). (The text has been edited slightly.)

Workers adopting the strategy of leaving clerical work hold a marked extrinsic orientation to their present employment. Since they only consider their present employment as temporary engagement, they keep themselves away from deep involvement in the work. They consider themselves not suited for the work they are doing. For instance, King-on does not like his present job because he thinks clerical work is not for him.

Interviewer: Do you think that your last job was better than the present one?

King-on: The last one was more comfortable. But it does not mean one is better than the other; both are more or less the same.

Interviewer: You said that this job is boring. Are you going to find another one after the double pay?

King-on: Maybe. I think I am not suited to being a clerk.

Interviewer: What kind of job is suitable for you?

King-on: Jobs that involve a lot of movement.

Interviewer: Why is clerical work not suitable for you?

King-on: I cannot sit for long. I think it's very tough. Having to stare at the monitor is tough!

(King-on, M, S, 24, pp. 26-27)

We can notice the helpless and contradictory attitude of King-on. On the one hand, he defines his job as unsuitable for him. On the other hand, he is still engaged in it since he has no better choice. In

this case, we can only understand his present
employment in terms of its material incentive. Indeed,
King-on explains that his first consideration of any
employment opportunity is the salary. He just wants to
accumulate enough money for his present tuition fee,
so he does not mind the work content of the job and
other long-term benefits offered by the job. He does
not value any intrinsic content of the job.

Sidney's attitude is interesting. During the
interview, he states several times that he does not
value anything of his post of clerical assistant. He
thinks that the salary is too little. He does not like
the work content and he describes it as "awful" when
facing the clients. At the end of the interview, he
reminds me that I must not use his real name in my
thesis because he does not want his friends to know
that he is so "wretched" that he has to work as a
clerical assistant. Apparently, he is staying in the
job only because he is looking for a chance to
transfer. He is holding an extrinsic orientation to
his employment. (pp. 100-101)

As you can see, the researcher in this example includes a dialogue between a subject and the "interviewer." The dialogue, like other dialogues and quotations in her report, is from Chinese transcripts of the interviews conducted for the research. In parentheses at the end of the dialogue (or quotation), information is given of the interviewee and the transcript: the interviewee's pseudonym, sex, marital status, and age, and the page number(s) of the original Chinese transcript. Thus, King-on (a pseudonym), in the text you just read, is male, single, aged 24, and the dialogue can be found on pages 26 and 27 of the original Chinese transcripts.

The second example is taken from Wong (1996), a Ph.D. thesis that studies the changes in nursing work at different levels that reflect the development of new roles. Wong conducted a case study of a hospital in Hong Kong that was one of the pilot hospitals introducing new management initiatives of the Hospital Authority. Being a qualified nurse herself, she was a participant observer in the study and interviewed various nursing personnel throughout 1995. In the following excerpt (slightly edited), Wong describes the work of nurse specialists (NSs), focusing on their initiation of formal referrals. (Note the abbreviations for some technical terminology: RENNS:

Nurse Specialist in Renal Nursing; DIABNS: Nurse Specialist in Diabetic Nursing; OPD: Outpatient Department.) In this example, you will see that Wong uses a quotation from a subject (a nurse specialist) to illustrate a point made in the first paragraph about the nurse specialist giving advice to ward staff. Then, Wong includes a passage from her field notes to describe the importance of clinical notes made by nurse specialists.

Frontline nurses seemed to lack confidence in making formal referrals to request service from the NSs. It might be because nurses were not sure about their own assessment and felt insecure about their own clinical judgement of patients' condition. They would prefer the traditional way of passing on information orally and asking for help informally. All the NSs in this study had acted as resource persons and given advice to ward staff in a less formal way of networking. For instance, the RENNS described one of her experiences as follows:

> Recently a member of staff in Ward Y told me that there was a patient with A-V (arterial-venous) fistula. The patient had a permanent catheter inserted and would be coming to us (the renal unit) for haemodialysis. The staff person from Ward Y was not familiar with the dressing. She was scared. I had previously told the staff person that she could contact me if necessary. That evening that staff person was on duty and she called me.

When formal referrals were initiated, the NSs wrote their clinical notes in the same place where the doctors wrote their notes. The correspondence of the NSs and the doctor in the same charting document signified their equal relationship in the referral system. In contrast, frontline nurses wrote on separate sheets and their notes were placed away from the main file of the patient's charts. The nurses' notes were not made accessible to the doctors who hardly requested to see nurses' documentation. When I was working in the ward, I observed a situation that supported the inference that NSs were maintaining parallel positions with doctors. I wrote in my field notes:

> I saw the DIABNS coming up to see a newly diagnosed young diabetic patient. The patient was referred by the doctor to see the Nurse Specialist. In the patient's chart, the diabetic nurse wrote: "The patient demonstrated Novapen skill. . . . I would make an appointment to see her [in OPD]. . . practise Novapen skill under supervision in ward." After the clinical notes of the DIABNS, the doctor wrote: "To practise [injection] skill in ward. Send home when ready." In this situation I see a mutual respect between the two practitioners—-the doctor and the nurse. The control of exit point of patient hospitali-zation still lies with the doctor. However, the DIABNS could initiate and continue her care for the patient at the OPD.

In this case, the doctor respected the expert opinion of the DIABNS's recommendation and reiterated in his notes that the patient would not be discharged until the patient had learned the skill of injection. It was more common to find nurses copying the doctor's clinical notes into nurses' charting. In this instance, however, the pattern was reversed. In his documentation, the doctor repeated what the DIABNS said. The doctor still maintained his authority to discharge the in-hospital patient, but he honoured the referral system by taking into account the expert opinion he solicited in his conceptualization of treatment plan for the patient.

(pp. 178-179)

9.8 Verb Tenses in Describing Findings

Verb tenses can be a problem for you if you are not careful or are not sufficiently clear about the conditions that justify the use of one tense rather than another when you report your findings.

What tense should be used when you present your findings? Use the following principles (9.8.1 to 9.8.4) to guide your decision. (See also Appendix 5 "Verb Tenses in Research Papers.")

9.8.1 Present Tense

Use the present tense for general statements that are supposed to be still valid when the reader reads your report. If what you say amounts to an overall pattern that summarizes the results indicated in a table, or an observation that is demonstrated by certain numerical figures in the table, it counts as a general statement since that pattern or observation is assumed to be generally true. In qualitative reports, using the present tense in the narrative means that what you describe or say represents conditions or behavioural patterns that are presumably still true or can be reasonably expected to be still true.

9.8.2 Past Tense

If you wish to describe how your subjects actually responded to a question or what emerged as a result of your choosing to analyze the data in a certain way, then you can use the past tense. In qualitative reports, use the past tense if you wish to present an event or describe a process as an historical record. Use the past tense if the emphasis is on what actually happened or how a person felt at a certain moment in the past.

9.8.3 Do Not Shift Tenses without Reason

As long as one of the above two situations applies to your writing, use the tense called for by that situation. Use the selected tense consistently and do not shift from the present to the past, or vice versa, for no particular reason. If, however, you genuinely need to change from one situation to another, then you may, of course, shift tenses accordingly, provided that such change is reasonable and clear from reading the context.

9.8.4 Antecedent Actions

If you are in the present tense mode, any antecedent action should be stated in the present perfect tense. For example:

```
The data suggest that teachers of School A have not
prepared themselves sufficiently when they counsel
their pupils.
```

Similarly, if you are in the past tense mode, any antecedent action is expressed using the past perfect tense. For example:

```
In contrast to men, most of the women said that they
had seldom thought of setting a time limit before they
went out shopping.
```

9.8.5 An Example in Quantitative Research

We shall now use an example to illustrate how you can use a short paragraph to describe the gist of the findings shown in a table. This time, the table is constructed somewhat differently from the ones you have seen earlier. The example will also illustrate the use of verb tenses in describing findings.

Table 8 is an example of a situation in which more than one dependent variable is included in the same table. Usually, the dependent variables so included are similar in some way, such as attitude statements soliciting degrees of agreement or disagreement from respondents. Placing them in the same table against the same independent variable(s) facilitates comparison. Thus, in Table 8, the rows are for three dependent variables (pro-divorce attitudes), and the columns for two independent variables (sex and age). The data are from the Hong Kong-wide Social Indicators Survey conducted in 1993 by researchers from The Chinese University of Hong Kong, the Hong Kong Polytechnic University, and the University of Hong Kong.

In this table, note that only percentages representing those respondents who disagree with the first two attitude statements and those who agree with the third attitude statement are shown, because these are the figures that the researcher wants to examine. Given the wording of the attitude statements concerning divorce, disagreement with the first two statements and agreement with the third all represent a pro-divorce disposition. It is not necessary to show, within each category of sex and age, the remaining percentages that would bring the total to 100 per cent. This is important since it makes the table less cumbersome to read and makes it easier for

Table 8 Pro-divorce Attitudes by Sex and Age

Pro-divorce attitudes (N = 344)	Sex[a]		Age[b]		
	Men	Women	Young	Middle	Old
The government should make divorce more difficult (% disagree)	36.7	38.2	43.8	44.1	12.3
Married people with children should not divorce (% disagree)	35.5	38.8	50.7	40.6	12.3
It is all right to marry a divorced person with children (% agree)	54.2	35.4	53.4	44.6	33.8

[a] Chi-square test significant at 0.05 level for third statement only ("It is all right to marry a divorced person with children.")

[b] Chi-square test significant at 0.05 level for all three statements

Source: Table 1.12 in Lee (1995)

readers to focus their attention on the part of the data—pro-divorce attitudes in the case of this example—that is most pertinent to the analysis.

The following are two versions of how the findings indicated in Table 8 may be described. You can study them closely to see differences in the use of verb tenses (note words in italics) and in the amount of details included.

VERSION 1

Gender differences in attitudes towards divorce *are* not substantial, except over marrying a divorced person with children (Table 8). Women *seem* less likely than men to accept this.

Age differences, by comparison, *are* more noticeable. Not only *are* younger people more inclined to think that marrying a person with children *is* not a problem, they *are* also more tolerant of divorce between people with children (second statement) and more opposed to government policies that *make* divorce difficult (first statement).

VERSION 2

We *can see* from Table 8 that there *is* a substantial

```
pro-divorce  sentiment  in  roughly  more  than  a  third  of
all respondents.
      Gender  does  not  seem  to  make  a  significant
difference  in  pro-divorce  sentiment  except  for  men's
stronger   tendency   (54.2   per   cent)   to   think   that
marrying someone with children is not a problem.
      Variation  by  age  in  such  sentiment  is,  however,
clearly   present.   When   presented   with   the   statement
"The   government   should   make   it   more   difficult   to
divorce,"  young  respondents  were  significantly  more
likely  than  the  old  (43.8  per  cent  vs.  12.3  per  cent)
to  express  disagreement.  Over  50  per  cent  of  the  young
respondents  thought  that  couples  with  children  could
seek  divorce  if  they  wanted  to,  or  felt  that  it  was
all right to marry a divorced person with children.
```

Of course, there can be other ways to describe the findings shown in Table 8. If you have examined the two versions carefully, you should have noticed the following:

- Version 1 describes the findings in very general terms, without mentioning any specific percentages. This has its own merit: it simplifies interpretation of the findings for the reader. (But you should not describe your findings always like this; numerical results, when quoted suitably and not excessively, add clarity and strength to your text.)
- Because of its presentation of the findings in the form of general statements, Version 1 uses the present tense throughout.
- Version 2 gives more details by referring to relevant percentages.
- In Version 2, part of the description takes the reader to the time when the data were collected to visualize how respondents reacted to certain items. Such description therefore uses the past tense.
- You may need to refer to the attitude statements in your own words or capture their meaning in some concise way. When making such a reference, take care to ensure that the whole sentence is grammatical. (Read, for instance, the last sentence of Version 2 again.)

9.8.6 An Example in Qualitative Research

Remember that in a qualitative research report, you often play the role of telling a story, which usually necessitates using the past tense because you are reporting what happened, including what your subjects (respondents) said or did. But the story-telling is often interrupted by comments you make to indicate a general observation or to interpret what happened in the "story" in the context of some broader or more general concerns. To do this, you shift to the present tense.

You can see this in the next example taken from an article (Becker and Moen, 1999) reporting, based on in-depth interviews, how married couples modify and restructure their commitment to paid work over their life course. The authors call such restructuring "scaling back."

```
The decision to scale back appears to be reflexive and
conscious. The couples we interviewed recognized the
demanding nature of contemporary careers and were
consciously trying to buffer family life from too many
work demands, while at the same time maintaining two
ties to the work-force. One woman in her 30s, without
children and on the staff of a major university, gave
a good summary of the tensions that most of the people
we talked to expressed when she told us that her
biggest challenge is:

    balancing the commitment I feel to both [my
    husband and my work]. Successfully doing my job
    to the point I feel it can be done, without being
    a workaholic, spending enough time with my
    husband. Getting out of work at a reasonable hour
    so that we can sit down every night and have a
    meal together and talk, see where we both are for
    the day. That's important to me. . . . but it's
    hard . . . The work drives my ability to get out
    of the office and spend time with family [italics
    added].

It was this sense of resisting the demands of a
greedy workplace that caused us to label these
strategies as scaling back. Respondents were resisting
the expectations of a 60-or more-hour work week
inherent in many professional careers. (p. 999)
```

In this excerpt, the first sentence, intended as a general statement to have current validity, uses the present tense. After that, the authors shift to the past tense because they present observations of what happened at the time of the fieldwork, including how the couples felt about their work. The quotation of what a woman said, however, is in the present tense as it represents what is generally true for her, at least up to the time when she was interviewed. In the paragraph after the quotation, the time reference is again the past, stressing what happened at the time of the fieldwork.

9.9 Expressing Numbers

When you describe and discuss findings, you are likely to refer to quantities expressed with numbers. You need to be careful with how you handle numbers, which you may indicate either through numerals (1, 2, 3) or through words (one, two, three). If you write a psychology paper, you should be particularly careful with describing such matters as measurements, statistical tests, and experimental designs. To ensure that you do it properly, you should consult the latest edition of the *Publication Manual of the American Psychological Association.*

In the following, you will see a list of some of the more important guidelines that should be useful to most social science students. Included are matters that are more pertinent to the description and discussion of findings.

9.9.1 Using Arabic Numerals to Express Numbers

9.9.1a Percentages (especially decimal percentages)

In the main text of a research report, write out the word *per cent* instead of using the percentage symbol %. You may use the % symbol in tables and in footnotes, if any, when you need to refer to percentages. However, the use of the % symbol is acceptable or standard in some professional journals.

- (In a footnote) The response rate was 72.5%.
- (In the main text) The response rate was 72.5 per cent.

Note that you can write *per cent* as one word *percent*. Either is acceptable, but you must stay with whichever form you choose throughout your report.

The number preceding the word *per cent* is never spelled out except when beginning a sentence. This number should be accurate to no more than one decimal place, but no decimal place is mentioned when the number is expressed in words.

- As many as 69.8 per cent of those with a primary education are satisfied with their leisure.
- Seventy per cent of those with a primary education are satisfied with their leisure.

The word "percentage" is never preceded by a number.

- Women now constitute a higher percentage of professional workers than they did thirty years ago.

9.9.1b Percentage points

The difference between two percentages is expressed in percentage points. Since a percentage can be thought of as a probability or likelihood, you can use percentage points to indicate the increase or decrease in likelihood. Thus, for example, if you find that women of every age group in your study are more likely to be satisfied with their life than are men in the same age group, you can first compute all the percentage differences, one for each age group, and then focus on the lowest and highest values. The following are possible statements about such a finding:

- Women are more likely than men to be satisfied with life, with an advantage of 8 to 23 percentage points.
- Women's likelihood to be satisfied with life is 8 to 23 percentage points higher than men's.

9.9.1c Probabilities

As percentages represent probabilities, sometimes percentages are shown as probabilities in tables. For example, 75.3 as a percentage is shown as .753 as a probability. If 68.6 per cent of all respondents indicate that they are happy with their life and 75.3 per cent of those who so indicate are also planning for leisure travel, then these percentages can be listed as probabilities in a table, if you so wish—.686 and .753 respectively. (But note that the probability of respondents' indicating that they are happy *and* also planning for leisure travel = .686 × .753 = .517)

A zero is not necessary in front of the decimal point for numbers whose values cannot exceed 1 (e.g., probabilities, correlation coefficients, and levels of statistical significance).

9.9.1d Fractional numbers

Fractional numbers are usually written in numerals (to one decimal place).

- an average family size of 3.2 persons

9.9.1e Ages, age groups

Note the variation in expressions indicating age:

- ages ranging from 18 to 64
- the average age at first marriage, 25.4, is an indication of . . .
- women in the 30-34 age group
- women aged 30 to 34
- women (ages 30-34)
- men in their 40s
- all the 25-year-olds (but: a 25-year-old graduate)

9.9.1f Statistics, ratios, percentiles and quartiles

- χ^2=18.4, df=4, N=368, p<.01
- χ^2(4, N=368)=18.4, p<.01
- a one-tailed test at the .05 level
- F(1, 820)=4.06, p<.05
- a ratio of 12:1
- the 3rd quartile
- the 70th percentile

9.9.1g Hypotheses

- Hypothesis 1
- Hypothesis 2a

9.9.1h Numbers representing time, dates, sample size, scale values

- In the preceding 3 weeks
- It took 1 hour 15 minutes to complete.
- August 15, 2003 (or: 15 August 2003 with no comma)
- 35 subjects, including 4 over age 80
- Work satisfaction is a 5-point scale (1=very dissatisfied, 2=dissatisfied, 3=average, 4=satisfied, 5=very satisfied)

9.9.1i Numbers referring to a specific table, page, or section in printed material

(Leave a space between the numeral and the word preceding it.)

- Table 8

- page 103
- chapter 12

9.9.2 Using Words to Express Numbers

9.9.2a Numbers smaller than 10 referring not to precise measurements

- **five** domains of life satisfaction
- Respondents were asked to recall their **two** most memorable leisure experiences in the past year.
- comparison of the **three** socioeconomic groups
- Each interview took about **an hour and a half** to complete.

However, when a small number (below 10) appears with a larger number (10 or above) for comparison, you may use Arabic numerals for both numbers:

- 3 of the 18 schools
- on a scale of 1 to 10
- 5 of the 21 leisure activities

but

- In the second test given six months later, only 35 of the 54 original subjects participated. [Here, test and months are different from subjects, and are thus not comparable.]

9.9.2b Fractions and multiples that are easily understood

- about **a quarter** of the respondents
- **two-thirds** of them
- The likelihood was almost **double** that of the previous group.

9.9.2c Any number, regardless of magnitude, that begins a sentence

Remember that you should never begin a sentence with a numeral. Either spell out the number or rephrase the sentence to have the numeral appearing not as the first word.

- Do not write: 54% of the men, but only 35% of the women, agreed with the statement.
- Write: Fifty-four per cent of the men, but only 35 per cent of the women, agreed with the statement.

If the numbers are part of the text, it is acceptable to round the numbers to the nearest integer. You can reword such a sentence to indicate the numbers more precisely:

- The likelihood of agreeing with the statement was higher among the men (54.3 per cent) than among the women (35.2 per cent).

9.10 Checklist for Reporting Research Findings

A social science research report is different from an essay. It requires that you give special attention to how to present the research findings to the reader so that they are readily understandable and that they may help the reader to see the research problem in the proper perspective. The following is a checklist containing the main points of this chapter:

Tables

1. Use tables and figures sparingly. Do not use them if results can be stated simply.
2. All tables and figures must be numbered and titled.
3. Use only horizontal lines in constructing a table.
4. Use the percentage symbol % in tables only; write out "per cent" in the text.
5. When percentages are shown in a table, give the relevant base number(s).
6. When you mention percentages in a statement, make sure that their base is clearly identified to avoid misinterpretation of the meaning of the percentage in question.
7. In a cross-tabulation, the independent variable is usually, though not always, the column variable; the dependent variable is usually (again not always) the row variable. In this format, percentages are computed down the columns and compared, in analysis, across the rows.
8. Where necessary, place notes at the bottom of tables. Notes include explanations of abbreviations and meaning of certain numbers; statistics (e.g., chi-square, significance levels) if used; and source of information if it comes not first-hand from the research itself.
9. Use your text to point out the main characteristics or patterns indicated by the numbers (percentages or otherwise) in any given table. You need not describe every detail.

Relationships between Variables

10. To detect the presence of a relationship (association) between two variables, compare the conditional distributions of the dependent variable across different categories of the independent variable. More generally, see if the values of the dependent variable vary systematically with those of the independent variable.

11. If you are testing hypotheses, present your findings according to some meaningful order of those hypotheses.

12. If you are not testing hypotheses, present your findings according to the main topics or themes that make up your research problem. This applies to both quantitative and qualitative studies.

13. Analyzing data is more than just describing them. Having described the findings, try to interpret what they indicate about your research problem.

Verb Tenses

14. Use the present tense for general statements that are supposed to be still valid at the time your report is read or valid for your subjects at the time when they responded to your interviewing (which, by extension, may be assumed to be valid at the time your report is read.).

15. Use the past tense to report what actually happened or how your subjects felt about something at some time in the past or during the fieldwork.

Expressing Numbers

16. Never begin a sentence with a numeral. Construct your sentence so that a number that you need to mention is not at the beginning of the sentence; if you must start with the number, spell it out in words.

17. A percentage figure or an average number usually contains no more than one decimal place.

18. Do not put a zero in front of the decimal point for numbers whose values cannot exceed 1.

19. As a general guideline, spell out numbers smaller than 10 that do not refer to precise measurements.

20. Put precise percentages or other figures in parentheses close to where you mention the presence or strength of a certain value or tendency.

```
Members of this group clearly prefer personal activi-
ties (38.4 per cent) to social activities (5.2 per
cent).
```

21. In your text you may use such easily understood phrases as "nearly half," "just over three quarters," and "roughly two-thirds" to describe quantities.

Revising, Editing, and Proofreading

In describing writing as a process in Chapter 3, I pointed out that revision is the most important part of the writing process. There I also pointed out that to revise is to re-examine and to improve, and gave, as examples, a few questions for your consideration regarding what tasks may be called for in revision.

In this concluding chapter, we want to distinguish more clearly between "revising" and "editing" although many people may think of revising as including editing. As you will see later (10.3), revising is more concerned with the writing's content and structure whereas editing focuses on the expression of this content through sentences and words. When these matters are settled, you will need a final round of proofreading to make sure that everything is in order and in correct form. All these tasks—revising, editing, and proofreading—are instrumental for turning your draft into a more satisfactory (though perhaps never really problem-free) final product.

We will first consider once again the importance of rewriting that all careful writers take the time to do, hoping that you, too, will practise it seriously as a matter of habit. Then, we will see more clearly what revision, editing, and proofreading involve. We will further consider each of the three tasks in the form of a detailed checklist.

10.1 Writing is Rewriting

Many students tend to leave little or no time for checking their written work to see if there are errors or if anything needs changing for better results. First, not a small number of them start working on their paper fairly late, with hardly any time or energy left for revision, especially when they are dealing with several term papers at the same time. Second, there is a strong urge to rid themselves of a burden as soon as they think the paper is done. No sooner has the paper been churned out from the printer than they rush to hand it in so that they will have one fewer thing to worry about. If this describes you, you should re-examine your time management and read this chapter seriously. Of course, not all students are like this, but unfortunately it is a rather common practice.

As mentioned in the opening chapter, writing for academic purposes is not only to demonstrate what you have learned but also to deepen your understanding and learning in what you write about. You cannot deepen your understanding and learning if you think that the draft, once completed, is good enough. On the contrary, if you take the time to look at your own writing from the perspective of a third party, you can take the written work as an object and scrutinize it in a different light. As you do so, you *detach yourself from your paper*, which enables you to see where you have done something improperly and what parts of the paper need some "repairing" or even more drastic change. You will be able to find ways to clarify your points with modified descriptions or explanations, to strengthen them with additional examples, and to perhaps vary the paper's organization so that it will become more effective. As a result, you will surely understand your material better and will probably gain valuable insights into certain aspects of your topic.

To revise a paper is, therefore, to give yourself the opportunity of demonstrating what you know—from study or from research—cautiously and responsibly. In revising, you make an effort to *rethink, reshape, and rewrite* ideas and organize them into a clearer and hence more effective statement. Only in this way can you claim to have truly learned. In his highly acclaimed book *On Writing Well*, William Zinsser (2001) asserts that "rewriting is the essence of writing well" (p. 84). No one can honestly believe that he or she can get everything right upon finishing the first draft. All professional writers rewrite their work until they feel that what they have comes reasonably close to what they really want to say. What you read in your books and journal articles are never first drafts but the result of often arduous labour of rewriting. If you value learning and quality work, you will indeed think of writing as very much rewriting. If you discipline yourself to practise it, and to do so consistently in all writing tasks, you will find the learning experience highly rewarding.

10.2 Basic Approach to Revising

Here are a few points about how you should approach revising your written work:

- Always leave ample time for revision. It is not something you can rush through in one sitting, but may require going through different parts of your paper a number of times.

- Revising means re-reading your draft carefully to see what its strengths and weaknesses are.
- Do not start revising immediately or soon after you have finished the draft. Put it aside for a day or two so that you will be able to read it not so much as the author but as an objective reader who can then be more critical.
- Keep asking yourself questions, such as Is this clear enough? Have I left out any important point? Can I reword this more concisely? Do I need to elaborate a certain part by adding new material and examples? Are there any inconsistencies in what I say at different places of the paper? (More checklist questions later.)
- Let one or two classmates or friends read it and ask for their feedback. They may have useful comments and questions for you.
- Exercise great care and patience as you revise.

10.3 Revising, Editing, and Proofreading

It makes good sense to start revising by examining the larger picture. Improve the overall structure before working on smaller details, or your may waste precious time on parts that you may discard later. Let me now describe briefly the main concerns of revising, editing, and proofreading.

10.3.1 *Revising*

When you revise, look for changes that will improve the organization and presentation of the paper as a whole. You should be concerned with whether the paper achieves its purpose you have set for yourself. For example, see if you need to shorten or condense parts that are too expansive; eliminate parts that are superfluous; clarify, elaborate, or rewrite parts that are unclear, using examples or analogies if necessary; and rearrange parts that are not in the proper place. These are "macro" matters that form the framework of the paper.

10.3.2 *Editing*

You will then re-examine your paper more closely, section by section and paragraph by paragraph, to edit for clarity, correctness, and effectiveness. When you have checked the basic structure of the paper and have made the necessary changes, you can turn your attention to smaller units: sentences and words. Editing is concerned with writing clear and effective sentences and using words correctly and adequately so that your paper will read smoothly. Editing is also concerned with ensuring that matters of format and style are attended to properly, such as citing and listing sources, page breaks, punctuation, and tables.

10.3.3 Proofreading

Having revised and edited your paper into a final draft, you still need to print it once more for proofreading, which is to ensure that everything is typed and arranged accurately. You will go over the final draft very carefully and patiently line by line to spot any errors, some of which may have occurred while making changes on the computer in the process of revising and editing. Some errors may also result from carelessness, fatigue, or from editing that is not sufficiently thorough. Whatever their cause, all errors, when spotted, must be corrected.

10.4 Managing your Drafts

If you have been using a computer to write your draft, make a printed copy from your first draft to do your revision. The printed copy allows you to see the whole draft at once, and you can mark desired changes (e.g., "add examples here," "move this to beginning of next section," "explain more clearly," "delete," "rewrite this paragraph to shift emphasis to . . .") on the copy. When ready, you can make the actual changes on the computer. But do take the precaution to leave the original first draft intact, and work on a copy of that draft under a different file name. This way, you can go back to the original draft for anything you may need. Indeed, you should keep all successive drafts under their own file names so that you can examine or reconsider any material included in an earlier draft if necessary.

10.5 Checklist for Revising

10.5.1 Purpose

- What is the purpose of your paper?
- Have you maintained that purpose consistently in your paper?
- Are there any parts of your paper that are irrelevant to that purpose?

10.5.2 Thesis

- What is the thesis (main idea, theme) of your paper?
- Do you have a well-specified thesis statement that indicates your stance on the problem and how you will approach the problem? (For discussion of thesis statement, see 5.5 in Chapter 5.)
- Does your paper treat its topic and present itself as promised in your thesis statement?

10.5.3 Audience

- Have you considered the interest and expectation of your audience? (not necessarily your professor personally but perhaps readers with a similar academic background as you or, as the case may be, members of a profession).
- Will they be able to understand you?

10.5.4 Organization

- What are your main points?
- Are they sufficient for the purpose of your paper?
- Does each main point support the thesis?
- Have you presented the main points in a logical sequence so that they help you achieve the purpose of your paper?
- Have you given the right amount of emphasis to different parts of your paper? (e.g., the balance between description and analysis in a research paper, and the balance between material quoted from other sources and your discussion of such material)

10.5.5 Development

- Do you have suitable and sufficient details, examples, and other evidence to support each main point?
- Have you explained or described these items clearly and documented them (recorded details) properly if necessary?

10.5.6 Unity and Coherence

- Is each paragraph unified and coherent so that its focus is clear and that it contributes to the purpose of the paper?
- Are there any non-essential or irrelevant points that should be deleted?

- Are there any parts that are awkwardly written and thus need to be rewritten?
- Are the paragraphs connected logically so that the whole paper is unified and coherent?

10.5.7 *Introduction, Body, and Conclusion*

- Is the length of the introduction just about right to introduce the topic and to engage readers' attention and interest?
- Is the body of the paper substantial enough and well integrated in itself?
- If you are writing a research paper, check the adequacy of each component, including the introduction and literature review, the methods section, the findings section, and the conclusion.
- Have you summarized your main points or main findings clearly in the conclusion?
- Does the conclusion bring everything to a smooth and natural close without leaving any loose ends?
- If yours is a research paper, have you made an effort to discuss the implications arising from your findings?

10.6 Checklist for Editing

Having revised your paper so that its purpose is maintained and its organization is sound, you proceed to re-read and edit it for clarity, correctness, and effectiveness. These are smaller-scale changes compared with revision, with focus on various aspects of language use, but are certainly very important for enhancing the quality of your paper.

When you have a revised draft on the computer, print a copy for editing. Mark the spots where you need corrections, and transfer the corrections onto the computer. Save this as an edited draft while still retaining the revised draft.

10.6.1 *Clarity* (See notes on writing clear and effective sentences in Appendix 7.)

- Are there any confusing, vague words? (Use a dictionary to check words you are not sure of.)
- Make sure there are no run-on sentences and comma splices.
- Are there any misplaced or dangling modifiers?
- Are pronoun references clear?

- If you have used nominalizations (e.g., *we conducted an investigation of this problem*), try rewriting with verbs (e.g., *we studied this problem*) so that actions are clearer and the text is more readable.

10.6.2 Effectiveness (See notes on writing clear and effective sentences in Appendix 7.)

- Avoid using informal or colloquial language (except when quoting conversations); use standard academic English instead.
- Check your choice of words to see if they mean what you want to say. See if they are precise and specific enough for the meaning intended.
- Improve conciseness. Eliminate unneeded repetition, empty words and phrases, and wordy constructions.
- Use transitional markers to ensure smooth connections between ideas.
- Combine sentences so that they are more tightly constructed and important ideas stand out more clearly. Use coordination and subordination tactfully.
- Check use of punctuation as you combine sentences, paying special attention to the possible use of the semicolon, the colon, and dashes for bringing out the effect intended. (See notes on punctuation in Appendix 6.)
- Have you got variety in sentence length and structure?
- Have you used parallel structure to express related ideas so that sentences containing them become more effective?

10.6.3 Correctness

- Are there spelling errors? (Your computer's spellchecker can help, but note whether it uses British or American spelling as standard. Either standard is acceptable, but be consistent.)
- Are there any contractions? Do not use contractions except when quoting conversations.
- Check verb forms. (Note –s and –ed endings and irregular verbs.)
- Check verb tenses, and avoid unjustified shifts in tense.
- Check pronoun forms. (Note, for example, the correct use of subjective and objective forms.)
- Are there errors in subject-verb agreement? (Check especially when a subject is separated from its verb by other words.) (See Appendix 1.)
- Are there errors in agreement between pronouns and their antecedents?
- Are there sentence fragments? If so, try to convert them to complete sentences. (Occasionally, sentence fragments may be used in informal writing to mark a

change in mood or to present a vivid image. Some examples are: *Not so. Quite a job! Too bad, as everybody else got a better deal.* You might use fragments in quoting conversations, but not in the regular text of formal or academic writing.)

- Check if you have misused articles. In particular, watch out for the excessive use of *the*. (See Appendix 4.)

- Are there any non-standard constructions that may be described as "Chinese-English"? (Examples: *I am agree towards this. This makes the public hard to show their critical mind.*)

- If you have in-text citations and a list of references at the end of your paper, check all of them very carefully. Make sure that all cited sources in your text appear in the list of references and that, conversely, all items included in the list of references have been actually cited.

- In-text citation of sources and quotations: Make sure that all citations and quotations are done according to the proper format as indicated in Chapter 7. In particular, check how you indicate author names, year, and page location where needed. For quotations, check whether they are integrated grammatically with your text and whether ellipsis points, if any, are used correctly.

- List of references: Have you prepared your list of references in accordance with all the applicable conventions? Check such matters as alphabetical order of the entries, spacing, punctuation, capitalization, and indentation. You may use the checklist at the end of Chapter 8 for a final check of all the major details.

10.7 Checklist for Proofreading

Proofreading for accuracy follows when you have revised and edited your paper. *Never submit a paper without proofreading it.* Although it is possible to proofread a paper on a computer screen, you are more likely to do a better job if you work on a printed copy of the edited draft. At the end of the proofreading, you will of course save the final draft on the computer and print it once more for submission.

Using a ruler to guide yourself line by line, read the paper *slowly* and *carefully*, preferably aloud so that you will have a better chance of catching errors. Do not overlook the importance of this action: it is quite effective in improving your visual contact with what is on paper. Check the following:

10.7.1 Words and Typographical Errors

- Have you forgotten to delete words that you have moved elsewhere or that you have decided to delete?

- Are there any needed words missing? (They may include words you have decided to add or change during editing.)
- Look for the following kinds of errors:

	What you typed	**What you intended or what you should have**
Transposed letters	*from*	*form*
	causal	*casual*
Missing letters	*accomodation*	*accommodation*
	close-end items	*closed-ended items*
	questionaire	*questionnaire*
Extra letters	*dinning*	*dining*
	ommit	*omit*
	liaisson	*liaison*
Missing or misplaced apostrophes	*McDonald*	*McDonald's*
	childrens' welfare	*children's welfare*

10.7.2 *Punctuation* (See notes on punctuation in Appendix 6 for more details.)

- Make sure that quotation marks, parentheses, and brackets are used in pairs. (You may sometimes forget to put in the closing quotation mark or the right parenthesis when you come to the end of a quote or some parenthetic material.)
- Are there any question marks missing at the end of direct questions?
- Look for comma splices not detected earlier.
- Check that a semicolon is used before a conjunctive adverb (e.g., *however, therefore, moreover*) that introduces a second independent clause after a first one. (*The problem was very serious; however, the government did nothing.*)
- Check that compound adjectives consisting of two or more words are hyphenated when used before a noun (e.g., *above-average performance, hard-working people, hard-to-find evidence, taken-for-granted assumption*).
- Check that the apostrophe is used correctly, especially when forming the possessive of plural nouns (e.g., *children's, members'*) and when indicating joint possession held by two persons (e.g., *Bowles and Gintis' book*).

10.7.3 *Numbers*

Use numbers (numerals or words) according to guidelines set out in Chapter 9 (9.9). You should also consider what is accepted as standard practice in the field you are writing in. The following are just several of the most important general points:

- Spell out numbers smaller than 10 referring not to precise measurements (*three months, five schools,* but *2.5 years, on a scale of 1 to 7*).
- Never begin a sentence with a numeral; always spell out any number that begins a sentence. Alternatively, try to recast your sentence so that it does not start with a number.
- Always use a numeral before the word **per cent** except when beginning a sentence.

10.7.4 Abbreviations

Abbreviations should be used sparingly in your text. Contractions such as *don't* and *it's* should not be used except in quoted conversations.

- Many familiar abbreviations and acronyms are written in capital letters without periods: *UNESCO, USA, ASEAN* (Association of Southeast Asia Nations), *ICAC* (Independent Commission Against Corruption), *IQ, AIDS, WHO, WTO, JP* (Justice of the Peace)
- Latin abbreviations may be used with comments in parentheses and in in-text citations: *i.e., e.g., et al., vs.* (Note the presence of one or two periods in each of these abbreviations.) In your text, do not use these abbreviations but use the English translation of the terms (*i.e.* = that is; *e.g.* = for example; *et al.* = and others; *vs.* = against).
- If you need to abbreviate a term, such as the name of a constructed index, the term must be spelled out in full when it first appears, followed immediately by its abbreviation in parentheses. You may later refer to the term by its abbreviation without further explanation.

10.7.5 Capitalization

The following are a few principles generally applicable:

- Capitalize personal names and initials, names of countries and places, and words that identify nationalities (*Chinese, Japanese*) and ethnic or religious groups (*the Hakkas, Asian-Americans, Christians*).
- Capitalize historical events and periods of time. (*May Fourth Movement, World War II, Cultural Revolution, the Renaissance, the Industrial Revolution*)
- Do not capitalize disciplines unless they are part of a proper noun, such as names of courses or academic departments. (*psychology, psychology students,* but *the Department of Psychology*)
- Capitalization of titles of books, book chapters, and articles may follow

different guidelines from one system to another. Check with the system that you are supposed to adopt. (See Chapter 8 for details.)

10.8 Preparing the Paper for Submission

When you have completed all revisions, editing, and proofreading of your paper, you will put its parts together and prepare the paper in a final form suitable for submission. As a standard practice, your paper should have a title page. In the case of longer papers such as theses and research reports, you may also need to insert a table of contents between the title page and the paper itself to indicate the page location of the main parts of your paper. When all is done, your paper should look neat, tidy, and professional. Use the following checklist to prepare your paper for submission.

10.8.1 Paper

- Use A4 (8.5 in. X 11 in. in North America, slightly shorter and wider than A4) standard white bond paper of 75 g/m^2 (20-pound in North America) weight.
- Do not use coloured paper.

10.8.2 Title Page

- Title page: Place the title (and subtitle, if any) of your paper about a third of the way down the page. Type double-spaced if it takes more than one line. Do not underline, boldface, or enclose it with quotation marks. About an inch below the title, place your name preceded by "By." If you have a student identification number that is regarded as important for confirming your student status, you can place it (just the number itself) double-spaced below your name. After that, starting about three inches below your name (and student ID number if you use it), type the course code and title, your instructor's name, and the date on which the paper is submitted.
- All the items appearing on the title page should be centred.
- Do not underline the title or any item appearing on the title page.
- Do not use ornamental typefaces, including script, and any decorative designs on the title page and any other part of the paper.

10.8.3 Table of Contents (for Long Papers and Theses)

- Print "CONTENTS" (all in capital letters) centred at the top of the table.

- List the parts of the paper (e.g., sections, chapters) with their headings on the left and the page numbers (just numbers without the letter *p*) on the right. Make sure the page numbers are correct.
- Capitalize the headings of chapters or main sections of your paper.
- Use double spacing for the entire table of contents.

10.8.4 Printing and Margins

- Use Times Roman, Times New Roman, or CG Times typefaces (11-point or 12-point font size), which are all highly readable. In principle, use the same typeface throughout your paper.
- For emphasis, you may italicize or underline but not both at the same time.
- Print on only one side of each sheet.
- Paper margins: Are the margins at least one inch on all four sides? If you plan to bind your paper with a binder, the left margin should be widened to 1½ inches.
- Spacing: Have you typed everything double-spaced? (Exceptions apply, such as single spacing for block quotations in ASA style. But APA style requires that block quotations must also be double-spaced.)

10.8.5 Indentation and Pagination

- Paragraph indentation: All paragraphs should be indented 5 to 8 spaces from the left margin. Maintain the same amount of paragraph indentation throughout the paper.
- Page numbering: Number the pages of your paper consecutively from the first text page in the upper right-hand corner. Alternatively, you may print your last name before each page number (so that the authorship of each page is always clearly marked). If there are others with the same last name as yours in your class, use your initials or first name as well. Place the page number at least two lines above the first line of text. You can do this more easily if you use the header feature of your word processing software.
- Page breaks: Avoid leaving the first line of a new paragraph, a heading, or a table title at the bottom of a page. Move it to the next page.
- Tables and figures: Make sure that all tables and figures have an appropriately worded title and that all columns and rows in a table, and all parts of a figure are clearly labelled. Tables and figures are numbered separately. Place each table or figure on a page all by itself immediately after the page that refers to it.

The Rise of the Middle Class in Hong Kong:
Fact or Fiction?

By
Pinky Wai-ling Woo
02654321

SOC 2201 Research Writing
Dr. Pedro Ng
December 5, 2003

A sample title page of a term paper

10.8.6 Final Check for Completeness

If you have followed all the guidelines faithfully in revising, editing, and proofreading, and have prepared the "final" version of your paper properly, your paper should be ready for submission. Just to be safe, however, you should give it a final check to ensure that it is complete: the title page, the table of contents (if necessary), the paper itself (check that all pages are there in the right sequence), and the list of references at the end. Staple your paper at the upper left corner. (Do not use a bent-wire paperclip as the pages may slip out.)

By now, what you have produced should have a reasonably good quality not only in content but also in appearance. It should look neat, sharp, and professional, marking a job well done.

Subject-Verb Agreement

General Remarks

All nouns and pronouns have number as a feature. When the noun or pronoun, as subject of the sentence, is singular, the verb that refers to it is singular; when the noun or pronoun is plural, the verb is plural. This is what we mean by subject-verb agreement.

To ensure that you recognize singular and plural verbs, study some illustrative sentences.

The verbs (including auxiliaries) in the following sentences are all singular verbs since they apply to singular subjects:

Sociology **is** a fascinating subject because it **studies** human social behaviour.

Durkheim's Suicide **was** the first empirical study in sociology.

Communication **becomes** easier with the use of computer technology.

The practice of e-commerce **has** given rise to new legal problems.

What **does** it mean to live in postmodern society?

The verbs (including auxiliaries) in the following sentences are all plural verbs because they apply to plural subjects:

Sociology students **are** all required to study statistics and research methods.

Living conditions in Hong Kong in the 1960s **were** generally much worse than what we **have** now.

We **become** more skilled as we **keep** on practising what we
have learned.

Status and role **are** actually two sides of the same coin.

Do teenagers act purely in response to their peers?

Some Important Principles

1. The verb agrees with the head (the main word) of the noun phrase preceding it.

    A **catalogue** of courses and requirements often **looks**
    (not **look**) confusing to students.

    The **changes** in Hong Kong society in the past three decades
    have been spectacular.

    A **list** of references **is** given at the end of the article.

2. Compound subjects usually take plural verbs.

    Durkheim and Weber **were** contemporaries.

    Weber and Marx **recognize** the economic aspect of
    stratification.

    2.1 But such phrases as **as well as**, **together with**, **in addition to** do not
         change the number of the subject:

         Weber, as well as Marx, **recognizes** the economic aspect
         of stratification.

         (Here, we do not really have a compound subject because the phrase **as
         well as Marx** is not part of the subject.)

         This **article**, together with the one distributed
         earlier, **explains** how documentation is done.

    2.2 When a compound subject is preceded by **each** or **every**, the verb is
         singular:

         Each student interest group and departmental organi-
         zation **has** to register with the university.

         However, a compound subject followed by **each** takes a plural verb:

```
The supervisor and her subordinate each have
different problems.
```

2.3   When parts of a compound subject are joined by **or** or **nor**, the verb agrees
      with the nearer part:

```
Neither he nor his friend is ready to take the test
today.
```

```
The chairman or his assistants are authorized to
issue work instructions.
```

3.   Most indefinite pronouns have a singular sense and therefore take a singular
     verb. (Some common indefinite pronouns with a singular sense are: **anybody,
     anyone, everybody, everyone, everything, nobody, nothing, one, somebody,
     someone, something**.)

```
Practically everybody in this neighbourhood goes to
work by the MTR.
```

```
Nothing describes the social nature of the self as
vividly as Cooley's notion of the "looking glass self."
```

```
Something unusual is happening in this organization.
```

```
One does not always know what one is doing.
```

4.   **All**, **any**, **some**, **most**. These quantity words have a singular sense when used
     with uncount nouns and a plural sense when used with plural count nouns.

```
Plural:    All citizens are expected to pay tax.
Singular:  All that discussion is nothing but empty talk.
```

```
Plural:    Any important decisions of the group have to
           have consultation with its members.
Singular:  There is no sign of any progress that is likely
           to resolve the conflict.
```

```
Plural:    After retirement, some people are uncertain
           about how to spend their time.
Singular:  Anxiety about how to spend their time is a
           common feeling among the retired; however,
           some of this feeling is actually unjustified.
```

Plural :   **Most** measures of socioeconomic status **include**
              income or education.

Singular :   **Most** of people's leisure time **is** spent on
              watching television.

5. **Who**, **which**, and **that** in relative clauses take verbs that agree with their antecedents. When you use **who**, **which**, and **that** to introduce a relative clause, these words refer to another word appearing earlier, called the *antecedent*. The verb should agree with the antecedent.

> The **costs** of emigrating to another society, **which are** measured in many ways, can be fearfully high.

> Any **student who takes** this course as an elective is putting in a great deal of effort.

6. **One of, the only one of, a number of, the number of**

6.1 The phrase **one of** is followed by plural count nouns. The verb used is plural in (a), but singular in (b) and (c):

(a) Wong is **one of the students who are** taking this course.

(b) Teresa is **the only one of the students who knows** who Erving Goffman is.

(c) **One of** the students **knows** the answer to this question.

6.2 The word **number** may be singular or plural in sense. Preceded by **a**, it is plural; preceded by **the**, it is singular.

> **A number of sociology students are** interested in improving their writing skills.

> **The number of students** who need to improve their writing skills **is** quite large.

7. When the verb **be** is used to link a subject to a complement (word or phrase that provides further information about the subject)**,** the linking verb agrees with its subject, not the subject complement.

> One **reason** for his success **is** his friends. (**His friends** is the subject complement.)

His **friends are** one reason for his success. (**One reason for his success** is the subject complement.)

The **cause** of downward mobility **is** market conditions.

Market conditions are the cause of downward mobility.

8. Inverted subject-verb order.

8.1 Sometimes the verb **be** comes before, instead of after, the subject. This occurs when you start a sentence with **There + be**. The verb **be** must agree with the subject (the head word if the subject contains a noun phrase):

There **is** a well-written **article** on universities as places of consumption.

There **are** many different **views** on this issue.

8.2 When you use the present perfect tense in a construction starting with **There**, you say **There has been** when the subject is singular and **There have been** when the subject is plural:

There **has been** little **attention** paid to the social significance of leisure.

There **have been** many **studies** done on the determinants of achievement.

8.3 Inverted subject-verb order also occurs when you write questions starting with **wh**-words (**what, where, when, why**), e.g., **What + be.** The verb **be** must agree with the subject (the head word if the subject contains a noun phrase):

What **is** the author's real **message**?

What **are** his **reasons** for not acting as requested?

8.4 The same principle governs **wh**-words followed by **have/has. Have/has** must agree with the subject:

What impact **has the Internet** brought to social life?

Why **have most of his followers** rejected him?

9. Nouns plural in form but singular in meaning take singular verbs.

9.1   Some words ending in **-s** (e.g., **economics**, **news**, **politics**, and **dynamics**) are actually singular in meaning:

> `Economics is` `one of the social sciences.`
>
> `Statistics is` `a course that many social science students need to take in their studies.`
>
> `It is not too exaggerating to say that` `politics is` `present in all organizations.`

9.2   Measurements and figures ending in **-s** may also be singular when the quantity they refer to is a unit.

> `Three years is` `really not a long time for university education.`
>
> `Three-quarters` `of this library's collection` `consists` `of reference books.`

10.   Collective nouns take singular or plural verbs depending on meaning.

10.1   When the group named by the collective noun acts as one unit, use a singular verb.

> `The` `committee decides` `who will take up this task.`
>
> `Our` `group believes` `that we should support such a noble cause wholeheartedly.`

10.2   When the collective noun refers to group members as individuals and their separate actions within a group, use a plural verb.

> `The` `audience have` `various reactions to the performance.`
>
> `Our` `family do` `not agree on where to take the next summer vacation.`
>
> `The` `committee` `have not come to any clear decision.`

11.   Phrases and clauses that function as subjects are treated as singular and take singular verbs.

> `To write well is` `an essential skill for professionals.`

> **That the two sides are willing to sit down and talk
> is** a good sign.
>
> **How much we understand depends** on our willingness to
> pursue knowledge.
>
> **What the survey results mean for policy has** to be
> considered carefully.

Exercise A

Use the correct form of the given verb in the following sentences.

1.   Sociology as one of the social science disciplines (have) _____ a history
     of about one and a half centuries.

2.   The structures of social life (include) _____ the relationships maintained
     by people.

3.   Our thinking about vacations (be) _____ filled with ideas of consumption.

4.   Interaction between strangers under certain conditions (tend) _____ to be
     ritualized.

5.   Values and norms (be) _____ perhaps the most important cultural ideas.

6.   What (do) _____ modernity and postmodernity have in common?

7.   Conflict theory, as well as functionalism, (treat) _____ society as a social
     system.

8.   Position in a group, together with the rights and privileges associated with the
     position, (form) _____ the basis on which interaction with others occurs.

9.   Members of this group each (have) _____ the same number of tasks to
     perform.

10. Each voluntary agency (have) _____ its own service programme.

11. In reviewing the relevant literature, there is no point in trying to examine everything that (have) _____ been written on the subject.

12. Anyone who (claim) _____ to be a sociologist must have read Weber.

13. All the negotiation between the two parties so far (have) _____ been a waste of time.

14. All values (be) _____ ideas about what is good or bad.

15. Any progress (be) _____ better than no progress.

16. (Be) _____ there any supporters of this view in the audience?

17. Some people (be) _____ more concerned with their rights than their obligations.

18. Some of the misunderstanding between parents and children (result) _____ from lack of communication.

19. Most institutions of higher education (place) _____ great emphasis on the training of professionals.

20. Most of people's energy (be) _____ spent not on self development but on acquisition of wealth.

Exercise B

Use the correct form of the given verb in the following sentences.

1. The rate of natural increase, which (be) _____ calculated as the birth rate minus the death rate, may look like a harmless small number.

2. Any student who (have) _____ read Mills ought to know the difference between "issues" and "troubles."

3. Euthanasia is one of those issues that (involve) _____ complicated moral and social considerations.

1. This is the only one of the university's rules that (allow) _____ students to take less than three years to graduate.

2. One of the articles reviewed (take) _____ a very different view of the problem.

3. One motivating force behind her achievement (be) _____ her parents.

4. The consequence of non-compliance (be) _____ less desirable customer relations.

5. There (be) _____ no further news about the establishment of private universities.

6. There (be) _____ a large variety of theories of social development.

7. Do you think there (be) _____ enough examples given in this article to illustrate the author's point?

8. Seeing the operation of social relations on different levels (be)_____ important for recognizing some of the different roles played by the mass media.

9. What influences (have) _____ the computer brought to our daily life?

10. Four years (be) _____ perhaps a more appropriate length of university study.

11. That we could retrieve so much information about so many different topics (indicate) _____ the power of the Internet.

12. In the 1950s, television (be) _____ marketed to women as something they could enjoy at the same time as they (be) _____ doing housework.

13. A number of reasons for the launching of the new benefits scheme (be) _____ given by the company director.

14. "Diploma mill" universities in the West, which cannot capture a sizeable portion of the higher education market there, (have) _____ expanded overseas with distance education programmes.

15. To be able to write well (require) _____ a heightened awareness of the importance of grammar and a willingness to read with involvement.

Using the Correct Word Form: Verbs, Nouns, Adjectives

Verbs, nouns, and adjectives are among the most often-used words in writing. (Together with adverbs, they account for the bulk of the vocabulary used in practically any kind of writing.) Your sentences will read well and will be more easily understood if you use words correctly. If, however, you use them incorrectly, such as using a noun when you should be using an adjective, your sentence will sound strange and interfere with understanding.

Look at the following sentence. What is wrong with it?

```
Interpretation is more convenience if we focus on the
main findings.
```

Obviously, the word **convenience** (noun) should be **convenient** (adjective) in the sentence. It modifies **interpretation** there. The sentence should therefore read:

```
Interpretation is more convenient if we focus on the
main findings.
```

Now see if you can spot the error in this sentence:

```
Do you know how to analysis the nature of news?
```

The phrase that starts with **how to** should remind you that what follows ought to be a verb (such as **how to remember**, **how to write**, **how to study**). But is **analysis** a verb? Certainly not. **Analysis** is a noun. You see the noun form of the word in such phrases as **analysis of social systems** and **analysis of poverty as a social problem**. You should note that **analysis** is often followed by **of**. The verb is **analyze** (AmE) or **analyse** (BrE). The corrected sentence should read:

```
Do you know how to analyze the nature of news?
```

Alternatively, you could change it to the following if you must use the noun form:

```
Do  you  know  how  to  do  an  analysis  of  the  nature  of
news?
```

This is more wordy and sounds a bit less direct in indicating what you mean. By comparison, the sentence that uses **analyze** is shorter and more direct. But do not take this to mean that using the verb form of a word is necessarily better than using the noun form. It depends on what you want to say. Compare, again, for example:

```
The  way  he  analyzes  the  problem  is  quite  different.

His  analysis  of  the  problem  is  quite  different.
```

Doesn't the second sentence, which uses the noun form, sound more direct now? But before you can choose between these constructions, you must first be able to identify the word form correctly and use the right one in your sentence.

The message, then, is that you should learn the different forms of a word. Recognize them visually, memorize their spelling (which is often different) and learn to use them correctly. Next time when you look up a word in the dictionary, be sure to check its part of speech (word form) and study any example sentences given there so that you will see clearly how the word is used.

It will be helpful if you collect certain words that are often used, and enter them into a table under the headings of *verb, noun,* and *adjective.* You can add a fourth one, *adverb*, if you like. Use a good dictionary to check the spelling and the part of speech. Not every word has all three or four forms.

Sometimes, there may be more than one word for a given form (e.g., **satisfied**, **satisfactory**, and **satisfying** are all adjectives). Where this is the case, you should learn to distinguish the differences in meaning and use by consulting your dictionary and studying its example sentences. If you do not do this, you will not understand these words well enough to use them correctly. (Thus, for example, if a waitress serves you well, you as a customer are **satisfied** with her **satisfactory** service. If the food is delightful and good, you will have a **satisfying** meal.)

The following is an example of such a table. Since it is an example, only a small number of words are included to give you a general idea.

Verb	Noun	Adjective
analyze	*analysis*	*analytical*
benefit	*benefit*	*beneficial*
compete	*competition*	*competitive*
differ	*difference*	*different*

Verb	Noun	Adjective
familiarize	*familiarity*	*familiar*
generalize	*generality* *generalization*	*general*
occur	*occurrence*	------
perceive	*perception*	*perceivable* *perceptible* *perceptive*
resist	*resistance*	*resistant*
separate	*separation*	*separate* *separated*
strengthen	*strength*	*strong* *strengthened*
succeed	*success*	*successful*
think	*thinking* *thought*	*thinkable* *thoughtful*

Exercise

Select the correct word to complete the following sentences.

1. Quiz shows have tremendous _____ for audiences because the shows offer large amounts of prize money to winners.
    A.   attractive
    B.   attract
    C.   attraction
    D.   attractment

2. It is many people's _____ that thirteen is an unlucky number.
    A.   believe
    B.   beliefs
    C.   believing
    D.   belief

3. Journal articles are now easily _____ on the Internet.
    A. accessable
    B. accessible
    C. accessing
    D. access

4. Citizens are becoming less _____ about the effectiveness of the government.
    A. confidence
    B. confidential
    C. confident
    D. confide

5. _____ behaviour is behaviour that departs from what social norms prescribe.
    A. Deviance
    B. Deviant
    C. Deviate
    D. Deviation

6. We were very _____ to hear that the Department will place greater emphasis on students' learning skills.
    A. exciting
    B. excitement
    C. excited
    D. excitedly

7. It is quite _____ how people can act under group pressure in ways contrary to their own preference.
    A. surprise
    B. surprised
    C. surprising
    D. surprisingly

8. With knowledge of statistics, you should be able to _____ the relationship between two variables.
    A. analyze
    B. analysis
    C. analyzed
    D. analyzing

9. In primary relationships, much _____ is placed on expressiveness rather than instrumentality.
    A. emphasize
    B. emphatic
    C. emphasized
    D. emphasis

10. That the two conflicting sides are willing to meet and present their views is a rather _____ sign.
    A. encourage
    B. encouraging
    C. encouragement
    D. encouraged

11. Interview surveys are more likely than mailed questionnaire surveys to elicit a higher _____ rate.
    A. respond
    B. responds
    C. responses
    D. response

12. In reviewing the relevant literature for a research paper, we should select sources that are particularly _____ in lending support to our theme.
    A. significant
    B. significance
    C. significantly
    D. signify

13. After 1997, the government of Hong Kong has actively _____ reforms in education with, however, limited success.
    A. pursuit
    B. pursue
    C. pursued

14. To start a project is not too difficult; to _____ in it is.
    A. success
    B. successful
    C. succeed
    D. succeeding

15. In explaining the cause of suicide, Durkheim _____ the role of social integration or the lack of it.
    A. emphasis
    B. emphases
    C. emphasize
    D. emphasized

16. That two variables are correlated is no _____ that one is a cause of the other.
    A. proof
    B. proofs
    C. prove
    D. proves

17. As Berger reminds us so clearly, we must know how a sociological problem _____ from what many people call a "social problem."
    A. different
    B. difference
    C. differs
    D. differ

18. We need only to observe carefully what we do every day to assert that our family, our friends, our colleagues, and others who serve us in various transactions all place some degree of _____ on our actions.
    A. constrain
    B. constraint
    C. constrains
    D. constraining

19. Concepts are tools that _____ analysis and understanding.
    A. facility
    B. facilitate
    C. facilitating
    D. facilitation

20. After a long and tedious process of negotiation, management and employee representatives worked out modifications of the employment terms that were _____ to both sides.
    A. satisfy
    B. satisfied
    C. satisfaction
    A. satisfactory

Uncount Nouns, Variable Nouns, and Plural Nouns

Uncount Nouns

Uncount nouns refer to qualities, processes, and ideas that are not normally counted or treated as individual items. They do not have a plural form and are used with a singular verb (e.g., **is, has, exists, continues**). They are not used with the indefinite article **a** or **an**.

advice   Parental **advice plays** a less important role as children are growing up.

progress   Slowly but surely, **progress** towards some kind of agreement **is** developing between the two conflicting parties.

knowledge   **Knowledge has** long been regarded as the basis of power and influence.

Other examples of uncount nouns:

beauty	confidence	education	equipment	information
news	patience	peace	survival	suitability
tact	unemployment	vulnerability	wastage	

Variable Nouns

Many nouns can have countable use in some contexts and uncountable use in others. When used as uncount nouns, they refer to abstract things such as **democracy** and **truth**. When used as count nouns, they refer to particular varieties or individual instances of that thing (thus use of the indefinite article **a** or **an** is possible).

democracy   The unification of Germany and the dissolution of the Soviet Union represented the spread of **democracy** in Europe. (Uncount)

Indonesia is one of the new **democracies** facing great challenge today. (Count)

truth   Some people find it difficult to distinguish between **truth** and hearsay. (Uncount)

Parkinson's law points to a **truth** about the way organizations operate. (Count)

Other examples of variable nouns:

behaviour	**comfort**	**concern**	**conflict**	**contact**
environment	**experience**	**performance**	**power**	**reaction**
reality	**research**	**strength**	**status**	**youth**

Plural Nouns

Plural nouns are nouns used only in the plural form with a particular meaning. (If used in the singular, the meaning is not quite the same.) They are used with plural verbs (e.g., **are**, **have**, **become**). If you use a pronoun to stand for a plural noun, it must be a plural pronoun (e.g., **they**, **them**).

authorities   The university **authorities** have decided to step up their efforts to strengthen students' language skills.

details   We have yet to work on the **details** of a plan to improve our bargaining power.

resources   Human **resources** are what a society must develop to improve its economic strength.

Other examples of plural nouns and phrases in which they may occur:

basics	*(the basics of writing a proposal)*
conditions	*(changing social conditions)*
contents	*(the contents of a book)*
essentials	*(the essentials of learning)*

feelings	*(having mixed feelings)*
goods	*(goods and services tax)*
interests	*(acting in the best interests of somebody)*
matters	*(doing something to improve matters)*
means	*(living within one's means)*
particulars	*(information concerning personal particulars)*
politics	*(the internal politics of higher education)*
relations	*(international relations)*
spirits	*(in high spirits)*
terms	*(the terms of employment)*

CAUTION

Some nouns ending in **-s**, seemingly plural in form, are in fact uncount nouns. They must be used with singular verbs.

civics   **economics**   **electronics** (as a technology)   **ethics** (as a study)
politics (as a study)   **statistics** (as a study, not figures)

news   `News is` constructed in social contexts.

ethics   `Ethics is` the study of what constitutes morally
right and wrong behaviour.

But **ethics** in the sense of a person's moral principles is a plural noun, as used in the following sentence:

> His professional **ethics** as a doctor **dictate** that
> saving lives has priority over everything else. (Note
> the use of the plural verb **dictate**.)

You may also come across **ethic** in the singular form when it means a system of moral behaviour, as in Weber's study of capitalism and the Protestant ethic.

We also refer to people's **work ethic**, **leisure ethic**, and the **ethic of public service** found in a community. In these expressions, **ethic** is a singular noun. It cannot have a plural form and is used in a singular sense.

Exercise

In each of the following pairs of sentences, identify the correct sentence.

1. (a) We can collect many informations from the Internet.
   (b) We can collect many pieces of information from the Internet.

2. (a) Middle class families can afford to have all kinds of equipments in their household.
   (b) Middle class families can afford to have all kinds of equipment in their household.

3. (a) Finding a decent job is of great concern to many young people.
   (b) Finding a decent job is of great concerns to many young people.

4. (a) Statuses are often compared and ranked by people of any society.
   (b) Status is often compared and ranked by people of any society.

5. (a) Because of his accomplishments, Mr. Chan is a person of high statuses.
   (b) Because of his accomplishments, Mr. Chan is a person of high status.

6. (a) In a time of economic downturn, it is not surprising to find many unemployments.
   (b) In a time of economic downturn, it is not surprising to find much unemployment.

7. (a) News have great influence on readers.
   (b) News has great influence on readers.

8. (a) Many Hong Kong people are discussing the integration of new immigrants into their society.
   (b) Many Hong Kong people are discussing the integrations of new immigrants into their society.

9. (a) Modern life style is actually endangering the environment.
   (b) Modern life style is actually endangering the environments.

10. (a) Characters are formed not by heredity but by environments.
    (b) Characters are formed not by heredity but by environment.

11. (a) To grow up well, children need happy home environment.
    (b) To grow up well, children need a happy home environment.

12. (a) What do you have to say in reaction to China's joining the WTO?
    (b) What do you have to say in a reaction to China's joining the WTO?

13. (a) She described to us one of her most memorable experience as a university student.
    (b) She described to us one of her most memorable experiences as a university student.

14. (a) The youth is a time of rapid growth and development.
    (b) Youth is a time of rapid growth and development.

15. (a) A labour union is supposed to act in the best interest of workers.
    (b) A labour union is supposed to act in the best interests of workers.

16. (a) The relations between China and the USA have been going through ups and downs.
    (b) The relation between China and the USA has been going through ups and downs.

17. (a) The conditions are now favourable for the establishment of a new department to promote the performing arts.
    (b) The condition is now favourable for the establishment of a new department to promote the performing arts.

18. (a) First we shall set up an overall outline, and then we shall look into the details.
    (b) First we shall set up an overall outline, and then we shall look into the detail.

19. (a) Lawyers' professional ethics requires them to keep their clients' case material strictly confidential.
    (b) Lawyers' professional ethics require them to keep their clients' case material strictly confidential.

20. (a) People who do not live within their mean will run into serious trouble.
    (b) People who do not live within their means will run into serious trouble.

21. (a) Like a book, a thesis should have a page that contains a table of contents.
    (b) Like a book, a thesis should have a page that contains a table of content.

22. (a) All social science students must take statistic as a required course.
    (b) All social science students must take statistics as a required course.

23. (a) As sample size increases, the value of the obtained chi-square statistics also increases.
    (b) As sample size increases, the value of the obtained chi-square statistic also increases.

24. (a) Whether nuclear weapons should be banned completely is a question of ethics.
    (b) Whether nuclear weapons should be banned completely is a question of ethic.

25. (a) Plagiarism is behaviour that involves the ethic of academic honesty.
    (b) Plagiarism is behaviour that involves the ethics of academic honesty.

Use of Articles

The Indefinite Article: a/an

The Definite Article: the

The Zero Article: No Article Is Used

The proper use of articles (**a/an**, **the**, and **zero article**) in English is a skill not easily mastered by students for whom English is not a first language. Improper use of articles (in particular, the indiscriminate use of **the**) is one of the most conspicuous deficiencies in their writing. Learn to use articles correctly, and your writing will read more smoothly and naturally.

Articles are words we use before nouns or noun phrases to indicate the kind of reference or meaning intended:

I have **a plan.** (some plan, but we do not know which one)

Is this **the plan** you have been working on? (we now know which one)

Plans are always necessary for greater efficiency. (a general statement)

A or **an**? **A** is used with words that begin with a consonant sound (remember: not letter):

a plan   **a concept**   **a game**   **a university**
a usual routine (as in **university, u** in **usual** is pronounced [ju], a consonant sound)

An is used with words that begin with a vowel sound:

an event   **an idea**   **an hour** (silent h)   **an honest** (silent h) **person**
an organization   **an unusual arrangement**   **an answer**

To help you understand the basics, let me draw your attention to three considerations governing the use or non-use of articles:

1.   The kind of noun used
2.   General or particular meaning
3.   Definite or indefinite reference.

1.   The Kind of Noun Used

1.1   The indefinite article **a/an** can only be used with singular count (countable) nouns:

a group   a problem   a value   an idea   an organization

1.2   The definite article **the** can be used with all kinds of nouns:

the group   the problem   the value   the values   the idea
the ideas   the organization   the organizations   (all count nouns)

the confidence   the cooperation   the patience   the knowledge
the progress   the resistance   the worth   (all uncount nouns)

1.3   The zero article is used with

(a) plural count nouns: **groups   problems   values   ideas**
organizations   people   phenomena   decisions
rules   consequences   effects

(b) uncount nouns: **confidence   cooperation   patience   knowledge**
progress   resistance   worth   information
evidence   advice   news

1.4   Never use **a/an** with uncount nouns.

We CANNOT say: **a confidence   a cooperation   a news**
an advice   a knowledge

However, when we have a noun phrase containing not only an uncount noun but also a count noun that becomes the main word of the phrase, we can put **a/an** before the main word.

Thus, **vote**, **instance**, **item**, and **piece** are all main words in the following phrases. Note that we can insert an adjective between **a/an** and the main word if needed. We CAN say:

a vote of confidence	**a strong vote of confidence**
an instance of cooperation	**a rare instance of cooperation**
an item of news	**an important item of news**
a piece of advice	**a valuable piece of advice**

1.5   Normally a singular count noun is preceded by either the indefinite article, the definite article, or some other determiner (e.g., **any**, **this**, **another**, **each**, **every**), but there are some exceptions. Certain nouns in expressions involving time, place, and movement are used without articles:

at night	**finish school**	**enter university**	**in class**
at work	**out of town**	**by train**	**on foot**
go home after school		**by phone**	**by fax**

2.   Particular Meaning

2.1   Particular meaning is expressed when we refer to particular, or specific, individual entities (objects, persons, ideas) rather than things in general or classes of things.

2.2   In referring to particular entities, we need to distinguish between definite reference and indefinite reference. Definite reference is used when the reader can identify the things or persons referred to (as in sentence (a) below). That is, the reader can tell which thing or person is referred to. By contrast, indefinite reference is used if the reader cannot identify them (as in sentence (b)).

(a) This is **the** student who has surpassed all others in the test.
(The **who**-clause indicates the identity of the **student**.)

(b) Some students have failed the test.
(Although we know that certain individual students have failed the test, we cannot tell who they are.)

2.3   **Particular meaning with definite reference**

2.3.1   Use **the** to indicate which one(s) we mean:

(a)   Back-pointing use of **the** (to refer to things or persons mentioned before)

First you select a destination and a travel
agency; then you go to **the agency** to ask for
information about **the destination**.

Sometimes you start with a good idea, but later
find that **the idea** is really too complex to
write about in a short paper.

(b)   Forward-pointing use of **the**

This is **the document** that has caused so much
controversy.

We are disappointed by **the response** the
legislator gave to our query.

Nobody is interested in **the story** about how
he came to power.

What is **the main feature** of the sociological
imagination that Mills discusses?

The opinions of others can affect how we see
ourselves.

2.3.2   Use **the** to refer to the only one(s) in existence (assuming our reader
understands what is referred to from general knowledge or from
knowledge of the situation concerned):

the digital age	the tourism industry	the arms race
the China market	the Internet	the West
the United Nations	the WHO (World Health Organization)	
the United States	the United Kingdom	the Renaissance
the Industrial Revolution	the May Fourth Movement	

The world has become much smaller because of the
convenience of communication.

After encountering so much criticism from
citizens, **the Government** has to consider adopting
new and better policies.

The Chief Executive is keen on improving the image
of Hong Kong.

> Sociologists are in a very good position to study
> the social impact of **the Internet.**
>
> Relations between the United States and Russia
> have improved greatly after the end of **the cold
> war.**

2.4 Particular meaning with indefinite reference

Use **a/an** or an indefinite determiner (e.g., **some, several, many, most, no**) to refer to certain individual entities (objects, persons, ideas) without really identifying which one(s):

> I came across **an interesting study** of tourism in a locally
> published journal.
>
> Everyone is looking for **a satisfactory solution** to this
> problem.
>
> You need to include **some discussion** of related issues
> toward the conclusion of your essay.
>
> **Some political leaders** speak of promoting **a society** of
> caring citizens.
>
> He had **several happy surprises** after joining the company.
>
> **No sensible person** would believe that the media can really
> print anything they want.

3.   General Meaning (All forms of the article may be used)

3.1 When we write not about particular or individual entities but about entities in general or about whole classes, we are expressing general meaning. Since the emphasis is on generalities or whole classes, the distinction between definite meaning (identifying which ones) and indefinite meaning (not identifying which ones) becomes unimportant.

> (a) **the: The university** is a place of higher learning.
>
> (b) **a: A university** is a place of higher learning.

    (c) **zero article: Universities** are places of higher learning.

Essentially the same general meaning is expressed in the above three sentences. Please note, however, that reference is to all universities generally as a kind of institution in (a) **the university** and in (c) **universities**, whereas reference is to *any* university in (b) **a university**.

3.2   Use zero article with an uncount noun or a plural count noun. This is the most natural way of expressing general or generic meaning.

> **Cooperation** between **management** and **workers** is necessary to minimize **industrial disputes**. (**Cooperation** and **management** are uncount nouns; **workers** and **disputes** are plural count nouns.)

> Both **employers** and **employees** are equally concerned about the Mandatory Provident Fund scheme.

3.3   Less commonly, we can use **the** with a singular count noun to indicate a generic class:

> **The primary group** is the most basic kind of collectivity.

As a statement that defines or classifies something, it is about the same in meaning as:

> **Primary groups** are the most basic kind of collectivity.

> **A primary group** is the most basic kind of collectivity.

Similarly, the following three sentences are similar in meaning:

> **The church** is an organization.

> **Churches** are organizations.

> **A church** is an organization.

3.4   Also less commonly, we use **a/an** with a singular count noun to make a generic phrase. Two examples (**a primary group**, **a church**) were given in 3.3; here is another example in which the generic phrase is used to define or classify something:

> **An opinion poll** conducted properly is supposed to be
> reliable.
> (=**Opinion polls** conducted properly are supposed to be
> reliable.)
> (=**The opinion poll** conducted properly is supposed to
> be reliable.)

But since **a** means "any," its use in some contexts cannot adequately express generic meaning, as when the statement is not used to define or classify something. In such a statement, we cannot use **a/an** in front of the noun.

We can say:

> **The computer** has brought pervasive changes to society.
>
> **Computers** have brought pervasive changes to society.

But not:

> **A computer** has brought pervasive changes to society.
> (Not acceptable)

3.5 Use **the** with certain adjectives (behaving as nouns) to refer to classes of people:

the rich	**the poor**	**the young**	**the old** **the religious**
the healthy	**the sick**	**the privileged**	**the deprived**
the better-educated		**the highly trained**	

> One often-heard criticism of the economy is that the
> gap between **the rich** and **the poor** is widening.

3.6 Use **the** with group nouns to refer to collectivities or aggregates taken as wholes:

the public	**the audience**	**the administration**	**the middle class**
the state	**the government** (to be distinguished from **the Government** or		

just **Government**, both indicating particular meaning)

> When the economy declines, people tend to blame it on
> **the government**.

3.7 Use **zero article** with **society** when it means "the society that we as human beings all live in." That is, **society** takes no article when it is used as a general and abstract idea that can include any society we can think of.

What is the relationship between **society** and the individual? (Notice that **the individual** refers to the entire class of human individuals.)

As concepts, culture and **society** are actually two sides of the same coin.

3.8 Use **the** with nouns that refer to our physical environment or to stereotypes or institutions that are part of our shared social world or our common experience.

the climate	**the weather**	**the future**	**the past**
the environment	**the media**	**the news**	**the cinema**
the city	**the bank**	**the paparazzi**	

Reports of the election will be in **the paper** tomorrow.

With the popularity of video rentals, people are going to **the cinema** less often.

Part of our social greeting is some brief talk about **the weather**.

People in North America like to live in **the suburbs**.

Exercise

Fill in the blanks with **a/an** or **the** if necessary and appropriate. If no article is needed, write **nil**.

1. Sociology offers _____ perspective or _____ view of _____ world.
                     (1)   (2)   (3)

2. _____ sociological perspective opens _____ window onto _____ unfamiliar
      (4)   (5)   (6)

    worlds and offers _____ fresh look at familiar worlds.
                      (7)

3. _____ social sciences examine _____ human relationships.
      (8)   (9)

4.   _____ scientists have to examine _____ evidence with _____ open mind.
        (10)   (11)   (12)

5.   So that we can interpret _____ facts, we must put them in _____ framework
                                            (13)   (14)

     called _____ theory.
                (15)

6.   Culture provides _____ lens through which we see _____ world and obtain our
                              (16)   (17)

     perception of _____ reality.
                        (18)

7.   _____ anthropologists tell us that our modern ideas about _____ privacy were
        (19)   (20)

     not present in_____ ancient and primitive societies.
                        (21)

8.   _____ television has become _____ inseparable companion for most people in
        (22)   (23)

     _____ home.
        (24)

9.   It is quite common for _____ university students to save enough money
                                    (25)

     working at _____ various jobs for about two months in _____ summer for
                    (26)   (27)

     _____ trip afterwards that may take up to _____ month.
        (28)   (29)

10. Individual access to _____ Internet has created _____ concern about _____ use
                              (30)   (31)   (32)

of cyberspace for _____ unregulated spread of pornography.
          (33)

11. _____ factories for textiles developed in _____early nineteenth century; it was
      (34)   (35)

_____ factory that made _____ new city.
 (36)   (37)

12. Rationalization involves _____ emphasis on _____ things that can be calculated
                              (38)   (39)

and quantified.

13. Some of _____ most troublesome ethical dilemmas have resulted from _____
             (40)   (41)

integration of _____ computers and _____ digital technology.
               (42)   (43)

14. With _____ advanced technologies, _____ modern shopping malls operate with
          (44)   (45)

such great uniformity that there is overall _____ unreal perfection about them.
                                             (46)

15. Of _____ special sense-organs, _____ eye has _____ uniquely sociological
        (47)   (48)   (49)

function: _____ union and interaction of _____ individuals is based on _____
          (50)   (51)   (52)

mutual glances.

Verb Tenses in Research Papers

General Remarks

Verbs are "action" words that give "flesh and blood" to your writing. Thus, you should treat verbs and their tenses with great care.

If you take a close look at verbs appearing in many social science articles or book chapters, chances are that you will find three tenses used more often than others. They are the simple present tense, the present perfect tense, and the simple past tense. But you should also be familiar with the present progressive and the past perfect tenses as they may sometimes be used, if conditions are appropriate.

Simple Present Tense

The simple present tense is frequently used in writing that describes and discusses concepts, ideas, and problems. Such description and discussion often include general statements concerning individuals, groups, or organizations taken to be true or applicable without any time constraint. The following are examples not taken from any particular source but are typical of sociological writing:

> The self **is** a notion that the individual **acquires** and **develops** in the course of living and communicating with others.

> Society and culture **are** like two sides of the same coin.

> As organizations **become** increasingly complex in structure, work procedures **need** to be formalized and standardized to ensure efficiency.

Curriculum reforms usually **reflect** changes in manpower requirements of the economy.

Weber **distinguishes** between charismatic, traditional, and legitimate forms of authority which **exist** in different combinations in a given society.

Present Perfect Tense

The present perfect tense is used when we refer to an action or event that has taken place over some period of time in the recent past. Of course, "the recent past" need not be specifically defined or indicated in the writing. In a way, the action or event in question is examined from the time of writing or the time when the writing is read. What the writer means to say is something like this: "It (the action or event) has been this way up to now." Study the following examples:

Sociologists **have studied** organizations for decades and **have found** much support for the contingency theory.

Different researchers **have come** to contrary conclusions.

Functionalist theory **has been criticized** for its over-emphasis on consensus.

Public activities such as going to the movies **have,** to some extent, **been replaced** by watching television or videos which we usually experience in the privacy of our homes.

As you can see from the examples given above, you may use the present perfect tense when you examine what researchers have done or found or how some problem has been treated. You do this typically when you review the relevant literature in a research paper. The present perfect tense may also be used in writing about social trends and their effects.

This does not mean, of course, that only the present perfect tense is used in reviewing the literature or describing social change. Sometimes, as you are in the present tense mode, it is quite appropriate to use the present perfect tense to state an antecedent action or trend, as in the following sentences:

The emergence of the Internet **has changed** the way we

live and **do** business. No one and no organization can really afford to ignore such change because, like it or not, it **has penetrated** into our lives.

Our data indicate that teachers of most schools in our study **have not prepared** themselves sufficiently when they **switch** to the new teaching method.

Present Progressive Tense

When you describe a phenomenon that is happening now and is likely to continue, the present progressive (continuous) tense is what you need:

The Internet **is becoming** an important part of our daily life. Children **are growing** up as the "Net generation" whose socialization experiences are vastly different from those of their parents many of whom **are trying** hard to be familiar with what they can do with the Internet.

Simple Past Tense

Sometimes we need to bring in the simple past tense to refer to actions or events that occurred in the past, even when the present tense is used elsewhere. Study the following passage written for this appendix:

Environmental protection **was** not an issue and **did** not even appear in the local language before the intro-duction of wireless television in Hong Kong in the late 1960s. The development of mass communication over the past three decades or so **has changed** all that. Through mass communication in its many forms, people **have** access to all sorts of information and ideas. In this process, new words and phrases **take** hold at the same time as attitudes and behaviour **change**. Whereas few people in the 1950s and 1960s ever seriously **thought** of the needs of the environment, almost every-one **is** now familiar with the term "environmental

```
protection" and knows that to protect the environment
is a good thing.
```

Time Sense

In this passage, you can see that all three tenses are used: the simple present, the present perfect (once), and the simple past. The choice of which tense to use is actually not difficult if you remind yourself clearly of the time sense that is associated with each action or event you want to write about. You must be consistent in your choice and use of tenses. That is, for example, you must make sure that the past tense is used for verbs indicating actions or events that occurred in the past. Once you forget this, you could get into trouble.

Past Perfect Tense

By comparison, the past perfect tense is used much less frequently in research papers. You need it, however, when you want to distinguish, in the same statement, between two different time points in the past. In general, if you are in the past tense mode, any antecedent action or event is expressed in the past perfect tense. For example:

```
We asked our respondents about what leisure meant to
them and whether any planning was involved when they
spent their leisure time. In contrast to respondents
who were better educated (secondary school graduation
or higher), most of those who were least educated
(primary education or less) said that they had rarely
planned about what to do before they did something for
leisure.
```

Choosing a Tense

I must point out, though, that when you review previous research or the content of others' papers, you have the option of using either the simple past tense or the simple present tense. Thus, you can write:

```
Goffman noted that . . . or Goffman notes that . . .
```

Whichever tense you choose, you must be consistent. Do not mix tenses for statements that have the same time sense.

While you have a choice of either the simple present or the simple past, it is customary among many professional writers to use the simple present tense when reviewing the literature or when discussing others' writing. Thus, in quoting a source, you may write:

> Berger (1963) asks "not what it is that the sociol-
> ogist is doing but what it is that drives him to it"
> (p. 17).

In summarizing an idea, you may write:

> In his classic, *The Sociological Imagination*, Mills
> (1959) points out that we must distinguish between
> personal troubles and public issues.

Some Guidelines

Use the Simple Present Tense

- to describe what your research is all about

> The primary objective of the study **is** to identify
> the general patterns of leisure behaviour of youths
> in Eastern District.

- to discuss the general nature of your research problem

> By placing leisure in a broader context, we **hope**
> that we **may** be able to produce a better under-
> standing of the nature of youths' leisure.

> While different measurements of socioeconomic
> status **capture** different aspects of the meaning of
> the concept, the reliability of any of these
> measurements **depends** on how cooperative, willing,
> and even capable respondents **are** in providing the
> information needed.

- to make theoretical statements

> The idea of "role career" **is** useful for understanding the meaning of life space because it alerts us to both continuity and change that **characterize** the social context of our lives.

- to describe certain phenomena or relationships that have been discussed or established empirically by some other scholars

> Kelly (1987) **argues** that leisure **can** occur any time, even if in "interstitial" form, in our daily life.

- to describe the research design (e.g., the major variables and their measurement)

> The questionnaire **contains** three main parts: (a) interviewees' background information, (b) various aspects of leisure behaviour, and (c) interviewees' perceived satisfaction with various life domains.

> In this study, 17 categories of leisure activity **are** given in a checklist.

- to describe your findings (including making references to figures in tables)

> As Table 5 **shows**, while the three SES profiles **are** quite similar in most activity types, they **tend** to differ most in media use.

- to interpret the meaning of your findings

> The finding that the great majority of the youths in our sample **do** not participate in organized leisure activities should be interpreted with care. **Does** it mean organized activities have little appeal to youths?

> Our findings **indicate** that the youths in our study **are** dissatisfied with various aspects of the environment. This **may** not mean a deterioration of the performance of the government: perhaps they **suggest** that today's youths **are** more conscious of the quality of the environment.

Use the Present Perfect Tense

- to introduce or emphasize what has been found or what has emerged either in theory or in research:

  > Research **has revealed** strong empirical associations between education and political liberalism.

  > It **has** long **been known** that there are social class differences in fertility behaviour.

  > Age and sex **have been found** to be important independent variables for understanding the variation in leisure activities.

  > Kelly (1990), like Rapoport and Rapoport (1975) before him, **has proposed** that leisure develops in close interaction with work and family roles.

- to state an antecedent action or trend when you are in the present tense mode:

  > The use of the mobile phone **has changed** how we **interact** with others and how we **conduct** our daily life.

  > Generally, people who **have read** much international news **seem** to be more self-confident than those who **have read** very little such news.

Use the Simple Past Tense

- to indicate a state of affairs or something that was true at a particular time in the past

  > Environmental protection **was** not an issue and **did** not even appear in the local language before the introduction of wireless television in Hong Kong in the late 1960s.

- to describe the actions taken in your research (e.g., how the sample was chosen, when fieldwork took place, and what respondents were asked to do)

  > With the assistance of the Census and Statistics Department of the Government, a sampling frame of

```
all permanent structure living quarters in Eastern
District was made available.
```

- to introduce what some other researcher or researchers found or advocated (Their names appear as subject in your sentence. Note that the simple present tense is used for the content of the finding or the researcher's view since such content is believed to have a large element of generality.)

```
Katz and Gurevitch (1976) found that, in general,
age is more important than educational attainment
in affecting participation in out-of-home activi-
ties.
```

If, however, you have reason to believe that the finding or the view should be understood in the context of the researcher's work itself only, then you should use the simple past tense for the clause describing the finding or view:

```
Katz and Gurevitch (1976) found that, in general, age
was more important than educational attainment in
affecting participation in out-of-home activities.
```

Exercises for Verb Tenses in Research Papers

In each of the following three exercises, choose the appropriate tense for the verbs (base form shown in parentheses) that are used in the numbered blanks. Keep in mind the purposes for which different verb tenses are used. If necessary, add words or modify word order to indicate properly the tense that you think ought to be used. If the context requires passive voice construction, indicate this accordingly.

Exercise A

In the literature on adolescence, considerable attention _____ (give) to
                                                                      (1)

the significance of peer groups in socialization. It often _____ (note) that in the
                                                                  (2)

process of identity-seeking, adolescents _____ (tend) to be highly self-
(3)

conscious. They _____ (be) sensitive to how they _____ (see) and
(4)   (5)

_____ (evaluate) others, especially their peers who _____ (serve) as their
(6)   (7)

reference groups (Roberts 1983). They do what they can to _____ (seek) peer
(8)

support and approval. Indeed, peer evaluation _____ (can) _____ (cause)
(9)   (10)

great anxiety. In their study of adolescents, Wright and Keple (1981) _____
(11)

(find) that adolescents _____ (spend) more time together with their peers than
(12)

with their parents and that their behavioural norms much _____ (determine)
(13)

the peer group. Wilson (1979) _____ (believe) that intergenerational conflict in
(14)

society is probably more significant than racial or interclass conflict. Further,

Coleman (1979) _____ (point out) that the three greatest problems of
(15)

adolescents _____ (be) troubles of heterosexual relationships, fear of non-
(16)

acceptance by peers, and conflict with parents.

Exercise B

The social indicators approach to life quality _____ (receive) many
                                                                (1)

criticisms. Researchers _____ (come) to realize that quality of life _____
                              (2)   (3)

(be) not necessarily directly related to material wealth. Hence, there _____ (be)
                                                                              (4)

an increasing tendency to study quality of life subjectively. The social well-being or

life satisfaction approach _____ (study) the subjective attitudes _____
                                 (5)   (6)

(hold) persons in a population. This method _____ (attempt) to unveil the
                                                  (7)

privately known and privately evaluated aspects of life by asking respondents

appropriate questions. It _____ (believe) that we _____ (cannot)
                              (8)   (9)

_____ (understand) the psychological quality of a person's life simply from
     (10)

knowing the circumstances in which that person _____ (live). The same
                                                      (11)

circumstances _____ (may be) satisfying and enjoyable to some people but not
                    (12)

others. Therefore it _____ (be) important to include perceptual and subjective
                          (13)

elements in the study of quality of life.

Exercise C

In this study, we _____ (intend) to examine a large number of life
                    (1)

concerns or "domains" which _____ (can) _____ (consider) as the major
                              (2)   (3)

divisions in a person's life. It _____ (be) important to tackle different domains of
                                  (4)

life separately because one _____ (may be) more satisfied and pleased with
                             (5)

some aspects of life than with others.

Respondents _____ (be) asked to rate their level of satisfaction with each
            (6)

of 26 different domains of life on the same seven-point scale ranging from 1 for

"very satisfied" to 7 for "very dissatisfied." The middle point on this scale

_____ (label) "neither satisfied nor dissatisfied." Then the respondents
  (7)

_____ (be) asked to describe their satisfaction with their life as a whole. The
  (8)

results _____ (be) listed in Table 3.
         (9)

We _____ (note) that responses across the 26 items _____ (tend) to
   (10)   (11)

cluster rather heavily around the more satisfied end of the scale. Amazingly, more

than 85 per cent of our respondents _____ (report) that they _____ (be)
                                               (12)   (13)

satisfied with their peer relationships. This, however, _____ (do) not mean that
                                                      (14)

they _____ (love) their peers and _____ (hate) their family. In fact, they
         (15)   (16)

_____ (report) very high satisfaction levels on the several items concerning
  (17)

family life.

                  (The exercises are adapted from Ng and Man (1988a, pp. 2, 3, 4, 15).)

Punctuation

If you want to write well, not only should you do your best to construct sentences that are clear and effective and paragraphs that are unified and coherent, you should also make every effort to use punctuation correctly. Indeed, the clarity, coherence, and effectiveness of your writing depend greatly on good punctuation.

The marks of punctuation do for writing what voice levels, facial expressions, gestures, and pauses do for speaking. Writing is silent, but you can give it "voice" so that it may be heard—not by ears but by the mind—when it is read. Your writing may be heard only when you punctuate it properly to achieve the desired effects. You use punctuation to help readers understand what you mean.

Learn the conventions of good punctuation to communicate effectively. When you revise your writing draft, always check whether you have been careless with punctuation. If your punctuation does not follow the proper conventions or if you have omitted a certain required punctuation mark, you may mislead or confuse your readers. Treat all punctuation marks with great respect, because they can make a considerable difference in the clarity of what you write.

In this appendix, you will find guidelines for using the following punctuation marks:

1. Period (full stop)
2. Question mark
3. Comma
4. Semicolon
5. Colon
6. Dash
7. Quotation marks
8. Hyphen
9. Apostrophe
10. Parentheses and brackets

1. Period (Full stop)

1.1 Use a period at the end of a statement or an indirect question.

```
We learn about ourselves through our perceptions of
what others say of us.

We asked our respondents whether they thought Hong
Kong had a promising future.
```

1.2 Place a period and a space after an initial in personal names:

```
C. Wright Mills   C. K. Yang   John F. Kennedy
```

1.3 Place a period after each lowercase letter of the following abbreviations:

```
a.m.    p.m.    i.e.    e.g.
```

1.4 Use periods to punctuate academic titles and titles before or after personal names:

```
M.Phil.    Ph.D.    Dr. Young    Ms. Li
Rev. Wong  M. Brown, Jr.
```

1.5 Many abbreviations consisting of all capital letters often do not use periods after the letters:

```
HKSAR    ICAC    JP    UNESCO    US    BBC
WHO      ASEAN
```

2. Question Mark

2.1 Use a question mark at the end of a direct question.

```
We asked our respondents this question: Do you
think Hong Kong has a promising future?
```

The following use of the question mark is incorrect because the question is indirect rather than direct. It should end with a period.

```
We would like to find out what drives the journa-
list in the search for news? (Incorrect)
```

> We would like to find out what drives the journa-
> list in the search for news. (Correct)

To use the question mark, you need to rephrase the sentence so that it contains or leads to a direct question, as in the following:

> The question we would like to ask is: What drives
> the journalist in the search for news?

2.2   For the use of question marks along with quotation marks, see 7.3 and 7.4 under "Quotation Marks."

3. Comma

3.1   Use a comma before a coordinating conjunction (e.g., **and**, **but**, **or**, **yet**, **so**) that joins two independent clauses.

> The functionalist perspective treats deviance as a
> product of society, **but** symbolic interactionism
> sees deviance as a process of interaction.

3.2   Use a comma to set off introductory words, phrases, and clauses.

> **Thus,** she feels deeply deprived compared with her
> friends.
>
> **In short,** social expectations are an essential
> element in the concept of "role."
>
> **Since the study uses a convenience sample,** we
> cannot be too assertive in our conclusions.
>
> **To the extent that care was taken in the design of
> the questionnaire,** we may expect that the data
> collected are both reliable and valid.

3.3   Use commas to set off a parenthetical element or a transitional expression.

> August Comte, **the father of sociology,** coined the
> word "sociology."
>
> This report, **we understand,** is taken very seriously
> by the Government.

> Americans, **for example**, have fewer public holidays
> than Hong Kong people do.

3.4   Use commas to set off a nonrestrictive clause. (See 12 (b) in Appendix 7 for more examples.)

> Sociology students, **who are supposed to be capable
> of critical thinking**, ought to be not easily
> deceived by claims in advertisements.

> The idea of anomie, **which Merton discussed in a
> paper published in 1938**, concerns the imbalance
> between cultural success goals and institutional-
> ized means.

3.5   Use commas between items in a series. (The comma before **and** in **A, B, and C**, called a serial comma, is more commonly seen in American usage than in British usage.)

> Leisure can be thought of as time, activity, **and**
> experience.

If an item in a series contains two elements that usually appear together (e.g., **research and development, law and order**) or that together represent a unit of an organization (e.g., **marketing and sales, scholarships and awards),** the two elements must not be separated by a comma. If such an item appears last in a series, place the final comma just before this item.

> To be competitive, technology companies must up-
> grade its human resources, hardware, **and** research
> and development.

4. Semicolon

4.1   Use a semicolon to join independent clauses (complete sentences) that are closely related. The second clause may be an elaboration or an alternative statement of the first.

> Parsons' writing is difficult and highly compli-
> cated; few students could understand his ideas.

```
A family is a simple structure; it is composed of a
few positions.
```

4.2 Use a semicolon to separate parallel clauses or strings of phrases.

```
Ex-convicts do get jobs and go 'straight'; drug
addicts do sometimes give up their habit and re-
enter conventional society.
```

4.3 Use a semicolon to present two or more contrasting ideas or statements.

```
Merton identified a single cause of deviance
(anomie) to explain deviance throughout a person's
life; Becker stresses that the reasons for deviance
might change as time passes and circumstances alter.
```

```
Bureaucracies do not simply form spontaneously from
what individuals do; it is what individuals do,
rather, that is shaped and conditioned by bureau-
cratic systems.
```

4.4 Use a semicolon between two independent coordinate clauses. The conjunctive adverb (e.g., **however, therefore, thus, consequently, indeed, in addition**) that introduces the second clause is customarily followed by a comma.

```
Social structures have a constraining effect on
individuals; however, individuals perceive and res-
pond to the same social structure in different ways.
```

See 11 (c) in Appendix 7 for more examples.

5. Colon

5.1 Use a colon to introduce a series or list of items. Note, however, that the lead-in text before the colon that introduces the list must be an independent clause and not a phrase or sentence fragment.

```
A research report usually contains the following:
introduction, literature review, method, findings,
and conclusion.
```

5.2 Use a colon to give an example of a general statement.

> Technology compresses time and space: what happens
> half a world away can be seen on television news at
> practically the same time by live transmission.

5.3 Use a colon to announce an important statement or question.

> There are real job opportunities for those with
> social science training: this will become clearer
> as you pursue such training further.

> Functionalism asks a basic and interesting question:
> What does a cultural or social phenomenon do for
> the maintenance and integration of society?

5.4 Use a colon to separate two clauses the second of which expresses an effect of the first.

> The government is cutting its funding of the
> universities: many postgraduate programmes can only
> continue if they are totally self-financing through
> tuition fees.

5.5 Use a colon to introduce material that explains or clarifies a point.

> Individuals do not react passively to external
> forces: they attach meanings to events before
> deciding how to respond.

5.6 Use a colon to introduce a subtitle after a main title of a book, an article, or any document.

> Effective Writing: A Guide for Social Science
> Students

5.7 The following are conventions concerning capitalization after a colon:
   - Do not capitalize the first word of a phrase after a colon.
   - You may begin the first word of a clause with a capital letter or a small letter, but you need to be consistent.
   - You must capitalize the first word of a subtitle after a colon.

6. Dash

The dash is a mark of separation stronger than a comma. There is some overlap in use between it and the colon although it is less formal and more relaxed than a colon. Both tend to draw attention to what you write after it.

The dash is a better choice than the colon if what you mention next contains an element of surprise. Type the dash with two consecutive hyphens, with no space before or after the mark. (Your word processing software may allow you to opt for the function that automatically links the two consecutive hyphens into an unbroken short line as you type.)

Single Dash

6.1   Use a single dash to introduce material that explains or further elaborates a preceding word.

> At the core of the functionalist view is the concept of a social system--a set of relationships that can be thought of as a functioning whole.

> News as we see it reported on television is not something that just happens--it is the result of what journalists and editors have agreed to put together so that there is a "story" to tell.

> Whereas children assimilate technology fairly easily as they grow up, adults must accommodate--a much more difficult learning process.

6.2   Use a single dash to introduce material that summarizes a series of words or phrases.

> Intimacy, informality, expressiveness, and unique-ness of relationship--all these are qualities of primary groups.

6.3   Use a single dash to introduce an afterthought.

> Politics is part of the culture of organizations--churches are no exception.

Two Dashes

6.4   Use a pair of dashes to set off parenthetical material that is nonessential and that interrupts a main clause. While you can also use a pair of commas to set off parenthetical material, the break produced by a pair of dashes is more distinct. That is, dashes are more emphatic than commas used this way.

```
What marks Durkheim's contribution to sociology is
the recognition that systems of cultural symbols--
that is, values, beliefs, religious dogmas, and the
like--are an important basis for the integration of
society.

In sociology or psychology, a general approach--the
scientific method--guides research.
```

7. Quotation Marks

7.1   If you follow British usage, use single quotation marks for quoted material and double quotation marks for words or phrases that appear as quoted in the original text. In American usage, it is just the reverse. However, it is now not uncommon to see the use of double quotation marks for quoted matter in British English.

```
BrE:   This view, he argues, 'gives a proper place
       to social control as a dynamic factor or
       "cause" of deviance'.

AmE:   This view, he argues, "gives a proper place
       to social control as a dynamic factor or
       'cause' of deviance."
```

7.2   Note that, in British practice, the full stop (period) appears outside the closing quotation mark. In American practice, the period appears inside the closing quotation mark. However, when a page location is given after the quotation, both American and British practice put the period after the parentheses in which the page location is given. Thus, using double quotation marks for the longer quoted matter, the above example reads:

```
This view, he argues, "gives a proper place to
social control as a dynamic factor or 'cause' of
deviance" (p. 614).
```

In this example, if the words **this view** are in the original text, you may express the quotation in either of the following two forms. Note that, in the second form, the comma after **this view** is placed *inside* the closing quotation mark, following American usage.

```
He argues that "this view gives a proper place to
social control as a dynamic factor or 'cause' of
deviance" (p. 614).
```

```
"This view," he argues, "gives a proper place to
social control as a dynamic factor or 'cause' of
deviance" (p. 614).
```

7.3 If a question mark is part of the quoted matter, place it *inside* the closing quotation mark.

```
Original text:    What   is   the   character   of   this
                  particular society as a whole?
```

```
Your quotation:   He  asks  the  key  question:  "What  is
                  the   character   of   this   particular
                  society as a whole?"
```

7.4 If a question mark is not part of the quoted matter, place it *outside* the closing quotation mark.

```
What does the author really intend to say in the
chapter on "the character of society"?
```

7.5 Use quotation marks to enclose the titles of journal articles, book chapters, reports, and conference papers (ASA style, but not APA style).

```
"The Importance of Writing"
```

7.6 Use quotation marks to enclose words or expressions used with a special meaning.

```
C. Wright Mills went to great length to distinguish
between public "issues" and personal "troubles."
```

8. Hyphen

Many compound words are written with hyphens. (However, some compound words that used to be hyphenated may now be written as one word. When in doubt, consult a good dictionary.)

8.1   Use a hyphen in the following types of compound adjectives when they are placed before a noun:

8.1.1   Compound adjectives ending with the present participle or the past participle of a verb.

```
self-fulfilling prophecy

face-saving act

data-processing skills

cost-cutting strategies

Hong Kong-based company

profit-oriented move

tertiary-educated professionals
```

8.1.2   Compound adjectives beginning with an adverb such as **hard**, **well**, **little**, **ill**, **half**, or **best**. (Do not hyphenate these compounds when they follow the noun they modify.)

```
hard-earned reputation  (reputation that is hard earned)

well-known achievements  (achievements that are well known)

ill-prepared document  (document that is ill prepared)

half-hearted attempt  (attempt that is half hearted)

little-understood theory  (theory that is little under-stood)

best-organized paper  (paper that is best organized)
```

8.1.3   Compound adjectives beginning with **all**. (Hyphenate these compounds whether they precede or follow the noun they modify.)

```
all-important

all-inclusive

all-powerful

all-purpose

all-round
```

8.1.4   Compound adjectives in which the first element is an adjective and the second element is another adjective with an **-ed** ending (formed from a noun or a verb).

> `closed-ended question` (`close-end` and `close-ended` are incorrect)
>
> `quick-tempered young people`
>
> `cold-blooded violence`
>
> `middle-aged man`
>
> `open-minded view`
>
> `far-sighted decision`

8.1.5   Compound adjectives in which the first element is an adjective and the second element is a noun.

> `public-sector organizations`
>
> `high-tech society`
>
> `long-term benefits`
>
> `mid-life crisis`
>
> `multi-group comparison`

8.1.6   Compound adjectives in which the first element is a number and the second a noun.

> `a five-day period` (a period of five days)
>
> `a three-person committee` (a committee of three persons)
>
> `a 50-page thesis` (a thesis of 50 pages)
>
> `a 14-year-old girl` (a girl 14 years old, or a girl aged 14)
>
> `first-term courses` (courses of the first term)
>
> `twentieth-century history` (history of the twentieth century)

Note that, as in the first four examples above, the noun is always in the singular when it is hyphenated with a cardinal number. (Never say `a three-persons committee.`)

8.1.7 Compound adjectives consisting of two nouns, two verbs, or two adjectives indicating two related or opposing elements.

```
East-West dialogue

cost-benefit analysis

love-hate relationship

nature-nurture issue

rural-urban continuum

win-win situation
```

8.1.8 Compound adjectives consisting of three or more elements.

```
hard-to-please audience

life-and-death struggle

middle-of-the-road beliefs

taken-for-granted assumptions

once-in-a-lifetime experience

now-or-never opportunity

matter-of-fact attitude

fifteen-to-nineteen-year-old group

on-the-job training

face-to-face negotiation

state-of-the-art equipment
```

8.2 Use a hyphen for fractions and numbers from 21 to 99.

```
one-third

one-half

three-quarters

two-fifths

twenty-eight

ninety-nine
```

8.3   Use a hyphen to indicate that two or more compounds have the same second
element.

```
short- and long-term consequences

15- to 24-year-old age cohort

pre- and post-1997 social conditions

mid- to late-1990's
```

Note that, when referring to two compounds, as in the above examples, there
must be a space after the hyphen following the first element of the first
compound.

The following is an example of three compounds:

```
first-, second-, and third-quarter figures
```

8.4   Do not use a hyphen in compound adjectives beginning with **very, much** or
with an adverb ending in **-ly**.

```
very controversial issue

much discussed idea

much researched topic

rapidly changing society

carefully designed study

jointly prepared proposal

convincingly argued point
```

8.5   Do not use a hyphen in familiar compound terms consisting of two nouns.

```
class structure            media event

construct validity         outreach service

consumer market            personality disorder

data analysis              questionnaire design

identity crisis            research method

information technology     response rate

intelligence quotient      role model
```

```
life expectation          sampling error

life quality              term paper

measurement level         theory construction
```

8.6   In general, do not use a hyphen after prefixes unless the prefix is followed by a capital letter. If the situation requires, use the hyphen to improve readability or to clarify meaning. In some cases, either the unhyphenated or the hyphenated form is acceptable. But you must be consistent in using the chosen form.

```
cooperate, coordinate (also co-operate, co-ordinate)

coworker              but co-author

extraordinary         but extra-curricular

multifunctional       but multi-disciplinary

nonconformity         but non-essential, non-Christian

overestimate          but over-optimistic

postwar               but post-Cold War

postindustrial        but post-colonial

(also post-industrial)

predominant           but pre-eminent

reproduce             but re-enact, re-enter, re-register

recreation (enjoyment) but re-creation (new creation)

semicircle            but semi-skilled, semi-professional

underdeveloped        but under-the-table
```

9. Apostrophe

9.1   Use the apostrophe to form the possessive of singular nouns.

```
the group's leader

the report's conclusion

a moment's joy

Mr. Jones' book
```

```
Parsons' theory

C. Wright Mills' ideas
```

Note that names ending in *s* may take either *'* or *'s*. (Just the apostrophe *'* is preferred.)

9.2   Use the apostrophe to form the possessive of plural nouns.

```
employees' union

board members' meeting

the Rapaports' study
```
(study by two authors with the same last name Rapaport)

```
children's development

women's status
```

9.3   Do not use the apostrophe for personal possessive pronouns.

```
This is your suggestion.
The suggestion is yours.

These are our results.
These results are ours.
```

9.4   To indicate joint possession held by two persons or parties, only the last person or party takes **'s** or the apostrophe only.

```
Falk and Campbell's book
```
(The book is co-authored by Falk and Campbell.)

```
Lee and Adams' article
```
(The article is co-authored by Lee and Adams.)

```
Hong Kong and Shenzhen's agreement
```
(The agreement is jointly signed by Hong Kong and Shenzhen.)

9.5   To indicate individual possession held separately by two persons or parties, both persons or parties take **'s** or the apostrophe only.

```
Durhkeim's and Weber's theories
```
(=Durkheim's theories and Weber's theories)

```
Mills' and Parsons' ideas
```
(=Mills' ideas and Parsons' ideas)

9.6 You may use the apostrophe for years in a decade, or to form the plural of numbers and individual letters. Alternatively, you may choose not to use the apostrophe. The choice depends on your personal preference. Not using the apostrophe seems to be more common now. In any case, you have to be consistent.

> the 1980's and 1990's (or: the 1980s and 1990s)
>
> men in their 60's (or: men in their 60s)
>
> You can check all items that apply with X's. (or: ... with Xs.)

9.7 Use the apostrophe with plural abbreviations that contain periods. For unpunctuated abbreviations, it is quite acceptable to omit the apostrophe. (This form is probably easier to read.)

> Ph.D.'s   PhDs
>
> M.B.A.'s   MBAs
>
> V.C.R.'s   VCRs
>
> J.P.'s   JPs

9.8 Use the apostrophe to indicate contractions.

> you're (you are)
>
> doesn't (does not)
>
> it's (it is)
>
> o'clock (of the clock)
>
> '97 (1997)
>
> class of '03 (class of 2003)

10. Parentheses ( ) and Brackets [ ]

10.1 Use parentheses to enclose explanations and additional information.

> Some definitions of leisure use a single criterion (such as time or function).

```
The second test (using the same instrument) was
administered two years later.
```

```
These places are where young people can associate
with their peers (rather than with adults).
```

10.2 If the material enclosed by parentheses comes at the end of a sentence, the period is placed outside the closing parenthesis. If the enclosed material itself is a complete sentence, the two sentences each have their own period.

```
Support for gender equality varies directly with
education (see Table 2).
```

```
Support for gender equality varies directly with
education. (See Table 2.)
```

10.3 Use parentheses to give citations. (See Chapter 7 for more details.)

```
Some have argued for studying leisure in the
context of larger social structures (e.g., Heywood,
1988; Kelly, 1992; Stokowski, 1994).
```

```
Brief moments of leisure, which Kelly (1987, pp.
126-127) calls "leisure episodes" may occur any
time.
```

10.4 Square brackets are used much less than parentheses. Use brackets to enclose words that explain, modify, or comment on quoted material. (See Chapter 7 for more details.)

```
According to Berger (1963), the sociologist is
"someone concerned with understanding society in a
disciplined way [italics added]" (p. 27).
```

Writing Clear and Effective Sentences

To write clear and effective sentences, you must first master the ability to write grammatical sentences. That is, sentences must be constructed according to the conventions of standard English grammar. Some of the most important aspects are the following, which you can examine in Appendices 1 to 5:

Subject-verb agreement
Use of uncount nouns, variable nouns, and plural nouns
Proper use of word forms
Use and non-use of articles
Verb tenses

Clear sentences are not only grammatically correct but also well structured to make the meaning clear. Clear sentences are easy to read and understand. But good sentences go beyond correctness and clarity. You should learn to use the appropriate strategies to construct your sentences in such a way that they indicate emphasis where needed and that they contain variety in length, structure, and other aspects. The principles explained below are some strategies you can use to write not only clear but also effective sentences.

1. Avoid writing sentence fragments (incomplete sentences).
2. Pronoun reference (including relative pronouns) must be correct and clear.
3. Avoid shifts in person, number, and tense.
4. Avoid run-on sentences and comma splices.
5. Avoid wordiness.
6. Avoid nominalizations: sharpen the "action" in your sentences by clarifying who is doing what.
7. Avoid starting a sentence with "it is" or "there is."
8. Prefer the active voice to the passive voice when it is important to emphasize the actor.
9. Avoid misplaced modifiers.
10. Avoid dangling modifiers.

11. Use coordination to show two equally important ideas.
12. Use subordination to show that one idea is more important than another.
13. Use parallel construction for coordinated elements.

1. Avoid writing sentence fragments (incomplete sentences).

A sentence is complete if (a) it contains both a subject and a verb, and if (b) it is not a subordinate clause. A subordinate clause begins with such words as **that, since, while,** and **because** (e.g., **while influence is a vague concept**). If you have a subordinate clause, it must be joined to a main clause to make a complete sentence.

Incomplete: Individuals constrained by the social system.

Complete: Individuals are constrained by the social system.

Incomplete (second part):   Sociology as a form of consciousness reveals many things we are not aware of. Especially those covered by ideology.

Complete (and revised):   Sociology as a form of consciousness reveals many things we are not normally aware of, especially those that are ideological.

Incomplete (first part):   Since the government does not have a well-considered population policy. The burden on social resources is becoming problematic.

Complete: Since the government does not have a well-considered population policy, the burden on social resources is becoming problematic.

2. Pronoun reference (including relative pronouns) must be correct and clear.

Remember two principles:

(a)   A pronoun and its antecedent (the noun it stands for) must agree in person, number, and gender.

> The **problems** found in this university are similar
> to **those** in other universities.

(b)   Try to place the antecedent close to the pronoun. If this is not possible, try replacing the pronoun with the appropriate noun.

> He submitted the **proposal that** was more likely to
> attract funding.

> He wrote the proposal modelled on the one submitted
> last year. We will study **the new proposal** carefully.

> Unclear: Mass communication makes people aware of
>   messages, but interpersonal relation-
>   ships are more influential in persuading
>   people to accept the ideas behind the
>   messages because **they** provide social
>   support. (What does **they** refer to?)

> Clear: Mass communication makes people aware of
>   messages, but interpersonal relation-
>   ships are more influential in persuading
>   people to accept the ideas behind the
>   messages because **interpersonal relation-
>   ships** provide social support.

> Clear: Mass communication makes people aware of
>   messages, but interpersonal relation-
>   ships, **which** provide social support, are
>   more influential in persuading people to
>   accept the ideas behind the messages.

3.   Avoid shifts in person, number, and tense.

Be consistent in referring to people, either in the third person (**a person**, **he or she**, **one**; **people**, **they**) or in the second person (**you**). Sometimes it is appropriate to use the first person (usually the plural **we**, **us**). Do not mix these references in the same sentence.

(a)   Shift in person

   Inconsistent: **One** may not be aware of how society
                     affects **our** lives other than thinking
                     of it vaguely as **people's** external
                     environment.

   Consistent: **We** may not be aware of how society affects
                     our lives other than thinking of it
                     vaguely as **our** external environment.

(b)   Shift in number

   Inconsistent: If **a person** does not comply with the rules
                     of society, **they** will face punishments
                     of one kind or another.

   Consistent: If **a person** does not comply with the rules
                     of society, **he or she** will face
                     punishments of one kind or another.

(c)   Shift in tense (when such shift is not justified by changes in actual or
      relative time)

   Inconsistent: In the first two chapters, Berger
                     basically **describes** the nature of
                     sociology and **clarified** the image of
                     sociologists as different from other
                     scholars.

   Consistent: In the first two chapters, Berger
                     basically **describes** the nature of
                     sociology and **clarifies** the image of
                     sociologists as different from other
                     scholars.

Note that in the following sentence the shift in tense from the past to the
present is justified because the meaning of the statement modifying
"leisure" is supposed to be unrestricted by time.

   Researchers in this new phase of development **treated**
   leisure as something intentionally created by people
   who **have** various group memberships.

4.   Avoid run-on sentences and comma splices.

If you write two independent clauses one after another without any punctuation mark between them, you have a run-on (or "fused") sentence.

You cannot use a comma to join two independent clauses unless they are joined by a coordinating conjunction (e.g., and, but, or). Otherwise, you make the error of a "comma splice."

Run-on: Weber wrote about bureaucracy as an ideal
                  type he believed that bureaucracy is a
                  characteristic of modern capitalism.

Comma splice: Weber wrote about bureaucracy as an ideal
                  type, he believed that bureaucracy is a
                  characteristic of modern capitalism.

You can correct a run-on or comma splice sentence by any of the following methods:

(a) Separate the two clauses into two sentences.

    Weber wrote about bureaucracy as an ideal type. He
    believed that bureaucracy is a characteristic of
    modern capitalism.

(b) Join the two clauses with a coordinating conjunction.

    Weber wrote about bureaucracy as an ideal type, and
    he believed that bureaucracy is a characteristic of
    modern capitalism.

(c) Join the two clauses with a semicolon.

    Weber wrote about bureaucracy as an ideal type; he
    believed that bureaucracy is a characteristic of
    modern capitalism.

(d) Join the two clauses with a suitable conjunctive adverb (e.g., **however, nevertheless, consequently, therefore, in addition, at the same time**). If you do so, you need to place a semicolon after the first clause and a comma after the conjunctive adverb.

```
Weber wrote about bureaucracy as an ideal type; at the
same time, he believed that bureaucracy is a charac-
teristic of modern capitalism.
```

(e) Treat one of the two clauses as subordinate and join it to the other clause with a subordinating conjunction (e.g., **although**, **while**, **because**, **since**, **if**). (Of course, you must ensure that the relationship—causal or conditional—between the two clauses indicated by the conjunction used is justified.)

```
Since he believed that bureaucracy is a characteristic
of modern capitalism, Weber wrote about bureaucracy
as an ideal type.
```

The following is also a case of comma splice:

```
This social phenomenon cannot be observed within a
short period of time, it is an ongoing process. (Faulty)
```

You can rewrite it as two sentences:

```
This social phenomenon cannot be observed within a
short period of time. It is an ongoing process.
```

You can insert a coordinating conjunction:

```
This social phenomenon cannot be observed within a
short period of time, for it is an ongoing process.
```

You can place a semicolon between them:

```
This social phenomenon cannot be observed within a
short period of time; it is an ongoing process.
```

You can also use a conjunctive adverb to join the two clauses:

```
This social phenomenon cannot be observed within a
short period of time; rather, it is a process.
```

5.   **Avoid wordiness.**

Do not use more words than are really necessary to express an idea. Writing concisely without losing any important meaning is effective writing. The following are several main types of wordiness.

(a) Redundancy. A word or phrase is redundant if a main word already implies the same meaning.

Wordy: We should **repeat** this study **again** next year.
Concise: We should repeat this study next year.

Wordy: **In addition to** describing the article, he **also** evaluated it.
Concise: He described and also evaluated the article.

(The word **also** is optional, depending on whether you want to emphasize that "he evaluated the article.")

Wordy: It is difficult to have **consensus of opinion** in a group of such a **large size**.
Concise: It is difficult to have consensus in such a large group.

(**Consensus** is, by definition, uniform opinion.)

(b) Circumlocution. A circumlocution is a roundabout expression that uses too many words to express an idea instead of indicating the idea directly.

Circumlocutory: His brother, **who is a student majoring in psychology**, likes to argue.
Concise: His brother, **a psychology student**, likes to argue.

Circumlocutory: We **are of the opinion** that the survey was not done properly.
Concise: We **believe** that the survey was not done properly.

Circumlocutory: The economy will probably improve **in the near future**.
Concise: The economy will probably improve **soon**.

AVOID THESE:	**TRY THESE:**
on more than one occasion	several times
to a certain extent	partly
to a large degree	largely
is at variance with	differs from
to make a long story short	briefly

AVOID THESE:	TRY THESE:
a sizeable (or considerable) number	many
in a similar way (fashion, manner)	similarly
from a sociological perspective	sociologically
it is evident that	clearly
a significant number of	many, most, dozens, hundreds

(c) **Words used too loosely.** Watch out for words that are used so much that they become vague. Many such words are adverbs (e.g., **actually, basically, really, totally, very**). Every time you use such a word, ask yourself whether you need it to add any specific meaning. Most likely you do not.

Wordy: **Basically,** there will be a discussion of anomie in this paper.

Concise: This paper discusses anomie.

Wordy: It is too early to tell whether the project will **actually** succeed.

Concise: We have yet to see whether the project will succeed.

(d) **Long-winded phrases.** Long-winded phrases are empty phrases that can be shortened or deleted without losing any meaning. Their presence only hinders reading. The following lists some such phrases.

WORDY	DIRECT
at the present time	now, today
in this day and age	now, today
at this point in time	now, today
due to the fact that	because
in order to	to
in order to utilize	to use
in view of the fact that	because
for the purpose of	for
in the event that	if
by means of	by
in the final analysis	finally
in connection with	about, on, for

WORDY	DIRECT
concerning the matter of	**about**
have the ability to	**can**
on a regular basis	**regularly**
in a useful way	**usefully**
reach a conclusion	**conclude**
with regard to	**of, on, for, about**
with the exception of	**except**
in spite of the fact that	**despite, although**
in fact	(often not necessary)
as a matter of fact	(often not necessary)
the point I am trying to make	(delete, because you would sound indecisive or not confident enough)
the process of modernization	**modernization**

5.   Avoid nominalizations: sharpen the "action" in your sentences by clarifying who is doing what.

Prefer verbs to nouns or "nominalizations" (nouns derived from verbs). This is yet another way of eliminating wordiness. Whenever you use a nominalization, you tend to use more words and the action becomes impersonal and abstract, making the sentence harder to understand.

Less clear: Since the experience of leisure is quite subjective, it is not easy to have a clear-cut **definition** and **measurement** of leisure.

Clear: Since the experience of leisure is quite subjective, it is not easy to **define** and **measure** leisure clearly.

Less clear: To be a good sociologist, the necessary **condition** is to engage in active **examination** of social issues.

Clear: To be a good sociologist, one **needs** to **examine** social issues actively.

7.   Avoid starting a sentence with "it is" or "there is."

You may sometimes use "it is" or "there is" to start a sentence to indicate a change in direction. But doing so may add words to weaken your sentence.

Wordy: **It is** a fact that traditions die hard.
Concise: Traditions die hard.

Wordy: **There is** an increasing number of teenagers who
            commit various crimes.
Concise: An increasing number of teenagers commit
            various crimes.

8.   **Prefer the active voice to the passive voice when it is important to emphasize the actor.**

By indicating the "doer" of the "action," your sentence is more vigorous and better understood.

Less effective: A new centre for policy research **will be
                   set up** by the university.
More effective: The university **will set up** a new centre for
                   policy research.

Less effective: The implications of the reduced funding
                   have been considered carefully.
More effective: We **have considered carefully** the impli-
                   cations of the reduced funding.

On the other hand, if it is important to emphasize the action rather than the actor, especially when it is not easy or possible to show who the actor is, you may use the passive voice.

Data for the study **were collected** in May of last year.
(emphasis on the action of data collection)

The Chinese University of Hong Kong **was established** in
1963. (It is quite cumbersome to name who was or were actually
responsible for establishing the university.)

9.   **Avoid misplaced modifiers.**

A modifier is a word or a phrase that describes or qualifies some other word or part of a sentence. Always place a modifier close to the word or the entity it modifies, or else the meaning becomes unclear.

Unclear: I agree with the author's statements **in principle**.

Clear: I agree **in principle** with the author's statements.

Unclear: We appealed for more volunteers to help with the rice-for-the-elderly programme **at last week's committee meeting**.

Clear: **At last week's committee meeting,** we appealed for more volunteers to help with the rice-for-the-elderly programme

10. Avoid dangling modifiers.

If you construct a sentence in such a way that the element to be modified is merely implied rather than clearly stated, the modifier is said to be "dangling." That is, it does not modify anything in such a sentence.

Examine this sentence:

Comparing television and newspapers, each type of medium has its strengths and limitations.

In this sentence, the modifying phrase, **comparing television and newspapers,** seems to describe **each type of medium**. But **each type of medium** does not and cannot compare television and newspapers; only people do. Thus, the sentence ought to be revised as:

Comparing television and newspapers, we can see that each type of medium has its strengths and weaknesses.

The following kinds of modifiers are likely to become dangling, especially when the verb in the main clause is passive:

(a) Participial phrases

Whenever you start a sentence with a participial phrase, ask yourself who is doing the action indicated in that phrase. Mention the doer at the beginning of the main clause (i.e., make the doer the subject of the main clause) that follows the participial phrase. If you do not do this, you will have a case of dangling modifier. (Use the same strategy in (b) and (c) below.)

Dangling: **Hoping to stimulate tourism,** more leisure attractions will be developed.

Revised: **Hoping to stimulate tourism,** the government
             (the doer) is planning to develop more leisure
             attractions.

Dangling: **Referring to Table 1,** there is a positive
             relationship between A and B.

Revised: **Referring to Table 1,** we (the doer) see that
             there is a positive relationship between
             A and B.

or: **Referring to Table 1,** we see that A and B
             are positively related.

(b) Prepositional phrases containing a gerund

Dangling: **After analyzing the data,** age does not
             affect leisure choice as much as education
             does.

Revised: **After analyzing the data,** we (the doer) find
             that age does not affect leisure choice as
             much as education does.

(c) Infinitive phrases

Dangling: **To check for defects and problems,** a pilot
             study will be conducted.

Revised: **To check for defects and problems,** the
             researchers (the doer) will conduct a pilot
             study.

11. Use coordination to show two equally important ideas.

If two ideas (each expressed in an independent clause) are equally important,
link them to form a compound sentence in one of the following ways:

(a) Use a coordinating conjunction (e.g., **and, but, or, nor, for, yet, so**)

Hong Kong is now part of China, **and** its legal system
remains as autonomous as before.

People come and go, **but** positions will always remain.

Students may choose to minor in any subject area, **or**
they may choose not to have any minor at all.

> Many people nowadays do not have a healthy diet, **nor** do they have enough exercise.

> Stress is not necessarily bad, **for** it may improve our ability to cope with difficulties.

> Japan is just as highly industrialized as the United States, **yet** these two societies are not alike in every way.

> He does not speak Chinese, **so** he has to have an interpreter when he interviews respondents in China.

(b) Use a pair of correlative conjunctions (e.g., **both ... and, either ... or, not only ... but also, just as ... so**)

> Reading widely can **both** broaden one's horizons **and** improve one's writing ability.

> We can use **either** a smaller sample to save money **or** a larger sample to strengthen the accuracy of our findings.

> **Not only** does conflict theory believe that there is lack of social consensus on values and interests, (**but**) it **also** maintains that stratification leads to a waste of talents. (In this construction, **but** may be omitted.)

> We **not only** completed the project in time, **but** (**also**) saved about ten per cent of the total cost. (In this construction, **also** may be omitted.)

> **Just as** the city centre has changed, **so** has the countryside.

(c) Use a conjunctive adverb (e.g., **however, otherwise, consequently, indeed, hence, therefore, as a result, in addition, nevertheless, similarly, moreover**)

Note that the conjunctive adverb typically follows a semicolon, which marks the relationship between the two clauses. A comma follows the conjunctive adverb to mark a pause in reading the sentence to give emphasis to the adverb, indicating such meanings as concession (**however**), result (**consequently, therefore**), condition (**otherwise**), or addition (**moreover**).

The proposal sounds wonderful; **however**, its feasibility is doubtful.

Roles compete for our time; **indeed**, we all play many roles every day.

The status of wife dominates a woman's relationship with her husband; **hence**, it is called the master status in such a relationship.

It was only an exploratory study; **therefore**, our conclusions were quite tentative.

12. Use subordination to show that one idea is more important than another.

The more important idea is contained in the main (independent) clause; the less important idea is contained in the subordinate (dependent) clause or phrase. Link the two ideas in one of the following ways:

(a) Use a subordinating conjunction (e.g., **although**, **as**, **assuming that**, **because**, **even if**, **even though**, **given that**, **if**, **now that**, **provided**, **since**, **so that**, **unless**, **when**, **whereas**, **while**) to introduce the dependent clause.

Although both ethnomethodology and symbolic interactionism study interpersonal interaction, they are quite different in one respect.

While the sociological perspective is very useful for a clear perception of social phenomena, it is not the only frame of reference with which society may be viewed.

Conflict theory is concerned with change **while** functionalism is concerned with stability.

If we can only see how the individual is influenced by society but not how he or she contributes to larger social processes, we have not fully acquired the sociological imagination.

Since sociological training tends to liberate the mind and sharpen analytical skills, it should be an important component of general education.

As there is no statistically significant difference, we cannot reject the null hypothesis.

Given that influence is often a matter of personal qualities, we cannot understand organizational behaviour fully by studying the organization's formal structure alone.

We need to revise our report **so that** it will be more detailed.

(b) Use a relative pronoun (**who**, **which**, **that**) to introduce an adjective clause as the dependent clause.

New immigrants, **who** lack language facility and social connections, have difficulty adapting to life in an unfamiliar society.

The **who-**clause here is a nonrestrictive or non-defining clause. It does not restrict the reference of the noun it modifies—**immigrants**—to particular individuals, and is thus not essential to the meaning of the sentence. A comma or commas must be used to set off such a clause.

This same sentence can be written without the commas to mean that only those new immigrants who lack language facility and social connections would have difficulty adapting to life in an unfamiliar society. Used in this manner, the **who-**clause becomes a restrictive or defining clause. It restricts the reference of the noun it modifies to particular individuals, and is therefore essential to the meaning of the sentence:

New immigrants **who** lack language facility and social connections have difficulty adapting to life in an unfamiliar society.

In the following sentence, you will see that the **who-**clause can only be restrictive and thus must not be set off by commas:

Students **who** have studied psychology should know what schizophrenia means.

Some more example sentences follow. Use **which** to introduce a nonrestrictive clause and **that** to introduce a restrictive clause.

The buildings in this area, **which** have been around for many decades, will be demolished. (nonrestrictive)

The buildings in this area **that** have been around for many decades will be demolished. (restrictive)

The central figure of our discussion is Durkheim, **who** has given us the concept "social fact." (nonrestrictive)

This is Peter Berger's Invitation to Sociology, **of which** we have heard a lot. (nonrestrictive)

This is one of the best studies of Chinese society **that** have appeared in a long time. (restrictive)

These are the issues **that** have generated much debate. (restrictive)

(c) Use a prepositional phrase (preposition + noun/noun phrase) (e.g., **because of . . .** , **according to . . .** , **in spite of . . .** , **as a result of . . .** , **like . . .** , **unlike . . .** , **in contrast to . . .** , **with . . .**) to express the less important idea.

Because of rising labour cost, manufacturers have to relocate their factories to places where there is cheaper labour.

According to this study, there is probably no relationship between gender and life satisfaction.

In spite of its shortcomings, the study is still a respectable pioneering effort.

As a result of obtaining the assistance of the Department of Census and Statistics, we were able to use an up-to-date sampling frame from which to select our sample.

Like symbolic interactionism, the developmental perspective on the family is interested in social processes and change.

> **In contrast to the economic downturns of many Asian countries,** China's economy has recorded phenomenal growth for at least three consecutive years.
>
> **With great care and attention to details,** our project proceeded relatively smoothly.

(d) Use a participial phrase to express the less important idea.

A participial phrase contains a participle, i. e., a verb in **-ing** or **-ed** form. The subject of such a phrase is usually a noun or pronoun in the main clause. The phrase can be made negative by placing **not** or **never** before the participle. There are four main types of use of participial phrases:

- (General form: active voice. Use the **-ing** present participle.) Time intended is shown by the verb in the main clause.

  > **Comparing the two views,** you **will see** that neither has a clear advantage over the other.
  >
  > **Taking all these reasons into consideration,** I **believed** we had to proceed as planned.
  >
  > **Being a prejudiced person,** he **refuses** to listen to opinions different from his.

- (General form: passive voice. Use the **-ed** past participle.) Time intended is shown by the verb in the main clause.

  > **Compared with secondary groups,** primary groups **are** more lasting and expressive.
  >
  > **Not discouraged by unfamiliarity with a strange culture,** she **tried** her best to adapt herself to her new surroundings.

- (Perfect form: active voice. Use the **-ed** past participle.) Time in the participial phrase precedes that shown in the main clause.

  > **Never having lived away from home,** the new students probably **felt** homesick.
  >
  > **Having seen the similarities between sociology and anthropology,** we will next **examine** their differences.

- (Perfect form: passive voice. Use the **-ed** past participle.) Time in the participial phrase precedes that shown in the main clause.

    Having been trained to identify unspoken mes-sages, she **is** a competent interviewer.

    Not having been told of the duration of the study, I **was** unable to decide if I could accept it.

(e) Use an appositive to express the less important idea.

An appositive is a word or phrase that describes or identifies a noun in a sentence. The appositive is often placed immediately after the noun it describes, although it can also come at the beginning of a sentence. In the following examples, the appositive is not essential (nonrestrictive) to the meaning of the noun it describes and is set off with commas or dashes.

    Talcott Parsons, **a leading figure in functionalist theory,** believed that value consensus is what makes any social system stable.

    My friend, **eager to get ahead in his career,** worked extremely hard.

    The new manager--**efficient and friendly**--soon gained the respect of the workers.

    A pioneer empirical study, Durkheim's work on suicide has long been a fine example of the research process in sociology.

The appositive in the next example is essential (restrictive) to the meaning of the noun it describes (**leaders**). It is not set off with a comma.

    One of the major difficulties of a developing country is the scarcity of able leaders **knowledgeable enough to run the government.**

Compare with the following sentence in which the appositive is not essential (nonrestrictive). It is thus set off with a comma.

    This country is ruled by able leaders, knowledgeable enough to run the government.

13. Use parallel construction for coordinated elements.

A parallel construction uses similar grammatical forms for two or more similar or closely related (parallel) elements. The parallel arrangement emphasizes that these coordinated elements have the same function and importance in the sentence. Any kind of sentence element (words, phrases, clauses) may be placed in a parallel construction.

You should use parallel construction for

(a) elements linked by coordinating conjunctions (e.g., **and, but, or, nor, yet**)

(b) elements linked by paired correlative conjunctions (e.g., **both . . . and; either . . . or; neither . . . nor; not . . . but; not only . . . but also; whether . . . or**)

(c) elements being compared or contrasted (introduced by, for example, **rather than; as opposed to; not; more . . . than . . .**)

Single words

Culture refers to the learned patterns for **thinking, feeling,** and **acting** that characterize a society. (Gerunds)

A primary group consists of people who enjoy a **direct, intimate,** and **cohesive** relationship with one another. (Adjectives)

His argument in defence of his innocence is **simple,** but **convincing.** (Adjectives)

The focus of this article is more on **actors** than on **action.** (Nouns)

Phrases

Formulating a research problem and **drawing up a research design** are the preliminary steps in the research process. (Gerund phrases)

To study the dynamics of interpersonal relationships in organizations, we use **the interview method** as opposed to **the questionnaire method.** (Noun phrases)

To lower costs and **to maintain operating efficiency,** organizations become increasingly McDonaldized. (Infinitive phrases)

Students spend their time **reading books, writing essays,** and **developing skills.** (Participial phrases)

Clauses

A group consists of people **who share a feeling of common identity** and **who are bound together in relatively stable patterns of social interaction.** (Adjective clauses)

Whether one examines the micro world of the individual or **whether one studies the macro context of social change,** it is always possible to find phenomena not explainable by common sense alone. (Adverbial clauses)

Travelling is rewarding **both because it allows you complete escape from the pressures of your normal work** and **because it gives you a total change of experience.** (Adverbial clauses)

It is very encouraging **that the university has decided to fund our study** and **that we have recruited enough student helpers to conduct the field work.** (Noun clauses)

Examples of Revision of Sentences with Comments

The twenty "cases" selected for inclusion in this appendix are all from actual student writing. Together, they illustrate many of the most common errors.

Sentence revision is more than just making the sentence grammatical; it should also aim at making the sentence convey the intended meaning clearly and directly, with just the right tone and the right force. Choice of words and sentence structure are equally important considerations in revising a sentence to make it work for you in the best way possible. Of course, a sentence does not stand alone but is an ingredient in a flow of ideas in a paragraph. If a sentence is in need of repair, there are usually more ways than one to "fix" it, taking into account the context in which it is placed. Some of these ways are better than others, depending on the effect (such as emphasis and logical relationship) desired. No wonder some people tend to think of sentence writing and revision as an art.

Art or not, the "model" revisions shown here will, I hope, help you learn something about correct and effective sentences. In some cases, I have given more than one revised version of the original sentence, just so that you will see that alternative revisions are possible.

Case 1

Original: Radical changes in the present social welfare system
            is very unlikely.

Revised: Radical changes in the present social welfare system
            are very unlikely.

Comments:
Errors in subject-verb agreement are very common in student writing. The principle is quite simple. A singular subject takes a singular verb; a plural subject takes a plural verb. Train yourself to be careful enough to see whether the subject of your

sentence is singular or plural. Sometimes the real subject may be separated from its verb by a modifying phrase or some other words, as is the case in this sentence. The subject is **radical changes.** It being plural (**changes),** you must use **are** (a plural verb) instead of **is** (a singular verb). For further details, see Appendix 1.

Case 2

Original: In any society, some form of regulations must present.

Revised: (a)   In any society, some form of regulation must be
                        present.
               (b)   Some form of regulation must be present in any
                        society.

Comments:
- The sentence intends to refer to **regulation** as control and not as individual rules. Thus, the singular **regulation,** an uncount noun, should be used to mean control as an abstract idea.
- **Present** in this sentence is an adjective used as complement of the subject, and thus needs to be preceded by a linking verb such as **be.**
- Sentence (b) is better than sentence (a) if you want to place greater emphasis on **some form of regulation** that starts the sentence.

Case 3

Original: In an open society, class system can has high social
                  mobility but racial system is something fixed at
                  birth and can never change.

Revised: In an open society, the class system allows high social
                  mobility although the racial system still tends to
                  affect a person's life chances.

Comments:
- The definite article **the** should come before **class system** and **racial system** since particular meaning is intended when referring to the various "systems" (including these and others such as religion and education) in any given society.

- Avoid the serious error of **can has.** After the auxiliary **can,** the main verb must be in its base form. The correct construction is **can have** for first, second, and third persons, singular and plural included.
- Race is an ascribed quality that may affect a person's life chances, but the racial system itself cannot be said to be "fixed at birth." That is, the racial system is not the same thing as the attribute of race. What we can say about the racial system is that it **affects** (or **constrains**, if you want a more emphatic word) a person's life chances.
- The pattern of emphasis is altered in the revision. In the original sentence, the coordinating conjunction **but** coordinates the two ideas (one about the class system and the other about the racial system) as equally important. In the revised sentence, the subordinating conjunction **although** introduces the less important second idea (racial system affects life chances), making the first idea (class system allows high social mobility) stand out as more important. This is perhaps what the sentence is intended to indicate.

Case 4

Original: All these controlling means are very powerful, that making every individual try not to break the social norms.

Revised: All these control mechanisms are very powerful in preventing individuals from violating social norms.

Comments:
- **Mechanisms** in a social system are arrangements designed to achieve a goal. It connotes the idea of structure in a way more distinctive than the word **means.**
- The second half of the original sentence is not grammatical. The **–that** construction is neither a phrase nor a clause, and the word **that** as used here cannot connect grammatically with the first independent clause.
- If something is powerful, remember that you can describe or specify the way **in** which it is powerful. That is, think about this: it is powerful **in** some way. That "some way" can be expressed with a gerund phrase beginning with an **–ing** word. To fit this sentence, the gerund phrase you want is **preventing individuals from violating social norms.**

Case 5

Original: To have this awareness is absolutely an advantage
             to students that alerts them to be careful and to
             develop more in-depth study on studying their
             professional fields.

Revised: (a) It is absolutely to students' advantage to have
                  this awareness as it prompts them to be careful
                  and to study their professional fields in greater
                  depth.
             (b) It is definitely to students' advantage to have
                  this awareness as it alerts them to the danger
                  of taking things at face value in their
                  professional study.
             (c) Students certainly have everything to gain from
                  this awareness, which prompts them to be careful
                  and more penetrative in their professional study.

Comments:
- The construction **it is to somebody's advantage** is an idiomatic way of saying that something gives somebody an advantage.
- **Alert someone to** is usually used in reference to some danger or risk. The expression should be followed by a noun phrase or a gerund phrase, as in (b).
- Sentence (c) uses a different expression (**students have everything to gain from . . .**) to indicate that something is to students' advantage.
- Note the replacement of **absolutely** by **definitely** or **certainly. Absolutely** means "completely, in every way" whereas **definitely** and **certainly** imply "without any doubt." Although these three words overlap much in meaning, the shade of "undoubtedly" or "surely" is probably more appropriate to the sentence.

Case 6

Original: Sociology will look at phenomena that other
             disciplines also interested but its angle of vision
             is different.

Revised: While sociology studies phenomena that other
disciplines are also interested in, its perspective
is different.

Comments:

- **While** is often used to introduce a clause of concession: it makes a statement admitting that some condition may be true without, however, invalidating the truth of the main clause. The main clause here is: **Its** (sociology's) **perspective is different.**

- The present tense is appropriate for a general statement that is supposed to be always valid.

- Note that **interested** takes the preposition **in** when your sentence includes either of the following two patterns:

  Somebody is interested in something.

  This is something that somebody is interested in.

- You can say that a discipline looks at something from a certain **angle** or **perspective**. The expression **angle of vision** is too cumbersome.

Case 7

Original: In reading newspaper, we should judge the news'
reliability and accuracy from its source, comparison
of different reporting . . . etc.

Revised: In reading newspapers, we should judge the news'
reliability and accuracy by checking its source and
comparing different versions of its report.

Comments:

- Use the plural **newspapers** both because this is a statement conveying general meaning and because the statement implies that comparison of different newspapers is necessary to check the reliability and accuracy of the news.

- Note the parallel construction using gerund phrases introduced by **checking** and **comparing.** Parallel construction often makes a sentence more readable because its points stand out more clearly. (Do you see the parallel construction contained in the preceding comment?)

- Avoid using contractions such as **etc.** (and so forth) in formal writing. Either write **and so forth** or, if you really must mention other examples, name them.

Case 8

Original: I am not disagree with the author's notion about
             television can stimulate conversation among family
             members.

Revised: (a) I do not disagree with the author's notion that
                  television can stimulate conversation among
                  family members.

             (b) I agree with the author's notion that television
                  can stimulate conversation among family members.

Comments:

- The error of using **be** (is, am, are) in front of a base verb (*I am agree; I am disagree)* is probably due to direct translation from Chinese (我是同意；我是不同意). Do not fall into the habit of translating word for word from Chinese to English. Sentence patterns in the two languages are often quite different. In English, the auxiliary verb **do** (**does**) is used in front of a base verb for emphasis: **I do agree; she does agree.** For the negative, use **do (does) not: I do not agree; she does not agree.**

- **I do not disagree** is, of course, a double negative construction. If it sounds somewhat confusing, consider changing it to **I agree**, although one can argue that the two constructions are not identical in meaning.

Case 9

Original: We will not feel strange about a-husband-a-wife
             marriage system in Hong Kong.

Revised: We do not feel strange about the monogamous marriage
             system in Hong Kong.

Comments:

- Do not use the future tense in a general statement. The simple present tense is used instead because it is usually intended to be "timeless."

- When there is a proper term for something, use it instead of making one up by yourself. The writer of this sentence probably translated directly from the Chinese expression 一夫一妻 when he or she wrote **a-husband-a-wife.** The correct English word is **monogamous** (adj.).

Case 10

Original: We should not involve in matters that are responsible by other service agencies.

Revised: (a) We should not get involved in matters that are the responsibility of other service agencies.

(b) We should not get involved in matters for which other service agencies are responsible.

(c) We should not involve ourselves in matters for which other service agencies are responsible.

Comments:
- **Involve** is a transitive verb which requires an object. You can say either **we should not get involved in something** or **we should not involve ourselves in something.**
- Using the correct word form (adjective, noun, verb) is very important for expressing yourself accurately. If you use the noun **responsibility**, write your sentence as in (a); if you use the adjective **responsible**, (b) or (c) is your choice.
- Ask yourself the question: Who is responsible for what? If P is responsible for Q, then Q is the responsibility of P. A sentence written like (b) requires that the preposition **for** is placed before the relative pronoun **which.** The following two sentences are similar in that the preposition, which normally follows the main verb or adjective in the relative clause (**based on**, **measured with**), is moved to the position just before the relative pronoun **which:**

  This is the idea **on which** his whole theory is based.

  Three items make up the index **with which** socio-economic status in the study is measured.

Case 11

Original: To further understand how people are control in the system of society, the writer continue to talk about social stratification.

Revised: To examine further how people are controlled by society, Berger continues to discuss the influence of social stratification.

Comments:

- Always refer to a writer or author by his or her last name (surname). The author referred to in this sentence is Peter Berger.

- In reviewing what Berger does in his text, it is safer to say that he attempts to **examine** rather than to **understand something** unless you see clear indications of the latter.

- Placing the adverb **further** after **examine** instead of between **to** and **examine** reads better in this sentence.

- **To talk about** is too casual and vague. Indeed, avoid using such an imprecise phrase when you review a source. Consider a more precise and meaningful word instead that captures the intention of the author whom you are reviewing. Choices include **argue, discuss, examine, describe, mention, propose, review, suggest,** and many others. These are called "lead-in verbs," which are useful for introducing an author's ideas. Besides the lead-in verb, you should specify the content succinctly. Thus, **to discuss the influence of social stratification** is certainly more specific than **to talk about social stratification.** In other contexts, the content might be described as, for example, **nature, complexity,** or **universality (to discuss the universality of social stratification).**

- Failing to use the past participle verb form for a passive voice action (**controlled**) and omitting the -**s** ending of a present tense singular verb (**continues**) following a singular subject are common errors that students make. These are serious but avoidable errors.

Case 12

Original: In a certain extent we can predict an individual choice
              by examine those institutions that constraining him.

Revised: (a)   To a certain extent we can predict an individual's
                    choice by examining the ways in which he or she
                    is constrained by various institutional ele-
                    ments.

              (b)   We can more or less predict an individual's choice
                    by examining the institutional constraints that
                    he or she encounters.

Comments:

- We act or do something **to** (not **in**) **a certain extent**, but **more or less** is less wordy than **to a certain extent**.

- Since **individual** is used as a noun rather than an adjective in the sentence, write **individual's choice** rather than **individual choice**.
- Pay attention to situations that call for the use of gerunds rather than the base verb form. The gerund form (**-ing**) is required after the word **by** if the sentence structure involves the construction of **we can do something by . . . .**
- Because **institutional elements** include a variety of entities such as cultural values and beliefs, behavioural norms, time-specific activities, economic and legal transactions, and political considerations, all of which exerting constraints on the individual in one way or another, reference to **institutional elements** rather than just **institutions** makes better sense.
- The verb **constrain** is usually used in the passive voice—**People's decisions are constrained by many factors**. Sentence (a) uses constrain in this manner.
- Alternatively, you can use the noun **constraint**, as in sentence (b).

Case 13

Original: University students are supposed to be the pillars of the future society, so the aim of tertiary education is enhancing general knowledge of society of students as well as preparing for future career.

Revised: University students are supposed to be the pillars of society in future, so the aim of tertiary education is to enhance students' general knowledge of society and to prepare them for a career.

Comments:
- Keep modifiers close to the words they modify. Whose general knowledge of society? Students'. Hence, put **students'** in front of **general knowledge**; otherwise, the meaning of **general knowledge of society of students** is not clear.
- The word **future** in **preparing for future career** is redundant: preparation is always getting ready for something to come.

Case 14

Original: As long as the government still concerns about

> juvenile delinquency, the importance of youth
> service will not change.

Revised: (a)   As long as the government **is** still **concerned
> about** juvenile delinquency, the importance of
> youth service will not change.

         (b)   As long as the government still **concerns itself
> with** juvenile delinquency, the importance of
> youth service will not change.

         (c)   As long as juvenile delinquency still **concerns**
> the government, the importance of outreaching
> social work will not change.

Comments:

- The original faulty sentence shows a tendency among many Chinese students to use **concern** as a verb but incorrectly. If you use **concern** as a verb, see sentences (b) and (c).
- **To concern yourself with something** is to become involved in something because you are interested in it or because it is something that worries you. Alternatively, if **something concerns you**, it involves you or it worries you.
- You can use **concerned** as an adjective. **To be concerned about something** is to be worried about it. For more examples, see **concerned** (adj.) in Appendix 9 (Use of Selected Words and Phrases).

Case 15

Original: The famous American restaurant, McDonald's, uses
> technology and computerized method in producing food.
> Its adopts a standardized and routine way in running
> business. "McDonaldization" is a process that
> institutions run their business like that of
> McDonald's: standardized and routine.

Revised: The famous American restaurant chain, McDonald's,
> uses technology and computerized methods in
> producing food. Indeed, it runs its business with
> a high degree of rationalization. In general,
> "McDonaldization" is a process in which more and more
> institutions operate like McDonald's.

Comments:

- Accuracy of reference and meaning counts importantly. Thus, McDonald's (note that the name contains the apostrophe **s**) is not just a restaurant but a restaurant chain.

- The second sentence is rewritten to stress how McDonald's runs its business. Changing the original second sentence to **it runs its business with a high degree of rationalization** captures the characteristic of McDonald's business style more accurately.

- The term **rationalization** is more precise and more forceful than such words as **standardized** and **routine** because **rationalization** implies more than **standardization** and **routine**. It is both general and concise enough to indicate what McDonaldization is all about.

- The **that**-clause in the third sentence of the original is a noun clause; it cannot be connected to **McDonaldization is a process.** What is needed is an adjective clause introduced by **in which.**

- To improve the flow of ideas, transition markers **indeed** and **in general** are added.

Case 16

Original: Nowadays, individualism is predominant that pave the way for worsening the interrelationship and enhance selfishness. People tend to emphasize self-fulfil-ment and self-satisfaction but ignore the public benefits.

Revised: Nowadays, individualism is prevalent and may lead to greater selfishness. People tend to emphasize self-fulfilment and self-satisfaction but ignore others' needs.

Comments:

- Again, as is so commonly overlooked, the verb **pave** does not agree with its subject **individualism.** If this verb remains in the sentence, it obviously should be **paves.**

- If you want to stress that individualism is more powerful than some other orientations, **predominant** would be an appropriate word to describe it. But if you are not comparing individualism with other orientations and simply want to say that individualism is quite commonly found in many societies, then it should be described as **prevalent.**

- The term **benefits** should be used carefully. In the plural, it often refers to such things as privilege allowances paid to employees and welfare payments to the umemployed. In place of **public benefits,** use **others' needs,** which are what people preoccupied with themselves tend to overlook.

- The first sentence is too wordy; the revised sentence is more concise and straightforward.

Case 17

Original: It is clear from Table 15 that half or over half of the people tended to satisfy with their leisure no matter which educational attainment group they are belonged to. However, people with lower educational attainment had a higher leisure satisfaction, whereas higher dissatisfied cases towards higher educational attainment groups.

Revised: It is clear from Table 15 that over half of the respondents tended to be satisfied with their leisure. However, the less-educated had a higher level of leisure satisfaction than the better-educated.

Comments:

Sentences like these two here are often found in students' research papers. In reporting findings, you must say exactly what you see in the figures as clearly as possible. Note the following problems present in the original sentences:

- Individuals under study are usually referred to as **respondents** or **subjects**, not **people**.

- **To satisfy with** should be **to be satisfied with**. Whereas something satisfies (v.) you, you are satisfied (adj.) with something. That is, you should distinguish between something arousing a feeling in you and your having a feeling. (See **satisfy** in Appendix 9.)

- If you are describing just the overall distribution of the dependent variable, you do not need to mention anything about the independent variable. Hence, **no matter which educational attainment group they are belonged to** (read **they belonged to**) should be deleted.

- The second sentence is not clear; its second half is not grammatical. **People with lower educational attainment** can be more directly rephrased as **those who were less educated**. This can be further simplified to **the less-educated**.

Case 18

Original: Owing to such a unique perspective of sociology thinking, it increases students' awareness to the reality of the society. As a result, it contributes to the development of independent and critical thinking of students.

Revised: The unique perspective of sociology increases students' awareness of the reality of society and contributes to the development of their independent and critical thinking.

Comments:
- Usually we refer to the **perspective of sociology** (or some other discipline) or **sociological thinking**, but not the **perspective of sociology thinking**. If you choose **sociological thinking**, you can say: **The uniqueness of sociological thinking** . . .
- In revising sentences, combining sentences is one very important strategy since it can sharpen what you want to say. The two original sentences intend to state the effects of the perspective of sociology; they can be simplified somewhat and combined into one sentence. The revised sentence indicates the cause and effect more directly.
- **Awareness** is often followed by **of**, not **to**.
- Do not use the definite article **the** before **society** if you refer to society in a general sense or as a general idea rather than a particular society. (See **society** in Appendix 9.)

Case 19

Original: Ritzer said that university would become a kind of consumption in the postmodern society. Students choose university base on cost, quality and

```
convenience. Universities need to have innovation
to meet the needs of students, reduce cost and became
more high technology. This kind of university likes
the format of McDonald's and Disney.
```

Revised: ```
              Ritzer said that the university will become a means
              of consumption in postmodern society. Students
              choose universities according to cost, quality, and
              convenience. Universities need to innovate to meet
              the needs of students; they also need to reduce costs
              and become more technology-oriented. This kind of
              university follows the model of McDonald's and
              Disney.
              ```

Comments:

*First sentence*

- The definite article **the** placed before **university** in this sentence indicates general reference to the university as a social institution, not a particular university. Any university can fit the bill.
- The term **means of consumption** stresses the institutional framework and the mechanisms therein that make consumption possible, and is thus more precise than **kind of consumption.** In his discussion, Ritzer uses the term **means of consumption.**
- As a general idea representing a type of society but not referring to any particular society, **postmodern society** should not be preceded by the definite article **the.**

*Second sentence*

- The phrase **base on** (should be **based on)** is inappropriate because it should be preceded by a noun or noun phrase plus the verb **be** (i.e., **something is based on**). This is not the case in the original. You could say: **Students' choice of universities is based on cost, quality, and convenience.** But using the verb **choose** instead of the noun **choice** expresses the action more clearly and gives a somewhat shorter sentence. So the revision is: **Students choose universities according to cost, quality, and convenience.**
- In American English usage, place a comma after each element in a series up to the second-to-last one—**cost, quality, and convenience.** The comma before **and** is called a "serial comma." But whether you use a serial comma is a style decision. You should, however, be consistent in either using or not using it.
              ```

Third sentence

- **Universities need to innovate** is better than **universities need to have innovation** because it is more direct and sounds more forceful.

- A semicolon is used in the middle of the third sentence to bring about a sense of equal importance between meeting the needs of students on the one hand and reducing costs and becoming more technology-oriented on the other.

- Never shift tenses without good reason. There is no reason at all for using the past tense **became** in the third sentence.

Last sentence

- **Likes the format of** is not as accurate in usage and meaning as **follows the model of**.

Case 20

Original: In his research, Becker finds that the dance musicians in the club have a very strong and isolate subculture. They regard themselves to be talented, and the other to be the outsiders (Square). In order to make themselves to be different, they also always break the obligation of the conventional society.

Revised: In his research, Becker finds that the dance musicians in the club have a very strong though isolated subculture. They regard themselves as talented, and others as outsiders (squares). To make themselves different, they always disregard the rules of conventional society.

Comments:

First sentence

- **Isolate** is a verb. Use the adjective **isolated** to modify **subculture.**

Second sentence

- **Regard** takes the preposition **as** in the construction **regard something as something**.

- Becker, the author of the article that these sentences refer to, uses the word **square** to describe a kind of person who is a kind of outsider to the dance musicians. The word should not be capitalized.

- All words referring to people should be in the plural: **they**, **others** (not **the other**), **outsiders**. Thus, the plural **squares** should be used.

Third sentence

- **In order to** is a long-winded phrase that can always be reduced to simply **to** without losing any meaning.
- The word **also** is out of place because nothing has been mentioned about how the dance musicians "make themselves different."
- **Rules** (note the plural)**, not obligation,** is the better word as the concept includes both obligations and rights.
- No article is placed before **conventional society** because **conventional society** has general rather than particular meaning.

Use of Selected Words and Phrases

Correct and idiomatic use of words and phrases is a significant indicator of good writing. This appendix serves to guide you in the proper use of English by showing you language in action as seen in illustrative sentences. The present list of over 300 words and phrases certainly does not include all the ones that you may want to look up, but it does include quite a variety to meet many of your writing needs. At the same time, you should always consult a good dictionary for information not given here.

Use the list of entries that precedes the usage list itself to have an overview of the words and phrases included in this appendix. It lists all the main entries and most phrases appearing under them.

For most entries in this collection, I have written explanatory notes to help you understand their meanings and uses. Study these notes and the example sentences to learn how to use the words and phrases correctly. If you have a problem word or phrase, try checking it here. Alternatively, you can flip open any page in this appendix and just read any entry or entries that attract your attention. Do this often and you will learn much to enhance the quality of your writing.

General Guidelines for Using This Appendix

1. The entries are listed alphabetically, letter by letter, disregarding articles (**a, the**), if any, that begin a phrase. (Thus, **a series of** is listed under S, and **the following** is listed under F.)
2. Where an entry lists more than one form of the same base word, it does not mean all the possible forms are there. Unlike a dictionary, this glossary selects only those word forms that are presumably more commonly used or more likely to cause problems for students.
3. Wherever appropriate, the part of speech or the grammatical function of an entry word or phrase is indicated. Knowing the grammatical function of a word or phrase in the context of a sentence should help you to write grammatically correct sentences.

4. Some entries contain related words or phrases. You may be directed to see another word (or phrase) with which the one you are looking for is related.

5. The explanatory notes of some entries contain phrases that illustrate various uses of the key word of the entry. For example, in the entry of **rise,** you will find such phrases as **rise to power, rise to fame, rise through the ranks.** They are intended to show you various ideas involving the verb **rise** and idiomatic ways of expressing those ideas. If you bear these in mind and learn to use the phrases in addition to the key word itself, you will know that word much better.

6. An x placed in parentheses (×) in front of an example sentence indicates that the use of a certain word or phrase in that sentence is incorrect or inappropriate, whereas (√) indicates the corrected version of a flawed sentence.

7. The following abbreviations are used:

n.	=	noun	n. plural	=	plural form of a count noun
v.	=	verb	plural n.	=	plural noun (used only in the plural)
adj.	=	adjective	adv. phr.	=	adverbial phrase
adv.	=	adverb	prep. phr.	=	prepositional phrase
prep.	=	preposition	AmE	=	American English
conj.	=	conjunction	BrE	=	British English
n. phr.	=	noun phrase			

List of entries

able (adj.), **capable** (adj.)
    be able to do something
    be capable of (doing) something

access (v. and n.)
    have access to

accurate (adj.), **precise** (adj.)

adapt (v.), **adopt** (v.)
    adapt to
    adopt something

advocate (v. and n.)
    advocate (v.) **something**
    advocate (n.) **of**

affect (v.), **effect** (n.)

aggravate (v.) See **exacerbate.**

agree (v.)
    agree with
    agree on
    agree on/about
    agree that
    agree to something
    agree to do something

all-round (adj.), **all round** (adv.)

alleviate (v.)**, ameliorate** (v.)

ambiguous (adj.)**, ambivalent** (adj.)

amount (n.)

analyze (v.), **analysis** (n.)

approach (n. and v.) See **perspective.**

as (subordinating conj.) See **because.**

as follows See **the following.**

as regards (prep. phr.) See **regard** (v.).

as well (adv. phr.)

as well as (prep. phr.)

at last (adv. phr.), **lastly** (adv.)

attitude (n.), **opinion** (n.)

aware (adj.)
    aware of
    aware that
    aware why/when/how
    awareness (n.)

basis (n.)
    basis for/of
    on the basis of
    on a regular basis

because (conj.), **as** (conj.), **since** (conj.), **for** (conj.), **therefore** (adv.), **so** (conj.)

because of (prep. phr.), **because** (subordinating conj.)

believe (v.), **belief** (n.)
>   **believe in**

beneficial (adj.), **benefit** (n. and v.)

besides (prep., adv.), **moreover** (adv.)

be used to (doing) something See **used to do something.**

both . . . and . . . (correlative conj.)

capable (adj.) See **able.**

characteristic (n., adj.), **characterize** (v.)

close (adj., adv.), **closed** (adj.)

common sense (n.), **common-sense** (adj.)

compare (v.)
>   **compare with**
>   **compare to**

complain (v.), **complaint** (n.)
>   **complain about**
>   **complain to someone about something**
>   **complaint about**

compose (be composed of) See **comprise.**

comprise (v.)

concern (n.)
>   **concern that**
>   **cause** (v.) **concern, be a cause** (n.) **for concern**
>   **be of concern to someone**
>   **not someone's concern** or **none of someone's concern**
>   **concern about/over something**
>   **concern for someone**
>   **concern with something**

concern (v.)
>   **concern something**

concern someone
concern oneself with

concerned (adj.)
   all (those) concerned
   be concerned with
   be concerned about
   be concerned for
   be concerned that
   be concerned to do something
   as far as (or **where**) **something/somebody is concerned**
   as far as I am concerned

concerning (prep.)

confidence (n.), **confident** (adj.)
   confidence in something
   be confident about something
   be confident that

consider (v.)
   consider as
   consider to be
   consider doing something

consist of (phrasal v.) See **comprise.**

constitute (v.)

constrain (v.), **constraint** (n.)

contingency (n.), **contingent** (adj.)
   contingent on (or **upon**)

continual (adj.), **continuous** (adj.)

continuance (n.), **continuation** (n.), **continuity** (n.)

contrary (adj.)
   contrary to
   on the contrary

contrast (n. and v.)
   contrast (n.) **between**
   in contrast to

by/in contrast
contrast (v.) with

contribute (v.)
   contribute to

convenience (n.), **convenient** (adj.)
   for convenience of

correct (adj.), **right** (adj.)
   taking a step in the right direction

cosmopolitan (adj.)
   cosmopolitan character/outlook

cost of living (n. phr.) See **standard of living.**

criterion (n.), **criteria** (n.)

data (n.)

decide (v.), **determine** (v.), **determined** (adj.)

deprive (v.), **deprived** (adj.), **deprivation** (n.)
   deprive somebody of something

depth (n.)
   in depth (adv. phr.)
   in-depth (adj.)

despite (prep.), **in spite of** (prep. phr.)

detail (n.), **detailed** (adj.)
   go into detail
   in (great/full) detail
   detailed (adj.) **description**

difficult (adj.), **easy** (adj.)

discuss (v.), **mention** (v. and n.)
   not to mention
   it is worth mentioning that
   mention (n.) **of**

distinguish (v.), **distinction** (n.), **distinct** (adj.), **distinctive** (adj.)
   as distinct from

easy (adj.) See **difficult.**

effect (n.) See **affect.**

effective (adj.), **efficient** (adj.)

effort (n.)
> **make an effort**
> **make every effort**
> **put much effort into something**

either . . . or . . . (correlative conj.)

emphasize (v.), **emphasis** (n.)
> **emphasize something**
> **emphasize that**
> **put/place/lay emphasis on**
> **with emphasis on**

essential (adj.) See **necessary.**

even if, even though (both subordinating conj.)

every day (adv. phr.), **everyday** (adj.)

everyone (indefinite pronoun), **every one**

evidence (n.)

exacerbate (v.), **aggravate** (v.)

examine (v.) See **study.**

excited (adj.), **exciting** (adj.)

experience (n., v.), **experienced** (adj.)
> **experienced in/at**

explanation (n.)
> **explanation of**
> **explanation for**

extent (n.), **extend** (v.), **extension** (n.)
> **to a certain extent, to some extent, to a large extent**
> **to the extent that**

facilitate (v.)

familiar (adj.), **familiarity** (n.), **familiarize** (v.)
  familiar with
  familiar to .
  all-too-familiar
  familiarity with
  familiarize oneself with

the following, as follows

for (coordinating conj.) See **because.**

for example

fourth (adj.), **forth** (adv.)

get used to (doing) something See **used to do something.**

given (adj., n., prep.)

grateful (adj.)
  grateful to somebody for something

a great deal, a great deal of

happen (v.)

have to (modal auxiliary verb) See **must, should, have to.**

horizons (n.)
  broaden one's horizons

impact (n., v.) See **influence.**

imply (v.), **infer** (v.)

in addition to (prep. phr.)

indispensable (adj.) See **necessary.**

influence (n., v.), **impact** (n., v.)

in itself (adv. phr.), **per se** (adv., Latin)
  in and of itself, in its own right
  an end in its own right.

in particular (adv. phr.) See **particular.**

in regard to (prep. phr.) See **regard** (n.).

in respect of (prep. phr.) See **regard** (n.).

in someone's own right See **right** (n.).

in spite of (prep.) See **despite.**

interest (n. and v.), **interested** (adj.), **interesting** (adj.)
>   **interest** (n.) **in**
>   **enduring interest**
>   **intense interest**
>   **interested to do something**
>   **interested in**
>   **interest** (v.) **somebody**
>   **interesting to**
>   **interested party**

investigate (v.) See **study.**

irrespective of (prep. phr.) See **regardless of.**

kind of (adv.), **sort of** (adv.)

kind(s) of

lack (v. and n.), **lacking** (adj.)
>   **through lack of** or **for lack of something**
>   **lacking in something**

lastly (adv.) See **at last.**

let (v.), **make** (v.)

lie (v.), **lay** (v.)
>   **lie on**
>   **lie in**
>   **lie at the heart of**
>   **lay the groundwork**

like (n., adj., v., and prep.)
>   **likes and dislikes**
>   **and the like**
>   **like-minded people**

likely (adj., adv.)
>   **likely consequences**

likely margin of error
as likely as not

lose (v.), **loss** (n.)

lots of, a lot of (determiner)

make (v.) See **let.**

make (be made up of) See **comprise.**

male (adj. and n.), **female** (adj. and n.)

many (adj.) See **much.**

may (modal auxiliary verb)

maybe (adv.), **may be** (**may** as a modal auxiliary verb)

media (n.)

mention (v. and n.) See **discuss.**

more . . . than . . .

more than one

moreover (adv.) See **besides.**

much (adv.)
much the same
much too difficult

much (adj.), **many** (adj.)

must, should, have to (modal auxiliary verbs)

must (n.)

necessary (adj.), **need** (v.)

necessary (adj.), **indispensable** (adj.), **essential** (adj.)
necessary for
indispensable for
indispensable to
essential for
essential to
essential that

not . . . but . . . (correlative conj.)

not only . . . , but also (correlative conj.)

one of

opinion (n.) See **attitude.**

outdated, out-of-date, out of date (all adj.)

particular (adj.), **particularly** (adv.), **in particular** (adv. phr.), **particulars** (plural n.)

per se (adv., Latin) See **in itself.**

perspective (n.), **viewpoint** (n.), **approach** (n. and v.)

phenomenon (n. singular)**, phenomena** (n. plural) See also **criterion, criteria.**

possess (v.)

possible (adj.), **probable** (adj.)

possibly (adv.)**, probably** (adv.)

precise (adj.) See **accurate.**

principal (n. and adj.), **principle** (n.), **in principle** (adv. phr.)

procedure (n.)

process (n. and v.)

provided that, **providing that** (both subordinating conj.)

pursue (v.), **pursuit** (n.)

raise (v. and n.) See **rise.**

rather than (coordinating conj., prep. phr.)

recent (adj.), **recently** (adv.)
    in recent years
    in recent decades
    until as recent as

regard (v.)
    regard somebody/something as
    as regards (prep. phr.)

regard (n.)
>   **with regard to, in regard to** (prep. phr.)
>   **with reference to, with respect to, in respect of** (prep. phr.)
>   **in this regard**

regarding (prep.)

regardless of, irrespective of (prep. phr.)

related to

relating to (two-word prep.)

relation (n.)**, relationship** (n.)
>   **in relation to**
>   **bear no relation to**
>   **relations between two countries**

relatively (adv.)

reliable (adj.) See **valid.**

replace (v.)**, substitute** (v., n.)
>   **X replaces Y**
>   **replace Y with X**
>   **Y is replaced by X**
>   **substitute X for Y**
>   **X is substituted for Y**
>   **X is a substitute for Y**

research (n. singular)**, researches** (n. plural)

result (n. and v.)
>   **result** (n.) **of**
>   **as a result of** (prep. phr.)
>   **result** (v.) **in**
>   **result** (v.) **from**

right (adj.) See **correct.**

right (n.)
>   **rights and obligations**
>   **in someone's own right**
>   **an end in its own right**
>   **an end in itself**

rise (v. and n.), **raise** (v. and n.)
    rise (n.) **in**
    rise (n.) **of**
    give rise to

satisfy (v.), **satisfied** (adj.), **satisfactory** (adj.), **satisfying** (adj.), **satisfaction** (n.)
    level of satisfaction
    satisfied with

search (v.), **search for**

a series of

since (subordinating conj.) See **because.**

so (coordinating conj.) See **because.**

so . . . that . . .

social (adj.), **societal** (adj.)

society (n.)

some (determiner)

someday (adv.)**, some day** (n. phr.)

sometimes (adv.)**, sometime** (adj., adv.), **some time** (n. phr.), **some time ago** (adv. phr.)

sort of (adv.) See **kind of.**

standard of living (n. phr.), **cost of living** (n. phr.)

statistic (n.), **statistics** (n.)

study (v.), **examine** (v.), **investigate** (v.)

substitute (v., n.) See **replace.**

succeed (v.), **success** (n.)
    succeed in something
    succeed in doing something

such that, such . . . that

suppose (v.), **supposed** (adj.), **supposedly** (adv.), **supposing** (conj.)
    be supposed to
    supposing (that)

surprise (n., v.), **surprised** (adj.), **surprising** (adj.)
  take somebody by surprise
  much to somebody's surprise
  surprised at
  surprised by

take something for granted
  take it for granted
  something is taken for granted
  it is taken for granted that
  take nothing for granted
  taken-for-granted (compound adj.)

tend (v.)
  tend to do something
  tend to be

therefore (conjunctive adv.) See **because.**

thought of as

time (n.), **times** (n.)
  there are times when
  at times

together with (prep. phr.) See also **as well as.**

towards (prep.)

twenty-four-hour (adj.)

understanding (n.)
  understanding of something
  understanding that (introducing a noun clause)

update (v. and n.), **up-to-date** and **up to date** (adj.)

used to do something, be used to (doing) something, get used to (doing) something

valid (adj.), **reliable** (adj.)

a variety of (followed by a plural noun)

a variety of (followed by a singular noun)

view (n. and v.)
  view of

view on/about

viewpoint (n.) See **perspective**.

vocabulary (n.)

with reference to (prep. phr.) See **regard** (n.).

with regard to (prep. phr.) See **regard** (n.).

with respect to (prep. phr.) See **regard** (n.).

worth (n. and adj.)**, worthy** (adj.)**, worthwhile** (adj.)
    great worth (n.)
    worth (adj.) **doing**
    worth something
    for what/whatever it is worth
    worthy (adj.) **of something**
    worthy of somebody
    worthy cause
    worthwhile thing
    worth your (or somebody's) while

youth (n.)

Usage List

able (adj.)**, capable** (adj.)
    be able to do something (= to have the skill or opportunity to do something)

> If we recruit at least fifty fieldworkers, we will **be able to** complete the data collection in time.

> Not knowing Japanese, we **were** not **able to** communicate with most local people when we visited Japan.

    capable (adj.)

> A **capable** researcher is always aware of the limitations of the method used.

be capable of (doing) something (= having the qualities to do something)

> Many women **are** now quite **capable of** pursuing a career and taking care of a family.

> With sincerity and discipline, some seemingly ordinary people **are capable of** great achievements.

> A socio-emotional leader is **capable of** boosting morale in his or her group.

access (v. and n.)

access (v.) (stress on the first syllable*)*

Used as a verb, **access** means to obtain or to find information stored on a computer. DO NOT confuse with **assess** (v. = to evaluate) (stress on the second syllable)

> You cannot **access** these databases unless you are a registered user.

have/has access (n.) to

> Only top-level managers **have access to** confidential documents.

> (×) With technological advancement, people can **access to** a great variety of information.

> (√) With technological advancement, people can **have access to** a great variety of information.

accurate (adj.)**, precise** (adj.)

Accurate emphasizes adherence to or reflection of fact or truth by exercising great care. It is used in phrases such as the following:

> **accurate time** (= true time)
> **accurate description**
> **accurate information**
> **accurate measurement**
> **accurate calculation**
> **accurate translation**

Precise emphasizes sharpness of definition or exactness of detail. You may come across it in the following phrases:

precise prediction (e.g., unemployment rate rising to anywhere between 5.2
per cent and 5.6 per cent next month")

precise date (e.g., "June 15, 2004" rather than "some day in June of 2004")

precise definition

precise nature of the task

precise reproduction of an original

The meaning of **precise** should be clear from the following sentence:

> It is more **precise** to say that the Chief Executive's
> approval rate is likely to be between 55 per cent and
> 57 per cent than to say that it is likely to fall between
> 50 per cent and 60 per cent.

If the Chief Executive's actual approval rate is 59 per cent, the less precise
description of 50 per cent to 60 per cent will be more accurate than the more
precise description (or estimation) of 55 per cent to 57 per cent! This shows that
precision does not guarantee accuracy.

> If **accuracy** is more important to the researcher, he
> or she may have to do with less **precision**.

adapt (v.), **adopt** (v.)

These two words are easily confused as they resemble each other both in
spelling and in pronunciation.

> If you **adapt** yourself to a new environment, you get
> used to conditions in that environment.

> Young immigrants are likely to **adapt** to the host
> country faster than do their parents.

If you **adopt** something, you have it or use it as your own.

> Now that government funding will be reduced, the
> universities in Hong Kong will have to **adopt** stringent
> measures in resources allocation.

adopt (v.) See **adapt.**

advocate (v. and n.)

To advocate X is to argue for X and to speak in favour of it. **Advocate** as a verb
is not followed by any preposition:

> They **advocate** qualified freedom of the press.

But **advocate** as a noun (a person who argues for something) takes **of** after it. Thus, we may say:

> He is an **advocate of** qualified freedom of the press.

affect (v.), **effect** (n.)

Affect (stress on the second syllable) is often used as a verb meaning "to influence."

> How do advertisements in the mass media **affect** our consumption behaviour?

Effect is usually used as a noun:

> Do advertisements in the mass media have any **effect** on our consumption behaviour?

Effect can be used as a verb:

> We usually need influential and trusted agents to **effect** behavioural change in a group.

aggravate (v.) See **exacerbate.**

agree (v.)

agree with

You can **agree with** something or **agree with** someone **about** something:

> No action will be taken unless everybody **agrees with** the plan.

> We **agree with** the author **about** the need to place teenage problems in the context of social relationships and social institutions.

Two things can be said to **agree with** (= to be consistent with or the same as) each other:

> Your description of yesterday's events **agrees with** theirs.

agree on

When you say that some people **agree on** something such as a date or an action, you mean that it is something these people decide together.

> After a long discussion, we **agreed on** using both

```
interview of informants and field observation to
gather data for our study.
```

agree on/about

If you want to stress that some individuals have the same opinion about something, then you can use either **agree on** or **agree about.**

```
They did not have to talk for long before they realized
that they actually agreed about whether universities
in Hong Kong should change from a three-year system
to a four-year one.
```

agree + that-clause

You can **agree that** something is true, acceptable, or feasible:

```
Not all politicians agree that the government should
interfere with the property market.
```

agree to

You can **agree to** someone's request or some new policy:

```
Staff members of the two universities should have the
right to vote to show whether they agree to the proposed
merger of their universities.
```

You can **agree to do something:**

```
It will be good if both Israel and the Palestinians
can agree to end all hostilities and conflicts.

We agreed to complete this project before the end of
this year.
```

Note that the use of **agree to**, as indicated in the preceding two example sentences, implies that the subject (**Israel and the Palestinians** in the first sentence and **we** in the second) is the doer or potential doer of the action mentioned. If the subject is not or cannot be the doer of the action, the use of **agree to** is inappropriate, as in the following sentence:

```
(×) As students, we do not agree to merge University A and
University B.
```

The sentence is not appropriate because the actual merging action, if ever implemented, is unlikely to be taken up by students. To make better sense, the sentence may be rephrased by using **agree** with a **that-**clause, as follows:

```
As students, we do not agree that University A and
University B should be merged.
```

Restated this way, the sentence no longer has the problem involved earlier since students can certainly indicate whether they agree that the two universities should be merged. The doer of the action (merging), as the sentence is written, is anybody but the students.

all round (adv.) See **all-round.**

all-round (adj.)**, all round** (adv.)

An **all-round** person is someone who is able to do many different things or who has many different skills. In AmE, the expression is also written as **all-around.** Do not write **all-rounded.**

```
A good all-round education consists of familiarity
with a wide variety of subject matter.
```

Note that **all-round** is used only as a premodifier (placed before a noun):

```
A liberal arts education aims at producing all-round
individuals.
```

An **all-round** person can be described as an **all-rounder.**

```
Given adequate training and opportunities, some people
can become all-rounders in sports.
```

When used without the hyphen, **all round** is an adverb meaning in all respects:

```
This is a well-written report all round.
```

alleviate (v.)**, ameliorate** (v.)

We speak of **alleviating** pain or suffering, meaning making it less severe. We also speak of **alleviating** a problem or making it less hurtful or serious.

```
The task of alleviating poverty is a difficult one for
any government.
```

Ameliorate has a similar meaning. To **ameliorate** is to make something better or easier. **Alleviate** is the word to use when you mean to say to lighten a burden or minimize trouble. If you have in mind a condition, rather than some specific pain or trouble, then **ameliorate** should be used instead of **alleviate.**

```
What can the United States do to ameliorate the
situation in the Middle East?
```

Note, however, that **ameliorate** is quite formal, perhaps more appropriate in literary writing. In the above sentence, you can use **improve** without changing the meaning:

> What can the United States do to **improve** the situation in the Middle East?

ambiguous (adj.)**, ambivalent** (adj.)

Anything that is **ambiguous** has more than one meaning or has an unclear meaning. We may speak of an **ambiguous** sign or an **ambiguous** role.

Whereas **ambiguous** refers to things, ideas, or positions, **ambivalent** refers to people when they are not sure what they want or when they have mixed feelings about something.

> The law can be **ambiguous about** what constitutes infringement of individual privacy.

> Although many people tend to support the legalization of sports gambling, some of them are actually quite **ambivalent about** it.

ambivalent (adj.) See **ambiguous.**

ameliorate (v.) See **alleviate.**

amount (n.)

Amount of is usually used with uncount nouns (e.g., time, work, wealth, influence, attention, energy).

> The **amount** of influence a person has over others in an organization depends on both knowledge and experience.

> Celebrity figures appearing in charity shows can attract a large **amount** of attention.

analysis (n.) See **analyze.**

analyze (v.)**, analysis** (n.)

Watch out when you use these words. Many students use them incorrectly. Keep in mind their difference. Being a noun, **analysis** (four syllables, stress on the second syllable) can be modified by an adjective (e.g., **thorough analysis, careful analysis**) or preceded by an article (e.g., **an analysis, the analysis**). Typically, you refer to **the analysis of** something. **Analyze** (three syllables, stress on the first syllable, spelled **analyse** in BrE) is a verb. You can **analyze** something, or **have** something **analyzed.** Having done so, you have an **analysis** of something.

analyze (v.)

> To **analyze** the production of news, we can start with the role of reporters.

> We plan to have the data **analyzed** differently to see whether we have the same result.

analysis (n.)

> We need to consider the role of social values in our **analysis** of news.

> All research reports contain a section on data **analysis**.

approach (n. and v.) See **perspective.**

as (subordinating conj.) See **because.**

as follows See **the following.**

as regards (prep. phr.) See **regard** (v.).

as well (adv. phr.)

Like **too**, **as well** is usually placed at the end of an affirmative statement.

> She gathered the data and wrote the report **as well.**
> (Writing the report is being emphasized.)

> She is our group's leader and a modest person **as well.**
> (That she is a modest person is being emphasized.)

The above two sentences can be reworded, using **as well as**, as follows:

> She wrote the report **as well as** gathering the data.

> She is a modest person **as well as** being our group's leader.

as well as (prep. phr.)

> Garfinkel, **as well as** Goffman, **is** (not **are**) interested in people as agents of action.

> Women's employment has symbolic **as well as** economic significance. (Symbolic significance is more important than economic significance.)

In the following two sentences, you must use an -**ing** word after **as well as**:

> She wrote the report **as well as** gathering the data.

> She is a modest person **as well as** being our group's leader.

Do not equate this in meaning with **and.**

Examine this sentence:

> Choice of measurement method, **as well as** defining the meaning of concepts under study, **is** a critical part of the research process.

In the phrase enclosed by commas, **as well as** introduces additional information which is considered less important than the information given in the opening noun phrase. The sentence means that choice of measurement method is a critical part of the research process, more so than defining the meaning of concepts under study.

Note that if the opening noun phrase is singular (as is the case in the sentence given), the verb is singular. In contrast, in a sentence using **and** to connect two nouns or noun phrases to produce a compound subject, the verb is usually plural. If **as well as** is replaced by **and,** the above sentence should read:

> Choice of measurement method **and** defining the meaning of concepts under study **are** critical parts of the research process.

When a verb is used in the phrase introduced by **as well as,** it should be in -**ing** form. This is shown also in the following sentences. Note that since **as well as** introduces a subordinated element, this element can be placed in initial or final position in the sentence:

> He wrote the report **as well as** gathering the data.

> **As well as** gathering the data, he wrote the report.

> She considers herself an individual with her own identity **as well as** being the manager's wife.

```
As well as being the manager's wife, she considers
herself an individual with her own identity.
```

at last (adv. phr.), **lastly** (adv.)

At last (= eventually) always refers to time:

```
At last we completed all the data processing required
by the project.
```

Lastly (= finally) refers to order in a list. When you come to the last item or point in a list, you use **lastly**, not **at last**.

```
Lastly, we will consider the relationship between
advertising and consumption.
```

attitude (n.), **opinion** (n.)

An attitude is basically a disposition in some general direction; an opinion is a view or position regarding an issue. For example, you may feel sympathetic with people who have lost their jobs. That is your **attitude towards** unemployment (in general). If someone asks you what you think about the usefulness of the government's retraining programmes for the unemployed, you may say that you think they are not very useful. That is your **opinion** (specific to an issue).

```
Beginning university students usually have a somewhat
relaxed attitude to their studies.
```

```
They are studying the attitude of Hong Kong people
towards new immigrants from China.
```

```
This is a survey that examines university students'
opinions of whether the government should support
associate degree programmes.
```

```
We can study the role of the mass media in helping
people to form opinions about issues and events.
```

aware (adj.)

Aware is not a verb and must not be used as such. The following constructions are all incorrect:

```
(×) I aware that writing well is important.
```

```
(×) We do not aware the difference between "organization"
and "association."
```

(×) She **awared** this could not be done.

The above three sentences should be revised as follows:

I am **aware** that writing well is important.

We are not **aware** **of** the difference between "organization" and "association."

She was **aware** that this could not be done.

aware of

A typical construction is **be + aware + of + noun phrase:**

Sociology trains us **to be aware of** the connection between individual actions and social processes.

Some students **are** not **aware of** the importance of time management.

aware that (**that** introduces a noun clause)

Some students are not **aware that** time management is important.

aware why/when/how (these words also introduce a noun clause)

They were painfully **aware why** they failed the test.

You do not seem to be **aware when** this study was conducted.

We need to be **aware how** critical funding is to this project.

You can begin a sentence with a phrase starting with **aware of:**

Aware of the urgency of the problem, we decided to adopt some rather drastic measures.

awareness (n.) (can be followed by a -**that** noun clause)

The **awareness** that personal choices are in fact affected by social factors is something all sociology students need to have.

basis (n.)

    basis for/of

> Functionalists believe that consensus is the **basis of** social stability.

> What do you think is the **basis for** their opposition?

    on the basis of

> **On the basis of** these reasons, we make the following recommendations.

> Better say (to be less wordy): **Considering** these reasons, we make the following recommendations.

    on a regular basis

> We visited the family **on a regular basis.**

> Better say (to be less wordy): We visited the family **regularly.**

because (conj.), **as** (conj.), **since** (conj.), **for** (conj.), **therefore** (adv.), **so** (conj.)

    because, as, since (all subordinating conjunctions)

These words all introduce a reason clause which is also a subordinate clause, with the main clause receiving greater emphasis. **As** and **since** (more formal than **as**) are more often used at the beginning of a sentence to refer to reasons that are supposed to be well known, as in the following two sentences:

> **Since** government funding for higher education will be reduced, all universities are implementing stringency measures to cope with the situation.

> **As** electronic resources are easily accessible, students find it very convenient to find material for their research papers.

Be careful with **as,** since it can mean both "because" and "while." Thus, the meaning of **as** is ambiguous in the following sentence. To remove the ambiguity, you can use **since** or **while,** depending on what you mean to say.

> **As** the economy continued to deteriorate, the government devised a package of actions to increase employment opportunities.

While **because** can also be used to introduce a reason clause at the beginning of a sentence, it comes more often after the main clause:

```
China at first adopted a secretive approach to the
coverage of news of the atypical pneumonia epidemic
because it feared that such news would jeopardize
national stability and commerce.
```

for (coordinating conj.)

For, even more formal than **since**, is not used at the beginning of a sentence. Whereas **because, as,** and **since** are subordinating conjunctions, **for** is a coordinating conjunction. This means you use **for** to give equal emphasis to both the reason clause and the consequence clause. Neither clause is subordinate.

```
We must hurry, for we have only little time left.

This is what the government must do, for there is really
no feasible alternative.
```

therefore (conjunctive adv.)

Therefore is a conjunctive adverb used to coordinate two equally important ideas:

```
It was a city-wide study; therefore, we needed more
research resources.
```

Do not use **since**, **as**, or **because** in the same sentence in which you use **therefore** for the consequence clause. Conversely, if you use **since**, **as**, or **because,** do not use **therefore**. Remember: **since**, **as**, **because** are used in subordinating one idea (cause) to another (consequence), but **therefore** is used to indicate that both ideas (cause and consequence) are equally important.

(×) ```Because the population is aging rapidly; therefore,
    more resources for services for the elderly are needed.```

(√) ```The population is aging rapidly; therefore, more
    resources for services for the elderly are needed.```
    (Note the use of a semicolon before **therefore**.)

(√) ```Because the population is aging rapidly, more
    resources for services for the elderly are needed.```

so (coordinating conj.)

So is a coordinating conjunction (in the same class as **and**, **or**, and **but**) used to link two equally important ideas. As in the case of **therefore**, do not use **so** to introduce the consequence clause if you use **since**, **as**, or **because** for the reason clause.

(×) **Since** communicating by email is very easy, **so** people seldom write letters by hand.

(√) Communicating by email is very easy, **so** people seldom write letters by hand.

(√) **Since** communicating by email is very easy, people seldom write letters by hand.

because of (prep. phr.), **because** (subordinating conj.)

As a prepositional phrase, **because of** takes a noun or a noun phrase as its object:

Because of rising labour cost, manufacturers have to relocate their factories to places where there is cheaper labour. (**Rising labour cost** is a noun phrase.)

Because must be followed by not a phrase but a clause with its own subject and verb:

Because labour cost is rising, manufacturers have to relocate their factories to places where there is cheaper labour. (**Labour cost is rising** is a clause.)

Both **because of** and **because** are used in subordination, as in the above two sentences.

belief (n.) See **believe**.

believe (v.), **belief** (n.)

Do not confuse the use of **believe** and that of **believe in**. You **believe** something if you think it is true. If you **believe** a person, you think that he or she is telling the truth:

You may find this overly zealous politician hard to **believe**.

I **believe** that politics exists wherever there is human activity.

If you **believe in** an idea or an activity, you think it is good or right and thus worth pursuing:

```
Pacifists believe in non-violence.

If more people believe in the value of reading, the
level of cultural literacy will improve.
```

If you **believe in** God and miracles, you believe that they exist. If you **believe in** someone, you have confidence in him or her.

```
It is such a comfort to hear that your friends believe
in you.
```

belief (n.) (*pl.* **beliefs**)

```
The belief that hard work will not be unrewarded is
what has sustained them in difficult times.
```

In the following two sentences, the plural **beliefs** is used:

```
Some athletes will not compete on Sundays because of
their religious beliefs.

Culture consists of beliefs, values, and norms.
```

beneficial (adj.), **benefit** (n. and v.)

If an action is **beneficial to** certain groups of people, it brings certain advantages or **benefits** (n.) to them. We say that the action will **benefit** (v.) those people, and those people will **benefit** (v.) **from** the action.

```
(×) Which groups of people will be the most beneficial by
    computer technology?

(√) Which groups of people will benefit most from computer
    technology?

(√) To which groups of people will computer technology be
    most beneficial?
```

benefit (n. and v.) See **beneficial.**

besides (prep., adv.), **moreover** (adv.)

Besides and **moreover** are used to indicate additional points. But many students tend to overuse them and often use them inappropriately.

besides (prep.)

As a preposition, **besides** means "in addition":

```
Television programmes can inform and cultivate tastes
besides providing entertainment.

Besides being diffuse, primary relations are highly
personal.
```

besides (conjunctive adv.)

As an adverb, **besides** is used not to add a point in a neutral way but to add a point against something. You may use it in this function to make a new statement that is related to a preceding one. Note that the preceding statement contains a negative idea about something; the statement introduced by **besides** adds another negative point about that something. Study the following sentences carefully. If you place **besides** in mid-sentence, you should use a semicolon before **besides.**

```
What we read in some newspapers is often not news in
the strict sense of the word but gossip; besides, it
does not do much to help us understand the more
important social issues.

Environmentalists argue that the proposed highway will
disrupt the serenity of the place. Besides, they warn
us, it will also destroy the habitat of a number of
rare species of birds.
```

The following use of **besides** (adv.) is inappropriate because it adds a point in a neutral way:

```
(×) News is what reporters tell us about events; besides,
its production depends on the editorial policy of the
newspaper.
```

moreover (conjunctive adv.)

Use **moreover** to introduce a *new* point which is *parallel* with a point already made. Like **besides, moreover** is a conjunctive adverb used to coordinate two equally important ideas. If you use **moreover** in mid-sentence, remember that you should use a semicolon at the end of the first idea before you introduce the second idea with **moreover.**

```
Every question included in a questionnaire must have
a purpose related to the research; moreover, the
researcher must ensure that the wording of each
question is simple and clear.
```

In the following, **moreover** is used incorrectly because the statement introduced by **moreover** is not really a *new* point but part of the same point:

(×) Questionnaires are often used in surveys. Researchers must ensure that the wording of each question is simple and direct. **Moreover,** the design of questionnaires can be quite time-consuming.

In the above passage, **moreover** should not be used. That designing questionnaires can be time-consuming is **because** much effort is needed to get the wording right. The following is an improved version of the passage:

Questionnaires are often used in surveys. The design of questionnaires can be quite time-consuming **because** researchers must ensure that the wording of each question is simple and direct.

If the point added is not really *parallel* with a preceding one, using **moreover** to mention the added point is incorrect:

(×) Questionnaires are often used in surveys. **Moreover,** researchers must ensure that the wording of each question is simple and direct.

be used to (doing) something See **used to do something.**

both . . . and . . . (correlative conj.)

As with other correlative conjunctions, you must use a parallel construction for **both . . . and . . .** That is, what follows **both** must be grammatically parallel with what follows **and**.

Reading widely can **both** broaden one's horizons **and** improve one's writing ability.

Care must be taken **both** when we conceptualize a problem **and** when we design an appropriate research instrument to collect the data we need.

(×) We can **both** learn important concepts **and** application to our daily life.

(√) We can **both learn** important concepts **and apply** them to our daily life.

   (×) Sociologists need to **both** think logically **and** to study
      events systematically.

   (√) Sociologists need **both to think** logically **and to study**
      events systematically.

   Or:

   Sociologists need to **both think** logically **and study**
   events systematically.

capable (adj.) See **able.**

characteristic (n., adj.), **characterize** (v.)
   characteristic (n.)
     A **characteristic** is a typical feature of something or someone.

       A distinguishing **characteristic** of a primary group is
       that relationships are very personal.

   characteristic (adj.)

       Personal relationships are a **characteristic** feature
       of a primary group.

       The Chief Executive started his speech with his
       characteristic smile.

characteristic (adj.) **of something/somebody**
   In its adjectival role, **characteristic** can be placed before or after the noun (or noun phrase) that it modifies. When placed after such a noun, use **characteristic + of something** (or **somebody**):

       Visitors to Hong Kong can easily sense a rapid pace
       of life that is so **characteristic of** Hong Kong. (Here,
       characteristic modifies the noun phrase **a rapid pace of life**.)

   The above sentence can be rewritten to place **characteristic** before the noun phrase it modifies. While the sentence becomes more concise, it loses some of the emphatic tone more readily carried in the last part of the original sentence.

       Visitors to Hong Kong can easily sense its **charac-
       teristic** rapid pace of life.

In the next four sentences, note that a slight difference in wording results from whether **characteristic** is used as a noun or as an adjective:

> In modern shopping malls, you will find standardized layout and equipment that are **characteristic of** a McDonaldized society. (Here **characteristic** is an adjective.)

> In modern shopping malls, you will find standardized layout and equipment that are **characteristics of** a McDonaldized society. (Here **characteristics** is a noun.)

> Adherence to formal rules is **characteristic** (adj.) **of** bureaucracies.

> Adherence to formal rules is **a characteristic** (n.) **of** bureaucracies.

characterize (v.)

You can **characterize** a concept or a theory (or anything) by describing its characteristic features. Certain features can be said to **characterize** something. Something is **characterized** by certain features.

> The omnipresence of societal forces **characterizes** Durkheim's theory.

> Hong Kong is **characterized** by a vibrant capitalist economy.

> Academic autonomy **characterizes** the role of university professors.

characterize (v.) See **characteristic.**

close (adj., adv.), **closed** (adj.)

These two words are easily confused if you are not careful.

The core meaning of **close** (adj.) is "near." You can **be close to** something by coming near it. When you are close to achieving something, you are almost there.

> We are **close** to reaching an agreement.

Given the core meaning of "near," **close** also means "careful" and "friendly" or "intimate." You pay **close attention** to something important, including perhaps how to stay **close to** members of your family.

> Let us take a **closer** look at the situation.

When in trouble, she wants to talk to a **close** friend.

In the following two sentences, **close** is an adverb:

Hong Kong is still an important economic and financial centre in Asia, but Shanghai is **close** behind.

Members of a **close-knit** (or **closely-knit**) group have a strong sense of belonging.

Closed (adj.) means "not open." A **closed society** is one that isolates itself from outside influences. A person who is not willing to consider different ways of doing things or new ideas has a **closed mind.** In social research, a questionnaire containing only questions with preset response categories is a **closed-ended** questionnaire.

The discussion is now **closed.**

One cannot approach this sensitive issue with a **closed** mind.

They will discuss the matter in a **closed-door** meeting.

This questionnaire contains only **closed-ended** items.
(NOT **close-end** or **close-ended**)

closed (adj.) See **close.**

common-sense (adj.) See **common sense.**

common sense (n.), **common-sense** (adj.)

Guided by **common sense,** we should be able to make a decent plan.

Use the hyphenated compound adjective **common-sense** (**commonsense** in AmE) when you place it as a modifier before a noun.

We are taking a **common-sense** approach to the problem.

compare (v.)
   compare with
When you **compare** A **with** B, you want to consider their similarities and differences:

You will find that functionalist theory is quite

```
conservative as a perspective compared with conflict
theory.
```

compare to

When you **compare** A **to** B, they are being likened to each other:

```
Charles Cooley compared people's influence on the
emergence of the self to the use of a looking glass.
```

complain (v.), **complaint** (n.)

Note that the noun **complaint** ends with a **"t"** which should be voiced when spoken. If you have the habit of dropping the **t** sound when using it as a noun (as in **my complaint**) in speech, chances are that you may forget the **t** when you write the word.

complain about

```
People are always complaining about the high cost of
living.
```

complain to someone about something

```
The employees complained to their boss about the poor
working conditions.
```

complaint about

```
These employees have no complaint about how they are
treated by their employer.
```

complaint (n.) See **complain.**

compose (be composed of) See **comprise.**

comprise (v.)

If A, B, and C are parts that make up a whole, W, we say that W **comprises** A, B, and C. Note that it is wrong to say **comprise of** or **is comprised of.**

(×) The company **is comprised of** five departments.

(√) The company **comprises** five departments.

You can express the same meaning using **be composed of, be made up of,** or **consist of:**

```
The company is composed of five departments.
```

```
The company is made up of five departments.
```

```
The company consists of five departments.
```

But you cannot write:

```
(×) The company is consisted of five departments.
```

concern (n.)

Many Chinese students have difficulty in using the word **concern** correctly. It is probably the word that is most frequently misused. You should therefore study carefully the example sentences in this and the next three main entries to recognize the patterns of construction associated with the various uses of **concern** as a noun and as a verb, **concerned** as an adjective, and **concerning** as a preposition. The following illustrates uses of **concern** as a noun.

A **concern** is something that is important enough to be considered seriously or worried about. You can use **concern** in either the singular or the plural form depending on the sense intended.

```
We all have concerns as citizens.
```

```
Grades are the main concern of many students.
```

```
It is our concern in this part of the report to explain
why the response rate was so low.
```

To specify a concern, you can use a **that**-clause. Note the changes in sentence construction in the following to express slightly different meanings:

```
There is widespread concern that the economy might
worsen.
```

```
Our greatest concern is that the economy might worsen.
```

```
Our concern that the economy might worsen is not
unfounded.
```

cause (v.) concern, be a cause (n.) for concern

```
The rapidly rising cost of rental properties in
Shanghai is causing (v.) much concern among foreign
business people living there.
```

```
To environmentalists, the proposed highway project
```

that requires the draining of marshland **is a cause** (n.) **for concern**.

be of concern to someone (usually with a modifier added before **concern**)

Finding a suitable job in a gloomy economy **is of** great **concern to** young graduates.

How workers feel about their job may **be of** little **concern to** their employers.

not someone's concern or **none of someone's concern**

We are contracting a specialist group to design the study; how it is funded is **not their concern**.

Some people feel that others' problems are **none of their concern**.

concern about/over something (= worry (n.) or anxiety about something) (Use **concern over** for a situation that causes anxiety.)

Sociologists have expressed **concern about** media violence.

There is growing **concern** in the academic community **over** the decline in students' language skills.

concern for someone (= worry (n.) or anxiety about someone's safety, happiness, or health)

Some people are dedicated volunteers who give their time and effort out of a **concern for** those who need help.

concern with something (= attention given to something)

An instrumental leader has great **concern with** getting things done.

concern (v.)

concern something (= be about something) (This "something" can be expressed in a short noun phrase or a much longer noun clause.)

This article **concerns** Goffman's concept of "region behaviour."

> The controversy **concerns** whether the government should
> reduce the salaries of civil servants immediately or
> gradually over a two-year period.

concern someone: (1) affect or involve someone, (2) make someone worried

> The new curriculum will **concern** only students admitted
> next year. (first sense)

> That we have to launch the interviews when it is
> especially difficult to recruit student interviewers
> really **concerns** me. (second sense)

concern oneself with

> Berger believes strongly that sociologists should
> **concern themselves with** methodological questions.

concerned (adj.)

everyone concerned, all (those) concerned: everyone or all those affected by or involved in something (Note that **concerned** in this sense is used after a noun or pronoun.)

> The agreement that resulted after a long negotiation
> process was a satisfactory arrangement for **all (those)
> concerned.** (The word **those** can be omitted.)

concerned (= worried or troubled) (used before a noun)

> She looked at me with a **concerned** expression.

be concerned with: (1) be involved with or in, (2) have interest in, (3) be about

> The Central Planning Unit **is concerned with** giving
> policy advice to the Chief Executive. (first sense)

> Social scientists **are concerned with** the practical
> implications of their research findings. (second sense)

> This study **is concerned with** how Hong Kong people
> perceive the meaning of leisure. (third sense)

be concerned about (= be worried about something)

> Upon discovering that some of his interviewers
> "manufactured" the responses to certain questionnaire

```
items, the researcher was quite concerned about the
reliability of his data.
```

Caution: Do not use **concerned about** to mean simply "about." Since **concerned about** means "worried about something," you cannot use it for inanimate subjects. You can say that, for instance, somebody's suggestion is **concerned with,** but NOT **concerned about,** public welfare.

be concerned for (= be worried about someone's welfare)

```
Parents are likely to be concerned for the health and
general welfare of their children who are studying
overseas.
```

be concerned that (introducing a noun clause)

```
Many people are increasingly concerned that environ-
mental conditions will deteriorate.
```

be concerned to do something

```
Some students are concerned to donate their pocket
money to help flood victims in China.
```

as far as (or **where**) **something/somebody is concerned** (can be placed at beginning or end of sentence)

```
As far as the needs of the poor are concerned, the
government has to re-examine its social welfare
policy.
```

```
Our social behaviour is much like performance on a
theatre stage, where the theory of Erving Goffman is
concerned.
```

as far as I am concerned

Use this phrase to indicate that you are expressing your opinion. Like the preceding phrase, it can be placed at beginning or end of sentence.

```
As far as I am concerned, the government is not doing
enough to help the poor and the elderly.
```

concerning (prep.)

Concerning means "about." Many students use this word improperly by putting **concerning** after the verb **be:**

(×) This question **is concerning** the meaning of higher
    education.

Such construction is always wrong. The correct construction is:

(√) This is a question **concerning** the meaning of higher
    education.

You can rewrite this sentence in any of the following alternative constructions
without changing its meaning:

This question **concerns** the meaning of higher education.
(**concern** as verb)

The **concern** of this question is the meaning of higher
education. (**concern** as noun)

This question **is concerned with** the meaning of higher
education. (**concerned** as adjective)

The usual pattern in using **concerning** is: noun/noun phrase + **concerning** +
noun/noun phrase
Study a few more examples illustrating this pattern:

There is very little information **concerning** the
reasons for the proposed action.

This is a problem **concerning** the economic future of
Hong Kong.

Have you read the clearly-written article **concerning**
human cloning?

confidence (n.), **confident** (adj.)

Do not confuse the noun **confidence** with the adjective **confident.** You have
confidence in (not **on**) **something** if you trust that it is good, strong, or reliable.

What can the government do to restore our **confidence
in** the economy?

Why do some students have insufficient **confidence in**
themselves?

Nobody can claim to have the **confidence that** the
economy will improve any time soon.

We use the adjective **confident** in two common constructions:

be confident about something

> Young people **are** generally more **confident about** using computers than are older people.

be confident that (introducing a noun clause)

> After a period of thorough preparation, we **are confident that** we will have a high response rate in the survey.

confident (adj.) See **confidence.**

consider (v.)

consider as (= think of someone or something as)

> We generally **consider** Auguste Comte **as** the father of sociology.

> Labelling theory is **considered as** part of the conflict perspective on social control and deviance.

consider to be (= have a particular opinion of something or somebody) The words **to be** may be omitted.

> Many students **consider** sociology (**to be**) the most useful subject in their education.

> Sociology is **considered** by many (**to be**) the most comprehensive discipline in the social sciences.

consider doing something (= think seriously about doing or having something)

> The researcher **considered taking** a systematic sample.

consist of (phrasal verb) See **comprise.**

constitute (v.)

The components of a whole **constitute** the whole:

> Middle-class families **constitute** the congregation of this church.

Another use of **constitute** is to indicate what something amounts to:

> Using an author's words or ideas without acknowledging the source **constitutes** plagiarism.

constrain (v.), **constraint** (n.)

Like **complain** and **complaint**, the verb **constrain** does not end in **t** but the noun **constraint** does. Make a habit of pronouncing the ending "**t**" when you use the noun **constraint** in speech.

> It is only by extending our perspective beyond the here and now that we come to appreciate fully the forces that **constrain** our lives.

> Women are often **constrained** by family commitments.

In the second of the above sentences, **constrained** is a verb. Compare with the following sentence in which **constrained** is an adjective:

> During the present economic recession, many companies feel **constrained** to lay off some of their employees to reduce costs.

The noun **constraint** can be countable or uncountable depending on how it is used. In the following, the first sentence uses **constraint** as an uncount noun whereas the second uses it as a count noun:

> Group membership exerts some **constraint** on the behaviour of its members.

> In performing their role, legislators face many **constraints** coming from both within and outside their own political party.

constraint (n.) See **constrain.**

contingency (n.), **contingent** (adj.)

A **contingency** is anything that might happen in the future.

> A careful researcher should prepare for all **contingencies** in planning how data are to be collected.

> If it rains, the University has a **contingency plan** to change the venue of the congregation from the mall to the auditorium.

A cross-tabulation of two variables is also called a **contingency table** because it shows the likelihood of the occurrence of any value of the dependent variable given a particular value of the independent variable. We thus speak of the occurrence of some value of one variable as being **contingent on** (or **upon**) the value of another variable.

> The success of the environmental movement is **con-**
> **tingent upon** the support of both citizens and the
> government.

The above sentence means that the success of the environmental movement will happen only when both citizens and the government support it.

contingent (adj.) See **contingency.**

continual (adj.), **continuous** (adj.)

Continual means "repeating frequently"; **continuous** means "happening without interruption." Thus, it makes better sense to describe an action as **continual** which is on and off many times over a period, as in the following:

> Customer service workers have to attend to **continual**
> complaints from all kinds of customers.

> Some school pupils are subject to **continual** harassment
> from gang members.

> Popular computer applications are **continually** (adv.)
> updated.

If, however, an action goes on with no interruption, use **continuous** instead:

> A social movement is a **continuous** programme of social
> action directed towards an issue that concerns large
> numbers of people. (Note the use of **concern** as a verb. See **concern**
> (v.) in this appendix.)

> In Japan, it is not surprising to find people who have
> worked **continuously** (adv.) for the same company all their
> working life.

continuous (adj.) See **continual.**

continuance (n.), **continuation** (n.), **continuity** (n.)

Distinguish carefully between these three nouns of **continue.**

Continuance, a rather formal word, refers to the act of continuing without interruption, as when we speak of the **continuance of war** or the **continuance in power of a political party.**

Continuation can also refer to the act of continuing without interruption or stopping. Thus, we may speak of the **continuation of war,** the **continuation of the dominance of a political party,** or the **continuation of a family line.**

If an action or event X follows another Y closely, we can say that X is a **continuation** of Y:

> The policies implemented by the new vice-chancellor of the university are essentially a **continuation** of those of his predecessor.

> Young adulthood is in some ways a **continuation** of adolescence. (Here **continuation** has the meaning of "extension.")

Continuation may also be the act of continuing something after a break:

> This week's class is a **continuation** of last week's discussion.

Continuity has two main meanings. First, it is the state of being **continuous:**

> Government institutions are so well established that **continuity** of operation is ensured regardless of who fill the key positions.

Second, **continuity** refers to the logical connection between parts of a larger entity:

> The writer maintains **continuity** throughout the paper by focusing clearly on three main ideas.

continuation (n.) See **continuance.**

continuity (n) See **continuance.**

contrary (adj.)
   contrary to

> Their approach to the problem is **contrary to** ours.

> **Contrary to** what some people might think, sociology is not simply "elaboration of the obvious."

on the contrary (used to indicate strong disagreement)

```
Interviewing senior executives is not as difficult as
it seems; on the contrary, it is rather exciting and
informative.
```

contrast (n. and v.)

contrast (n.) (stress on the first syllable)

contrast between

```
Let us examine the contrast between "community" and
"society."
```

in contrast to

```
In contrast to Durkheim, Weber's treatment of "action"
lays emphasis on the individual's interpretive
understanding.
```

by/in contrast

```
Behaviour is essentially biological. By contrast,
action is inherently social.
```

```
Common sense seems to be quite straightforward without
requiring much rethinking. Scientific attitude, in
contrast, takes nothing for granted.
```

contrast (v.) (stress on the second syllable)

contrast with

```
Their approach to the problem contrasts sharply with
ours.
```

contribute (v.) (stress on the second syllable)

contribute to (**contribute to** + noun/noun phrase)

```
The work of sociologists has contributed enormously
to our understanding of the nature of society. (Note
```
the non-use of articles before **sociologists** and **society**.)

convenience (n.), **convenient** (adj.)

Confusing these two words is quite common in the writing of Hong Kong
students. Distinguish between the adjective **convenient** and the noun
convenience. Form a clear impression of how the two words end: the adjective
ending in **-t** and the noun ending in **-ce.** (Other noun-adjective pairs with similar

endings include **presence**, **present**; **patience**, **patient**; **prevalence**, **prevalent**; and **resistance**, **resistant**.)

convenient (adj.)

> Interpretation will be more **convenient** if we focus on the main findings.
>
> Clear signs make it **convenient** for visitors to find their way.
>
> We find it **convenient** to write about familiar topics.
>
> NEVER write: We are **convenient** to write about familiar topics.

This is a very common error among students. You need to understand that it does not make sense to refer to people as being convenient; only conditions or situations can be described as convenient. This is similar to the use of **easy** and **difficult** (see these entries for more examples):

INCORRECT	CORRECT
We are convenient to . . .	We find it convenient to . . .
	It is convenient for us to . . .
We are easy to . . .	We find it easy to . . .
	It is easy for us to . . .
We are difficult to . . .	We find it difficult to . . .
	It is difficult for us to . . .

convenience (n.) In the following, the first two sentences use **convenience** as an uncount noun, and the third uses it as a count noun:

> For **convenience** of interpretation, the table of findings is somewhat simplified.
>
> **Convenience** is important to Hong Kong people who lead busy lives.
>
> The quality of modern living is marked by such **conveniences** as air-conditioning, mobile telephones, credit cards, and palmtop computers.

convenient (adj.) See **convenience**.

correct (adj.)**, right** (adj.)

These two words are sometimes used as synonyms, as when we refer to a **correct answer** or a **right answer,** but there is a subtle difference between them. **Correct** stresses freedom from error; **right** stresses being in full accordance with fact, truth, or a standard.

We speak of **correct manners** rather than **right manners**, **correct** (or **accurate**) **calculations** rather than **right calculations.** When a person does not make any mistakes in doing something, **correct** is the word to use. When the government implements a policy judiciously and appropriately, it is said to be **taking a step in the right direction** (rather than **in the correct direction).**

In the following sentences, **right** is used **correctly** to imply the ideas of "morally good," "desirable," or "suitable."

> This is the **right** thing to do given the situation.

> We are looking for the **right** person for this new position.

> Making the **right** decision at the **right** time is not easy.

cosmopolitan (adj.)

A **cosmopolitan** society is one in which there are people from different countries, thus bringing with them different cultural traditions and outlooks. We can refer to such places as Hong Kong, New York, Vancouver, and London as **cosmopolitan** cities because they all have a **cosmopolitan** character.

> People living in cities like Hong Kong and New York are likely to have a **cosmopolitan outlook** because they are exposed to people, things, and ideas from many different countries.

cost of living (n. phr.) See **standard of living.**

criteria (n.) See **criterion.**

criterion (n.)**, criteria** (n.)

Remember that **criterion** is singular and **criteria** is plural. (The other pair of words with similar endings often used in social science is **phenomenon** and **phenomena.**) NEVER say: **a criteria.**

> We have chosen p < .05 as the **criterion** for asserting whether any observed difference is significant.

> These are the **criteria** we use to assess the quality
> of the report.

data (n.)

Careful writers use **data** as a plural noun, taking a plural verb:

> These **data have** been checked carefully before analysis
> begins.

> The **data** of that study **are** now outdated.

Compounds formed with the word **data**, however, take a singular verb if the key word is singular: **data collection, data analysis**, **data manipulation**, **data processing.**

> **Data processing** begins as soon as fieldwork is
> completed.

In phrases such as **type of data**, **form of data**, and **batch of data**, the key word is not **data** but **type**, **form**, and **batch**, which are all singular in meaning (and form) and thus take a singular verb.

> The **type of data** obtained **determines** what kind of
> analysis is most appropriate.

decide (v.), **determine** (v.), **determined** (adj.)

To **decide** is to make a choice about what you should do.

> When people **decide** whether to emigrate, they usually
> consider both pull and push factors.

Determine has several somewhat different shades of meaning:

(a)   to ascertain or to find out the facts about something

> It is not easy to **determine** what causes deviant
> behaviour.

(b)   to control something so that it will occur in a particular way

> Socialization **determines** a person's character.

> There is much truth in saying that both competence
> and luck **determine** career success.

(c)   to make a firm decision to do something

> Knowing that we had limited time, we **determined** to
> start the project immediately.

This meaning is also expressed by using **determined** as an adjective:

> She was **determined** to meet the challenge no matter what
> happened.

deprive (v.), **deprived** (adj.), **deprivation** (n.)
deprive (v.) The verb **deprive** is usually used in this pattern: **deprive somebody of something.**

(x) Routinization **deprives** the autonomy and dignity of
workers.

(√) Routinization **deprives** workers **of** their autonomy and
dignity.

deprived (adj.)

> Large cities are likely to contain contrasting areas:
> some are affluent while others are **deprived**.

> We may feel **deprived** if we compare ourselves with the
> very wealthy and powerful.

deprivation (n.) (stress on the third syllable /vei/)

> Many people living in remote areas in south-western
> China suffer from economic **deprivation**.

> Relative **deprivation** results from comparing with those
> who have more than we do.

deprivation (n.) See **deprive**.

deprived (adj.) See **deprive**.

depth (n.)
in depth (adv. phr.)
Do not hyphenate the phrase if you use it as an adverbial phrase following an action:

> We need to study the proposed plans **in depth** (or **in some
> depth**).

Caution: The phrase is perhaps so overused that its meaning becomes vague. Consider other more precise modifiers, such as **careful, detailed, intensive, substantial**, and **thorough**. Using **careful** or **carefully**, for example, you may say:

> We need a **careful** study of the proposed plans.

> We need to study the proposed plans **carefully**.

in-depth (adj.)
Hyphenate **in-depth** when you use it as an adjective placed before a noun.

> This report is an **in-depth** study of the problems of higher education in Hong Kong.

Again, consider other modifiers if they can express your meaning more precisely.

> This report is a **thorough** study of the problems of higher education in Hong Kong.

despite (prep.), **in spite of** (prep. phr.)
Despite means the same as **in spite of,** but **despite** is not followed by a preposition. (DO NOT write **despite of**.) Both **despite** and **in spite of** are followed by a noun, noun phrase, or noun clause. You can use **despite** to start a sentence or in mid-sentence.

> **Despite** Government's effort explaining why the proposed pay-cut was necessary, tens of thousands of civil servants still decided to mobilize a protest march to voice their discontent.

> Reading culture is underdeveloped in Hong Kong **despite** (the fact) that there is no shortage of published material. (The words **the fact** are optional.)

detail (n.), **detailed** (adj.)
Detail is used as a count noun in the following two sentences:

> This is one **detail** that I missed.

> We should provide the **details** of the fieldwork in an endnote.

go into detail (used as an uncount noun)

The announcement did not **go into detail** about the new project.

Without **going into detail,** the study has found support for our hypothesis.

in (great/full) detail (used as an uncount noun)

You need not describe the design of the questionnaire **in such great detail** (not **details**).

detailed (adj.)

In the methods section there should be a **detailed** description of how the main variables are measured.

detailed (adj.) See **detail.**

determine (v.), **determined** (adj.) See **decide.**

difficult (adj.)**, easy** (adj.)

Like **convenient, difficult** and **easy** are adjectives that are often used to describe not people but conditions or situations if getting something done is what you want to say. See **convenient, convenience.**

difficult (adj.)

(×) They are **difficult** to get another job.

(√) They find it **difficult** to get another job.

Or: It is **difficult** for them to get another job.

(×) We didn't **difficult** to find some connection between them.

(√) We didn't find it **difficult** to see some connection between them.

Or: It was not **difficult** for us to see (or find) some connection between them.

easy (adj.)

(×) We are **easy** to see that uncontrolled expenditure causes deficit.

(√) We find it **easy** to see that uncontrolled expenditure causes deficit.

    Or: It is **easy** for us to see that uncontrolled expenditure causes deficit.

    Or: We can **easily** see that uncontrolled expenditure causes deficit. (**easily** is adverb)

The construction **X is easy to V** is possible only if **V** is a transitive verb (which takes an object to complete its meaning).

(√) This article is fairly **easy to understand.** (**Understand** is a transitive verb.)

(√) Short papers are actually not **easy to write.** (**Write** is a transitive verb.)

(×) Conflict becomes **easy** to happen. (Incorrect, because **happen** is an intransitive verb.)

We can say "understand an article" or "write short papers," but we cannot say "happen conflict." A conflict simply **happens** (intransitive verb, requiring no object to complete its meaning). Thus, the sentence needs to be rewritten as:

    It becomes **easy** for conflict to happen.

    Or: As a result, conflict happens **easily.**

discuss (v.), **mention** (v. and n.)

Do NOT use **about** after **discuss** or **mention**. We **discuss a problem** or we have a **discussion of** (or **about**) the problem. We **mention an idea** or we **mention something about** that idea. To **discuss** something implies that we examine it in some detail whereas to **mention** something means to write or speak about it briefly without giving many details.

(×) The author **discusses about** the effects of work on leisure.

(√) The author **discusses** the effects of work on leisure.

(√) We had a useful **discussion about** the meaning of postmodernism.

In the following sentence, **mention** is used correctly and appropriately to indicate the difference between **mention** and **discuss**.

> The author **discusses** the effects of work on leisure, but only **mentions** briefly that leisure can also affect work.

Do not use a **that**-clause immediately after **discuss.** You need to place such words as **the idea**, **the proposal**, or **the suggestion** before the **that**-clause.

(×) We will **discuss** that educational attainment is most important for career advancement.

(√) We will **discuss the idea** that educational attainment is most important for career advancement.

not to mention

You can use this phrase to refer to extra information to emphasize the main point you are making:

> The atypical pneumonia epidemic has greatly affected our social life, **not to mention** the economy that was ailing already even before the outbreak.

it is worth mentioning that

> While Hong Kong is very much autonomous as a special administrative region of China, **it is worth mentioning that** the economic and social link between the city and the mainland of China is ever increasing.

Mention can be used as a noun, as in the following two examples:

> Throughout the article, there is no **mention of** the very large body of work on the same subject done in non-Western societies.

> It is unfortunate that the report **makes no mention of** why the response rate was so low.

distinct (adj.) See **distinguish.**

distinction (n.) See **distinguish.**

distinctive (adj.) See **distinguish.**

distinguish (v.), **distinction** (n.), **distinct** (adj.), **distinctive** (adj.)

  distinguish (v.)

> It may not be easy to **distinguish** between "modernism" and "postmodernism."

> Can you **distinguish** "postmodernism" from "modernism"?

distinction (n.)

 In the first of the following two sentences, **distinction** means difference or contrast between two things. In the second sentence, **distinction** means quality of being outstanding.

> The **distinction** between primary groups and secondary groups lies in how people relate to one another.

> Hong Kong has the **distinction** of being one the world's major financial centres.

  distinct (adj.) (= clearly different)

> These are two quite **distinct** subcultures.

> University graduates have a **distinct** advantage when applying for jobs.

  as distinct from

> Adolescence, **as distinct from** childhood, is a period in which identity becomes a preoccupation.

  distinctive (adj.) (= having a special quality, feature, or character that is different from others)

> Japanese organizations, like other aspects of life in Japanese society, have a **distinctive** group-orientation.

> Group-orientation is a **distinctively** Japanese cultural trait. (Here, **distinctively** is an adverb modifying the adjective **Japanese**.)

easy (adj.) See **difficult.**

effect (n.) See **affect.**

effective (adj.), **efficient** (adj.)

To be **effective** is producing the desired result; to be **efficient** is producing desired results through sensible and economical use of resources such as time and money. We usually speak of a plan or an action as being **effective,** but people or a system as being **efficient.**

> We wonder if the government's plans to revitalize tourism and the economy will be **effective**.

> The university has already implemented an **efficient** on-line course registration system.

The noun of **effective** is **effectiveness;** that of **efficient** is **efficiency.**

> We need to test the **effectiveness** of the new fiscal policy in reducing the budget deficit.

> Unparalleled **efficiency** is achieved by writers using the computer in their work.

efficient (adj.) See **effective.**

effort (n.)

Many students write **pay an effort**. This is incorrect. The correct expression is **make an effort**. You can say that you are prepared to **make an effort** or **make every effort** to do something. You can also say that you want to **put much effort into** something.

> The government under Mr. Tung has pledged to **make a great effort** to ease the woes of economic stagnation.

> Why are the "abode seekers" **putting so much effort into** their struggle?

either . . . or . . . (correlative conj.)

Use **either-or** to refer to two and only two alternatives. Place the first alternative after **either** and the second alternative after **or**. The two alternatives must be grammatically parallel.

> We can **either** use a smaller sample to save money **or** use a large sample to strengthen the accuracy of our findings.

> **Either** you begin with a general statement and follow with supporting details **or** you start with specific

observations and proceed to a general conclusion.

We can vote **either for** candidate A **or for** candidate
B but not for both.

Alternatively:

We can vote for **either** candidate A **or** candidate B but
not both.

emphasis (n.) See **emphasize.**

emphasize (v.)**, emphasis** (n.)

Distinguish carefully between the verb **emphasize** (rhymes with *size*) and the
noun **emphasis** (rhymes with *crisis*). A very common error is the use of **on** after
emphasize. You can say that you want to **emphasize something**, but you must
NOT say that you want to **emphasize on something.** However, you do use the
preposition **on** when you use the noun **emphasis,** as you can put **emphasis on** a
point.

emphasize (v.)

emphasize something

(×) The conflict perspective **emphasizes on** inequality in
    society.

(√) The conflict perspective **emphasizes** inequality in
    society.

emphasize that

The conflict perspective **emphasizes that** there is
inequality in society.

emphasis (n.)

put/place/lay emphasis on

The conflict perspective **places** great **emphasis on**
inequality in society.

with emphasis on

Goffman discusses impression management **with emphasis
on** the distinction between "front region" and "back
region."

In the above two sentences, **emphasis** (singular) is used as an uncount noun. Sometimes **emphasis** (plural: **emphases**) is used as a count noun, as in the following sentence:

> In proposing to merge the two organizations, the special task force has outlined five main **emphases** that have to do with efficiency and productivity.

essential (adj.) See **necessary.**

even if, even though (both subordinating conj.)

Both **even if** and **even though**, as subordinating conjunctions, introduce a subordinate clause containing an idea that is less important than that contained in the main clause of a sentence.

Even if introduces something that may happen:

> **Even if** the Palestinians and Israelis are willing to negotiate peace, true peace between them will remain difficult to attain.

Even though introduces something that happens or has happened:

> **Even though** many students recognize that critical thinking is an important learning skill, most of them do not know exactly what constitutes critical thinking.

In other words, you use **even if** to introduce a condition that is hypothetical or not yet true:

> The unemployment rate is not likely to be reduced **even if** the government introduces more retraining programmes.

You use **even though** to introduce an actual condition that provides some kind of contrast:

> **Even though** high technology products are popular in Hong Kong, little emphasis is given to research and development in local industries.

> Many people like to read sensational reports about movie stars, **even though** they know that such reports may not be all true.

even though See **even if.**

every day (adv. phr.), **everyday** (adj.)

Write **everyday** as one word if you use it as an adjective that can only be used before a noun. If you use it to describe an action, it must be written as two words and placed after the action it describes. In this role, **every day** is an adverbial phrase.

> **every day** (adv. phr.)
>
> > Read something **every day** to keep well informed. (Do not hyphenate **well informed** because the phrase is used adverbially. But do hyphenate it when you use it as an adjective, as in **a well-informed person.**)
>
> **everyday** (adj.)
>
> > Reading should be part of our **everyday** life.

everyday (adj.) See **every day.**

every one See **everyone.**

everyone (indefinite pronoun), **every one**

Like **everybody**, **everyone** is spelled as one word.

> Nearly **everyone** in the neighbourhood is not happy with the resettlement policy.

When you use **every one**, make sure its reference is clear.

> There are three main reasons for the adoption of the new policy, but you can find something wrong in **every one** of them.

evidence (n.)

This is normally an uncount noun that should be used in the singular form (and thus takes a singular verb if used as a subject).

(×) The findings of this survey may serve as **evidences** to support the thesis that sense of political efficacy increases with education.

(√) The findings of this survey may serve as **evidence** to support the thesis that sense of political efficacy increases with education.

Examples of adjectives that may be used to describe **evidence** include the following: **clear, compelling, concrete, conclusive, hard, indisputable, reliable, strong, suspicious, shaky, weak,** and **unsatisfactory.**

> The **evidence** based on recent research **is** not strong enough to establish the claim that there is direct connection between violence in television programmes and violent behavioural tendencies in real life.

exacerbate (v.)**, aggravate** (v.)

Both **exacerbate** and **aggravate** mean to make a bad condition even worse.

> The closing of a large restaurant chain **exacerbates** the economic downturn.

> The plight of property owners with negative equity is **aggravated** by the fall in rents.

Aggravate also means to annoy or to irritate. **Exacerbate** cannot be used in this sense.

> The behaviour of a few individuals who use cell phones in cinemas **aggravates** others in the audience.

examine (v.) See **study.**

excited (adj.)**, exciting** (adj.)

Like the pairs **interested** and **interesting,** and **surprised** and **surprising, excited** and **exciting** are words that have to do with our emotional response to some event or experience.

It is very important that you distinguish between (a) our response (**interested, surprised, excited**) and (b) the event or experience that causes our response (**interesting, surprising, exciting**). Thus, something can be **exciting** to us, and we can become **excited** or feel **excited** as a result.

> Young people are easily **excited** (not **exciting**) by the presence of popular idols.

> They find popular music quite **exciting** (not **excited**).

exciting (adj.) See **excited.**

experience (n., v.)**, experienced** (adj.)

Experience (n.) can be used as an uncount noun to refer to knowledge and skill gained in an activity, or to all events and knowledge obtained from the past making up a person's life.

> It is difficult for new immigrants to get jobs because employers prefer people with local **experience**.

> If we learn from **experience**, we will become wiser.

Experience (n.) can also be used as a count noun to refer to something that affects you or a situation you get involved in.

> Being in an unfamiliar culture can be an unnerving **experience**.

> As an outreach social worker, he has many **experiences** of dealing with problem teenagers.

experience (v.)

> By working as a temporary marketing assistant in the summer, she **experienced** the business world at first hand.

> Like many other places, Hong Kong is now **experiencing** an economic recession.

experienced (adj.)

> Students will benefit greatly if they are taught by **experienced** and dedicated teachers.

If a person has much knowledge or skill in a particular activity, he or she is **experienced in** (or **at**) that activity.

> Schools need not only teachers but specialists who are **experienced in** dealing with crisis situations involving students.

experienced (adj.) See **experience**.

explanation (n. of **explain**)

> Can you offer a reasonable **explanation of** (not **about**) why some young people become addicted to drugs?

> That is a psychological, rather than sociological,
> **explanation of** suicide.

> There is no simple **explanation for** any given social
> problem.

extend (v.) See **extent.**

extension (n.) See **extent.**

extent (n.), **extend** (v.), **extension** (n.)

Do NOT confuse **extend** (v.) with **extent** (n.). **Extend** means to continue or to make longer; **extent** means degree. The word is **extent,** not **extend,** in these phrases: **to a certain extent, to some extent, to a large extent,** and **to the extent that.** You can replace **extent** by **degree** in all these phrases.

to a certain extent, to some extent, to a large extent

> **To a large extent,** the developmental perspective in
> the study of the family shares with symbolic
> interactionism an interest in social processes.

to the extent that (= as far as, so far as)

> **To the extent that** our research results have policy
> implications, we should be careful in presenting our
> interpretation of what those results mean.

extend (v.)

> Our research project **extended** over a period of more
> than a year.

> One student asked the professor to **extend** the deadline
> by two days.

extension (n.)

> Mead's theory of the self may be regarded as an
> **extension** of Cooley's idea of the "looking-glass
> self."

facilitate (v.)

Use **facilitate** for actions or processes, not people. When something or somebody **facilitates** an action or process, that action or process is made possible or easier. That is, you can make something more likely to happen when you **facilitate** it.

> Many argue that the Internet has **facilitated** self-learning by making information easily available.

> To **facilitate** economic growth, increase in both consumption and employment opportunities is necessary.

If ever you find yourself using **facilitate** before a pronoun or some reference to people, you are using the word incorrectly. Try to rephrase your sentence to make the action rather than people the object of **facilitate**, or you can replace **facilitate** with **help**.

> (×) His experience in survey research **facilitated** us in the planning of our study.

> (√) His experience in survey research **facilitated** the planning of our study.

> (√) His experience in survey research **helped** us in the planning of our study.

familiar (adj.)**, familiarity** (n.)**, familiarize** (v.)
familiar (adj.) **with**

As **familiar** is an adjective, you cannot use **do** or **does** before it. Instead, you need to use the verb **be: be** + **familiar with** + noun/noun phrase

> (×) Students **do not familiar with** this subject.

> (√) Students **are not familiar with** this subject.

> (√) If you **are familiar with** the concepts of rationality and efficiency, then Ritzer's McDonaldization thesis is not difficult to understand.

familiar (adj.) **to**

Note the use of prepositions after **familiar.** While people are **familiar with** an object or someone, an object or someone is (or looks) **familiar to** people. An idea may sound **familiar to** people.

> This place **looks familiar to me:** I may have been here before.

> This argument **sounds familiar** (**to us**). Is it not basically a functionalist view?

all-too-familiar (compound adj.) (hyphenated when used before a noun, not hyphenated when used after a noun)

> That the government is always slow in its response to problems and crises has become an **all-too-familiar** accusation.

> Whether the comprehensive social security assistance scheme has been abused is an issue that is **all too familiar**.

familiarity (n.) **with**

> Whether we are misled by survey results published in the media depends on our **familiarity with** sampling procedures and the use of statistics.

familiarize (v.) **oneself with**

> As sociology students, we must **familiarize ourselves with** the notion of "sociological imagination."

familiarity (n.) See **familiar.**

familiarize (v.) See **familiar.**

female (adj. and n.) See **male.**

the following, as follows

You use **the following** in mainly one of two ways. First, **following** is used as an adjective pre-modifying a noun:

> The results are shown in **the following** table.

> The unemployment rate in 1999 was 5 per cent. In **the following** year, it started to rise.

Second, **following** is used as a noun:

> **The following** is an account of what happened.

> **The following** (not **followings**) are examples of variables measured at the ordinal level.

Note that **the following** is used for both singular and plural meanings. There is no -**s** ending in **following. The followings** and **the followings are** are always wrong.

as follows

The verb in this phrase is always singular—**follows**—whether you have one or more than one item to refer to. The phrase means "as in the list (or description) that follows" or "as what follows." You can see, then, that **follows** in this context is a singular verb following an understood but unstated singular noun (*list, description*) or relative pronoun (*what = the thing that*).

```
The argument is as follows.

The findings are as follows.

My decision is as follows.

My reasons for making this decision are as follows.
```

for (coordinating conj.) See **because.**

for example (= **for instance**)

The word **example** (n.) in this phrase is always singular, even if it is followed by several items that are the actual examples.

```
(×) Values are what we treasure, for examples, honesty,
    integrity, and modesty.

(√) Values are what we treasure, for example, honesty,
    integrity, and modesty.
```

Or you can say the following if you wish to use the plural **examples:**

```
Values are what we treasure. Examples include honesty,
integrity, and modesty.

Honesty,  integrity,  and  modesty  are  examples  of
values.
```

Remember then that **for examples** is always wrong. It should always be **for example.**

Likewise, you must not say **for instances,** but say **for instance.**

forth See **fourth.**

fourth (adj.)**, forth** (adv.)

There is a **u** in **fourth** if you mean "4 th."

```
This is her fourth attempt to win the competition.
```

Forth is the word to use in sentences like the following:

```
Many different suggestions were put forth in the
meeting.

Sanctions of non-conformance with norms include
criticism, ridicule, isolation, and so forth.
```

get used to (doing) something See **used to do something.**

given (adj., n., prep.)
   given (adj.)
      As an adjective meaning "specified" or "previously arranged," **given** is used only before a noun.

```
We will explain the details of the questionnaire to
student interviewers at a given time and place.

For given values of a set of independent variables,
regression analysis allows us to estimate the value
of the dependent variable.
```

   given (n.)
      If we accept something as a basic fact without query, we may say that it is a **given.**

```
We take it as a given that doctors are motivated by
the desire to help relieve pain.

No business can last long if it is not profitable. That
is a given.
```

   given (prep.)
      You can use **given** as a preposition to mean "considering" to introduce a condition or reason for something else. In this use, **given** is followed by a **that**-clause.

```
Given that funding for the universities will be reduced,
they will all have to consider consolidating their
educational programmes.
```

grateful (adj.)

    grateful to somebody for something

> The school was **grateful to** the Jockey Club **for** their financial support of building a new school library.

a great deal, a great deal of See also **lots of, a lot of.**

    A great deal is used adverbially to mean "very much" or "very often":

> Background variables are used **a great deal** in studies of social behaviour.

    A great deal of something is very much of something. The noun following **a great deal of** should be uncount.

> Davis and Moore's classic article on the functionalist explanation of social stratification caused **a great deal of** debate on the subject that went on for many years. (**Debate** is an uncount noun in this sentence.)

happen (v.)

    Happen is an intransitive verb: it does not take an object. Like other intransitive verbs, it cannot be used in the passive voice.

> (×) Government is allowing inequality **to be happened** among secondary schools.

    In this sentence, it is better to use **exist** instead of **happen.** Alternatively, you can do without such a verb; the meaning of the sentence stays the same:

> (√) Government is allowing inequality **to exist** among secondary schools.

> (√) Government is allowing inequality among secondary schools.

    Some words or phrases have a meaning similar or related to **happen.** They include **occur, exist, arise, emerge, result, take place,** and **take shape.** The choice of word or phrase depends on the subject. The following are some typical combinations:

    A condition **exists.**
    A conflict **breaks out** or **erupts.**
    A consequence **results** from some action.

A discussion **develops.**

An event or process **happens** or **occurs.**

An idea **emerges** or **evolves.**

A meeting **takes place.**

A pattern or trend **emerges.**

A plan or programme **takes shape.**

A problem **exists** or **arises.**

A project **gets off the ground** or **is launched.**

A suggestion is **made** or **put forward**

have to (modal auxiliary verb) See **must, should, have to.**

horizons (n.)

broaden one's horizons

Note the word is **horizons**, not **horizon**, in this expression.

> The study of sociology **broadens** (or **expands**) our **horizons**.

> The study of sociology contributes to **broadening our horizons**.

(The construction of this sentence calls for the use of **broadening**, a gerund, which combines with **our horizons** to form a gerund phrase that becomes the object of the preposition **to.**)

impact (n., v.) See **influence.**

imply (v.), **infer** (v.)

To imply is to suggest an idea without saying it directly.

> If you say that a certain movie is "alright," you may be **implying** that it is mediocre.

If you say that X implies Y, you mean that Y is likely to be true.

> The brevity of the discussion section of a research report **implies** that you do not think there are any serious problems in your research or that you have not made an effort to evaluate your research in a broader context.

To infer is to guess that something may be true on the basis of the information you have. If an author implies something in what he or she writes, the reader tries to infer what that something is. Thus, **imply** and **infer** are used from two different points of view.

> We can **infer** from what he said about the movie that it was rather boring.
>
> What can you **infer** from the shortness of the discussion section of the report?
>
> Given the prevalence of English signs in the city, we **inferred** that there was an effort to boost tourism.

The noun of **imply** is **implication;** the noun of **infer** is **inference.**

in addition to (prep. phr.)

This means **as well as** and is used similarly. Remember that **in addition to** is followed by a noun, noun phrase, or gerund phrase.

> Migration of people can be explained by push factors **in addition to** pull factors.
>
> She wrote the report **in addition to** gathering the data.
>
> She is a modest person **in addition to** being our group's leader.
>
> **In addition to** alerting us to changes in society, sociology also sharpens our analytical mind.

in-depth (adj.), **in depth** (adv. phr.) See **depth.**

indispensable (adj.) See **necessary.**

infer (v.) See **imply.**

influence (n., v.), **impact** (n., v.)

Use **influence** to mean "effect" generally.

> She lives in a family in which the **influence** of parents is very strong. (Here **influence** is a noun.)
>
> How do parents **influence** children? (Here **influence** is a verb.)

Use **impact** only when you refer to a very powerful effect.

> The scandals of mismanagement of a number of corporations in the United States have a disturbing

> `impact` on the stock market. (Here **impact** is a noun, pronounced with stress on the first syllable. Note also that the key word of the subject, **scandals**, takes a plural verb **have.**)

> `Management scandals as well as political upheavals can` **impact** `the stock market seriously.` (Here **impact** is a verb. Pronounce it with stress on the second syllable.)

in itself (adv. phr.)**, per se** (adv., Latin)

When you consider something (P) in its own terms, without taking into account anything else that may be related to it, you say that P **in itself** has a certain quality or is, for instance, worth doing or achieving. **Per se,** a more formal expression, means **in itself** or **by itself.**

> `Rationalization` **in itself** `is a valid principle of organization although excessive adherence to it could bring about undesirable consequences.`

> `Knowledge` **in itself** `is the result of exploration and understanding; whether it becomes power is another matter.`

> `Social statistics as figures reflecting the social condition are not problematic` **per se,** `but may become tools of deception if they are misused by people and groups with vested interests.`

in and of itself, in its own right

You can use either phrase to stress that you want to consider something by its own nature.

> `Leisure may be regarded as valuable` **in and of itself.**

> `Leisure may be pursued as` **an end in its own right.**

For more examples see sentences at **right** (n.).

in its own right See **in itself** and **right** (n.).

in particular (adv. phr.) See **particular**.

in regard to (prep. phr.) See **regard** (n.).

in respect of (prep. phr.) See **regard** (n.).

in someone's own right See **right** (n.).

in spite of (prep.) See **despite**.

interest (n. and v.), **interested** (adj.), **interesting** (adj.)
    interest (n.)

       People **have interests in** many things. You may **have no interest in** an activity now, but may **develop an interest in** it in due course. Once you have **picked up** an interest, you may decide to **keep it up.** Of course, it is also possible that you may **lose interest in** something if something else draws your attention away from it.

> Hong Kong people's leisure **interests** are much more diversified than what they were in the 1960s.

       An interest in a given activity may be described by such adjectives as **absorbing, brief, deep, enduring, great, intense, keen, passing, passionate, real, serious, slight, strong,** and **sustained.**

> As a result of her family upbringing as well as exposure to cultural activities as a student, she has developed an **enduring interest** in music.

> Many teenage girls have an **intense interest** in collecting Hello Kitty paraphernalia.

    interest (v.)

> The seventeen-year-old girl who has dropped out from school told the social worker, "School does not **interest** me a bit; it's such a bore!"

> It may **interest** the reader to know that a study of this kind has never been attempted before.

    interested, interesting (both adj.)

       It is important to distinguish between these two adjectives. An object of interest can be said to be **interesting to** a person; a person is **interested in** an object. A person can also be said to be **interested** to do something.

> Many students find psychology as **interesting** as sociology.

> **Interesting** as this topic is, it is, however, a difficult one to study empirically. (Note the punctuation,

using three commas that are all necessary to convey the meaning of the sentence.)

Difficult as this topic is, we are **interested to** pursue it in some way.

Growing numbers of researchers are **interested in** qualitative studies of behaviour.

People who are affected by a particular situation or who may expect to gain from it are called an **interested party** or **interested group.**

The MTR Corporation will discuss this proposal with all **interested parties**.

interest in (not **on**) (**interest** as noun)

Students' **interest in** a subject is determined in part by how that subject is taught.

interested in (**interested** as adjective)

How a subject is taught partly determines how **interested** students are **in** that subject.

interested (adj.) See **interest.**

interesting (adj.) See **interest.**

investigate (v.) See **study.**

irregardless of

This is an erroneous phrase. The correct phrase is **regardless of.**

irrespective of (prep. phr.) See **regardless of.**

kind of (adv.), **sort of** (adv.)

Used as adverbs in very informal speech, both **kind of** and **sort of** mean "slightly," "to some extent," "in a way," "somewhat," or "rather." You should not use these phrases in formal academic writing except when quoting conversations in reporting qualitative research.

We were **kind of** confused and desperate when our business failed.

I **sort of** wished that something like this would not happen; but it did.

kind(s) of

Pay attention to the number of the noun that follows **kind(s) of.** For example, when you think of a particular kind of problem and this kind alone, you may say:

This kind of problem is difficult to deal with.

When you think of different kinds, the phrase becomes **kinds of problems.** You then say:

These kinds of problems are difficult to deal with.
(Note the subject-verb agreement between **kinds** and **are.)**

You cannot say:

(×) This kind of problems are difficult to deal with.
(subject-verb agreement violated)

But you can change the construction somewhat to say the following although the meaning is not the same as **These kinds of problems are difficult to deal with**. (referring to problems of multiple kinds)

(√) Problems of this kind **are** difficult to deal with.
(referring to problems of only one kind)

When you have an uncount noun or a variable noun used in an uncount sense, the noun should remain in the singular form for both **kind** and **kinds.** In the following, **beauty** is typically an uncount noun while **authority** and **conflict** are variable nouns (having both count and uncount uses):

Different **kinds of beauty** are associated with different objects.

Weber speaks of three **kinds of authority** in connection with social organization.

Conflict between the wife and the husband's mother is a **kind of conflict** much depicted in fiction about traditional Chinese families.

lack (v. and n.), **lacking** (adj.)

A common error is using **lack** as an adjective which it is not:

(×) Most people are **lack** of critical thinking.

To correct the above sentence, the simplest way is to use **lack** as a verb which it can be:

(√) Most people **lack** critical thinking.

lack (v.)

> Those who **lack** managerial skills cannot expect to advance very far in large corporations.

> Critics say that Hong Kong films may excel in fast action choreography but **lack** depth in the portrayal of characters.

lack (n.) (Uncount)

> The school counsellor told the student that most of her problems are probably caused by a **lack** of confidence.

> The **lack** of effective coordination among government departments can have serious consequences.

You can say that something happened **through lack of** or **for lack of** something, as in:

> The proposition to stage a protest was dropped **through** (or **for**) **lack** of support.

lacking (adj.)

> Students accustomed to rote memorization are usually **lacking in** inquisitiveness and critical thinking.

> Why is courtesy in public places so **lacking?**

lacking (adj.) See **lack.**

lastly (adv.) See **at last.**

let (v.), **make** (v.)

You CANNOT use **to** in front of the verb after **let** and **make.**

(×) Sociological imagination can **let** us **to** see the hidden social reality.

(√) Sociological imagination can **let** us see the hidden social reality.

(×) This study can **make** us **to** understand the problem better.

(√) This study can **make** us understand the problem better.

lie (v.), lay (v.)

Be very careful when using these words. First, remember that **lie** is always intransitive (taking no object) and **lay** is always transitive (taking an object). Second, examine the following principal forms of the verbs (**lie** has two sets of verb forms depending on its meaning).

	Base form	-ing participle	Past form	Past participle
lie (= to say something that is not true)	**lie**	**lying**	**lied**	**lied**
lie (= to be on a surface; to be in a particular place; to consist of or to exist)	**lie**	**lying**	**lay**	**lain**
lay (= to put down; to plan and prepare)	**lay**	**laying**	**laid**	**laid**

lie (= to say something that is not true)

> We went to great lengths to guard against respondents **lying** about personal information such as age and income.

lie (= to be on a surface)

> As we entered the apartment to do the interview, we saw clothes and newspapers **lying** on the floor.

lie (= to be in a particular place)

> Guangzhou **lies** about one hundred miles to the north-west of Hong Kong.

lie (= to consist of or to exist): **lie in, lie at the heart of**

> The difficulty of measuring an abstract concept **lies in** finding suitable indicators.

> Frustration with the way the government is handling unemployment **lies at the heart of** all these protest demonstrations.

lay (= to put down)

> She **laid** piles of newspaper clippings on the desk and started to sort them by topic.

lay (= to plan and prepare)

> This preliminary study **lays** the groundwork for future research on a larger scale.

like (n., adj., v., and prep.)

  like (n.)

> We all have our **likes** and **dislikes** in food.

> She is now studying modern means of consumption, such as shopping malls, fast-food restaurants, theme parks, **and the like**. (**and the like** = and similar things)

  like (adj.)

> People of **like** mind communicate with each other easily. (**People of like mind** can also be written as **like-minded people**.)

  like (v.)

> Why do people **like** to watch such television programmes as "The X-Files"?

> Parents **like** their children to succeed in school.

  like (prep.)

> What is the experience of a substitute teacher **like**?

> Some hospitals that cater to the needs of the wealthy are built to look **like** hotels.

> Countries **like** South Korea and Singapore are among the most developed in Asia.

> **Like** most Hong Kong people, they are interested in making money and improving their life quality.

likely (adj., adv.)

  likely (adj.)

    As an adjective, **likely** is often used in statements that some behaviour or consequence will probably happen.

You can put **likely** before the word it modifies:

> What do you think is the **likely** consequence of this new policy?

> In statistical estimation, one must consider the **likely** margin of error.

You can also place **likely** after the word it modifies:

> Social unrest is **likely** if the economy worsens.

> It is very **likely** that the government will pass legislation to reduce civil servants' pay.

> Many people believe that women are more **likely** than men to enjoy shopping.

Sentences like the last example above are used in comparing characteristics or probabilities of obtaining certain results among various groups. To be more specific in such statements, you can add an appropriate adverb (e.g., **more, less**) in front of **likely**:

> Women are certainly more **likely** than men to enjoy shopping.

> The better-educated are much more **likely** than the poorly-educated to understand and enjoy classical music.

> Young people are perhaps less **likely** than old people to believe that having children is important for a happy marriage.

likely (adv.)

> Given the present conditions, unemployment will most **likely** rise. (Here **likely** as an adverb modifies the verb **rise.**)

> **As likely as not** (= very probably), the demise of dictatorship in Iraq will not mean the solution of all problems in that country.

> Will merging two organizations bring about a stronger
> organization? Quite **likely**, many people believe.

lose (v.), **loss** (n.)

Some students confuse these two words, often using **loss** as a verb. Remember that **loss** is noun and **lose** (pronounced /luːz/) is verb. The past tense of **lose** is **lost** (also past participle), which sounds like **loss** and may partly account for the confusion.

(×) Many people **loss** their loved ones in a war.

(√) Many people **lose** their loved ones in a war.

This sentence, written in the simple present tense, amounts to a general statement to mean that people generally will lose their loved ones if there is a war. If you want to refer to a specific war in the past, such as World War II or the Vietnam War, you can rewrite the sentence using the simple past tense and use the definite article **the** before **war**:

> Many people **lost** their loved ones in **the** war (you can name the war here) .

If, however, you are referring to a war that has recently ended, say the war in Iraq (March to April 2003), you can use the present perfect tense. As in the preceding example, use **the** rather than **a** before **war**:

> Many people in Iraq **have lost** their loved ones in **the** war.

The following sentences use **loss** correctly as a noun. In the first sentence, it is a count noun; in the second, it is uncount.

> When the economy is not going well, there will be many job **losses.**

> War brings about suffering and **loss** of life.

lots of, a lot of (determiner)

These expressions, while common in spoken English, should not be used in formal writing. When referring to count nouns, use **many** or **a large number of**; when modifying uncount nouns, use **much** or **a great deal of**. Some examples are:

> **a large number of** supporters of the policy

> **many** different explanations
>
> **a great deal of** discussion
>
> **much** research

a lot of (determiner) See **lots of.**

make (v.) See **let.**

make (be made up of) See **comprise.**

male (adj. and n.)**, female** (adj. and n.)

In social science writing, these words are used more commonly as adjectives than as nouns, as in these expressions: **male dominance**, **male representation**, **male bias, female submissiveness, female workforce,** and **traditionally female areas of work.**

In the biological sciences, the use of the words as collective nouns (**the male** or **males**, **the female** or **females**) is quite common, as in the following:

> The genes are passed on through the male or the female.

If you want to refer to females and males as persons, better use **women** and **men** respectively:

> Our findings show that **men** are not as involved as **women** in household chores.

many (adj.) See **much.**

may (modal auxiliary verb)

You cannot put a past tense verb or a verb ending in **-s** after **may.**

(×) It may happened.

(×) It may happens.

(√) It may happen.

It may happen indicates present or future possibility. To indicate possibility in past time, you can say **it may have happened** or **it might have happened.**

may be (may as a modal auxiliary verb) See **maybe.**

maybe (adv.)**, may be (may** as a modal auxiliary verb)

Spelled as one word, **maybe** is an adverb that means "perhaps" or "possibly." Use it in informal speech only. In formal writing, use **perhaps** or **possibly.**

Do not confuse **may be** with **maybe.** Distinguish between the following two sentences:

> **Maybe** the rating of the Chief Executive will be more favourable if the economy recovers soon enough. (not recommended in writing)

> (√) The rating of the Chief Executive **may be** more favourable if the economy recovers soon enough.

Alternatively, the meaning of the preceding sentence is more accurately expressed as follows:

> The rating of the Chief Executive will **perhaps** be more favourable if the economy recovers soon enough.

media (n.)

Media (television, radio, newspapers and other means of mass communication) is the plural of **medium,** and thus should take a plural verb.

> The mass **media have** often concerned themselves more with what is newsworthy than with what is educational.
> (Note the use of parallel structure in **more with . . . than with . . .**)

However, many people use the word **media** as a singular collective noun taking a singular verb (e.g., **the media has indicated**). Careful writers consider this unacceptable. You should avoid such use. In his *The New Fowler's Modern English Usage*, Burchfield (1996, p. 488) advises: "When in doubt use the plural [verb]. Above all, never write **a media or the medias.**"

Media (rather than **medium**) also appears in many compounds such as **media content, media use, media event** (created deliberately for coverage by the media), **media culture, media environment**, **media imperialism, media technology,** and many others.

Note that when you use such compounds, the number (singular or plural) of the verb they take depends on the number of the main word (second word) of the compound. Thus, for example, you write **media use is** but **media events are**.

mention (v. and n.) See **discuss.**

more . . . than . . .

You may use **more . . . than . . .** to compare two things or two persons in terms of some characteristic, as in the following sentence:

```
Conflict theory is more interested in explaining
change than functional theory (is).
```

In this construction, the meaning is: X is **more** P **than** Y is. (Subjects compared: X and Y; characteristic compared: P)

Another way of using **more . . . than . . .** is when you want to say that a given subject is more likely to be P than it is to be Q. The following three sentences all use **more . . . than . . .** in this sense. Note that this construction requires parallel elements. That is, the element after **more** must be of the same grammatical form as that after **than.**

```
People eat at McDonald's more for convenience than for
saving money.

Hong Kong people's preference for one television
station over another is arguably more habitual than
rational.

The modern household is more like an entertainment
centre than (it is) a place of residence.
```

more than one

Although plurality comes to your mind when you use the phrase **more than one**, you cannot say **there are more than one.** Instead, you should say **there is more than one.** The noun that immediately follows is always singular.

```
(×) There are more than one way to define culture.

(×) There are more than one ways to define culture.

(√) There is more than one way to define culture.
```

Alternatively, you can write:

```
There are more ways than one to define culture.
```

If you have an actor in the sentence, the following are different ways of saying the same thing:

```
There is more than one person who supports the new
policy.

More than one person supports the new policy.

More persons than one support the new policy.
```

In the above three sentences, note carefully the agreement between the subject (**person/persons**) and the verb (**supports/support**).

moreover (adv.) See **besides.**

much (adv.)

Much in the following three sentences is an adverb, because it modifies a verb (**discussed,** first sentence), an adjective (**same,** second sentence), or another adverb (**too,** third sentence).

> The implications of labelling theory were **much discussed** in the conference.
>
> The news is **much the same** as usual.
>
> This task is **much too difficult** for a small group to accomplish.

much (adj.)**, many** (adj.)

Be very careful not to use **many** when you should use **much** and vice versa. The general guideline is that **many** is used for count nouns and **much** for uncount nouns.

CORRECT	INCORRECT
many questions	**much** questions
many ideas	**much** ideas
many people	**much** people
many times (here **time** means occasion)	
much time	**many** time
much labour	**many** labour
much energy	**many** energy
much effort	**many** effort
much argument (as an activity)	**many** argument

but:

many arguments (here "argument" refers to
   a statement offered as evidence)

Note that for variable nouns, which can be countable in some contexts and uncountable in others, you should use **many** when they are used as count nouns and **much** when they are used as uncount nouns.

> **Much time** can be spent on the design of a questionnaire.

```
Hong Kong has experienced many tough times before,
including civil disorders and epidemics.
```

must, should, have to (modal auxiliary verbs)

Modal auxiliary verbs (e.g., **can, may, ought to, should, have to, must**) bring additional meanings to verbs to express such ideas as ability, permission, obligation, and necessity. **Should,** like **ought to**, expresses obligation or advisability:

```
We should cite all sources used when writing academic
papers.

Most respondents in the survey indicated that heavy
penalties should be imposed on people who litter the
streets.
```

In the above two sentences, you can substitute **ought to** for **should** without changing their meaning. Whereas **should** or **ought to** suggests that some action is desirable as a matter of duty or doing what is right, **must** indicates a more definite and compelling course of action because the sense of duty or doing what is (morally) right is considerably stronger. If you say that you **must** do something, you are saying that there is no alternative: it is a matter of sheer necessity.

```
We must not think that the government can do nothing
about unemployment.

In traditional Chinese culture, children are taught
that they must obey their parents.
```

Like **must, have to** is used to indicate necessity. But **must** is stronger than **have to** in that **must** implies that the necessity arises from a constraint we impose on ourselves whereas **have to** suggests that the necessity is caused by some external factor (e.g., law, others' wishes). Thus, there is some difference between the following two sentences:

```
We must obey our parents.  (because we love them)

We have to obey our parents. (because this is what our parents
and relatives expect us to do)
```

Must signifies the highest degree of probability (as opposed to **may**).

You can use **must** to indicate present time and future time:

> The government **must** step up its measures to improve
> the economy. (now and in the near future)

To indicate past time, use **must** + **have** + past participle:

> Those who emigrated from Hong Kong to countries such
> as Canada and Australia in the mid- to late-1980s **must**
> **have** felt uneasy about the uncertainty of Hong Kong's
> political future at that time.

must (n.)

As a noun, **a must** is something you must do or must have—something that is absolutely necessary. But the expression is an informal one which should be avoided in formal academic writing. There are other words to choose from, such as **necessary**, **need**, **indispensable**, and **essential**. You can say this, for instance: **To make such a decision was necessary.**

necessary (adj.), **need** (v.)

Be careful NOT to use **necessary** in the following way:

> (×) We are **necessary** to change our approach to this
> problem.

The correct construction is any of the following:

> It is **necessary** for us to change our approach to this
> problem.

> We find it **necessary** to change our approach to this
> problem.

> We **need** to change our approach to this problem.

> We **need** (to take) a different approach to this problem.

necessary (adj.), **indispensable** (adj.), **essential** (adj.)

If you say that X is **necessary** for Y, it means that X is needed for Y to happen. The use of **necessary** implies a pressing need or constraint. But it need not connote that you cannot do without X, although X is highly desirable.

> Some knowledge of statistics is **necessary for**
> understanding the meaning of research findings.

Sometimes we say that **it is necessary for somebody to do something**:

> It is **necessary for** journalists to report news both
> promptly and accurately.

Indispensable implies a stronger urgency. If X is **indispensable** for Y, you cannot do without X in your effort to have Y.

> It seems that nowadays the MBA degree is **indispensable**
> **for** a managerial position in a large company.

If Y is a person or organization, we say "X is **indispensable to** Y."

> She has become so experienced that she is practically
> **indispensable to** her company.

Essential also implies strong urgency. It refers to elements that are fundamental aspects of some larger pattern. It implies inherent necessity.

> Shared goals and adequate socialization are **essential**
> **for** a social system to function smoothly.

> Reduction of interference is **essential to** effective
> communication.

> It is **essential that** we have ways of checking the
> validity and reliability of the measurement of key
> variables.

need (v.) See **necessary.**

not . . . but . . . (correlative conj.)

Whenever you use a pair of correlative conjunctions, you are joining sentence elements that are grammatically equal (to form a parallel structure). (See more details in 13 of Appendix 7.) Note that, in the following three sentences, the elements after **not** and **but** are grammatically parallel:

> Education is important **not** because it makes you a more
> respectable worker **but** because it makes you a better
> thinker.

> Authority lies **not** in the person **but** in the position.

> The larger problem is **not** poverty **but** illiteracy.

not only . . . , but also (correlative conj.)

You must use grammatically parallel elements after **not only** and **but also.**

We study sociology **not only to understand** the nature
of social forces **but also to recognize** the interrelationship between the individual and society.

Not only has the computer made life more comfortable,
but it has also changed the way we communicate with
others.

Note that in the second sentence, the normal order of "the computer has
made. . ." is changed to "has the computer made . . ." in the first clause. This is
called "inversion," a way to create emphasis. You will see a similar construction
in the next two sentences in which "do" or "does" is used to create emphasis:

Not only does sociology train us to think critically,
(**but**) **it also helps us** to distinguish between personal
problems and social issues. (The word **but** is sometimes omitted
in sentences starting with **not only**.)

Not only do Garfinkel and Goffman treat the individual
as an agent of action, **but they also consider** that the
individual's action is guided by a kind of rationality
different from that assumed in functionalist theory.

one of

Logically, **one of** must be followed by a noun phrase referring to a multitude of
items, objects, or people. Whether the verb that appears after that should be
singular or plural depends on the pattern of construction of the sentence.

PATTERN 1: X is **one of the (**multitude of items) **that/who** + plural verb

Participant observation is **one of the methods** that **are**
used to collect qualitative data.

"Privacy" is **one of those concepts** that **require** great
care in defining and explaining.

Kelly is **one of the few sociologists** who **devote** great
attention to the study of leisure.

PATTERN 2: **One of the** (multitude of items) + singular verb

One of the best known economists is John Maynard
Keynes.

> **One of the messages of this book concerns** how advertising affects our consumption behaviour.

PATTERN 3: X is **the only one of the** (multitude of items) **that/who** + singular verb

> This is **the only one of the questionnaire items that uses** closed-ended response categories.

> She is **the only one of over 50 student participants who has** travelled widely.

opinion (n.) See **attitude.**

out of date (adj.) See **outdated.**

out-of-date See **outdated.**

outdated, **out-of-date**, **out of date** (all adj.)

Outdated means very much the same as **out-of-date** or **out of date**: "no longer useful" or "old-fashioned." But if you want to mean that something is no longer useful or good because a specific date has passed, then **out-of-date** or **out of date** is the more suitable expression.

> You cannot use these figures for your paper because they are **outdated.**

> In many rural areas of China, **outdated** methods of farming are still in use.

> We cannot find the name Hong Kong Special Administrative Region in an **out-of-date** map.

> Technical knowledge can become **out of date** in a short time.

Note that the phrase **out of date** is not hyphenated if used as a postmodifier, that is, after the noun it modifies. If you use the phrase as a premodifier, before the noun it modifies (e.g., **out-of-date** map, **out-of-date** technology), insert hyphens. This convention of hyphenation applies to many other compound adjectives.

particular (adj.), **particularly** (adv.), **in particular** (adv. phr.), **particulars** (plural n.)

particular (adj.)

> Do you have any **particular** suggestion?
>
> This is a **particular** case quite unlike the others.
>
> We took **particular** care in coding the open-ended responses.

particularly (adv.)

> Karaoke singing is **particularly** popular with young people.
>
> Groups play an important role in social life, **particularly** in Japan.

in particular (adv. phr.)

   In particular may be replaced by **particularly** in the first but not the second of the following two sentences:

> Writing research reports, and qualitative research reports **in particular**, requires both organization and imagination.
>
> Is there anything **in particular** we can say about the implication of such a finding?

particulars (plural noun)

> This report concerning the progress of the case is complete in all **particulars**.

particularly (adv.) See **particular.**

particulars (plural noun) See **particular.**

per se (adv., Latin) See **in itself.**

perspective (n.), **viewpoint** (n.), **approach** (n. and v.)

   All three words, **perspective**, **viewpoint**, and **approach**, refer to a way of dealing with or studying something. You can say **from the perspective/viewpoint/approach of** a certain theory, before delving into your analysis of something.

   Perspective is the more common word when referring to a theory or a "theoretical framework." **Viewpoint (**or **point of view**) can sometimes refer to a very specific point, such as the interest of consumers or that of social welfare. **Viewpoint** implies an attitude or opinion, and therefore is more applicable to persons. Thus, we speak of agreeing or disagreeing with a person's **viewpoint** but not **perspective.** If, however, the emphasis is on how things look from a person's given position (e.g., parent, member of a religious faith, someone recently laid off), we speak of the perception or meaning of these things from the person's **perspective.** This implies that given that position, which is an objective fact, things are likely to be seen in a certain way, whether we agree with it or not.

> Psychology and sociology provide different **perspectives on** (not **towards**) suicide.

> Members of the same group may not have the same **viewpoint on** an issue.

> In the face of economic depression and the onslaught of the SARS epidemic, we need to take a fresh **approach to** education.

Approach is also a verb, as in the following sentence:

> How do historians **approach** revolutions differently from sociologists?

phenomena (n.) See **phenomenon.**

phenomenon (n. singular)**, phenomena** (n. plural) See also **criterion, criteria.**

> Rumour is a social **phenomenon** that is likely to occur when there is high anxiety accompanied by a lack of information.

> Fads and crazes are short-lived **phenomena** that come and go.

Do NOT say: **this phenomena** (should be **these phenomena** for plural and **this phenomenon** for singular)

possess (v.)

Do not confuse **possess** (v., stress on the second syllable) with **process** (n. and v., both with stress on the first syllable)

> A charismatic leader **possesses** great influence based on personal qualities.

possible (adj.), **probable** (adj.)

When something is **possible,** it can be done or it can happen. When something is **probable,** it is likely to happen or to be true. Note, however, that what is possible in principle or in theory may not be probable.

> Although it is **possible** for an unpopular candidate to get elected, that is not **probable.**

> The most **probable** way for the organization to cut operating costs is not to fill positions left vacant by retirements, but other more drastic actions are also **possible.**

We can distinguish between **how frequently** an event occurs and **how likely** or **probable** an event will occur, although the notion of **probability** is often built on the actual **frequency** that we can observe or have knowledge of. When we describe events, we may sometimes refer to frequency and sometimes to probability. Given their close relationship, we may also make statements in which both frequency and probability are indicated.

The following is a partial list of words referring to **frequency** grouped roughly in descending order:

Group I: **always, constantly**
Group II: **generally, normally, regularly, usually**
Group III: **frequently, often**
Group IV: **occasionally, sometimes** (a very often-used word!)
Group V: **hardly ever, rarely, seldom, scarcely ever**
Group VI: **never**

Here is a partial list of words referring to **probability**, also grouped roughly in descending order of likelihood.

Group I: **absolutely, certainly, definitely, surely, undoubtedly**
Group II: **most likely, probably**
Group III: **maybe, perhaps, possibly**
Group IV: **improbable, unlikely**
Group V: **certainly not, definitely not**

Study the following sentences that use various words of frequency of occurrence and probability:

> Young people are **normally** driven by curiosity to participate in activities with their friends. They

```
will probably become members of groups in which their
friends are already members.
```

```
If you seldom participate in religious activities, it
is still possible for you to remain as a believer, but
it is unlikely that you give substantial support to
an evangelical movement.
```

```
In the 1960s, Hong Kong people hardly ever travelled
to Europe for pleasure; now they do that quite often.
```

possibly (adv.)**, probably** (adv.)

Both words are used to indicate the likelihood that something is true or will happen. If you have no idea at all as to how likely this is, use **possibly;** if you have reason to believe that such likelihood is quite high (say more than 50 per cent), then you should use **probably.**

```
Some economists believe that the economy will possibly
improve next year.
```

```
Although property prices have recently risen somewhat,
they will probably never return to the levels of 1997.
```

```
If you hear some news on CNN, it is probably true.
```

You can use **possibly** to stress that some people tried as hard as they could to get something, but use **probably** to underscore that the actual chances of succeeding are slim:

```
Abode seekers in Hong Kong have done everything they
possibly can to persuade the government to grant them
their wish to stay. Despite that, most of them will
probably not succeed in reaching their goal.
```

precise (adj.) See **accurate.**

principal (n. and adj.)**, principle** (n.)**, in principle** (adv. phr.)

As a noun, **principal** is the amount of money you borrow or invest. A **principal** is also the head of a school or the most important part in a play or opera, or the leader of an orchestra section. More commonly, **principal** is used as an adjective meaning "most important" or "main":

```
The principal advantage of the questionnaire is that
it allows for standardized measurement of variables.
```

What   are   the   **principal**   characteristics   of   a profession?

Principle is always a noun, meaning a basic belief, assumption, rule, or standard. It may be used in the singular if you refer to one clearly identifiable belief or standard:

Timeliness is a widely accepted guiding **principle** for defining what news is.

If you refer to a number of basic beliefs and assumptions, such as those of a given discipline, use the plural **principles.**

The **principles** of functional theory are both different from and similar to those of conflict theory.

in principle (always singular) (= in general or in theory)

A longitudinal study of how children develop socially during their schooling years is possible **in principle**, but it will be difficult to execute.

principle (n.) See **principal.**

in principle See **principal.**

probable (adj.) See **possible.**

probably (adv.) See **possibly.**

procedure (n.)

A procedure is a set of actions or steps for doing something. If you refer to the steps as a set or a sequence, use the singular **procedure,** not **procedures.** Different sets of actions constitute different **procedures.**

Used as a count noun:

Our respondents were selected according to the following **procedure.**

Calculating a chi-square statistic for a multi-cell table can be a cumbersome **procedure.**

The universities have different **procedures** for admitting new students.

Used as an uncount noun:

> Knowledge of parliamentary **procedure** is important in
> formal meetings.

> Standard **procedure** is present in any bureaucracy.

process (n. and v.)

Do not confuse **process** with **possess**. (See **possess** (v.).) In the following, **process** is a noun in the first sentence but a verb in the second.

> Strictly speaking, identity construction is a life-
> long **process**.

> The human mind **processes** information in a highly
> sophisticated way.

provided that, **providing that** (both subordinating conj.)

These two expressions are interchangeable, and both can be used without **that.** As subordinating conjunctions, they introduce a subordinate clause referring to a condition for something to be possible.

> Our informants will answer our questions **provided**
> (**that**) we guarantee them total confidentiality.

> **Providing** (**that**) Hong Kong succeeds in controlling the
> atypical pneumonia epidemic within a short time,
> confidence in revitalizing the local economy will
> return.

providing that (subordinating conj.) See **provided that.**

pursue (v.), **pursuit** (n.)

Do not confuse these two words: **pursue** is verb, **pursuit** is noun. Note carefully the difference in spelling between them.

> People usually want to **pursue** their own interests
> during their leisure.

> Young people love outdoor **pursuits** on weekends.

> He is the kind of person who would go to extremes **in**
> **pursuit of** a dream.

pursuit (n.) See **pursue.**

raise (v. and n.) See **rise.**

rather than (coordinating conj., prep. phr.)

    Rather than is more commonly used as a coordinating conjunction, requiring parallel elements before and after it:

> It is a longitudinal study **rather than** a cross-sectional survey. (parallel noun phrases)

> Some employees prefer to get pay in lieu of leave **rather than** to take their earned leave. (parallel infinitive phrases)

> Killing the proposed new rail project is probably angering many people **rather than** pleasing a few. (parallel verb phrases)

    If you use **rather than** as a preposition (phrasal preposition) to introduce a subordinate clause, it can connect nonparallel constructions:

> **Rather than** risking being infected in public places at the height of the SARS epidemic, many people chose to stay at home.

> It is better to learn something useful during the long summer vacation **rather than** spending most of the time hanging around aimlessly.

recent (adj.), **recently** (adv.)

    These words refer to the near past. Note the use of the present perfect tense or the simple past tense associated with these two words.

recent (adj.): **in recent years, in recent decades, until as recent as**

> **In recent decades,** gender role attitudes of both men and women in Hong Kong **have changed** greatly. (present perfect tense)

    If you use the phrase **until as recent as,** you must specify a time point (e.g., **a year ago, 2001, last month**). It is less wordy, however, to omit **as recent as.** Alternatively, if the specific time point is not important, you can simply say **until recently.**

> **Until (as recent as)** about a year ago, many local residents **used** the accident and emergency services of

```
public hospitals as ordinary health clinics for all
kinds of ailments.  (simple past tense)
```

recently (adv.)

The single adverb **recently** is equivalent to such adverbial phrases as **since last year, in recent years,** and **in the past few years.** There is, of course, no absolute norm of what constitutes **recently.** It is possible, therefore, that **recently** may mean **since last summer, since two months ago,** or **in the past few weeks.**

```
Recently, an increasing number of researchers have
found that stress plays a significant role in mental
health.  (present perfect tense)
```

```
The SARS epidemic erupted in Hong Kong and other
countries only recently.  (simple past tense)
```

regard (v.)

regard somebody/something as

```
In traditional Chinese society, parents regard
arranged marriage as a means to strengthen the social
status of the family.
```

```
Adam Smith is generally regarded as one of the most
important figures in classical economic theory.
```

as regards (prep. phr.) (= in connection with)

```
Rules are quite clear as regards (or concerning) how sources
should be cited in research papers.
```

regard (n.)

with regard to, in regard to (prep. phr.) (= in connection with)

These phrases have the same meaning and are used in the same way as **with reference to, with respect to,** and **in respect of.** They may be used at the beginning of a sentence or in mid-sentence.

Although you may see these phrases in certain formal documents, avoid using them because they are wordy. To write concisely and directly, consider using **of, on, for, about, concerning,** or **regarding,** depending on the situation.

```
With regard to the performing arts in Hong Kong, the
future is uncertain.
```

> Better say: The future **of** the performing arts in Hong Kong is uncertain.

> What can we conclude **in regard to** the meaning of this article?

> Better say: What can we conclude **about** the meaning of this article?

in this regard (= in this aspect/matter; in this connection)

> The employment rate of married women in Hong Kong is quite high. **In this regard,** the availability of domestic helpers is an important factor.

You can combine the two sentences. One way is to link them with the phrase **contributing to:**

> The availability of domestic helpers is an important factor **contributing to** the high employment rate of married women in Hong Kong.

Note that the first sentence has been changed to a noun phrase that becomes the object of the preposition **to.**

regarding (prep.) (= concerning)

> Information **regarding** how data will be gathered must be clearly given in a research proposal.

regardless of, irrespective of (prep. phr.) (= without being influenced by something)

    Regardless of and **irrespective of** are both prepositional phrases with the same meaning and used in the same manner. It must be followed by a noun, a noun phrase, or a noun clause.

> Big corporations employ people who are qualified and experienced, **regardless of** age, gender, race, or nationality.

> **Regardless of** its shortcomings, the study is still a respectable pioneering effort.

> If you believe that something is really worth doing, you will do it **irrespective of** what it will cost you.

related (adj.) **to** (= causally connected to)

    The typical construction is: **be + related to**. If you say A is related to B, you mean that A is in some way caused by B.

> We suspect that the lack of an interest in reading among students is largely **related to** the immense appeal of video games and popular culture.

relating to (two-word prep.) (= about, concerned with)

    The typical construction is: noun/noun phrase + **relating to** + noun/noun phrase

> In this paper I shall discuss the main issues **relating to** the role of information technology in society.

The above sentence is equivalent to the following in which **relate** is a transitive verb:

> In this paper I shall discuss the main issues that **relate** to the role of information technology in society.

relation (n.), **relationship** (n.)

    Relation refers to the connection between people, things, or factors. A **relation** may exist because of some situational reason, such as the **relation** between employer and employee or the **relation** between teacher and student. The plural form "**relations**" is used to refer to the contacts between two parties and how they behave towards each other. Thus, we speak of the **relations** between two companies, two countries, or the government and its people.

relation (n.)

> It is not difficult to see the **relation** of politics to economics.

in relation to (three-word prep.)

> Women's social status **in relation to** men's has changed greatly.

bear no relation to

> It seems that this study **bears no relation to** Hong Kong society.

relations (n.)

> The **relations** between China and the USA are reasonably good now.

relationship (n.)

Relationship refers to the condition describing how two parties or factors interact given the fact that they are in some kind of connection. A warm and impersonal **relationship** may exist between an employer and his/her employees; a friendly and congenial relationship may develop between a teacher and his/her students. But whether or not such **relationships** will result from the given **relations** is an open question.

Coming to variables, we speak of the presence of a positive or a negative **relationship** between them. Both the direction and the strength of the **relationship** between two variables are matters we examine through empirical research.

The word **association** (n.) is often used as equivalent to **relationship.** Thus, we may also speak of the **association** between variables. In using the term **association** rather than relationship, we tend to give more attention to how differences in the values of one variable are associated with (accompanied by) corresponding differences in the values of another variable. (See 9.5.3 in Chapter 9 for details.) In particular, the word **association** is often used in referring to **measures of association** (e.g., *Gamma, Lambda, Coefficient of rank correlation*).

> With the passage of time, a **relationship** of trust develops between two business partners.
>
> Sociologists and other social scientists study the **relationship** between social variables.

relationship (n.) See **relation.**

relatively (adv.)

Use a non-comparative adjective, not a comparative one, after the word **relatively.**

(×) Discussion is active in a **relatively** smaller group.

(√) Discussion is active in a **relatively** small group.

(√) This case involving only a couple and their only daughter is **relatively** uncomplicated.

reliable (adj.) See **valid.**

replace (v.), **substitute** (v., n.)
    X replaces Y

        (a)   Here is the revised question that **replaces** the original one.

        (b)   Although new recruits **replace** organization members who have left, the organization will continue to operate with little or no difference.

    replace Y with X (Note how the above two sentences are rewritten to use this construction.)

        (c)   Here is where we **replace** the original question **with** the revised one.

        (d)   Although we can **replace** organization members who have left **with** new recruits, the organization will continue to operate with little or no difference.

    Y is replaced by X

        (e)   Here is where the original question is **replaced by** the revised one.

        (f)   Although organization members who have left are **replaced by** new recruits, the organization will continue to operate with little or no difference.

Substitute (v.) is always used with the preposition **for,** not **with** or **by.**

substitute X for Y (= put X in the place of Y)

        (g)   Let us **substitute** the revised question **for** the original one.

             DO NOT say: Let us **substitute** the original question **with** (or **by**) the revised one.

X is substituted for Y (= X is put in the place of Y)

        (h)   The revised question is **substituted for** the original one.

DO NOT say: The original question is **substituted by**
(or **with**) the revised one.

In (a), (c), (e), (g), and (h), we refer to the act of removing the original question and putting the revised question in its place.

substitute (n.)

If the revised question is indeed better than the original version of the question, you can say:

The revised question is a good **substitute for** the
original one.

research (n. singular), **researches** (n. plural)

When **research** is used as a noun, the singular form is far more common than the plural form.

You use **research** as an uncount noun when you refer to it as an activity in a general sense, regardless of the number of studies or researchers involved:

Past **research** shows that educational attainment is the
most important factor affecting social mobility.

This is what social scientists typically do in their
research.

More **research** is needed to clarify the concept of
serious leisure.

When you want to stress the existence of different studies or research efforts, you may use "**researches**" (more common in BrE), as in:

His **researches** have been mostly in the problems of
identity in a globalized world.

researches (n. plural) See **research.**

result (n. and v.)

result (n.) **of**

His success is a **result of** patience and hard work.

as a result of (prep. phr.)

As a result of rising costs, taxi fares will be
increased soon.

result (v.) **in**

When you say P results in Q, P is the cause and Q is the effect.

Frequent interaction among group members **results in**

greater coherence of the group. (Note that the subject **interaction,** being singular, takes a singular verb, **results.**)

Everyone tried to speak at the same time, **resulting in** complete chaos. (Note the use of a participial phrase here.)

result (v.) **from**

When you say B results from A, A is the cause and B is the effect.

Grave consequences **result from** careless and irresponsible decisions.

right (adj.) See **correct.**

right (n.)

Right is something considered good, moral, and acceptable. Thus, the things that people claim they can justifiably do because such things are morally or legally acceptable are their **rights.**

All social norms consist of both **rights** and obligations.

in someone's own right

If you say that you have a certain claim in your own right, you mean that you are entitled to it because of your own ability or achievement, rather than because of someone else's help.

With her long experience working with school dropouts, she has become a kind of youth expert **in her own right.**

an end in its own right, an end in itself (Both phrases have the same meaning.)

Sometimes we may characterize something as **an end in its own right.** This means that it is valuable or significant in itself to be considered an end (aim, purpose).

Those who love learning believe strongly that knowledge is **an end in its own right.**

Alternatively, you can use **an end in itself** to express the same idea:

```
Those who love learning believe strongly that
knowledge is an end in itself.
```

rise (v. and n.), **raise** (v. and n.)

Distinguish between the two words as verbs: **rise** is intransitive (not taking an object), but **raise** is transitive (taking an object).

Some ambitious and hard-working people may **rise to power**, or **rise to fame**. Sometimes, a person who starts as a junior employee may **rise through the ranks** to become chief executive officer. The past tense of **rise** is **rose,** the perfect tense is **have/has risen.**

A high-ranking officer of a company may have the authority to **raise the price** of a certain product. A college president may work actively on how to **raise scholarship money**. Workers may **raise objection** when they hear about a pay cut proposed by the management. As a student, you can **raise questions** in class. (Did you spot the objects of **raise** in the preceding sentences?)

```
Well-disciplined people may rise early in the morning.

The unemployment rate is expected to rise if
consumption continues to be weak.

The students raised many important questions during
last week's seminar.

Raising taxes is one way of increasing the government's
revenue.
```

rise (n.)

You usually quote the relevant statistics when you refer to the **rise in** the number of people out of work, the proportion of secondary school graduates who go on to university, or the age of first marriage. If you study the power or influence of something, you refer to its **rise**. Thus, for instance, you may study the **rise of** consumerism, environmentalism, nationalism, or some other social movement.

```
The government is considering a rise in taxes to reduce
the amount of its financial deficit.
```

give rise to

Use this phrase to refer to why something unpleasant happens:

```
The outbreak of atypical pneumonia in Hong Kong has
```

> `given rise to` widespread anxiety and nervousness in
> the population.

raise (n.) (= rise in the amount of money paid for work, especially in AmE)

> In a weak economy, people cannot expect to get a `raise`.
> They should count themselves fortunate if they are not
> laid off.

satisfaction (n.) See **satisfy.**

satisfactory (adj.) See **satisfy.**

satisfied (adj.) See **satisfy.**

satisfy (v.), **satisfied** (adj.), **satisfactory** (adj.), **satisfying** (adj.), **satisfaction** (n.)

These words occur rather frequently in writing about social phenomena. To use them correctly, it may be helpful to first understand the context in which these words bear some relationship to one another. Think of an activity (such as watching a film) in which you participate. As a result of participation, you have an experience. The following statements are relevant in this context:

- The activity gives you some amount or degree of **satisfaction**.
- You may feel **satisfied with** the activity.
- The activity (more particularly, the film itself) may be described as **satisfactory.**
  (To say that something is **satisfactory** does not mean that it is "wonderful" or "outstanding," but that it is only "acceptable." Thus, it may not be a very complimentary remark.)
- The activity **satisfies** you. If so, it gives you a **satisfying** experience. That is, it makes you feel pleased.

Now think of a community or neighbourhood in which you live. You can make such statements as the following:

> As a living environment, my neighbourhood is
> `satisfactory.`

> People living here generally have a fairly high `level`
> `of satisfaction with` what they can get from this
> neighbourhood.

> It is `satisfying` that my neighbourhood is so pleasant.

> It has a variety of shops and facilities that can **satisfy** our daily needs.
>
> I **am satisfied with** the quality of life in this environment.

When using **satisfied,** remember that you need the preposition **with** after it if you want to specify the object of satisfaction. If you put a modifier before **satisfied,** it must be an adverb, not adjective. Thus, in the following sentence, you must write **easily satisfied** instead of **easy satisfied.**

(×) The better-educated are not so easy **satisfied** their leisure.

(√) The better-educated are not so **easily satisfied with** their leisure.

Sometimes, you can use **satisfied** without **with,** as in the following:

> The management offered a new benefits package, but the employees were still not **satisfied.**

Note that, in the above example, it is clear that the employees were still not **satisfied with** what the management offered them. Of course, you need not write this all out, which would be repeating the first clause of the sentence. The sentence as you just read already means that.

satisfying (adj.) See **satisfy.**

search (v.), **search for**

When you **search** something, you look through it carefully, hoping to find something in it.

> Students can **search** the electronic resources of the library to find the relevant literature for their research.

When you **search for** something, you try to find something.

> We spent weeks **searching for** a suitable village to conduct our fieldwork.

search for See **search.**

a series of

This phrase can be used either in a singular or in a plural sense.

Singular sense:

> The new **series** of documentaries on Nature **is** very entertaining as well as educational. (All the episodes of the series together are considered as one unit.)

Plural sense:

> **A series of** events **have** occurred that will eventually lead to the conflict of civilizations.

since (subordinating conj.) See **because.**

so (coordinating conj.) See **because.**

so . . . that . . .

Use this construction when you want to say that a certain thing is **so** true (in some aspect or way) **that** some consequence follows.

> The World Cup football matches were **so** important to many people **that** they took time from work to watch the matches on television with sympathetic support from employers.

> Emphasis on monetary value is **so** strong in this society **that** everything is seen as having some connection with it.

social (adj.), **societal** (adj.)

Social refers to any situation or process in which people are involved in some kind of interaction or are related in some way. Any phenomenon that results from such involvement or relationship is described as **social.** Thus, we have **social interaction, social groups, social network, social organization, social learning, social movement, social innovation,** and many others.

Societal describes any characteristic or phenomenon that pertains to a particular society or to social systems in general. Thus, **societal** is more appropriate than **social** in the following sentence:

> For Parsons, integration and adaptation are important **societal** functions.

General attitudes towards the environment are referred to as **societal attitudes** towards the environment if they represent what most, if not all, members of a society think about the environment. Change that is broad enough to indicate how a society as a whole changes is described as **societal change.**

Given this distinction, all **societal change** is certainly **social change** because it involves people and their interaction, but not all social change is societal change because the change may be only that of certain specific areas of social life.

societal (adj.) See **social.**

society (n.)

The following guidelines under five main situations can help you decide whether to use or not to use an article before the word **society.** They are worth studying since you may write about society rather often. (For details on the use of articles, see Appendix 4.)

1.   Use **society** (singular) without any article when you refer to it as an abstract idea, a collectivity of people and their social institutions *generally*:

> To understand human behaviour, sociologists stand back and look at individuals as members of **society**.
>
> **Society** can be thought of as a set of interrelated institutions.
>
> Using the sociological imagination, we can contemplate the relationship between individuals and **society**.
>
> The idea of traditional **society** is usually contrasted with that of modern **society**.

2.   When you describe what is characteristic of, or what may happen in, any society, you use the indefinite article **a** in front of **society**:

> What goes on in **a society** is influenced greatly by what happens between societies. (Notice that no article is used in front of **societies**.)
>
> The development potential of **a society** depends heavily on the quality of its manpower.

3.   Use the indefinite article **a** in front of **society** when you insert a restrictive adjective clause (see 12(b) in Appendix 7 for the meaning and use of

restrictive and nonrestrictive clauses) to describe the kind of society it is: (Emphasis is placed on characteristics of a general type.)

```
New immigrants find life difficult in a society that
treats them as outsiders.

We are now living in a society that is undergoing
rapid and drastic change.
```

4. Use the definite article **the** to refer to a particular type of **society** in a sentence that describes that type of **society**:

```
The postindustrial society, according to Daniel Bell,
is one in which service work is predominant.

The explosive growth of information has caused our
society to be called the information society.
```

5. Use **societies** (plural) without any article when you refer to societies (rather than the idea of "society" expressed in the singular) of a certain type in general:

```
One has to be highly adaptable and resourceful living
in modern complex societies.

The group is regarded as more important than the
individual in Asian societies.

Service work is predominant in postindustrial
societies.  (Compare this with the example of the postindustrial
society in 4 above.)
```

some (determiner)

When **some** is used with an uncount noun, it takes a singular verb:

```
Some of the conflict is a result of misunderstanding.

Some of her work has nothing to do with her training.

Some hardship comes with this particular position.
```

When **some** is used with a plural count noun, it takes a plural verb:

```
Some of the studies reviewed in the article are
classics.
```

> **Some** of the company's problems **have** been around a long time.

> **Some** data collected under unfavourable conditions **are** not reliable.

some day See **someday.**

someday (adv.)**, some day** (n. phr.)

You can use **someday** and **some day** as a standard to check whether you are a careful writer.

someday (adv.) (= at an uncertain time in the future)

> We will succeed **someday**.

some day (n. phr., in which **some** is a determiner modifying **day)**

> Let us pick **some day** (not **someday**) next month to launch our fieldwork.

sometimes (adv.)**, sometime** (adj., adv.)**, some time** (n. phr.)**, some time ago** (adv. phr.)

sometimes (adv.)

> **Sometimes** it is difficult to tell whether a respondent is telling the truth.

sometime (adj.) (only before noun)

> He is the **sometime** (= former) chairman of the students' sociology association.

sometime (adv.) (= at some point in time)

> We need to complete this project **sometime** in August next year.

some time (n. phr.) (= a period of time, usually implying that the period is not a short one)

> They have been studying the problem for **some time** now.

some time ago (adv. phr.)

> We started writing this paper **some time ago**.

sometime (adj. and adv.) See **sometimes.**

some time (n. phr.) See **sometimes.**

some time ago (adv. phr.) See **sometimes.**

sort of (adv.) See **kind of.**

standard of living (n. phr.), **cost of living** (n. phr.)

   The **standard of living**（生活水平）is the level of wealth and material comfort that a person or a group has. It refers, therefore, to the quality of life enjoyed by individuals or social categories. This is not the same as the **cost of living** （生活 費用）, which is the cost of buying food and other things that the "average" person in society needs to live. That is, the **cost of living** is a composite indicator of how expensive or inexpensive it is to live in a given society, whereas the **standard of living** can vary from person to person depending on the preferred or chosen way of life.

   Thus, if you are thinking of the price of meals, clothing, and transport, use **cost of living:**

> The **cost of living** (not **standard of living**) in Hong Kong is higher than that in Mainland China.

   If you are thinking of the way of life some people experience, use **standard of living:**

> People with homes in the Peak District of Hong Kong enjoy a high **standard of living** (not **cost of living**).

   Changing the scene to a well-known exclusive residential area in the United States, the sentence becomes:

> People with homes in the Beverley Hills area of Los Angeles enjoy a high **standard of living**.

statistic (n.), **statistics** (n.)

   A **statistic** is a number representing the measurement of something, e.g., the fertility rate in a population or the correlation coefficient between two variables. You can use the plural **statistics** to refer to a collection of such numbers:

> Our **statistics** show that the ratio of female students to male students in our department has been about 5 to 1 in each of the past five years.

Statistics is the subject that studies and explains numbers used for measurement. Used in this sense, **statistics** is an uncount noun (hence singular) that always takes a singular verb. Compare and study the following two sentences:

> `Statistics` is (not **are**) `an important course for social`
> `science students because they need statistical skills`
> `to do research.`

> `The` **statistics** `that you read in the papers about`
> `popularity ratings of government officials` **are** `(not` **is**`)`
> `often not very reliable.`

statistics (n.) See **statistic.**

study (v.), **examine** (v.), **investigate** (v.)

When you **study** a problem, you want to learn all its aspects.

When you **examine** a problem, you want to look at it carefully. The difference between **examine** and **study** is indicated in the following sentence:

> `In` **studying** `the problem of deviance, some sociologists`
> `are interested in` **examining** `its causes in the social`
> `structure.`

To **investigate** is to conduct a methodical, searching inquiry into a complex situation in an effort to uncover the facts. In short, to **investigate** is to **examine** thoroughly.

> `A research team of sociologists and psychologists is`
> **investigating** `how "normal" individuals become members`
> `of religious cults.`

What adverbs may you use to qualify **examine** or **study**?

You can **examine** (or **study**) something **attentively, carefully, closely, critically, fully, intensively, meticulously, painstakingly, rigorously, seriously, systematically,** or **thoroughly** (but NOT **widely** or **deeply,** although you can study something **extensively** or **in depth**).

substitute (v., n.) See **replace.**

succeed (v.), **success** (n.)

succeed in something

We can say that someone **succeeds in business, in a career,** or in a certain field.

```
It is not so easy for a married woman to succeed in
a professional career in a field dominated by men.
```

succeed in doing something

Succeed in must be followed by a noun, noun phrase, or gerund phrase. **Doing something** is a gerund phrase, which starts with an **-ing** noun.

```
Our interviewers succeeded in gaining entry into over
70 per cent of the sampled addresses.
```

Remember that **success** is a noun, and **successful** is an adjective. You can rewrite the above sentence using **success** or **successful,** as follows:

```
Our interviewers had much success in gaining entry into
over 70 per cent of the sampled addresses.
```

```
Our interviewers were successful in gaining entry into
over 70 per cent of the sampled addresses.
```

such that, such . . . that

Such is a pronoun (referring forward) in the following two sentences. (As you read them, you should pause momentarily after **such** before carrying on with the **that**-clause. As a pronoun used this way, **such** refers to the content of the **that**-clause.)

```
The nature of social work is such that participants
in this service profession need to have good people
skills and great patience.
```

```
The topic of the term paper is such that much empirical
evidence is necessary.
```

In the following two sentences, constructed somewhat differently, **such** is a determiner placed in front of a noun phrase to which it refers:

```
The influx of new immigrants has brought such a demand
for social services that the government must re-
consider its population policy.
```

```
Critical thinking is such an important skill that it
should be discussed and used in just about any subject.
```

such...that See **such that.**

suppose (v.), **supposed** (adj.), **supposedly** (adv.), **supposing** (conj.)

suppose (v.)

To **suppose** is to believe or to think in some way, implying that there is some uncertainty in what you believe or think.

> I **suppose** that nothing can be done about this case.

supposed (adj.)

You use **supposed** as an adjective to mean "expected" in the phrase **be supposed to**:

> We **are supposed to** complete the data analysis for this project in the first week of August.

> This proposal **is supposed to** boost employment and encourage consumption.

As an adjective, **supposed** can also be used in front of a noun:

> We have yet to see whether the **supposed** benefits of the new training programme will actually occur.

supposedly (adv.)

In the following, **supposedly** is used as an adverb modifying a verb (first sentence) or a whole statement (second sentence):

> As Chief Executive of the Hong Kong Special Administrative Region, Mr. Tung Chee Hwa has the responsibility, with the help of his top officials, to identify the factors that **supposedly** are threatening Hong Kong's social stability.

> **Supposedly,** a large organization runs not by individuals' whims but by impersonal rules.

supposing (conj.)

You can use **supposing (that)** in the sense of "if" or "assuming" to introduce a situation that can be imagined to be true. In this sense, it serves as a conjunction linking two elements, one being the situation and the other being the thought that arises if that situation occurs.

> **Supposing (that)** the government decides to levy goods and services tax, what would be the strongest argument in its favour?

supposed (adj.) See **suppose.**

supposedly (adv.) See **suppose.**

supposing (conj.) See **suppose.**

surprise (n., v.), **surprised** (adj.), **surprising** (adj.)

Many students have difficulty with these words. To overcome the difficulty, you should first realize that they have to do with our emotional response to some event. There are three elements involved: (a) the person, (b) the event, and (c) the emotional experience. (See similar discussion at the entry **satisfy, satisfied, satisfactory, satisfying, satisfaction.**)

Using this framework, the four words may be characterized as follows:
- The event **surprises** (v.) the person.
- The event gives the person a **surprise** (n.). (the emotional experience)
- The event is **surprising** (adj.) to the person.
- The person is **surprised** (adj.) **by** the event. (He does not at all expect it.)
- The person is **surprised** (adj.) **at** the event. (He is amazed by it.)

Note the difference in meaning between **surprised by** and **surprised at** in the last two sentences.

Now you can see how the words are used in the following sentences. They are all about the same idea, but are worded somewhat differently.

```
It does not surprise (v.) us to find people working
hard in a competitive environment.
```

```
That people are working hard in a competitive environ-
ment comes to us as no surprise (n.).
```
(Note that the **that**-clause as a whole is a singular subject, which takes a singular verb.)

```
We are not surprised (adj.) that people are working
very hard in a competitive environment.
```

```
That people are working hard in a competitive
environment is not surprising (adj.) to us.
```

```
It is not surprising (adj.) that people are working
hard in a competitive environment.
```

The last sentence can be recast by using the adverb **surprisingly:**

```
Not surprisingly (adv.), people are working hard in
a competitive environment.
```

take somebody by surprise (= happen so unexpectedly that somebody is surprised)

```
Their success took us by surprise.
```

much to somebody's surprise

```
Much to our surprise, they finally succeeded.
```

Study these other ways of using **surprised (**adj.):

```
We were happily surprised to learn that they finally
succeeded.

We would not be surprised if Shanghai catches up with
Hong Kong.

We would not be surprised at Shanghai's catching up
with Hong Kong in a decade or so.

Surprised by the negative results, the researcher had
to rethink the study's design.
```

surprised (adj.) See **surprise.**

surprising (adj.) See **surprise.**

take something for granted

To **take something for granted** is to accept something as unquestioned fact. Study the following sentence patterns:

```
We must not take his reasons for granted; they may be
nothing more than excuses.

Most people take it for granted that suicide is purely
an individual act.
```
(Note that the noun clause **that suicide is purely an individual act** is the something that is **taken for granted**. Hence in the main clause you need to say "**take it for granted**.")

something is taken for granted

```
His reasons must not be taken for granted; they may
be nothing more than excuses.

Since she is such a well-known scholar, it is taken
for granted that her talk will be well attended.
```

take nothing for granted

To take nothing for granted is to adopt a very cautious approach without accepting too easily anything as true or valid.

> In studying the social causes of crime, sociologists **take nothing for granted.**

taken-for-granted (compound adj.) (hyphenated only when placed before a noun)

> As students of sociology, we need to study carefully the **taken-for-granted** aspects of society.

Note the use of the hyphenated phrase **taken-for-granted** as a compound adjective to qualify **aspects**. The phrase is hyphenated only when used before the noun it modifies. The above sentence can be rewritten with the phrase placed after the noun. In this case, the phrase must not be hyphenated:

> As students of sociology, we need to study carefully the aspects of society that are **taken for granted.**

Many phrases containing hyphenated compound adjectives are available for use in writing. Some examples follow. (For more examples, see 8.1.1 to 8.1.8 in Appendix 6.)

> **much-discussed issue**
> **long-overlooked problem**
> **closed-ended question**
> **little-understood theory**
> **well-organized groups**
> **high-tech society**
> **face-to-face interaction**
> **hard-to-please employer**
> **once-in-a-lifetime experience**
> **often-quoted words**
> **on-the-job training**
> **trial-and-error approach**

tend (v.)

> You should recognize two basic constructions using **tend** as a verb:
> **tend** + **to do something**
> **tend** + **to be** + adjective

In comparing different social groups, we often want to know how likely they are to do something (thus using a verb) or how likely they are in a certain state or of a certain quality (thus using an adjective). To describe tendencies or likelihoods, **tend** and **likely** are often used.

Using a verb:

```
Women tend to enjoy shopping more than men (do).

Women are more likely to enjoy shopping than men (are).
```

Using an adjective:

```
Chinese  people  tend  to  be  more  reserved  than
Westerners.

Chinese people are likely to be more reserved than
Westerners.
```

See more examples at **likely** (adj., adv.).

therefore (conjunctive adv.) See **because.**

thought of as (= **considered as**)

To use this construction correctly, first examine the following sentence:

```
We can think of society as a system.
```

Now turn the sentence into passive:

```
Society can be thought of as a system.
```

Similarly, you can have the following two sentences:

```
Some young people think of shoplifting as nothing too
serious.

Shoplifting is thought of by some young people as
nothing too serious.
```

time (n.)**, times** (n.)

As an uncount noun, **time** is always used in the singular:

```
Given the right conditions, it does not take too much
time for a new immigrant to be integrated into the host
society.

Time is often a critical factor in crisis management.
```

You can use **time** as a count noun to mean "occasion" (thus it can take an -**s** ending in the plural), as in the following:

```
The government is handling the problem more cautiously
this time.
```

```
There are times when parents learn much from their
children.
```

```
At times, the pressure to conform to social norms is
obvious and strong.
```

In the following sentences, **time** is also a count noun meaning "period" (in a person's life, in the history of a society):

```
He described his adolescent years as the happiest time
of his life.
```

```
Hong Kong had gone through many difficult times in the
1950s and the 1960s before the economy improved
significantly in the 1970s.
```

Other phrases using **time** in this sense include **wonderful time, good times,** and **hard times.**

times (n.) See **time.**

together with (prep. phr.) See also **as well as.**

Be careful when you use the prepositional phrases **together with, along with,** and **as well as** to join two nouns. If the first noun or noun phrase is singular, the verb must be singular:

```
The clarity of the writing, together with the abundance
of examples used, makes this article a joy to read.
```

towards (prep.)

Towards (variant spelling: **toward,** especially in AmE) means "in a particular direction" or "in relation to something or someone." The following are some common idiomatic uses of **towards:**

```
Restructuring is an important step towards the merging
of two organizations.
```

```
We are planning a study of Hong Kong people's attitudes
towards new immigrants from China.
```

> The United States is formulating a policy **towards** North
> Korea.
>
> Hong Kong is implementing measures **towards** controlling
> the SARS epidemic.

You can also use **towards** to mean "close to a certain time":

> You should complete a report on this case **towards** the
> end of the month.

Chinese students may sometimes use **towards** unidiomatically, especially when the idea in Chinese is expressed by the character 對 (*dui*), which is often directly translated to **towards**. The problem is, the idea of 對 (*dui*) is not always expressed by **towards** in English. Although it is quite possible to use *dui* to express the meaning of the following sentences in Chinese, using **towards** in English is inappropriate:

(×) Let me explain my view **towards** this matter.

(√) Let me explain my view **on** (or **about**) this matter.

(×) Its function **towards** society is doubtful.

(√) Its function **in** society is doubtful.

(×) Ordinary people are naïve **towards** statistics.

(√) Ordinary people are naïve **in** their understanding of
statistics.

(×) Citizens' confidence **towards** the government has
fallen.

(√) Citizens' confidence **in** the government has fallen.

twenty-four-hour (adj.)

This is a compound adjective that expresses measurement. When placed before the noun it modifies, the compound requires hyphens, and the unit of measurement is singular. Thus, **hour** is singular in such expressions as **twenty-four-hour business** and **twenty-four-hour operation.**

You can place the compound adjective after the noun it modifies. The unit of measurement then becomes plural. In the following example, additional words have to be supplied to make the meaning clear. Hence, it is often more straightforward to use the compound adjective as a premodifier (i.e., a modifier placed before the noun it modifies).

an operation that runs for twenty-four hours a day = a twenty-four-hour operation

Other examples of compound adjectives indicating measurement:

- **a ten-year-old child** (= a child who is ten years old)
- **a four-member group** (= a group with four members)
- **a five-stage project** (= a project consisting of five stages)
- **a three-part paper** (= a paper containing three parts)

understanding (n.)
understanding of something

(×) Writing about a topic helps to deepen our **understanding** towards it. (**Towards** cannot be used this way. See **towards** (prep.) in this appendix.)

(√) Writing about a topic helps to deepen our **understanding of** it.

understanding that (introducing a noun clause)

Most opinion leaders share the **understanding that** an overhaul in the government structure is needed.

up to date (adj.) See **update.**

up-to-date (adj.) See **update.**

update (v. and n.), **up-to-date** and **up to date** (adj.)

Many people, including students, in Hong Kong erroneously use **update** as an adjective when speaking in Cantonese interspersed with English words. For example:

呢個 software 唔夠 update. (x) This software is not update enough.

Although few people seem to see or mind the error, it can affect your writing seriously if you do not recognize it. The sentence in question should be:

(√) This software is not **up to date.**

Note that the phrase **up to date** is not hyphenated if used after the noun it modifies. If you use the phrase before the noun it modifies, insert hyphens.

> By reading the relevant literature, you will have
> **up-to-date** knowledge of your field.

To **update** (v.) something is to make it more modern or **up to date** by adding something new or changing it to meet new requirements.

In the following sentences, **update** is a verb:

> This software has not been **updated** for nearly two years.
> (Be sure to pronounce the third syllable /tɪd/ of **updated.**)

> We need to **update** our other group members **on** the latest
> developments that may affect us.

Update is also a noun, as in this sentence:

> The late news on television is supposed to give us an
> **update** on the events of each day.

used to do something, be used to (doing) something, get used to (doing) something
used to do something

The modal auxiliary verb **used to** exists only in the simple past tense. Using **used to** implies that the past condition described by **used to** no longer exists. It is usually followed by an infinitive (base verb form).

> Up until the late 1980s, the British **used to have** a
> prominent presence in the senior levels of the civil
> service.

> Did university students in the 1970s **use to** be more
> interested in politics? (The past tense is indicated by **did,** so you
> must write **use to** instead of **used to** in this question form.)

be used to (doing) something

In the phrase **be used to, used** is an adjective that modifies the subject placed before it. **To** is a preposition (unlike **to** as an infinitive marker in **used to do something)** which is followed by an object (a noun phrase or a gerund taking the **-ing** form). You use the phrase **be used to doing something** the same way you use the phrase **be accustomed to doing something.**

> The Chinese **are used to** drinking tea without sugar.

```
City dwellers are not used to the simple way of life
of rural villages.
```

You can place **be used to** at the end of a sentence in which **be used to** typically becomes part of a noun clause, as in the next example:

```
Life in a foreign country can be completely different
from what we are used to. (What we are used to is a noun clause.)
```

get used to (doing) something

You may use **get used to something** when you want to refer to the effort needed to become used to something, as in the following sentence. Remember that after **get used to** you must use a noun phrase or a gerund (**–ing** form).

```
Students who have not studied sociology or any social
science before have to learn to get used to thinking
about society and human behaviour in new ways.
```

```
If you live in a foreign country for the first time,
you have to get used to new customs and standards of
behaviour.
```

valid (adj.), reliable (adj.)

Do not confuse these two words. If you claim that a statement is **valid**, it must have some "truth" in it. That is, there is some concrete or clear evidence to support it. At least, it should sound sensible based on what we know or common sense.

On the other hand, if you say that a statement is **reliable**, you mean that it can be trusted because of various reasons, for example, that it is based on research or that it originates from an authoritative source.

```
We shall demonstrate that this is a valid (not reliable)
argument.
```

```
These statistics showing GDP growth over the years are
quite reliable (not valid).
```

Note that **reliability** implies good quality of performance of a statement (since you can expect to get the same result through repeated verification), but **validity** stresses the truthfulness or reasonableness of what is contained in the statement. Consequently, you should always remember the following two points:

(a)   A **valid** statement must also be **reliable** (otherwise you can hardly show what it attempts to say).

(b)   A **reliable** statement can be not valid if it is propaganda "manufactured" by some authority.

This is similar to the distinction between the concepts of **reliability** and **validity** in the measurement of social variables: a valid measurement must be reliable, but a reliable measurement may or may not be valid. Put differently, reliability is a necessary, but not a sufficient, condition for validity.

a variety of (followed by a plural noun)

When this phrase is used to refer to a multitude of a particular type of things, it requires a plural noun and takes a plural verb. Used in this sense, **a variety of** can be replaced by **various,** if you want your sentence to be less wordy.

> Students can participate in **a variety of** extra-curricular activities.

> Students can participate in **various** extra-curricular activities.

> **A variety of** interest clubs **are** trying to recruit new members.

> **Various** interest clubs **are** trying to recruit new members.

> We need to study **a large variety of** theories that **have** been formulated in the past three or four decades.

In the last sentence, some of the original meaning will be lost if you substitute **various** for **a large variety of.** To keep the original meaning, you can consider using **many different.**

> We need to study **many different** theories that have been formulated in the past three or four decades.

a variety of (followed by a singular noun)

When **a variety of** is followed by a singular noun, it refers to a particular type of thing:

> There are **several varieties of** conflict theory. (not **theories**)

> **Each variety of** conflict theory has its own special concern.

view (n. and v.)

    view of (not **towards**)

        This is Parsons' **view of** social structure.

    The above sentence means:

        This is how Parsons **views** social structure. (In this sentence, **view** is a verb. The sentence means: This is how Parsons **understands** social structure.)

        A doctor's **view of** the role of doctors may change if he or she becomes seriously ill.

    view on/about

    If you refer to your belief or opinion that you have about something, you should use **view on** or **view about** rather than **view of**, as in the following sentence:

        We need more information before we can arrive at some **view on** this issue.

viewpoint (n.) See **perspective.**

vocabulary (n.)

    A **vocabulary** is the collection of words that a person knows or uses. We speak of the **vocabulary** of a well-educated person as being both larger and richer than that of someone who has only a primary education. As you read more and listen more to what is said on television and in films, both your written **vocabulary** and your spoken **vocabulary** grow.

    Note that in the sense just mentioned, **vocabulary** is used in the singular. You may learn many new words, but they are still part of your **vocabulary**.

    (×) Reading social science books can increase my **vocabularies**.

    (√) Reading social science books can increase my **vocabulary**.

    You can use the word **vocabulary** to refer to the words and expressions used in a particular field. Different fields then may have quite different vocabularies, such as **advertising vocabulary, diplomacy vocabulary, medical vocabulary, and legal vocabulary.** People of different ages can also have different vocabularies. Young people's vocabulary may contain many fashionable words and phrases used in popular culture and in their peer circles. Their vocabulary is thus not quite the same as their parents'.

with reference to (prep. phr.) See **regard** (n.).

with regard to (prep. phr.) See **regard** (n.).

with respect to (prep. phr.) See **regard** (n.).

worth (n. and adj.), **worthy** (adj.), **worthwhile** (adj.)

These three words are often used incorrectly in students' writing. Study them carefully.

worth (n.)

> Wealthy people are likely to have items of great **worth** in their homes.

> We have put in a month's **worth** of work in drawing up this proposal.

Adding the suffix -**less** to **worth** gives the word **worthless**, an adjective:

> Our effort in the past two months has been quite **worthless**. We never got what we wanted.

worth (adj.) (= having a certain value) Used after **be**: **be** + **worth** + gerund or noun phrase

> This book **is** really **worth** reading.

> Any method that can maximize questionnaire response rates **is** well **worth** a try.

> If a question is so designed that it will minimize response error, it **is worth** all the effort.

for what/whatever it is worth

You use this phrase (especially when speaking) to indicate that your suggestion or idea is only your personal view and may not be very useful. Yet you are still willing to share it with others.

> Here is my plan for whatever it is **worth**.

> **For what it is worth,** I propose that we do a careful pilot study to test what people think of these sensitive questions.

worthy (adj.)

worthy + of + something

When you say that a certain quality or action is **worthy of admiration/attention/consideration/mention/note/praise/respect/support,** you mean that it deserves admiration or some of the other responses named.

> His leadership during such a time of crisis is **worthy of** praise.

Words ending in -**worthy**

The -**worthy** suffix is commonly seen in such words as **newsworthy, noteworthy, praiseworthy,** and **trustworthy.**

> His leadership during such a crisis is indeed **praiseworthy**.

> The findings of the survey are **noteworthy** because they have answered some vital questions.

> Journalists have their criteria for deciding whether an event is **newsworthy**. (= Journalists have their criteria for deciding whether an event is **worth** reporting as news.)

worthy + of + somebody

You can say that some performance is **worthy of** somebody if you think that such performance is up to the standard you would expect from that person or some other person of fame.

> It was a most cordial and enthusiastic reception that the Nepalese extended to Sir Edmund Hillary (the first man to conquer Mount Everest in 1953), **worthy of a hero**, when he visited Nepal recently.

Worthy (adj.) can also be placed in front of the noun it modifies.

> We are donating our time and money for a **worthy** cause.

worthwhile (adj.)

> Considering the policy implciations of the study, all the effort made has been **worthwhile**.

> This has been a **worthwhile** project because we obtained much needed and useful information.

> It is **worthwhile** to make employees happy if this means higher productivity.

worth your (or somebody's) while

Something is **worth your while** if it is useful, good, or important enough for you to do.

> It is **worth your while** to formulate your research problem carefully before launching your thesis work.

worthwhile (adj.) See **worth.**

worthy (adj.) See **worth.**

youth (n.)

You can use **youth** to refer to young people collectively. Used this way, it takes a plural verb.

> The **youth** of today **are** generally more fortunate than those a few generations ago.

> The results of this survey indicate the opinions of the **youth** of Hong Kong today who **have** much to say about their wants and needs.

Like many other nouns, **youth** can be a premodifier placed before another noun (e.g., **youth culture, youth hostel, youth services, youth training**).

> **Youth** services require a vast amount of resources contributed by both the public and the private sectors.

You can use **youth** (uncount noun, singular form only) to refer to (a) the period of time between childhood and adulthood, or (b) the quality of being young.

(a) **Youth** is the time when the individual is particularly interested in his or her peers.

(b) Do you think that girls, more than boys, are obsessed by **youth** and beauty?

When used as a count noun, a **youth** is a young man (rather than woman) in his teens.

It is easy for **youths** to get into trouble even without
their own knowing.

This means that if you want to include both young men and young women, you
should use **youth** (plural in meaning).

Many recreational facilities and services are available for the community's **youth** (not **youths**) to express
themselves.

Answers to Exercises

Appendix 1 Subject-Verb Agreement

Exercise A

1 has   2 include   3 is   4 tends   5 are   6 do   7 treats

8 forms   9 have   10 has   11 has   12 claims   13 has   14 are

15 is   16 Are   17 are   18 results   19 place   20 is

Exercise B

1 is   2 has   3 involve   4 allows   5 takes   6 is   7 is

8 is   9 are   10 are   11 is   12 has   13 is   14 indicates

15 was, were   16 were   17 have   18 requires

Appendix 2 Using the Correct Word Forms: Verbs, Nouns, Adjectives

1C (attraction)   2D (belief)   3B (accessible)   4C (confident)

5B (Deviant)   6C (excited)   7C (surprising)   8A (analyze)

9D (emphasis)   10B (encouraging)   11D (response)   12A (significant)

13C (pursued)   14C (succeed)   15D (emphasized)   16A (proof)

17C (differs)   18B (constraint)   19B (facilitate)   20D (satisfactory)

Appendix 3 Uncount Nouns, Variable Nouns, and Plural Nouns

1b   2b   3a   4a   5b   6b   7b

8a   9a   10b   11b   12a   13b   14b

15b   16a   17a   18a   19b   20b   21a

22b   23b   24a   25a

Appendix 4   Use of Articles

(The numbers refer to numbered blanks in the exercise.)

1 a	2 a	3 the	4 The	5 a	6 nil	7 a
8 The	9 nil	10 nil	11 nil	12 an	13 nil	14 a
15 a	16 the	17 the	18 nil	19 nil	20 nil	21 nil
22 nil	23 an	24 the	25 nil	26 nil	27 the	28 a
29 a	30 the	31 a	32 the	33 the	34 nil	35 the
36 the	37 the	38 an	39 nil	40 the	41 the	42 nil
43 nil	44 nil	45 nil	46 an	47 the	48 the	49 a
50 the	51 nil	52 nil				

Appendix 5   Verb Tenses in Research Papers

(The numbers refer to numbered blanks in the exercise.)

Exercise A

1 has been given	2 has often been noted	3 tend
4 are	5 are seen	6 evaluated by
7 serve	8 seek	9 can
10 cause	11 found	12 spend
13 are much determined by	14 believed	15 pointed out
16 are		

Exercise B

1 has received	2 have come	3 is	4 is
5 studies	6 held by	7 attempts	8 is believed
9 cannot	10 understand	11 lives	12 may be
13 is			

Exercise C

1 intend	2 can	3 be considered	4 is
5 may be	6 were	7 is labelled	8 were
9 are	10 note	11 tend	12 reported
13 were	14 does	15 loved	16 hated
17 reported			

References

Abercrombie, Nicholas. 1996. *Television and Society.* Cambridge, England: Polity Press.

American Psychological Association. 2001. *Publication Manual of the American Psychological Association*, 5th ed. Washington, DC: American Psychological Association.

Barber, Benjamin R. 1992. "Jihad vs. McWorld." *The Atlantic Monthly* 269 (3): 53–65.

Becker, Penny Edgell and Phyllis Moen. 1999. "Scaling Back: Dual-Earner Couples' Work-Family Strategies." *Journal of Marriage and the Family* 61: 995–1007.

Berger, Peter L. 1963. *Invitation to Sociology: A Humanistic Perspective.* New York: Doubleday Anchor Books.

Best, Joel. 2001. *Damned Lies and Statistics: Untangling Numbers from the Media, Politicians, and Activists.* Berkeley, CA: University of California Press.

Burchfield, R. W. , ed. 1996. *The New Fowler's Modern English Usage,* 3rd ed. Oxford: Oxford University Press.

Campbell, Colin. 1997. "Shopping, Pleasure and the Sex War." Pp. 166–176 in *The Shopping Experience*, edited by Pasi Falk and Colin Campbell. London: Sage Publications.

Chao, Paul. 1983. *Chinese Kinship.* London: Kegan Paul International.

Croteau, David and William Hoynes. 2000. *Media/Society: Industries, Images, and Audiences,* 2nd ed. Thousand Oaks, CA: Pine Forge Press.

Gibaldi, Joseph. 2003. *MLA Handbook for Writers of Research Papers,* 6th ed. New York: The Modern Language Association of America.

Gill, Tom. 1998. "Transformational Magic: Some Japanese Super-heroes and Monsters." Pp. 33–55 in *The Worlds of Japanese Popular Culture: Gender, Shifting*

Boundaries and Global Cultures, edited by D.P. Martinez. Cambridge, England: Cambridge University Press.

Huntington, Samuel P. 1993. "The Clash of Civilizations?" *Foreign Affairs* 72 (3): 22–50.

Johnson, Allan G. 1991. *The Forest for the Trees: An Introduction to Sociological Thinking.* San Diego, CA: Harcourt Brace Jovanovich.

Kelly, Bill. 1998. "Japan's Empty Orchestras: Echoes of Japanese Culture in the Performance of Karaoke." Pp. 75–87 in *The Worlds of Japanese Popular Culture: Gender, Shifting Boundaries and Global Cultures*, edited by D. P. Martinez. Cambridge, England: Cambridge University Press.

Krenzin, Joan and James Kanan. 1997. *Handbook of the Mechanics of Paper, Thesis, and Dissertation Preparation*, 2nd ed. Washington, DC: ASA Teaching Resources Center, American Sociological Association.

Lee, Ming-kwan. 1995. "The Family Way." Pp. 1–19 in *Indicators of Social Development: Hong Kong 1993*, edited by Siu-kai Lau, Ming-kwan Lee, Po-san Wan and Siu-lun Wong. Hong Kong: Hong Kong Institute of Asia Pacific Studies, The Chinese University of Hong Kong.

Mills, C. Wright. [1959] 1967. *The Sociological Imagination.* London: Oxford University Press.

Ng, Pedro Pak Tao. 1974. "The Learning of Population-Related Norms: Some Problems for Research." Paper presented at the Conference on Population Socialization, 16–21 December, at East-West Center, Honolulu, Hawaii.

———. 1997. "Leisure: A General Profile of Behaviour, Perceptions, and Satisfaction." Pp. 255–295 in *Indicators of Social Development: Hong Kong 1995*, edited by Siu-kai Lau, Ming-kwan Lee, Po-san Wan and Siu-lun Wong. Hong Kong: Hong Kong Institute of Asia Pacific Studies, The Chinese University of Hong Kong.

———. 吳白弢 1998. "Xianggangren dui xianxia de qiwang ji manzu" 香港人對閒暇的期望及滿足 (Leisure Expectations and Leisure Satisfaction of Hong Kong People). Pp. 399–420 in "Huaren shehui de bianmao: shehui zhibiao de fenxi" 華人社會的變貌：社會指標的分析 (*Changing Chinese Societies: Social Indicators Analysis*), edited by Siu-kai Lau, Ming-kwan Lee, Po-san Wan, and Siu-lun Wong. 劉兆佳、李明堃、尹寶珊、黃紹倫 編 Hong Kong: Hong Kong Institute of Asia-Pacific Studies, The Chinese University of Hong Kong.

Ng, Pedro Pak-tao and Peter Jic-leung Man. 1988a. "The Effects of Peer Orientation, Parent Orientation, and Schooling Subculture on Leisure Behaviour and Life Satisfaction of Youths in Hong Kong." Occasional Paper No. 27. Hong Kong: Centre for Hong Kong Studies, Institute of Social Studies, The Chinese University of Hong Kong.

_____. 1988b. "Leisure Behaviour and Life Satisfaction of Youths in Eastern District." Occasional Paper No. 25. Hong Kong: Centre for Hong Kong Studies, Institute of Social Studies, The Chinese University of Hong Kong.

Pearson, Veronica. 1996. "The Past Is Another Country: Hong Kong Women in Transition." *Annals of the American Academy of Political and Social Science* 547: 91–103.

Ritzer, George. 1993. *The McDonaldization of Society.* Thousand Oaks, CA: Pine Forge Press.

_____. 1999. *Enchanting a Disenchanting World: Revolutionizing the Means of Consumption.* Thousand Oaks, CA: Pine Forge Press.

Rubington, Earl and Martin S. Weinberg, eds. 1995. *The Study of Social Problems: Seven Perspectives,* 5th ed. New York: Oxford University Press.

Schor, Juliet B. 1992. *The Overworked American: The Unexpected Decline of Leisure.* New York: Basic Books.

Thurow, Lester C. 1996. *The Future of Capitalism: How Today's Economic Forces Shape Tomorrow's World.* New York: William Morrow.

Turabian, Kate L. 1996. *A Manual for Writers of Term Papers, Theses, and Dissertations,* 6th ed. Chicago: University of Chicago Press.

Wan, Po-san. 1997. "Subjective Well-Being: Now and Then." Pp. 49–81 in *Indicators of Social Development: Hong Kong 1995*, edited by Siu-kai Lau, Ming-kwan Lee, Po-san Wan, and Siu-lun Wong. Hong Kong: Hong Kong Institute of Asia-Pacific Studies, The Chinese University of Hong Kong.

_____. 2001. "Subjective Well-Being and Discrepancy Perceptions." Pp. 159–181 in *Indicators of Social Development: Hong Kong 1999*, edited by Siu-kai Lau, Ming-kwan Lee, Po-san Wan, and Siu-lun Wong. Hong Kong: Hong Kong Institute of Asia-Pacific Studies, The Chinese University of Hong Kong.

Wong, Frances Kam Yuet. 1996. *Health Care Reform and Transformation of Nursing in*

Hong Kong. Unpublished Ph.D. thesis. Hong Kong: Division of Sociology, Graduate School, The Chinese University of Hong Kong.

Yuen, Siu Man Amy. 1997. *Gendered Job and Clerical Workers in Hong Kong.* Unpublished master's thesis. Hong Kong: Division of Sociology, Graduate School, The Chinese University of Hong Kong.

Zinsser, William. 2001. *On Writing Well: The Classic Guide to Writing Nonfiction,* 25th anniversary ed. New York: HarperCollins.

INDEX

(The numbers after each entry are section numbers)